AN ADAMS BUSINESS ADVISOR

Do-It-Yourself Advertising, Direct Mail, and Publicity

Other titles in
THE ADAMS BUSINESS ADVISOR SERIES

AN ADAMS BUSINESS ADVISOR

Do-It-Yourself Advertising, Direct Mail, and Publicity

READY-TO-USE TEMPLATES, WORKSHEETS, AND SAMPLES FOR

- CREATING ADS
- DIRECT MAIL PIECES
- PRESS RELEASES, and
- OTHER PROMOTIONAL ITEMS

Sarah White & John Woods

ADAMS PUBLISHING
Holbrook, Massachusetts

Published by Adams Media Corporation, 260 Center Street, Holbrook, MA 02343

ISBN: 1-55850-488-5

Printed in the United States of America.

J I H G F E D C B A

Library of Congress Cataloging-in-Publication Data
White, Sarah (Sarah E.)
Do-it-yourself advertising, direct mail, and publicity : ready-to-use templates, worksheets, and samples for creating ads, direct mail pieces, press releases, and other promotional items / Sarah White & John Woods
p.   cm. — (An Adams business advisor)
Includes index.
ISBN 1-55850-488-5
1. Advertising, Direct mail. 2. Sales promotion. 3. Advertising copy. I. Woods, John A. II. Title. III. Series.
HF5861.W52   1995
659—dc20   95-9328
CIP

This publication is designed to provide accurate and authoritative information with regard to the subject matter covered. It is sold with the understanding that the publisher is not engaged in rendering legal, accounting, or other professional advice. If legal advice or other expert assistance is required, the services of a competent professional person should be sought.
— From a *Declaration of Principles* jointly adopted by a Committee of the American Bar Association and a Committee of Publishers and Associations

Cover design by Marshall Henrichs

This book is available at quantity discounts for bulk purchases.
For information, call 1-800-872-5627.

Visit our home page at http://www.adamsonline.com

Contents

Preface

Advertising is the rock 'n' roll of the business world. Compared to managing the other aspects of your business—finances, operations, personnel—this is a gas. Lust, greed, fear, desire—advertising takes our animal motivations and shapes them into the desire to purchase. Being involved in that process is as much fun as work gets.

This animal behavior takes place in the modern jungle we call Main Street. Main Street is a way of thinking about the people you do business with. If you consider the folks you talk to on a regular basis either as buyers or sellers, you've got a group of people who resemble a small town. You learn what's new from one another; you react to what's bad; you exchange gossip and tips and real information. You know one another.

What's the "Main Street" of your business? If you're a retailer, it may be a literal place. For those of us selling services or products business-to-business, it's a "virtual reality" that may come together only a few times a year, at conferences and trade shows. Sometimes it's a well-read trade journal.

Whatever your Main Street, it offers many products to buy and many suppliers to buy from. Day in and day out you try to get along and maybe get ahead in this community. On Main Street you're competing for attention, competing for a sale.

In a competitive environment like this, you have to take a proactive approach. If you believe there's something wrong or embarrassing about "having to advertise," get real! In your personal life, a sense of modesty is an admirable characteristic. In business, modesty is inappropriate and self-defeating. Put aside your childhood instructions about "don't blow your own horn" as you start this book. We're going to discover how you can play lead trumpet in your own band.

What We'll be Covering

Analysis, strategy, creativity—that's the model for your advertising activity. The first two are planning steps; the last puts that plan into execution. If you analyze your situation and strategize intelligent responses to it, it follows that you will create executions that accomplish your goals.

This book is organized into three sections. It starts with broad concepts, moves into specific executions, and finishes up with related topics. But I don't think many of you will actually read this book in the order in which it's written. With a subject like advertising, you have to know a little about everything before you know which area is important for you to study in depth. This book is meant to be browsed through. Then you'll turn your attention to different chapters for closer study as you create your advertising plan and execute its various components. For instance, you might scan the radio chapter when you're trying to decide between radio and newspaper ads for your general strategy. You'll look more closely at the radio chapter when you decide that you do want radio, and it's time to negotiate your contract with the radio station. And you'll return to it again when it's time to go into the studio and record your commercial.

In the first section of this book you will learn about the underlying structure that supports creative advertising. We'll lay the groundwork by talking about goal setting, choosing strategies, developing a positioning statement, using promotions, planning media usage, and developing your advertising message. (That's Chapters 1 to 5.)

In the next section, we'll get specific about each medium you might choose for your advertising. We'll take you behind the scenes to learn about tasks that ad agencies usually perform for their clients, and show you how you can do each of these tasks yourself. You'll learn how to negotiate your media buys, and then how to craft the ad message for print, radio, TV, and direct mail advertising. (That's Chapters 6 to 9.)

In the last section we'll explore the other components of marketing that fall outside "pure" advertising: how to use publicity, what you need from your corporate image, how you should shop for an ad agency or other professional service, and how to get the best results from the team you build. (That's Chapters 10 to 12.)

We'll close with a return to the big picture: a summary that reviews how these pieces fit together. Throughout the book you'll find examples and templates that show you step by

step how to plan and execute your advertising. Some of the templates are designed to clarify your thinking on certain topics. Others are important to your overall planning: statements of strategy, calendars, and budgets. The summary shows you how to use these templates to build a solid overall plan.

Who Do I Think You Are?

Retailers. Service providers. Hospitality and tourism businesses. Manufacturers. Professional offices. Nonprofit organizations. You might be from any of these. Your gross sales might be anywhere from $100,000 to $4,000,000, as a ballpark estimate; your advertising budget might be from 0.5 to 10 percent of gross, or you might have no idea what your budget is or should be. In short, you have some resources to allocate to advertising, but you're "small fry" to most advertising agencies.

I have made these generalizations, as I think about you:

- You are either the owner of the business or close to it—you're responsible for all aspects of advertising. Your business is new or unfamiliar with advertising, so that you can't rely on doing things the way they've always been done.

- You will be doing this work yourself, not supervising others. You have no formal training in marketing. You have limited time and resources to apply to it. Your other job responsibilities are many and will constantly compete for your attention.

When You Finish This Book

You'll have a background of knowledge from which to operate. You'll be benefiting from many other businesses' experiences. I think you'll be able to:

- Apply basic concepts of advertising to your real-world situation.

- Develop specific goals and objectives.

- Select applicable techniques, then develop budgets, calendars, and creative executions.

- Manage a year's activities.

- Monitor results and use that information to improve your next year's activities.

- Start all over again.

As your competitive environment changes—and it always does—you will need to repeat the cycle of analyzing, strategizing, and creating advertising. This book is a tool kit. Occasionally you will need to pull out your tools and craft a new approach. My goal is to see that you are well trained in the use of your tools. If I've done my job well, you'll build solid, long-lasting strategies, resulting in ad campaigns that command attention. You'll experience the creative satisfaction any craftsman feels at a job well done. With that attitude, you'll be eager to begin each new cycle, bringing your enthusiasm and creativity to the task. Out of that you will generate ever more successful results. And you'll find this one of the most enjoyable aspects of your business day.

Why You Should Listen to Me

I have spent ten years listening to and working with people like you. My advertising business, White Space Design & Advertising, provides consulting, writing, graphic design, art direc-

tion, and related services to businesses like yours. I have a small staff who help me in this work. I encourage my clients to do as much or as little of the process as they are comfortable with, and I coordinate and provide the rest of the services needed. I have a background in journalism, advertising, and marketing, but most of what I know I learned from my clients and my peers, not from a textbook. Many of the examples in this book come from my practice, some from my colleagues'. Acknowledgments follow this preface. Please call each of these people and tell them how grateful we are for their help.

The last sentence of this book is, "Let me know how it all works out." I'm serious. Send me your thoughts, your filled-in templates, examples of the advertising you create. Send me your criticisms too, if you find information here that is confusing, unclear, or just plain bad advice. You can help me improve, just as I hope I've helped you improve the way you do business.

Remember, this stuff is fun. What you're about to do might not be Madison Avenue advertising, but it's going to make you a bigger player on your Main Street. Let's get going.

I want to hear from you!

Sarah White
White Space Design & Advertising
849 E. Washington St. 202
Madison, WI 53703

Acknowledgments

Jeff Berry assisted with many points throughout the book, and I'd like to recognize his contribution start-to-finish. Also, I'd like to thank John Beale and the staff of the Stardust Corporation, and Jerry Smith and the staff of First Business Bank, for allowing me the opportunity to be part of the exciting growth of their respective businesses. Many observations and techniques in this book were developed as we grew together.

Chapter 1—My thanks go to the following: P. S. Mueller.

Chapter 2—My thanks go to the following: J. Kinney Florist.

Chapter 3—I'd like to thank Sandy Besler of West and Zajac Advertising, Inc. for sharing her expertise with me. In addition, my thanks go to the following: M&I Bank; P.S. Mueller; Ralph McCall and Mike Couey, Heartland Litho; Espresso Royale Caffe; Mason Shoe Comfort Footwear; Phillips Distributing Corp.; SuperSaver Food Stores; Taverne Room Grille.

Chapter 4—I'd like to thank Gwen Jones, of Time and Space Media Service, for taking time to discuss the media buyer's role with me. In addition, my thanks go to the following: SRDS, Inc.; Adams Outdoor Advertising.

Chapter 5—My thanks go to the following: Columbia County Economic Development Corp.; J. Kinney, Florist.

Chapter 6—My thanks go to the following: Anchor Bank; Firstar Bank; The Park Bank; In Business Magazine; KMS Alternative Shampoo; Leisure Concepts; The Madison Advertising Federation; Midelfort Clinic Health Plan; James B. Beam Distilling Co.; The Royle Group; Cloud 9 Productions; Workbench; Captain's Chair Salons; Ginza of Tokyo; Stardust Corporation; Adams Outdoor Advertising; Milan's Restaurant; Geneva Lakes Greyhound Racing; Schoeps Ice Cream; Fruit of the Loom Activewear.

Chapter 7—I want to thank Carl Ames of Carl Ames Communications, Bob Abella, of Abella Audio, Lisa Fichter of Q106, and Greg Rittman of WTDY, for taking time to help me understand the finer points of radio. Also thanks to Scott Rippe, Ralph McCall and Mike Couey at Heartland Litho for working with me on the case study for this chapter. In addition, my thanks go to the following: Independent Bankers Association of Wisconsin; WHIT/WWQM-FM Radio; First Business Bank of Madison; Captain's Chair Salons; Michael's Frozen Custard; Holmes Tire; The Munz Corporation; Heartland Litho.

Chapter 8—I want to thank Bob Wickhem and Katherine Corneille from Channel 47, our local Fox affiliate, for taking time to work with me on this project. Also thanks to Jan Zajac of West and Zajac Advertising for Surma's Restaurant, Jim and Marcia Klinke of Klinke Cleaners and Joe Goldy of The Bedroom Store for contributing case studies.

Chapter 9—My thanks to Pam Bell of Soccer Notes, and Kathryn Leide of BiFolkal Productions for contributing case studies. In addition, my thanks go to the following: Jefferson Home Health Care; Great Wall Systems; Stardust Corporation; Thompson Publishing Group; Heartland Litho; ERIC Clearinghouse on Higher Education.

Chapter 10—My heartfelt thanks to George Cutlip for his collaboration on this chapter. A public relations consultant with almost 25 years of practical media relations experience, George learned the business at his father's knee. Portions of this chapter are extrapolated from suggestions found in several editions of "Effective Public Relations," by Cutlip, Center, and Broom, now in its seventh edition from Prentice Hall. I would also like to thank David Williams of Broadbent & Williams Inc., and Derrick Van Mell for their contributions to the case studies. In addition, my thanks go to the following: Independent Bankers Association of Wisconsin; The International Crane Foundation.

Chapter 11—My thanks go to the following: Columbia County Economic Development Corp.; Domus Equity Corp.; Wisconsin Whey International, Inc.; Space-Metrics; Metro Ride; Great Wall Systems, L.L.C.; Datakeep, Inc.; 35 West Productions; Skyline Displays, Inc.

The most thanks of all go to my beloved husband Jim, who brewed most of the espresso and offered his support in many other ways as well. If I have inadvertently omitted anyone who assisted in the course of this project, I apologize profusely and promise to do better next time.

Chapter 1

Before You Advertise: Determine Your Marketing Objectives

I have trouble with marketing language. I can't make a meaning stick to a phrase like "determine your marketing objectives."

What I know is, there's some promise you make to yourself that keeps you working the way you do, that comforts you when you wake up with knots from the tension of all you've undertaken. You're going to sell that extra thousand units, so that you can take some time off this summer. You're going to close the deal on a good repeat job, so that you can even out the peaks and valleys in your workflow. You're going to do the work to reach the next level, whatever that might be for you.

That's what this chapter (and all the ones that follow it) is about: ways to grow your business through advertising and promotion. To do that takes a plan, and that's why we start with determining marketing objectives.

A friend of mine says there's only one thing you need to know about marketing: "Spread the hay where the mules can find it." That's essentially true. Marketing activity (at least metaphorically) is basically just studying the mules and making sure the hay is the kind they like and where they want it.

But why do the mules get all the attention? Don't you deserve a say in the matter?

You want to make your particular type of hay, then market it to the mules that find they like it. And that's where marketing gets more complicated. You want to be a customer-driven organization, but you don't want to hand the reins over to the mules. Determining marketing objectives is really about finding a way to connect your overall business goals with your marketplace. It's all about finding a direction that leads you somewhere you want to go.

If you've never thought about marketing, your business is an unexplored territory. Before you start on a trip, you have to know where you are—and where you want to get to. Your marketing plan is the map that you'll follow to get from here to there. But there's a difference between the map and the territory. If your map doesn't match the terrain, you're unlikely to reach your destination. Sometimes you think your map is accurate but find you are misinformed. Perhaps a competitor brought a new product to market without your knowledge. Maybe road construction is literally changing the route to your business. Your marketing plan is a map derived from your knowledge of your business, your competitive environment, and your audience. As this landscape changes, you will have to keep replotting your map.

Expect to review the exercises in this chapter every two or three years, or whenever you are considering a new advertising campaign.

The marketing activity consists of learning your territory, choosing your direction, and then planning and organizing and making the trip. In this chapter we'll look at the stages in this activity in four sections:

- How to focus your marketing efforts: understanding your market, your image, and your competition

- The Four P's: your marketing mix

- Market research: what it is, when to do it yourself

- How to develop a functional marketing plan

When you finish this chapter, you will have a basic foundation of marketing knowledge. You'll understand the *marketing mix* of product, place, pricing, and promotion. You'll discover ways to do informal market research without hiring consultants or spending a fortune. And you'll summarize your knowledge in a marketing plan ready to be put into action by using advertising. The goal of this chapter is to give you focus as you read the rest of the chapters, so that you can decide which of my suggestions to try out with your business.

Focusing Your Marketing Efforts: The Business Review

We start with a business review, an exercise to help you get a precise fix on who you are and how you're doing business.

Use Template 1-1 to write out your answers to these questions. In future chapters we'll come to many branching paths of action, and your answers here will act as guideposts to help you choose your course.

Template 1-1: The Business Review

The Business Review

Who You Are:

Significant Chronology

Year established _____

Change/addition of physical location _____

Change of ownership _____

Change/addition of product or service offerings _____

Significant milestones _____

_____

_____

Mission Statement

Four aspects of value:

Form and function _____

Time _____

Place _____

Ease of possession _____

Audience profile _____

_____

Product or service offering _____

_____

Technology _____

_____

Self-concept _____

_____

Plans for growth _____

_____

_____

(more)

Where You Are:

What is your geographic domain? _____

What do you know about your competition? _____

_____

_____

_____

Industry's cycle _____

What's your current sales strategy? _____

_____

_____

What Needs to Change?

Where does it hurt?

SWOT exercise (Summarize results from Template 1-3)

Strengths _____

Weaknesses _____

Opportunities _____

Threats _____

Where Are You Going?

Goal setting (Summarize results from Template 1-4).

_____

_____

_____

The budget: _____

Date: _____

Prepared by: _____

Who You Are

Significant Chronology. All good stories begin at the beginning. So we begin by stating the year your business was established, followed by a chronological summary of any major events: changes of location, changes of owner-ship, and changes of focus in products or services. Any of these events may be relevant to your positioning strategy. (We'll talk more about that in Chapter 2.)

Mission Statement. A mission statement acts as a compass, to guide actions and decisions. It connects what a business is capable of doing with the needs of potential customers. It defines the business's purpose and provides direction for business decisions. How do you develop a mission statement?

At some point in their growth, most businesses will invest the time and attention of top management in writing a mission statement. Workshops and seminars are available, as are consultants who can guide a corporate visioning/mission-building process. What you are buying is essentially a process leading to a paragraph summarizing your chief contribution to your customer (see Example 1-1).

Example 1-1: Mission Statement

MISSION STATEMENT

Revised November 1994

The mission of First Business Bank of Madison is to provide premium quality service and products that meet selected financial needs of our clients in an accessible and responsive manner, as a locally owned independent bank.

ACTION STATEMENTS:

We will:

1   Offer non-labor intensive deposit and loan services to responsible businesses, business people and individuals.

2   Have strong local ties which will enrich their respective economic and cultural development and enhance the goals of the Community Reinvestment Act.

3   Provide a challenging and rewarding work environment that will promote personal growth, retain experienced personnel and create a team spirit.

4   All be empowered to utilize our creative resources to meet the needs of our clients, community, personnel and the bank.

5   Provide the quality of service that we would want to receive ourselves.

Not every mission statement includes action statements, as this one does. Look at each action step in relation to the questions on the business review section on the Mission Statement. Which statements derive from the audience, which from the product or service offering, and which from the self concept?

1. Product/service offering. 2. Audience. 3. Self-concept. 4. Self-concept. 5. Product/service offering.

A statement like this is deceptively simple. To arrive at it, you may have to consider a number of aspects of your business, and focusing your answers will be difficult. Businesses often invite key staff and stakeholders as a group to engage in this process. Usually a trained facilitator guides the work. Even if you don't want to buy a formal process, consider this: A few hours spent together with your staff, at a meeting room away from the usual workplace, discussing your mission in light of each of the following topics can bring new vision to your business.

Your mission statement reflects your business in terms of

- Audience profile
- Product or service offering
- Geographic domain
- Technology
- Plans for growth
- Philosophy/self-concept

These areas and more are part of the business review. We're about to look at each in more detail. As we go, use Template 1-1 to record your answers, whether you consider these areas alone or with a group. At the end, you should be able to write a mission statement that describes what you do as simply as possible, and defines the benefit your customer receives from you.

First we look at the marketplace. What do you know about your customers? How does the product or service you are selling help solve their problems? Why do they place value on what you offer? Value is a balance of several elements—quality and price certainly, but there's more to it than that.

The Four Aspects of Value. We have already stated that customers buy the problem solutions and benefits that a product or service offers. How do they judge those benefits or the quality of that solution? By breaking down (often not consciously, but they do it nonetheless) the value of what you offer in terms of four aspects: form and function, time, place, and ease of possession.

Form and function includes whether the item is consistent with a person's self-image, but it also includes how well the item per-

forms, how easy it is to use, and other characteristics that are tangible. For instance, a microwave oven that attaches to the underside of a cabinet offers a tangible functional benefit: It helps keep the counter area free. If it is available in a range of colors, that is a benefit of form. Either might be the persuading factor in a purchase decision, or one of these other aspects of value might tip the scale.

Time has to do with having the product or service available *when* a customer wants it. If you are out of stock when a customer comes in to buy, your offering loses value compared to that of your competitor who has the item in stock. If you run a repair business, can you respond to an emergency within two hours, or even immediately? Any aspect of a service or product tied to when it is available fits here.

Place has to do with *where* the product or service is available. Is your place of business easy to get to? Is parking available? Will you deliver to your customer's place of business? In other words, does your location make it easy for people to do business with you?

Ease of possession includes price, credit terms, and guarantees that make taking possession of your offering simple and reassuring to your customers. They want to be sure that their purchase will perform and that they are getting a fair price. If they don't feel comfortable on these points, they will deal with someone else.

So, in considering what you offer, break it down in terms of these elements to help you understand how your customers decide to buy one offering over another. Use Template 1-2 to describe the value you offer, then prioritize the aspects of value as you think your customers would.

Template 1-2: The Four Aspects of Value

Form and Function

Describe unique features and their benefit to your customer. If you have trouble with this, read Chapter 2 and return to this exercise.

_____

_____

_____

Time

Describe the timeliness of your product or service offering (when and how it is available). How can you improve versus your competition?

_____

_____

_____

Place

Describe where your product or service is available.

_____

_____

Ease of Possession

Describe the price, credit terms, and guarantees related to taking possession of your offering.

_____

_____

_____

Prioritize these aspects of value: Rank them in terms of their importance to your customer.

1. _____

2. _____

3. _____

4. _____

You should appreciate which of these four elements are most important to your customers. Different products and services have different selling dynamics. What dynamic affects you? Put yourself in the shoes of a typical customer. What is the customer going to emphasize when making a buying decision?

For example, people shop for loans based on interest rates. We shop for clothes based on our self-image, price, and the roles we play. We look for a new car based on our self-image, its reliability and safety, and its price. Looking for a computer, we research functions, speed, upgradeability, compatibility, and price—we want to make an educated decision.

That's the kind of information you're looking for: How conscientious will your customers be at looking at the value of your offering? What are their priorities concerning form and function, time, place, and ease of possession? Will your prospects take the time to research and learn about your product and/or service? Do they buy with loving care, or act on a whim? In your marketing, you'll look for ways to make these characteristics work to your advantage.

Audience Profile. Who buys from you, and what are these people like? What are they *really* buying? Customers don't buy products, they buy the benefits that products convey. They buy services to help them solve problems or do something they want to do. Each prospect in your audience has a self-image that he or she is trying to project into the world. Your customers buy the products and services that include the benefit of being consistent with that self-image. Shoes cover their feet—but the decision to buy high-top sneakers or stiletto heels is driven by self-image.

Even when you sell only to other businesses, people are still people. Businesses buy only those things that will help them solve their problems. So you have to answer the question: How does your offering help solve their problems? The answer is your *key benefit*—a concept we'll talk about much more in Chapter 2, "Positioning."

What is your customer base like? Look at where your sales come from. Learn what you can from the different levels of business. Who are your volume buyers? If yours is a service firm, ask yourself which are the most satisfying—and rewarding—customer relationships. Describe two or three success stories. Any type of business can benefit from asking this question: What would you see if you could videotape "Customer Bob" from Day One, happy with buying from someone else, to now, being a satisfied customer of yours instead of

your competitor's? What would have happened to bring about this change?

Find out everything you can about the interests, attitudes, and lifestyles of your customers. Where are they located geographically, and is that critical to your relationship? If you're a direct mail merchant, probably not. If you're a bank, probably so. That's the "place" aspect of value. Studying your customers' geographic distribution can help you decide when and where to build a new branch.

How often, and how many units, do your customers buy? Even if you're in a law practice selling billable hours, you can learn from looking at usage rates. What about loyalty? Hair styling salons typically experience great customer loyalty—but it's loyalty to the individual stylist more than to the firm. Customers will follow the artist who controls their "look." A self-service photocopy shop might experience almost no customer loyalty—the equipment and service are perceived as being no different from one place to the next. In that case, price becomes the major determinant of how the customer decides, all other things being equal (though they seldom are). You need to know how susceptible your customers are to the offers of your competitors. And you need to be continuously enhancing your offerings in terms of the four aspects of value to compete successfully and hold on to your customers.

Think about a current customer who's a profitable, steady source of business for you. How did you come together? Was it your location or your reputation? Your advertising? If you don't do it already, start asking every new contact, "How did you hear about us?" You'll find out which advertising methods are a good investment of your time and money. The answers might guide you to placing bigger ads in the Yellow Pages, or to dropping your newspaper advertising contract and relying on networking for referrals.

By looking at current customers, you draw conclusions about how to find more like them—and how to help them find you. This is equally true whether you're talking about business-to-business selling or consumer products and services. The difference is this: If you are selling a consumer offering, your customers' self-interest propels their search for solutions to problems. With business-to-business marketing, customers are making decisions about your offering as part of their jobs. They are expected to have the best interests of their employers in mind. In either case, the four aspects of value are equally important in how they make their buying decision.

People don't stop being people when they take on job functions. What you learn about your buyers as individuals is as important as what you learn about the businesses they represent. The buyers are still just people pursuing solutions to problems. And the way you let them know about your offering will be tailored to their habits as individuals, not their job descriptions. Media habits—the traits that will drive your choice of print, radio, TV, direct mail, or publicity vehicles—are intensely personal. We'll talk about surveying your customers' media habits later in this chapter.

And one more important thought about your current customers: If you don't have their names and addresses stored in a database, make it a priority to do so. You can set up fields for this and other information, such as how often and how much they purchase. Your current customers are your best source of new sales and a rich resource of information about your business. Tap into this power!

Product or Service Offering. Your business review will include a concise description of your outputs, the tangible products or services that contribute to your cash stream. Break your list into two categories. Start with core products—those that drive your operation from the standpoint of sales, capital investment, and day-to-day activity. Then list related products—items or services that you offer because it is convenient for your customer to buy them through you, but that are not essential to your operation.

For a computer retailer, the list might be: "Core products: Macintosh systems and peripherals. Related products: Software, software installation, and training."

For a bank, the list might read, "Core products: Deposit accounts, including money market accounts, CDs, and checking accounts; loan accounts, including "bricks and mortar" loans, operating capital loans, and revolving lines of credit. Related products and services: Courier pick-up and delivery to businesses, and VISA/MasterCard processing."

A florist—we'll look at her case more closely in Chapter 2—might answer this question, "Core products: Fresh flowers and plants. Related products: Gifts and cards." The live things she sells are core because the majority of her capital investment and day-to-day activity go to that area. She needs to own a walk-in cooler to keep the stock fresh. She needs to devote time daily to buying from wholesalers, choosing that day's best picks. Trimming and arranging the fresh flowers takes up more of her time than maintaining her gift and card displays. And at the cash register at the end of the day, the receipts tell her that she's primarily in the fresh flower business and only peripherally in the general gift category.

Technology. In this era, every business needs a master plan for its use of technology. For most of us, that means personal computers. Some companies make a conscious commitment to stay at the leading edge of technology. That demands capital reinvestment, sometimes to the tune of thousands of dollars each year. That in turn affects profit goals and sales goals, and therefore marketing goals. That's why the topic is relevant to advertising. If you are a desktop publisher, for example, you may feel the pull to upgrade your system radically every time there's a new technological breakthrough. New scanning equipment, faster processing speed, additional memory, more accurate color monitors—your wish list will never end.

For many professionals, such as accountants or free-lance writers, the basic system requirements haven't changed much in years. If you are one of these, your technology demands are not going to put the same strain on your cash flow.

Manufacturers will have more complicated technology issues to consider. If you manage a T-shirt silk-screening company, for example, your art room might benefit from computers, but then there's your production shop, which could benefit from automated screeners, drying ovens, solvent venting booths, and more. You may or may not be planning to reinvest in new equipment for your manufacturing process. My point is this: Your plans concerning your use of technology should be summarized in your business review.

Self-Concept. What's your attitude? How formal is your workplace, your business's body language and style of dress? These are intangibles, but worth exploring. The answers will guide the advertising work you're about to do. You can't graft a humorous ad campaign onto a law firm so stuffy that the average age of the lawyers is dead. You can't name your business "Elegant Edibles" and serve soup in tin cups.

Plans for Growth. Do you have plans for growth? How rapid? Your business may be planning to grow from zero to twenty-five locations in one year. Or you may be involved in a craft business that's happily refining the quality of its output without increasing in size or volume—that's growth of a different kind. You may be converting staff positions to outside contract labor, and thus actually shrinking, according to the traditional measures of jobs and square feet of real estate. Now more than ever, business strategists appreciate the concept of "right-sized" companies.

Your advertising must work hand in hand with your long-range plans. Growth doesn't happen without marketing, advertising, and publicity to fuel the engine. You've got to undertake these activities to let your customers

and potential customers know what you can do for them. How aggressive your plans are can help you determine how much of your resources you'll devote to an ad budget.

With the preceding questions, we've been looking at who you are and how you're doing business. We're getting a pretty good picture of the car you're driving. Now let's look at the landscape you're driving through.

Where You Are: The Marketplace

What Is Your Geographic Domain? How far will you go (in terms of physical area) to serve a customer? From how wide a radius do you draw customers? This might be a question of drive time, or retail location, or national or even international business segments. With the technological revolution around us, the concept of geographic domain is suddenly much more fluid than it used to be. If you haven't asked yourself this question lately, think about it now. Are you overlooking a potential market that's waiting for you just beyond your obsolete, self-imposed boundaries? Using communication technology and rapid delivery services, perhaps you can reach a much larger market than you thought. You have to advertise to take advantage of that possibility, though.

A couple of farmers began growing popcorn and distributing it themselves through grocery stores. Their geographic domain was basically as far as they were willing to travel on sales calls—about 100 miles from their base in central Wisconsin. Then they came up with a new marketing idea. They offered the product as a fund-raising device to groups like the Boy Scouts, high school bands, and similar groups. They developed a simple mailer, bought a national mailing list, and took their business to a whole new level. That's a low-tech example of how decisions regarding geographic domain affect the marketplace for a product.

How do the plain facts of your geographic domain fit with the "place" aspect of value to your customers? Can you improve that fit?

Keep this in mind during our discussion of SWOT analysis, coming up.

What Do You Know about Your Competition? Who, how many, how fierce? When you lose to a competitor, is it on the basis of price, a more attractive combination of form and function, or some other combination of the components of value? If you aren't doing the follow-up to find out this information, you're missing the boat. Look around you now, and list all the businesses that compete with you. Rank the three businesses that present the stiffest competition. In Chapter 2, Template 2-4 will help you assess your competitors' positioning strategies. You will discover what dimensions of competition are working to your advantage.

Find out everything you can about your competition. I've found that when you are the loser in a bid process, the client tends to feel some obligation to soften the blow. When you hear that you've been turned down, ask about the other proposers' materials and the criteria by which the selection decision was made. If you are in a governmental bid process, ask what materials might be available to you under the open records law. You can learn a lot by swallowing your pride and pursuing information from "the one that got away."

Look at your competitors' advertising; get copies of their brochures; visit them and check out the image they project. You must have a good idea of how you are like your competition and how you are different. As you develop advertising, brochures, and press kits, the samples from your competition will help you know what you want to do—and what you want to avoid.

Industry's Cycle. You can have aggressive plans for growth, but if your industry is in a steep decline, you're in dreamland. Where is your industry in its growth cycle? The personal computer industry was hot news five years ago, is a steady business today, and is likely to be as strong or stronger tomorrow. But if you're selling electric typewriters, you've got some challenges ahead. There are creative ways to prosper in a declining industry. But it's a challenge you'd better know you've taken on. They say the video rental business is headed for a big shake-up when cable pay-per-view becomes available. Yesterday's hot franchise opportunity may be tomorrow's linotype operators. Make sure your marketing plans are rooted in a real-world understanding of the challenges you face.

What's Your Current Sales Strategy? Many businesses get by with a haphazard sales strategy. They advertise in whatever vehicle seems affordable at the time the sales rep calls on them, and they stop advertising whenever the cash flow gets tight. They send people out to make personal sales calls without the backup of a good lead-generation program to send them in the right direction, or a good brochure to leave behind if they get in the door. The goal of this book is to help you avoid that kind of wasted effort.

Before you picked up this book, you had some kind of marketing going on. Evaluate it now. What are you doing, what are you spending, and how is it working out? How do you measure results? What do you wish worked better?

What Needs to Change?

Where Does It Hurt? "Marketing is a function of pain. Where does it hurt?" Kim Babler, the marketing director for Wisconsin Housing and Economic Development Authority, taught me to ask this question, and it always leads me straight to the heart of a client's needs. People don't get up and decide to do marketing because it feels right that day. They do it because the competition is gaining ground, or the new store isn't getting the traffic it needs, or something.

I wish I could tell you this isn't true. I'd like to think that most businesses take a proactive approach to marketing, but my experience says no. Businesses begin to examine their marketing needs when they are called to respond to a challenge. The first marketing plan is almost always reactive. The success of that plan leads to more proactive planning in the future. The goal of sound marketing and advertising is to minimize unanticipated onslaughts. When you have a sound marketing plan in place, you lessen the pain your business is likely to feel from potential challenges.

You probably picked up this book because there's a pain in your business some-where—otherwise you'd be reading something more fun! Now is the time to be blunt about what needs to change. Where does it hurt, and what can advertising do to make it better? Let's use a "SWOT" analysis to answer that question.

SWOT Analysis—Strengths, Weaknesses, Opportunities, Threats

Strengths and weaknesses exist within your company. They are *internal* influences—factors that are under your control. Strengths often have to do with your ability to create a product. Weaknesses often have to do with your ability to sell it. Our goal is to discover how you can exploit your strengths and correct your weaknesses.

Opportunities and threats are *external* influences—factors that are outside your control in their origin, but not in the way you respond to them. Opportunities are unfilled needs that your product or service can fulfill. Opportunities are problems your customers experience that your product or service can solve. Opportunities are combinations of circumstances that have been overlooked in one way or another by your competition. You might discover an opportunity by reassessing your sales boundaries. You might find an opportunity in exploiting a weakness of a competitor, such as in the areas of time or place value. Creative thinking and observation will reveal the openings in the landscape that suggest new opportunities for you.

Threats are market conditions that put you at a disadvantage. Threats come from competition, or financial risk, or a declining industry cycle. By solving these problems, you correct negatives and set things on the right track.

Thorough business planning requires a good understanding of SWOT analysis—I've only touched on a subject that deserves your deeper attention. You should find a good book on business planning to complement your study of advertising and promotions. (One book that might help you here is *Marketing Magic* by Don Debelak, also published by Adams Publishing.)

When you can be specific about your strengths, weaknesses, opportunities, and threats, you are better able to pick a destination on your marketing map.

Take this example: A company started up selling blank T-shirts to silk-screening and embroidering companies. As its advertising consultant, I asked, "Where does it hurt?" The answer: "Orders are slow because customers wrongly assume that a new company can't have much inventory." In Template 1-3A we look at this company's SWOT analysis. I'm leaving a lot out here, but basically the SWOT analysis suggested that we focus our marketing efforts on conveying the company's size to potential customers. "If they could just see how big our warehouse is, they'd know we've got the goods," my customer said in one of our meetings. And that sparked the idea for a marketing strategy and a creative approach. We decided to send prospective customers a picture. We created an attention-getting direct mail piece that spoofed roll-out postcards from old tourist attractions; it got attention, and the business got the change of perception it needed.

Here is an exercise to demonstrate the SWOT process. As you answer the questions in Template 1-3B, write your answers down. Keep your statements short, stay factual, and focus on one factor at a time.

Template 1-3A: SWOT Analysis Example.

"SWOT" Analysis

Consider each of these categories. State a strength, weakness, opportunity, or threat in each area.

Target market (for example, its size, location, demographics)

S W O (T)   Nationwide. Mostly men, 25 to 35, with about two years of college. About 30,000 potential buyers in the marketplace (individual firms and multiple buyers within large firms)

Buying habits

S W (O) T   Customers for this product typically choose one major supplier to use steadily, and maybe one for backup. If we get a trial order and do well, we have a good chance to make the customer's "short list."

Sales analysis

(S) W O T   Our sales have been strong since day one. We can afford a reasonable marketing budget—we don't have to operate on a shoestring.

Past marketing

S (W) O T   Because this company is only two years old, we don't have years of past marketing momentum behind us. Our ads in the first year were only half-page black-and-white—not too high-profile.

Product knowledge

(S) W O T   We carry a very wide product line and stock it deep. Computerized inventory control gives each phone operator instant knowledge of what's in stock, and details about that product.

Competitor strategies

S W O (T)   Competitors are known to make deals by asking what we're charging, then offering to match our price.

Template 1-3B: SWOT Analysis Blank.

"SWOT" Analysis

Consider each of these categories. State a strength, weakness, opportunity, or threat in each area.

Target market (for example, its size, location, demographics)

S W O T   _____

_____

_____

Buying habits

S W O T   _____

_____

_____

Sales analysis

S W O T   _____

_____

_____

Past marketing

S W O T   _____

_____

_____

Product knowledge

S W O T   _____

_____

_____

Competitor strategies

S W O T   _____

_____

_____

Add your own categories to this list.

Where Are You Going? Setting Objectives

That example doesn't tell the whole story. We had a hunch about what we needed to do, but we didn't plan a way to measure how successful we were. In the end, we had a gut feeling that the mailing was successful, because sales increased and we heard favorable comments at the next trade show. But we weren't maximizing our efforts. Since we didn't state a desired result in a measurable way, we didn't learn as much as we could from this experience.

We might have said, "We want fifteen new customer accounts established, with an average order size of 100 dozen pieces, and an average of two repeat orders by the end of the third month from the mail date." This type of goal would require work to meet it—for example, rigorous mailing list management, and backup from the sales staff. But if we did this work, at the end of the year we would know whether to do more of the same or look elsewhere for better results. By committing to this kind of goal, we would give direction to our work, and have a standard to see how well we did. And we could learn more from the experience. Next year we could develop more informed goals and more effective activities to meet them.

A marketing objective is a specific, measurable goal. Statements like "We need to have more accounts" are incomplete. You have to complete that thought in a measurable way. Say, "Three hundred new accounts opened in six months will be a good return on the investment we've planned in this advertising campaign." Setting measurable goals helps you justify budgets and measure progress; it tells you when to celebrate your accomplishments. (However, as any astute marketer will tell you, never settle for your successes. There is always a competitor just around the bend ready to learn from your successes and take customers away. So you have to keep learning from your experiences and keep getting better.)

A marketing objective provides overall direction. Time periods can stretch to two or three years ahead. For the shorter term, we think of specific strategies, means to that end. We'll talk about strategies later in this chapter.

Establishing revenue goals is an important part of the goal-setting process. You must choose a time period (typically a year, or the length of your budgeting cycle) and a dollar figure or percentage of gross for your business growth goal. By definition, goals must be quantifiable, measurable, and attainable.

If your business has several core products or services, describe where the growth is to take place. Here's an example. I handle the advertising for First Business Bank, a business you'll hear more about in examples in upcoming chapters. This bank focuses on attracting and serving business accounts only, a niche marketing strategy that is unusual but that has proved to be very effective. In the five years since its inception, the bank has grown by an average of 67 percent per year. That's remarkable performance! In 1995's annual planning session, the bank set a more conservative, but still aggressive, growth goal of 35 percent in gross revenue. We specified that this increase should be roughly balanced between growth in deposits and growth in loans. With that 35 percent figure in mind, we have a yardstick to apply to our budgeting process. The bank's budget for advertising will not increase by more than 35 percent to be consistent with its goal for growth of revenues. Like many businesses, the bank has chosen to determine the advertising budget as a percentage of gross revenue, which can also be stated as a percentage of gross sales. This is a useful means of comparison with past performance and with industry averages. In the last section of this chapter we'll talk more about setting budgets for marketing.

Use Template 1-4A as you think about your goals and objectives. Then use Template 1-4B to set your revenue goals and your proposed marketing budget.

Template 1-4A: Goal Setting: Why Statements

Goal Setting: Why Statements

Business goals: Why do you want to employ marketing?
Marketing in itself does not create revenue. Marketing affects the strength of selling points, which in turn affects sales. These are goals that marketing can help achieve:

1. Increase name awareness
2. Increase location awareness
3. Communicate positioning
4. Build current customer confidence or loyalty
5. Generate leads (replace cold calls with warm calls)
6. Cement long-term business relationships through image building

Write down your top four in order of priority, with any relevant details.

_____

_____

_____

_____

Personal goals: Why do you want to increase revenue?

1. So that the owners can enjoy a more comfortable lifestyle
2. To reinvest in the company's facilities and equipment
3. To add staff positions
4. To create seed money for future marketing

List those that are applicable, in order of priority.

_____

_____

_____

_____

Template 1-4B: Goal Setting: Revenue Goals Blank

Goal Setting: Revenue Goals

Goals must be quantifiable, measurable, and attainable.
A revenue goal: to increase revenue by *X* percent in *Y* amount of time.

Translate your sales goals into dollar volume, using the calendar year as the time period.
Here's how:

1. Last year's gross revenue: $ _____

2. What is your average annual growth percentage *without marketing*?

   (Look at last year's percentage of growth over previous year's): _____

3. Expected gross this year *without marketing*: $ _____

4. Annual growth percentage goal this year *with marketing*:   _____

5. Expected gross revenue this year *with marketing*: $_____

6. Subtract Item 3 from Item 5. $_____
   This is your projected revenue *with marketing* minus projected revenue *without marketing*. This
   number represents, in dollars, the annual difference you expect your marketing to make.

Review
Compare your projected revenue to your budget.
You are spending (line 6) $_____ to make (line 5) $_____ .
When you prepare your marketing budget (see Template 1-10), check that the "bottom line"
marketing total dollar estimate is not greater than the number on line 6.

Revenue Goal:
To increase revenue by $ _____ over the time period from _____ to _____ .

Total marketing budget will be no more than $ _____.

Template 1-4C: Goal Setting: Revenue Goals Example

Goal Setting: Revenue Goals

Goals must be quantifiable, measurable, and attainable.
A revenue goal: to increase revenue by X percent in Y amount of time.

Translate your sales goals into dollar volume, using the calendar year as the time period.
Here's how:

1. Last year's gross revenue: $ _____ *100,000*

2. What is your average annual growth percentage *without marketing*?
   (Look at last year's percentage of growth over previous year's): _____ *5%*

3. Expected gross this year *without marketing*: $ _____ *105,000*

4. Annual growth percentage goal this year *with marketing*: _____ *35%*

5. Expected gross revenue this year *with marketing*: $_____ *135,000*

6. Subtract Item 3 from Item 5. $ _____ *30,000*

   This is your projected revenue *with marketing* minus projected revenue *without marketing*. This number represents, in dollars, the annual difference you expect your marketing to make.

Review

Compare your projected revenue to your budget.
You are spending (line 6) $ *30,000* _____ to make (line 5) $ *135,000* _____ .
When you prepare your marketing budget (see Template 1-10), check that the "bottom line" marketing total dollar estimate is not greater than the number on line 6.

Revenue Goal:
To increase revenue by $ *30,000* over the time period from *Jan. 1, 1996* to *Jan. 1, 1997* .

Total marketing budget will be no more than $ *30,000* .

Summary: The Business Review

Now you have the first tool of Marketing 101: the elements of a business review. If you've followed the exercises, you have used specifics to describe your business, the landscape in which you operate, the characteristics of your potential customers, and how you'd like to influence their behavior. Here's a tip: Don't overlook your current customers. It costs less to develop a current user than to recruit a new one. Many people are so focused on the bird in the bush that they forget to serve the bird in the hand.

The Four P's: Your Marketing Mix

For decades marketers have been using the model of the "Four P's" to describe marketing activity. The P's are product, place, pricing, and promotion. Your marketing plan will describe each of these dimensions of your business. It's time to get specific; if you are unable to answer these questions clearly, do the homework necessary to make firm decisions.

The Four P's are closely related to the four aspects of value. Here is how they're different: The four aspects of value described your offering from the perspective of your customer, whereas the Four P's describe your offering from the perspective of internal operations.

Product (or Service)

In the business review I asked you to define your core and related products or services. After you have done your SWOT analysis, review your answers; do you see changes in your product or service offering that you would like to make? Think about how you select the right offering to meet your customers' needs. How do you generate ideas for new products? How about making your products easier to use? And how about enhancing their functionality? How are you packaging your existing products? (If you want to explore a company with an extraordinary record for product improvement, check out the appliances and power tools offered by Black & Decker. This company is continuously coming up with new versions of toasters, hand mixers, and power drills.) Your decisions here affect your marketing. Revamping your product might be the core of a marketing strategy.

Place (Distribution)

If you're in a retail business, then place is a straightforward question. Where is your physical location? Is it the right one, or is it presenting challenges to you? Are parking hassles or inconsistent hours keeping customers away? If your business is not dependent on store traffic, your P is a D—distribution. How are you getting your products to the right customer at the right time? Describe your operations strategy from the vantage point of "where the rubber meets the road"—how the product gets to the customer.

Price

Price is a decision you make based on both tangible and intangible factors. Somewhere between "what the traffic will bear" and "what it costs me to make it" lies your price—and your pricing strategy. Your production, advertising, and distribution costs go into the equation, but so do less quantifiable factors. What factors do your customers consider important? Value is the key: not just how much your product costs, but what quality is delivered at that price.

How does pricing affect your business image? You can charge too little. Underpricing your service when you wish to be perceived as prestigious can be a disastrous marketing strategy. Pricing for profitability, image, and value is a critical business decision. You might find it beneficial to work with your accountant and also consult advisers from your trade association when you establish your pricing strategy.

Promotion

Your promotion decisions are the fourth P—and the subject of the rest of this book. Which promotional vehicles should you use to reach your customers—print advertising, broadcast, direct mail, publicity, networking? See Chapter 4. What creative message will move your customers to buy? See Chapter 5. Where, when, and how often should the campaign run? See Chapters 6 to 10. If you can't answer these questions now, keep reading. Use Template 1-5 to summarize the Four P's of your marketing mix, or to make notes for areas that deserve further study.

Template 1-5: 4 P's

Your Marketing Mix: The Four P's

Product or service:

_____
_____
_____
_____
_____

Place (distribution):

_____
_____
_____
_____
_____

Price

_____
_____
_____
_____

Promotion

_____
_____
_____
_____
_____

Now you have two tools for marketing: your business review and your marketing mix. The third tool is marketing research—a tool you'll need if you're having trouble answering the questions raised by the first two.

Market Research: What It Is, When to Do It Yourself

Used by permission of P.S. Mueller.

Why do market research? What can it do for you? The obvious truths about your market you already know—such as that nobody would buy the machine pictured above. The purpose of researching your market is to find out the subtler truths. Market research can help you spot opportunities and problems. It can uncover useful information from data that you already have, such as customer sales records. It can enrich your understanding with insights that only an outsider's perspective could bring.

Research can be *primary*: original work compiled to meet your specific needs. Or research can be *secondary*: using existing information available through outside sources. Both types can use either of two techniques: *qualitative* or *quantitative* research methods. Quantitative research consists of gathering data through surveys of a random sample that represents the universe you're studying. You could choose to do customer-based research, which provides information about your own customers that can be used to extrapolate an understanding of the general market. Or you could choose to do marketwide research, gathering your information from the broader population that makes up your target market. The

goal of all quantitative research is to gather data that can be used to predict market behavior. The answers are numeric totals or percentages—quantifiable measures.

Qualitative research uses methods such as focus groups and telephone surveys that include open-ended questions. These methods don't try to statistically represent the market universe. Qualitative research typically involves small groups of customers who are asked to share their likes and dislikes on a particular subject, and to provide insight into how they choose one product over another. Qualitative research, by its more open-ended nature, can uncover problems and opportunities that quantitative research cannot. It can answer questions you never thought to ask. For instance, if your customer service is not what it should be, you will find this out quickly from a focus group. If your only research had been a quantitative survey, and you didn't include a question like "Please rate our service from 1 to 5," this problem would never have come to your attention.

These are some types of information you can learn from primary research, whether you use qualitative or quantitative methods to collect the data:

- Demographic and socioeconomic characteristics
- Psychological/lifestyle characteristics
- Attitudes and opinions
- Awareness/knowledge of a product or concept
- Intentions regarding purchases, travel, etc.
- Purchase motivators (the four aspects of value)

How do you choose which research techniques to use? Marketers find it wise to start with qualitative methods, to get a sense of the right questions to ask. After qualitative research has made clear to you which are the key issues, you can design a truly useful quantitative research study.

Focus groups are a popular means of doing qualitative research. But focus groups can be misleading. You don't have a statistically accurate sample. The personalities of the participants and the skill of the facilitator can have a big impact on the direction the conversation takes. I observed a focus group assembled to judge the general perception of a small community bank approaching its hundredth anniversary. One participant related a very negative experience with the bank twenty years in the past. Another chimed in with a story to top the first one. The session degener-ated into a grand bank-bashing. Could a better facilitator have gotten the conversation back on track? Maybe, maybe not. My point: If you're planning to use the focus group technique, plan to do it several times, and do it well. I think hiring a marketing firm with expertise in facilitation is definitely worth the expense. If that's beyond your budget, simply do personal interviews with a few customers that you consider typical. This is a very inexpensive method of research that you can do by yourself. The knowledge you gain will be admittedly idiosyncratic, but it will be valuable just the same. I highly recommend that you try this. You will quickly see how different a customer's perspective is from your own.

The questionnaire in Template 1-6 might be helpful in a focus group or single interview. Note: Whether or not you reveal the name of your business is a decision you will have to make. Obviously, in do-it-yourself interviews, it is nearly impossible not to reveal who you are and why you are asking these questions. Pure market researchers try to avoid making the client firm known, because it might skew the data collected. However, I feel there is much to be gained from informal discussions with people who know who you are and what business it is you're trying to improve. Let your instinct guide you as to how secretive you need to be.

Template 1-6: Focus Group Questions

Qualitative Questionnaire

Suitable for Focus Group or Personal Interview

How do you make a buying decision for this type of product or service?

      Price?   Convenience?   Perception of value*?

                                                      *Form and function
                                                      *Timeliness
                                                      *Place
                                                      *Ease of possession
                                                      Guide the discussion so that you can assess customers' priorities in terms of these aspects of value.

How do we compare with our competition in these dimensions?
    Packaging
    Follow-through (support after the sale)
    Image
    Price
    Quality of product or service
    Innovations
    Reputation

What benefit does this product or service give you?
What problem does it solve for you?

What do you wish was different about this product or service?
How could it be tailored better to your needs?

How does it fit into your image of who you are?

Interests, attitudes, and lifestyle questions
What media do you see?
    Print: What magazines, newspapers do you read?
    How thoroughly do you read?
        (example) Read 10 percent of all editorial, skim the ads
        Read most of the editorial, glance at about half the ads
        Read cover to cover
    Radio: What stations do you listen to? Where? (In the car, at home, at work?)
    TV: What programs do you watch?
        News
        Entertainment
(Make up more questions of your own that might help you advertise to reach buyers like these.)

When you've done your qualitative research, then you can design your quantitative research tools. Many businesses use simple questionnaires to gather data. You can distribute your questionnaire through the mail or by asking the questions over the phone. (A phone survey is quantitative if the questions are yes/no or multiple choice, qualitative if the answers are open-ended.)

Template 1-7 should get you started with ideas for your quantitative research questionnaire. Remember, each question must be given a numerical score. Your questions should be phrased so that respondents pick from multiple-choice answers, from which you can gather total and average scores.

Template 1-7: Quantitative Questionnaire

Quantitative Questionnaire: Sample Questions

Type of Question	Example
Implied alternatives	Yes/No Male/Female
Middle ground	Is the price higher than, lower than, or about the same as a year ago?
Multiple choice	Which of the following varieties of cheese have you used within the past year?
	Gouda Cheddar Mozzarella Swiss Muenster
Questions of degree/intensity	How likely do you think you will be to buy this product the next time you are shopping for products in this category?

A quantitative study is a good way to rate a product or company on a list of attributes.

Example:

Strongly Agree	Agree	Neutral	Disagree	Strongly Disagree	
☐	☐	☐	☐	☐	The step-by-step instructions on this package are easy to use.
☐	☐	☐	☐	☐	It is easy to exchange this product after the sale if necessary.
☐	☐	☐	☐	☐	This product conveys prestige upon the person who uses it.
☐	☐	☐	☐	☐	The price of this product is lower than that of other comparable products.
☐	☐	☐	☐	☐	The quality of this product is higher than that of other products available at the same price.

Add your own questions about product or company attributes.

A quantitative survey can assess demographic and lifestyle factors, media usage, and purchase characteristics, such as how frequently a product is bought or where it is typically used. This type of survey can help you weigh your market's perception of your product versus those of your competitors. See Chapter 2, "Positioning," for a discussion of the dimensions of competition you might wish to survey. You will find Template 2-4 particularly relevant.

How do you choose whom to survey, how many, what questions to ask? For starters, look at the questions about your marketplace in the business review. If there are any of these questions that you can't answer, they belong on your survey. For example, you might ask about an individual's media habits, or product usage, or self-image. How do you phrase the questions so that the answers are useful to you? That can be difficult. It helps to keep the entire data collection process in mind. Don't ask a question if you don't know what you would do with the answer.

To develop a questionnaire, follow these steps:

1. Determine what information is needed.

2. Determine the content of your questions.

3. Decide the type of questions you'll use: agree/disagree statements, multiple choice, etc.

4. Decide the wording of the questions. Questions should be easy, relevant, brief, and neutral—not sales-sounding in tone.

5. Decide the sequence of the questions.

6. Produce, test, revise, and distribute the questionnaire. Note that I said "test"! If you can't actually mail your questionnaire to a test audience, at least try it out on someone unfamiliar with your project. You may have included unclear or misleading questions. Try to catch these errors before they affect the data you collect.

After the surveys have been returned, you still have a big task ahead of you. It's time to tabulate the results and draw your conclusions. Transfer your responses to a tabulation spreadsheet. For each question, calculate the number and the percentage giving each response. For example, let's assume you mail out a survey in which Question 1 has five possible answers (strongly agree, agree, neutral, disagree, strongly disagree). Your spreadsheet would show a total for each of the five possible answers, and then give each as a percentage of total responses to Question 1. Likewise for Question 2, and so on throughout your survey.

The next step is to analyze the tabulated responses and group them into meaningful categories. Look for significant differences— for example, half the respondents to Question 1 strongly agree and the other half strongly disagree, with no middle ground. Think about why these differences might exist. Draw your conclusions, then write up your results. A good research report is complete, accurate, clear, and concise.

Using your common sense, it's possible to do quantifiable research on your own. But before you try, consult the professionals who specialize in this field. Make an information-gathering visit to a marketing firm or advertising agency with expertise in primary research. Ask to see samples of questionnaires and other research tools the firm has used for previous clients. You'll get many ideas for do-it-yourself research—or you may find that hiring professional expertise is the right direction for you. There are also many useful books available on this subject that can help, and I recommend that you look for these in a bookstore with a good business section.

The cost of formal research can be prohibitive for many small businesses. That leaves you with the responsibility to be well informed about your business, your customers, and your marketplace. Read up or look for seminars on grass-roots market research techniques. Be sure to listen to your customers. If you keep a list of questions in mind, every interaction can be part of your private focus group. At trade shows, on the showroom floor, behind the cash register, ask questions that can help you know your customers better. The results of this type of research are hard to tabulate, but doing it will stimulate your thinking in a number of ways.

We've been talking about primary research techniques. Your other option is secondary market research. This is probably easier for the individual without a marketing research background to do. Secondary research involves gathering information from sources that already exist, such as census information. Combining secondary research with information gleaned from your own company's data can help you find your answers. Some sources of information include the following:

For Consumer Information

Simmons Market Research Bureau (information on demographics, size, media habits for users of consumer products)
380 Madison Avenue
New York, NY 10017
212-916-8900

SRDS (information on population, income, and general household purchasing traits for geographic areas)
1700 Higgins Road
Des Plaines, IL 60018
708-375-5000

For Business-to-Business Information

Dun's Marketing Services (a division of Dun and Bradstreet)

This mailing list rental company has information about the number and size of businesses within specific Standard Industrial Classification (SIC) codes by category and by Zip code.

Check your phone book or call 1-800-234-3867 for the office nearest you.

Nielsen Test Market Profiles

This is the company that provides ratings information for radio and television stations. It has demographic, retail sales, and media information broken down by DMA (designated market area, basically communities and surrounding suburban areas) nationwide.

A.C. Nielsen Company
1290 Avenue of the Americas
New York, NY 10104
212-708-7500

Your community will probably have several local companies that rent mailing lists. You may find that they can sort for information that is useful to you; call and ask questions about how their databases are organized.

For more information on marketing as a whole, you will find the American Marketing Association extremely useful. As a member for years, I have learned a lot from the monthly meetings and newsletters, and in particular have found its library to be a tremendous resource. Able researchers are only a phone call away. Membership in your local chapter is a quick way to learn relevant marketing ideas for your business.

American Marketing Association
250 S. Wacker Drive, Suite 200
Chicago, IL 60606-5819
312-648-0536

There's much, *much* more you can do with market research. The overview to keep in mind is this: What you're trying to do through research is to discover the problems and opportunities facing you. By solving problems and exploiting opportunities, you will meet your goals.

That's three tools for successful marketing: the business review, the marketing mix, and research. Now it's time to pull these together into the fourth tool: the written marketing plan.

Developing A Functional Marketing Plan

To get where you're going, you have to know the lay of the land. A functional marketing plan is the route to your long-term success. As you might suspect, I'm going to recommend that you organize your plans and projections into a written document. I suggest you set up a Marketing Plan ring binder, with sections for

- Marketing background
- Marketing objectives and strategies
- Positioning
- Promotional plans
- Media strategy
- The advertising message
- Executions: a section for each advertising medium to be used, in which you will keep budgets, calendars, and creative work

- Master calendar
- Master budget

Does that look a little like the table of contents of a book? Not surprising. My goal is to help you find ways to effectively compete through advertising, and to document and learn from your experience, so that you get better and better at this. Here, in your marketing plan, you will organize your activity. This notebook will help you keep on task and on target.

I know you're overworked. Your marketing will be an activity that you pick up and put down between other activities of your business. Your well-organized notebook is the key to being effective with the time you do spend on marketing. Let's look at what you'll be putting in each of these sections.

Marketing Background. As you complete the templates in this chapter, place that information here. Your business review and your marketing mix—whether working drafts or final decisions—belong here. If you've done market research, that report goes here, too.

You may find it helpful to summarize your conclusions. Write a brief two- or three-page summation of your offering, your competitive environment, your customer base, and your SWOT analysis.

Marketing Objectives and Strategies. Templates 1-4A and 1-4B should be the first items in this section. Use them to define your goals and how you will measure them. Remember, goals must be quantifiable, attainable, and measurable. Summarize your primary marketing goal using Template 1-8.

Template 1-8: Statement of Marketing Objective

Statement of Marketing Objective

The goal of our marketing is to increase gross revenue by _____
(dollars)

in the time period beginning _____ and ending _____.
(dates)

This increase in sales will accomplish _____
(summarize "why statements" from Template 1-4.)

_____

We will measure our performance against this goal by _____
(quantifiable measurement method)

_____

We feel this goal is attainable because_____
(rationale: past performance, projections, etc.)

_____

The objective is where you want to go; the strategy is the route by which you will get there. Here's an overview of strategic thinking as it applies to marketing. A strategy is a description of the steps a company will take to realize its objectives. Obviously there are many ways to get from point A to point B, whether you're talking about marketing or finding your way to Tuscaloosa. Choosing your strategy requires a foundation of knowledge: You need to know what you want to get out of the trip. The fastest route? The most scenic? A stop at Aunt Tillie's on the way? You get the point. Your objective must include those "why" goals that help you vote yes or no on each strategy under discussion.

All marketing strategies fall into one of two categories. Either you're going to help the entire market grow, or you're going to steal customers from your competition. When some people reported that Avon Skin So Soft lotion repelled mosquitoes, the universe of potential customers for this lotion instantly grew. These people had discovered a new function for the product, and this caused the market for the product to expand. On the other hand, when a grocery store advertises that it will honor coupons from a competitor's store, that is a strategy designed to steal customers from the competition. There's nothing unsavory about stealing in this context. If your industry is stable or declining, this may be the best road to growth available to you.

In any business cycle, enhancing the quality and value of your product and finding new market segments are strong marketing strategies.

Some Example Strategies

Depending on the problems and opportunities you've identified, you might choose a marketing strategy that addresses one of these areas:

- *Focus on seasonality.* You might choose to focus on building sales during a traditionally slow season, or alternatively, you might focus on maximizing sales during your annual busy season. A Christmas tree farm would obviously choose the latter. For an example of the former, see Chapter 7, "All About Radio Advertising." The case study on Heartland Litho tells how a printer used radio as part of a marketing strategy to boost business during slow seasons.

- *Attack the competition.* Others may be attacking your unique position, claiming to match offers you have made, for instance. Or mergers and changes at your competition may be claiming the spotlight, and you'd like to counter with some excitement of your own. The competitive situation described at the beginning of Chapter 6, "How to Create Print Ads that Sell," is an example showing how this strategy fits in the competitive marketplace. In Chapter 2, "Positioning," you can read more about choosing a positioning strategy in relation to your competitors.

- *Use packaging to sell.* You might decide that changing the way your product looks will increase sales. Sometimes a "tune-up" of the graphic design of the package is all your product needs to get new buyers' attention.

    There is another strategic opportunity in packaging to consider. Look for creative ways to boost the appeal of your product. Packaging your home-remodeling kits with clean-up supplies enclosed might give you the unique angle you need. Packaging your chewy dog biscuits in stay-fresh six-packs might do it. How can you improve the form and function of your product through packaging? You might find the unique selling proposition you need by making your product a better value.

- *Special promotions.* If incentives—offers of discounts, rebates, extras, and so on—seem to work in your industry, here's another subject you'd better plan to study. Promotions can also involve special events like a Grand Opening or Open House. Chapter 3 discusses promotional strategies in detail.

    Your advertising message, like your packaging, reflects an underlying strategy. Should you be using a long-term image-building campaign or shorter, more hard-sell promotional advertising? Your choice of advertising media as well as your choice of message springs from the marketing objectives and strategies you choose. Chapters 4 and 5 are designed to help you make these choices.

The next sections in your Marketing Plan notebook relate directly to the work you'll do in these upcoming chapters. Your positioning strategy, your promotional plans, your media strategy, and your advertising message will each require a tab in the binder. As you work through the templates in each chapter, keep your notes in the appropriate sections.

Master Calendar. As you decide your schedules for the different media you plan to use, keep a summary of that activity on a master calendar in this section. Templates 1-9A and 1-9B will show you how. In the chapters on the various media you'll find more templates and planning tools for scheduling.

Template 1-9A and B: Master Calendar

MARKETING PLAN

Master Calendar Example

	January	February	March	April	May	June	July	August	September	October	November	December

Media Calendar

Print — See Template 6-3D
- Magazines
- Newspapers
- Other

Radio — See Template 7-2B
- Station #1
- Station #2

TV — See Template 8-1B
- Station #1

Direct Mail — See Template 9-12
- First mail drop
- Second mail drop

Promotional Program — See Template 3-5

Publicity Program — See Template 10-4

Template 4-5 is a media calendar like this one.

Worksheets in the appropriate chapters will help you plan the schedule for each component of your marketing plan.

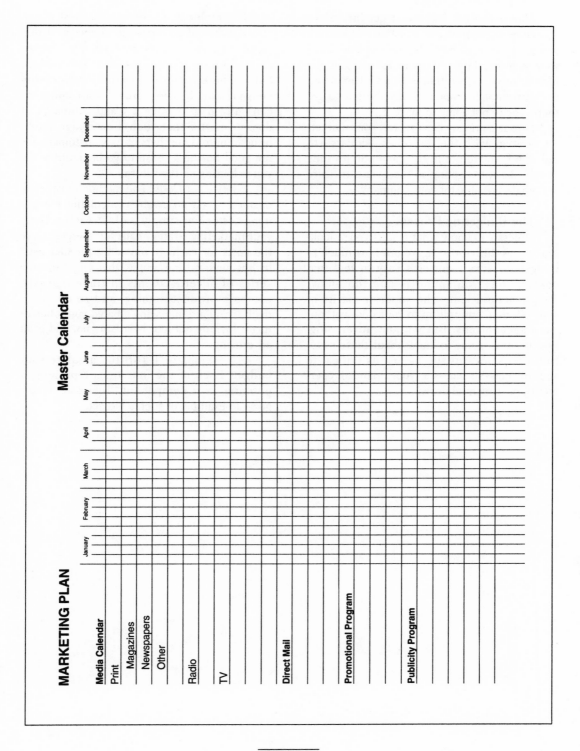

Master Budget. You won't get far before you come up against the question, "What's all this going to cost me?" No matter how good your road map or your reasons for going, if you plan to drive from Albuquerque to Tuscaloosa without enough money to buy the gas to get there, you're not going to make it.

If your company can't match your marketing strategy with the resources—dollars—to pull it off, you're not in the game. So it's time to talk about budgeting so that you can figure out what's possible for your company.

The Budgeting Process

Unless you know what results you're looking for, it's difficult to figure out how much to budget for advertising. It's easy to feel that every penny you spend is one too many: People should know the superior merits of your offering, and roll up to your door without such shenanigans. But without advertising, how are they going to know about those superior merits? Advertising is just as critical to your business's success as your financial, operations, or personnel decisions.

The problem: There's no real test of the affordability of advertising. You've probably heard the joke, "I know only half my advertising budget is working. I just don't know which half." There's another saying: "Advertising doesn't cost, it pays." But if your company can't afford to finance a grand campaign, it doesn't matter that such a campaign might bring in untold numbers of new customers. It's not good business sense to go bankrupt while you're betting on the future.

Component Costs. The method most small businesses rely on involves calculating component costs. You simply look at each activity your marketing strategy calls for, then estimate the costs for each. If you sell a product used by businesses, for example, that might mean a series of advertisements in trade journals, maybe a product catalog, and some direct mail. If you are managing a bank, your choices might include outdoor boards, radio, and print advertising.

Use Template 1-10B to calculate your budget. Each of the line items represents a potential cost component. Template 1-10A gives an example of such a budget.

Template 1-10A: Component Costs Budget Category Checklist

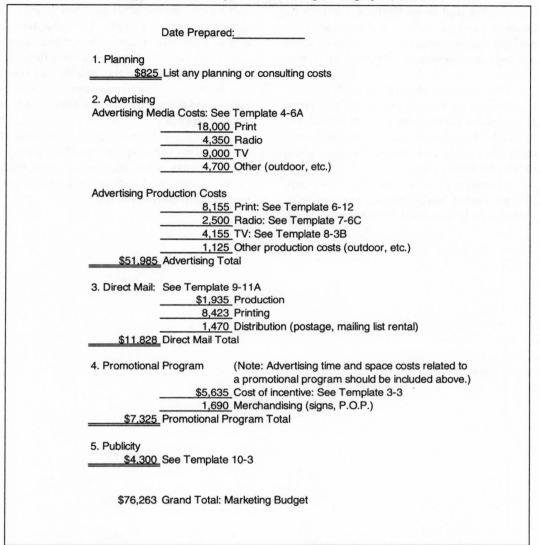

Date Prepared:_____

1. Planning
_____$825 List any planning or consulting costs

2. Advertising
Advertising Media Costs: See Template 4-6A
_____18,000 Print
_____4,350 Radio
_____9,000 TV
_____4,700 Other (outdoor, etc.)

Advertising Production Costs
_____8,155 Print: See Template 6-12
_____2,500 Radio: See Template 7-6C
_____4,155 TV: See Template 8-3B
_____1,125 Other production costs (outdoor, etc.)
_____$51,985 Advertising Total

3. Direct Mail: See Template 9-11A
_____$1,935 Production
_____8,423 Printing
_____1,470 Distribution (postage, mailing list rental)
_____$11,828 Direct Mail Total

4. Promotional Program   (Note: Advertising time and space costs related to
                               a promotional program should be included above.)
_____$5,635 Cost of incentive: See Template 3-3
_____1,690 Merchandising (signs, P.O.P.)
_____$7,325 Promotional Program Total

5. Publicity
_____$4,300 See Template 10-3

$76,263 Grand Total: Marketing Budget

Your dollar estimates in each of these areas, plus a "fudge factor" of 2 to 5 percent overall, will add up to your marketing budget. Arriving at good estimates may require research on your part. If you define what you need in each area well enough, you can get a great deal of free advice from potential vendors. Contact ad agencies, graphic artists, mailing houses, promotions special-ists, etc. Chapter 12 deals with this more specifically.

Explain that you are trying to arrive at a budget, and ask for proposals. You can probably get very rough ballpark figures over the phone—enough to help you decide whether to explore that area further.

Are you hearing figures that are out of your league? Check your sources and perhaps ask for a new proposal from a different vendor, but be prepared to go back to the drawing board if need be. Advertising is an arena of professional competition, and it's difficult to accomplish champagne objectives on a beer budget.

The upcoming chapters on each advertising medium include templates for budgeting. When you've finished the relevant worksheets in this book, you won't find it difficult to create a component costs budget for this section of your marketing plan.

Advertising-to-Sales Ratio. The other popular method of budget setting used by businesses is to look at industry averages. Usually there is an industry standard that represents "what works for the other guy." Your community may have its own quirks that make national averages less than relevant, but at least this is a place to start. Professional service firms, for example, vary wildly in the amount they spend on advertising. What competitors in your community are doing will be more important than national averages.

Example 1-2 shows the advertising-to-sales ratio for some typical retail businesses. If your business is not on this list, your trade association or your banker can probably provide the information you need.

Example 1-2: Retail Advertising-to-Sales Chart

Apparel	
Women's Wear Stores	2.9%
Men's Wear Stores	3.4%
Shoe Stores	2.9%

Automotive	
Auto Dealers	1.1%
Auto Service & Repair	3.4%
Tire & Auto Parts Dealers	1.7%

Health Care	
Drug Stores	1.4%
Hospitals	3.2%

Home Furnishings	
Appliance Stores	5.7%
Carpet Stores	2.4%
Furniture Stores	5.8%

Retailers	
Department Stores	3.5%
Discount Stores	2.3%
Mail Order Firms	13.5%

Building & Housing	
Real Estate Agents	1.7%
Lumber/Bldg. Stores	2.7%
Hardware Stores	2.3%
Mobile Home Dealers	2.3%
Moving Van Lines	2.4%

Financial	
Banks (% of assets):	
$1 Billion+	0.04%
$25–999 Million	0.08%
$10–25 Million	0.01%
Under $10 Million	0.14%
S&Ls	0.7%
Insurance Agents	0.8%
Stockbrokers	0.6%

Electronics	
Computer Stores	2.9%
Hi-Fi, Video Stores	4.6%

Business Services	
Office Supply Stores	0.4%
Employment Agencies	1.9%

Food Industry	
Supermarkets	1.4%
Convenience Stores	0.4%
Dairy	5.1%
Bakery	1.5%
Meat	1.7%
Beer	8.4%
Soft Drinks	6.6%
Restaurants:	
Full Menu	2.1%
Fast Food	2.8%

Leisure Market	
Hotels & Motels	3.5%
Movie Theaters	4.1%
Night Clubs	6.2%
Camera Stores	2.0%
Photofinishing Labs	4.7%
Travel Agents	5.0%
Sporting Goods Stores	3.0%
Lawn & Garden Stores	3.8%
Fabric & Sewing Stores	3.8%
Pet Shops	1.8%

Media	
Newspapers	2.5%
Magazines	4.0%
Broadcasters (Radio, TV)	3.8%
Cable TV	2.3%

Miscellaneous	
Jewelry Stores	6.2%
Schools	4.1%
Rental Equipment Firms	2.5%
Funeral Homes	3.4%
Invisible Fencing	2.7%

Our Source: Radio Advertising Bureau

The problem with the advertising-to-sales method is this: It creates a situation in which sales drive the marketing function. When problems arise and sales slow down, there is less money available to solve the problems causing the drop. You may want to have a fall-back plan in mind.

The advertising-to-sales method is useful as a first step. If your firm is new and has no history to fall back on, this method will help you have confidence that you're in the right ballpark with your budget.

If you're using the component costs approach, this method can act as a reality check. Does the budget you've established work out to a reasonable percentage of gross sales, given your industry and situation?

Whichever method you use, compare your budget to your previous year's expenditures. Does the budget you're considering represent a steep jump over last year's budget? This is not necessarily a bad thing, but it is something that you'll want to be able to explain. Look at your marketing objectives and put this budget to the test. Is this a reasonable amount to spend to accomplish those goals?

Template 1-4B, Goal Setting, includes a calculation that shows that you are spending X dollars to earn Y dollars. Your budget for advertising and promotion should not exceed that expenditure.

As you complete your budget process, you should be able to fill in Template 1-10B.

Template 1-10B: Master Budget

Date Prepared:_____

1. Planning
$_____ List any planning or consulting costs

2. Advertising
Advertising Media Costs: See Template 4-6A
     $_____ Print
     $_____ Radio
     $_____ TV
     $_____ Other (outdoor, etc.)

Advertising Production Costs
     $_____ Print: See Template 6-12
     $_____ Radio: See Template 7-6C
     $_____ TV: See Template 8-3B
     $_____ Other production costs (outdoor, etc.)
$_____ Advertising Total

3. Direct Mail: See Template 9-11A
     $_____ Production
     _____ Printing
     $_____ Distribution (postage, mailing list rental)
$_____ Direct Mail Total

4. Promotional Program (Note: Advertising time and space costs related to a promotional program should be included above.)
     $_____ Cost of incentive: See Template 3-3
     $_____ Merchandising (signs, P.O.P.)
$_____ Promotional Program Total

5. Publicity
$_____ See Template 10-3A

$_____ Grand Total: Marketing Budget

Calculating Payback

Despite the unscientific nature of advertising, you can attempt to calculate the income your ad campaign will generate. You must first anticipate the response your advertising will pull. Like all business projections, you will do this in terms of worst-case, most probable, and best-case scenarios. State this projected response in terms of a sales total.

Estimate your cost of goods sold related to these sales. Subtract that from the sales total. Add up all areas of your marketing budget. Subtract this from your last total. The dollar figure remaining is your campaign's contribution to profit. Is the number an attractive one? Keep working with this calculation until the results are both desirable and achievable.

Templates 3-3 and 9-11 explain in detail how to calculate cost and payback.

Scheduling for Cash Flow

Refer again to the master calendar for the months you intend your advertising strategy to cover. You've scheduled the appearance or "drop" dates for each activity. Now work backward and write in the costs associated with each at the point in time at which those costs must be paid. You now have a prediction of the cash flow required as well as the payback anticipated. Are your resources adequate to cover the outlay as it becomes due? Do not proceed until you can answer yes.

The Marketing Plan: A Summary

The following chapters will help you through the work of planning and executing an advertising campaign. But it's up to you to take the last step—*you* must measure sales and evaluate the effectiveness of your work. The cycle is not complete until you can answer the question, "Would I do this again?" Only careful tracking of costs and results will lead you to the answer. If your answer is yes, this means your campaign has been successful. But you can still do things better. If your answer is no, this does not mean that you shouldn't advertise. It means that you need to figure out what went wrong, and do it better next time.

You need measurable results from your advertising. As we discuss the different media, I'll mention specific ways you can craft your strategy so that the results are measurable, like putting a coupon in a print ad or a code number on a direct mail reply card. But I really can't say this often enough, and I can't do the work for you. Make projections. Measure

results. Compare the two. Learn from it. Adjust and try again. That's the substance of marketing as it applies to advertising and promotion.

There are other areas of marketing strategy that don't relate so directly to advertising: There's merchandising, and operations strategies, and much more to pricing and distribution than I covered in the section on the marketing mix. These subjects are beyond the scope of this book, but nonetheless worthy of your attention.

This list summarizes the actions you need to take before you truly have a marketing plan in place.

- Complete the business review, including:
  Write a mission statement (optional, but recommended)
  Define your four aspects of value
  Prepare your SWOT analysis
  Complete the goal-setting worksheets (why statements and revenue goals)
- Analyze your marketing mix in terms of the Four P's
- Do marketing research to enrich your perspective on customer behavior
- Choose strategies
- Develop a master calendar
- Develop a master budget

A good marketing plan is an essential tool for the small-business owner or manager who wants a profitable business. If you intend to flourish in both the short term and the long term, you need to follow these steps to develop a plan that is a vital and practical expression of your business goals. But the written plan is only half the battle; putting the plan into action is just as important. The rest of this book is devoted to helping you do just that.

Chapter 2

Positioning: The Heart of Creative Promotions

After reading this chapter, you will know how to:

1. Define what positioning does for your business.

2. Describe your unique position in terms of these components:
   - Your features/benefits
   - Your target market's needs/wants
   - Your competitors' positions

3. Choose a positioning strategy.

4. Write a positioning statement for your business and turn it into a tagline.

A flower shop opens in a crowded downtown area. Most shoppers here are office workers who come out for lunch and errands. There is good pedestrian traffic, but there are several competitors within a few blocks of this new shop, and many others available in town that take orders by phone. This new store advertises with a tagline that captures its difference from its competitors: "European-style flowers by the stem." Business grows steadily, and J. Kinney, Florist becomes a success.

What's the secret? Call it *positioning*, or *finding your unique selling proposition (USP)*. It's really just defining your own uniqueness and presenting it to your potential customers in a way that captures their interest. J. Kinney,

Florist carries an unusual selection of flowers and presents them in a way that makes the shopping experience as pleasant as the product. Her tagline conveys her uniqueness with precision. That's the essence of positioning.

"European" conjures up a world of taste and style more sophisticated than our own, one that we can enter by shopping at J. Kinney, Florist. "By the stem" implies a self-indulgent little browse, followed by an inexpensive, if impulsive, purchase. Häagen-Dazs used practically the same positioning to take its upscale ice cream all over America.

Positioning: The Art of Finding Your Unique Selling Proposition

Positioning is about making your offering different from, and more valuable than, your competitors' offerings—and placing that idea in the minds of a target group of customers. Positioning attracts customers by creating a positive and unique identity for your company and its offerings. Positioning is vital for distinguishing your offering from everybody else's.

In a world where there are more and more products and services every day, your customers are on advertising overload all the time. So they pick something to believe and hold that notion until a message breaks through and persuades them to change.

People can't hold warring ideas in their heads. They can't believe that the Norton Anthology is the best study guide for English literature, then study from a set of Cliffs Notes and believe they're doing the best they can to pass their exams. They can't believe that all paper towels are pretty much alike, buy one that costs more than most, and think that they are wise shoppers. The point is, positioning is your effort to claim a high ground in that overloaded prospect's head and hold it against competition.

There may be very little difference between your product and your competitors'— but if you can't find a way to communicate uniqueness and connect it to a need of your target, you might as well quit fighting your competition and sell out to them. There are many different ways to stake out a position. Just remember, your position reflects your unique selling proposition, and it is what makes your offering more valuable to your customers than what's being offered by your competition.

How will you be perceived as different from your competition in the minds of your targeted customers? To figure this out, you must look for your *best* customer and then design a position that matches *his or her* wants

and needs to an advantage that *only you* can offer. Remember, you can't be all things to all people, but you can be the vendor of choice for some group of them.

Positioning Affects Every Aspect of Your Communications—And Your Business

Positioning is the basis for all your communications—your packaging and product design, sales promotions, advertising, and public relations. Everything you do must reinforce that position—otherwise you just undermine your marketing efforts and sow confusion instead of confidence. Positioning is serious business. You must choose the *right* position, for now and down the road.

Do the work now to develop a clear position for your business vis-à-vis your competitors. You'll ensure that you get the most from your advertising budget. The truth is that with enough money, you can *buy* success in advertising. Mediocre, unfocused messages from a company without a clear position will generate sales surprisingly well if that company buys enough time or space to pound the message home. But think how much farther that budget could take you if you had a focused message, a unique selling proposition, and a target audience for your offering. Positioning—and the creative approach that grows from it— make the difference.

Developing the Positioning Statement—And the Tagline

Template 2-1A: Positioning Statement

Positioning Statement

1. What does your business do?

Whole Earth Market sells natural foods.

2. For whom? (Describe target market with a short phrase)

Neighborhood residents and health-conscious commuters.

3. What is your biggest benefit to them?

We offer fresh, wholesome alternatives to regular groceries.

4. Prove your claim. To what do you attribute that benefit?

Membership in a national natural foods distribution co-op, plus a network

of local organic food growers and a knowledgeable staff.

5. How will your customers perceive this benefit, relative to the competition?

Customers are healthier physically (quality of the food) and spiritually

(the small-community atmosphere of the store is satisfying).

Consider this business: A local natural foods market on a busy thoroughfare serves neighborhood residents and health-conscious commuters. It offers fresh, wholesome alternatives to regular groceries. Membership in a national natural foods distribution co-op, plus a network of local organic growers, and the store's hard-working and knowledgeable staff enable it to maintain its product-quality edge. Customers perceive themselves to be healthier physically for shopping here, but also healthier "spiritually" from participating in the small-community atmosphere of the store.

This short description has all the elements of a positioning statement. Later we'll refine it into a tagline that this business could use in its advertising to help distinguish itself to customers. These two concepts always go together: the positioning statement and the tagline. A tagline is just the positioning statement phrased in a way that makes it a memorable advertising slogan.

To begin creating your own sense of positioning for your business, answer the following questions with short, articulate answers that relate your offering to your customers' needs.

1. What does your business do?

2. For whom?

3. What is your biggest benefit to them?

4. Prove your claim. To what do you attribute that benefit?

5. How will your customers perceive this benefit, relative to the competition?

Templates 2-1A and 2-1B answer these questions for Whole Earth Market and J. Kinney, Florist. Use Template 2-1C to answer these questions for your own business. This won't be your final draft. It's just a start. Later in this chapter we'll analyze these questions in greater depth. Hang in there, and see how your understanding of positioning develops.

Template 2-1B: Positioning Statement

Positioning Statement

1. What does your business do?

J. Kinney, Florist sells flowers, greeting cards, and gifts.

2. For whom? (Describe target market with a short phrase)

Men and women with sophisticated tastes.

3. What is your biggest benefit to them?

Satisfy their need for a unique gift that is a good price/quality value.

4. Prove your claim. To what do you attribute that benefit?

We carry unusual flowers (even growing the prairie flowers ourselves), and we custom-design each bouquet individually (no menu!).

5. How will your customers perceive this benefit, relative to the competition?

Customers know that their gifts are individually designed, and they recognize the good value received in terms of price and quality.

Template 2-1C: Positioning Statement

Positioning Statement

1. **What does your business do?**

   _____

   _____

2. **For whom? (Describe target market with a short phrase)**

   _____

3. **What is your biggest benefit to them?**

   _____

   _____

4. **Prove your claim. To what do you attribute that benefit?**

   _____

   _____

   _____

   _____

5. **How will your customers perceive this benefit, relative to the competition?**

   _____

   _____

   _____

The USP—Unique Selling Proposition

In the 1950s, Rosser Reeves, then chairman of the Ted Bates & Co. advertising agency, was credited with inventing the USP. His ground rules for what makes a USP hold true today:

- All advertising must make a proposition to the customer: Buy this product, and you will get this specific benefit.

- This proposition must be unique, something the competition cannot or does not choose to promote.

- It must be so compelling that it can motivate consumers to answer a call to action.

The USP should be a brief and colorful statement of your positioning. It's the seed from which your creative approach will grow.

Components of Positioning

In determining how to position your offering, there are three components you need to consider:

- Features/benefits
- Target market
- Competition

All positioning is a matter of balancing these components, varying the emphasis placed on each to describe a position that uniquely defines your offerings and distinguishes them from your competition.

Features into Benefits

A feature is anything inherent in your product or service, what you have designed into it—for example, eight-power zoom on a video camera, or extra stain-dissolving power in a laundry detergent.

A benefit is what the customer gets out of it—for example, easy-to-get close-ups of sporting events from the stands, or cleaner clothes. A benefit statement tells you what need is met by using the product or taking advantage of the service. Consider these feature and benefit statements:

Feature: New X9 is a strong all-purpose cleaner.

Benefit: You clean quicker with X9 cleaner.

Feature: The Ross and McCarrier legal practice handles business, family, and accident law.

Benefit: At work, home, and play, Ross and McCarrier have your legal needs covered.

In the first example, the benefit is tangible—faster performance. But benefits don't have to be tangible. Often they appeal more to the emotions. In the second example, the benefit is the secure feeling the clients of Ross and McCarrier have, twenty-four hours a day.

Car advertising is a great arena in which to observe the difference between tangible benefits and emotional benefits. Cars are sold on both. We want to be sure we're choosing the right features: air bags for the safety of our family, antilock brakes, good acceleration—but wait. Acceleration is also an emotional benefit. Car commercials sell the great feeling of taking off on the open road. You've seen plenty of commercials in which the announcer talks about safety features while the visual is pure emotional appeal. The car you choose to drive is one of the most powerful statements you make about your personality and standing in the world. Compare the advertising for different makes of cars if you want a quick course in positioning. Watch how they balance the components of features, target markets, and competitors.

Now try this with your business. Using Template 2-2, prepare a list of features of your offering, whether it is a product or a service. Of each, ask the question: What is it about this feature that gives it value in the mind of the customer? Make up a list of at least five features and a benefit statement for each.

Template 2-2: Features into Benefits

Features into Benefits

Feature:

Example: Dry cleaning machines at multiple locations

Benefit:

You can have your clothes back sooner.

1. _____ _____

2. _____ _____

3. _____ _____

4. _____ _____

5. _____ _____

If this seems difficult, try thinking about interactions you've had with your clients. Which of your features do they talk about? Listen for the benefit statements in their comments. "I never would've switched to your bank if you hadn't opened an East Side branch" translates a street address into a compelling benefit: convenient location.

The Target Market

Who cares if your hotel serves the best prime rib in town, if you're trying to sell it as the headquarters for a conference of vegetarians? You've got to match the benefits of your offering to the needs of your target customers. To do that, you need to look at your potential customers in terms of the following:

- *Demographics.* This includes the data the census bureau collects—age, sex, income, education level, marital status, family size, home ownership, occupation, and similar characteristics that influence potential needs. For example, low- to middle-income high school graduates working in blue-collar jobs are more likely to patronize convenience stores, and such a business will want to create a product mix and advertising that appeals to these customers.

- *Lifestyle.* This includes the values and attitudes that influence customers' needs and purchase decisions. For example, people who value a health-conscious lifestyle are likely to be good customers for a natural food store or a health club.

- *Media usage.* Brides suddenly read bride magazines; first-time home buyers suddenly read shelter magazines in a way they never did before. Business decision makers read the financial pages of their local newspaper more closely than the lifestyle section. What patterns might help you find your target customers through media?

- *Purchase characteristics.* Do your best customers actually buy what you sell? Toddlers don't buy Cap'n Crunch—their parents do, although the parents would never eat the stuff. Families usually make vacation decisions as a committee. These are examples of products and services that are sold through clusters of purchase influencers and purchase decision makers. If you're in this situation, you might need to reach and influence several different generations with your advertising. For example, suppose you operate a theme park within a short drive of several major markets. You buy cable TV time in those markets, and you air a mix of spots. Some emphasize the excitement of your rides and attractions in a fast-paced style. Other spots highlight the *value* of your offering—one family ticket gives you

unlimited all-day admission. The net result: Kids and parents agree that a day at your park is a great idea.

- *Geographic location.* Where people live— the city, suburbs, or country— affects their needs. People who live in urban environments are more likely to be customers for restaurants and small grocery stores, and will be more likely to rent minivans for the weekend.

These kinds of characteristics help you identify the customers you can serve best, and in whose minds you must create your unique selling proposition (USP).

I touched on the need for market research in Chapter 1. I'll say it again here: Expending your energy doing research will be well worth the time and investment. Most entrepreneurs I know have trouble swallowing that idea. "I know my customers," they tell me. "I'll just go by what my gut says." Sometimes you can do that. If you're good at what you do, and you're on the front lines selling it to your customers and supporting them after the sale, then it's likely that you have a good grasp of their concerns. Otherwise, doing some customer research will help. At the very least, be sure to listen to what customers tell you at the trade show, on the showroom floor, at the teller's window, at the cash register, in personal discussions—wherever you or your employees have contact with customers. Analyze their comments in relation to the topics we just discussed. Build a database that gives you detailed knowledge of your best customers. It will help you find many more like them.

Consider using a market research firm. Tell the firm that you are working on a positioning strategy, and you'd like a survey designed to help you match your offering to some customer group's needs. You will expand your knowledge of research methods and results just by talking with the firm. And you might find you want to take the next step and use its services.

If you can't spend the time or money to survey your market, at least capsulize what you know. Imagine your ten best customers. Then, using Template 2-3, write out your answers to these questions about those customers.

1. What benefit are they purchasing? (Can you match this with anything on your benefits list from Template 2-2?)

2. Where is it purchased, and where is it used?

3. When is it purchased, and when is it used?

4. How is it purchased and used? Alone, or with other people?

5. How frequently is it purchased?

6. How is the market changing? What trends are affecting your customers? How will the answers to the previous questions change over the next three years?

Remember, in answering these questions, you need to focus on the *benefits* your customers purchase, not your product itself.

Template 2-3: Target Market

What Do You Know about Your Target Market?

1. What benefit are they purchasing?

_____

_____

2. Where is it purchased?

_____

Where is it used?

_____

3. When is it purchased? (Time of day, time of year, at time of what need?)

_____

When is it used?

_____

4. How is it purchased and used? Alone, or with other people?

_____

_____

5. How frequently is it purchased?

_____

6. How is the market changing? What trends are affecting your customers?

_____

_____

How will the answers to the previous questions change over the next three years?

_____

_____

_____

_____

The Competition

Study your competition! Try their products. Collect their ads. Analyze your conclusions. If you've decided to use a market research firm to study your target market, you might expand the scope to include researching the competition while you're at it.

You're curious not just about what your competitors offer, but about what position they hold in the mind of the target market. From physics we know that two objects can't occupy the same space at the same time. That's true of space in the mind, as well. You have to find an *unused* position for your offering, one that has a compelling appeal to the target market. What gap has the competition left uncovered? It's your mission to find out.

Define your competition by category and by name. If you compete in multiple markets or with multiple locations, your list may be different for each. Our European-style florist, for instance, competes in two categories; flowers is the obvious one, but there's also the cards-and-gifts category. Her list of competitors will include both.

If you can recognize the positioning of a competitor, from its advertising or from what you've learned about it, write a short statement summarizing it. To do this, answer the questions we discussed before for understanding your business (Template 2-1C).

1. What does the business do?
2. For whom?
3. What is its biggest benefit to its customers?
4. How does it support that claim? To what does it attribute that benefit?
5. How will its customers perceive this benefit, relative to your own key benefit? And how would *your* customers perceive this benefit?

The florist knew that her biggest competition came from Freeman's, a well-established family business started in the 1940s. She answered the questions as follows:

1. Freeman's sells a small range of familiar flowers and a wide range of gifts. It also grows its own plants for sale.
2. Its market is "our parents' generation"—the older, conservative, well-to-do population.
3. Its biggest benefit is dependability—its customers are confident that Freeman's can meet any need, with competent service and the expected range of choices in flowers and gifts.
4. Freeman's could attribute this benefit—the ability to do anything for any-one—to its size. It has seven locations, plus flower farms outside of town, and a fleet of vans.
5. Its customers perceive this benefit as sufficient to earn their loyalty. They don't realize the value of unique flowers, sold with a custom approach; they do value the reliability and predictability Freeman's has offered over its fifty years in business.

Our florist's customers feel that Freeman's size is a drawback. They sense that sheer size dictates an "assembly-line" process, resulting in a lack of individuality in Freeman's products.

Return to your positioning statement (Template 2-1), where you answered these five questions for your business. Revise your comments if your perspective has changed after learning more about your target market and the benefits they value.

Uncovering Your Advantage over Your Competition

You're looking for a sustainable competitive advantage, a position you can claim and hold for years to come. Explore your points of difference from your competition, whether positive or negative. By that comparison you will discover what position your competitors leave uncovered, and find where your opportunity lies.

You should consider these dimensions:

- Your packaging. Your product *is* its packaging. Is it prettier? Is it more informative? Does it appeal to a younger/older segment of the overall market?

- Form and function characteristics. These are performance attributes, such as reliability, speed, or ease of use.

- How's your follow-through? People buy complicated products on the basis of follow-up support or training. Can you add value by increasing your service here? For example, could you include free installation with a software purchase?

- Your image—the ambiance, or cachet, you convey. How's the appearance of your store or office? Are you participating in your community in a way that enhances your public image? This is especially important to service businesses.

- Your distribution. Are you everywhere your competitor appears? Or are you the local best-kept secret? Are your locations appropriate, convenient, and well known? Are you timely in your delivery? Do you have what your customers want, when they want it?

- Your price point and your level of quality. That combination defines your *value*. This is an important point. We tend to think of a high-value product as "something that costs more and is worth it." Low quality at a low price can be a good value too, but in a different way. Take kids' shoes, for example. If Johnny is going to outgrow a pair of sneakers in six months, why buy the more expensive brand that won't wear out for years? That higher quality simply has no advantage for you. Your better *value* will be cheaply made shoes at cheap prices.

- Ease of switching products. How common is it for purchasers to substitute one competitor's product for another? If you're out of toothpaste, and the store you visit does-

n't carry your favorite brand, you will probably buy a brand you've never heard of rather than go home with none. Conversely, if you came for a sundress and didn't find anything you liked, you would probably go away empty-handed rather than settle for a suit. The "ease of possession" aspect of value is relevant here as well.

- The "new" edge. Do you have new products, improvements, or innovations you plan to introduce?

- The value of your name and reputation. In retail, this might be called a brand identity. In service, it's a component of your image.

- Any functional benefits to your customers that are not covered under one of the categories above.

Maybe you recognized among the items on this list the four aspects of value we discussed in Chapter 1. Determine where you outperform your competition in ways your customers value, and you'll have a good idea what your positioning opportunities will be.

Dimensions of Competition

To compare yourself with your competitors, use Template 2-4. This template asks you to rate your competitors on the dimensions we've just discussed. You will also rate your company. These ratings help you discover where your advantages may lie.

The dimensions included are relevant to most businesses, but there will usually be some dimensions particular to your field. Include those in the "Other" section and make appropriate ratings. I have included two filled-in examples of this template, Templates 2-4A and 2-4B. These examples will help you see how filling out this template reveals competitive weaknesses and positioning opportunities for you to explore.

Template 2-4A: Dimensions of Competition

Find where your opportunity lies: Compare yourself to your competition. Where do you have positive answers compared to their negative answers? That's an advantage you can claim and sustain.

Competitor Name: J. Kinney, Florist

Dimension	Negative					Neutral				Positive		Comments
Packaging	5	4	3	2	1	0	1	2	(3)	4	5	Our wrapping is beautiful, but doesn't have our logo.
Form/function	5	4	3	2	1	0	1	2	3	(4)	5	
Follow-through	5	4	3	2	1	0	1	2	(3)	4	5	We expect customers to try to care for their flowers.
Image	5	4	3	2	1	0	1	2	3	4	(5)	Stylish & earthy: we have cats, birds, etc.
Distribution	5	4	(3)	2	1	0	1	2	3	4	5	We use a variety of services; sometimes it's awkward.
Price	5	4	3	2	(1)	0	1	2	3	4	5	We're pricey…
Quality	5	4	3	2	1	0	1	2	3	4	(5)	…but great.
Ease of switch	5	4	3	2	1	0	1	2	3	4	(5)	
Innovation	5	4	3	2	1	0	1	2	3	4	(5)	We grow our own prairie flowers and hand-make gifts.
Reputation	5	4	3	2	1	0	1	2	(3)	4	5	Very good among those who know us.
Other												
_____	5	4	3	2	1	0	1	2	3	4	5	
_____	5	4	3	2	1	0	1	2	3	4	5	
_____	5	4	3	2	1	0	1	2	3	4	5	

Template 2-4B: Dimensions of Competition

Find where your opportunity lies: Compare yourself to your competition. Where do you have positive answers compared to their negative answers? That's an advantage you can claim and sustain.

Competitor Name: _Freeman's Flowers_

Dimension	Negative					Neutral				Positive		Comments
Packaging	5	4	3	2	1	0	1	2	(3)	4	5	All the packaging has the logo, but it's ugly.
Form/function	5	4	3	2	1	0	1	2	3	(4)	5	
Follow-through	5	4	3	2	1	0	1	2	3	4	(5)	They replace anything for any reason.
Image	5	4	3	2	1	0	1	(2)	3	4	5	Widely known, but seen as "old guard."
Distribution	5	4	3	2	1	0	1	2	3	4	(5)	Locations all over town and a fleet of trucks
Price	5	4	3	2	1	0	1	2	3	4	(5)	Inexpensive
Quality	5	4	3	(2)	1	0	1	2	3	4	5	Their flowers don't last.
Ease of switch	5	4	3	2	1	0	1	2	3	4	(5)	
Innovation	5	4	(3)	2	1	0	1	2	3	4	5	Boring old mums!
Reputation	5	4	3	2	1	0	1	(2)	3	4	5	Well known by "old guard." Unquestioned choice.

Other

	Negative					Neutral				Positive		Comments
_____	5	4	3	2	1	0	1	2	3	4	5	_____
_____	5	4	3	2	1	0	1	2	3	4	5	_____
_____	5	4	3	2	1	0	1	2	3	4	5	_____

As you look at these examples, do you see the competitive opening for the florist? In most dimensions, J. Kinney and Freeman's are pretty closely ranked. But compare the rankings in the areas of price, quality, ease of switch, and innovation. What I see tells me that for J. Kinney, her prairie flowers are an opening to distinguish her offering from her competitor's. This is a way for the company to position itself, creating its USP. She tells us that she can position herself as an innovative florist, and that because it is easy to switch florists, this might attract new business. Further, this suggests a potential advertising approach. She should consider advertising a price discount coupon on prairie flowers. How did we come to that conclusion?

1. Her price and quality answers tell me that she has a product of good value to offer, but its retail price is higher than Freeman's.

2. The "ease of switch" answers indicate that Freeman's customers are likely to respond to an offer, since doing so involves little risk or change in their overall beliefs.

3. Her product innovation—prairie wildflowers—has real news value; she is the only florist carrying these unusual flowers. They may have broad market appeal, since current lifestyle trends, such as the popularity of "country" decorating motifs and a heightened awareness of ecology, make these flowers desirable to her competitor's customers.

If this florist's marketing objective is to attract customers from competitors like Freeman's, a sales promotion advertising price discounts on prairie flowers would be an on-target strategy for doing so. Ranking the dimensions of competition for comparison helped our florist to uncover this opportunity.

Template 2-4C: Dimensions of Competition

Find where your opportunity lies: Compare yourself to your competition. Where do you have positive answers compared to their negative answers? That's an advantage you can claim and sustain.

Competitor Name: _____

Dimension	Negative					Neutral				Positive		Comments
Packaging	5	4	3	2	1	0	1	2	3	4	5	_____
												_____
Form/function	5	4	3	2	1	0	1	2	3	4	5	_____
												_____
Follow-through	5	4	3	2	1	0	1	2	3	4	5	_____
												_____
Image	5	4	3	2	1	0	1	2	3	4	5	_____
												_____
Distribution	5	4	3	2	1	0	1	2	3	4	5	_____
												_____
Price	5	4	3	2	1	0	1	2	3	4	5	_____
												_____
Quality	5	4	3	2	1	0	1	2	3	4	5	_____
												_____
Ease of switch	5	4	3	2	1	0	1	2	3	4	5	_____
												_____
Innovation	5	4	3	2	1	0	1	2	3	4	5	_____
												_____
Reputation	5	4	3	2	1	0	1	2	3	4	5	_____
												_____

Other

	Negative					Neutral				Positive		Comments
_____	5	4	3	2	1	0	1	2	3	4	5	_____
_____	5	4	3	2	1	0	1	2	3	4	5	_____
_____	5	4	3	2	1	0	1	2	3	4	5	_____

If some of your answers on Template 2-4C were "We do pretty well, and the competition does too," don't give up there. Most product categories have become much more crowded in recent years.

Take athletic shoes. Five years ago it was possible to come up with a real innovation—a shoe specifically designed for women's aerobics, for example. But today shoes have gotten about as good as they need to be, given what we're willing to pay for them. Today the innovations are more likely to be small refinements, or even decorative elements. We're offered either air pumps and flashing lights as new benefits or a positioning strategy like Nike's "Just Do It" campaign—a creative approach that stresses the emotional, not the tangible, benefits of the product.

Compare the benefit you feel is your key advantage to your competition's offerings. Have you staked out a territory where you can stand alone? Have you found your *unique* position? What does that difference mean to the customer? Remember, your customers' perception about you and your offerings *is* the truth, as far as they are concerned. It doesn't matter whether you think it's accurate or not.

An important goal of advertising is creating a positive perception about your offering. To do that, you have to start from where the customer is.

Market research can dramatically increase the odds that you will position your offering successfully. But whatever the grounds on which you make a decision, whether analyzing your own gut instincts or studying the market through research, do something! All your subsequent work will be built on this foundation. Make sure you lay it properly and build it to last.

Choosing Your Positioning Strategy

Your positioning strategy will reflect these components:

- The target market
- The product and its key benefit
- The competition

What makes your positioning strategy unique is the degree of emphasis you place on each of these facets.

Positioning strategies can fall into some common categories, which I've numbered and located on Templates 2-5A and 2-5B. The position on the chart reflects the degree of emphasis on the components target market, key benefit, and competition. But remember, the positioning you develop will probably not fit neatly into one of these slots. There are many combinations and variations on types of positions. See which of these are relevant to your business, then try them on for size. Try writing a positioning statement for each of several strategies. Then you will have several options to compare and evaluate.

First, we'll talk about the extremes. The positions described below reflect an emphasis on one component to the exclusion of the other two components.

Template 2-5A: Positioning Strategies 1-3

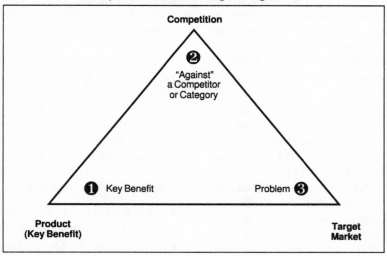

1. Key Benefit/Attribute

I can't say it often enough: There should be some sort of compelling benefit implied by your position. Depending on what you sell, it will probably be some variation on one of these attributes.

- Quality—the offering meets customers' needs and expectations—works right, looks right, fits, etc.

- Selection—there is a large variety of offerings so that customers can find what they are looking for.

- Price—the cost to the customer is commensurate with the value placed on the purchase.

- Service—the company provides support, training, delivery, etc., to make it easy for customers to buy and use the offering.

- Location—the company is located to give customers easy access or makes it easy to buy from home, as with mail-order companies.

Which attribute or combination of attributes you emphasize will depend on what you sell, what your customers expect, and what your competition is doing.

Are you competing in a crowded niche, like the athletic shoes we were talking about? You might create your positioning based on price (low), service (informed salespeople), selection (lots of styles and brands), or location (shopping mall). Or you may want to go after special groups of customers, such as athletic teams in your area. These are ways to create a key benefit out of fairly generic attributes.

Key benefit positioning is not a good strategy for products that are competing against very similar offerings. If you are in a commodity market, you are likely to find another strategy or combination of strategies to be more successful.

2. Against a Competitor or Category

We still remember the Avis car rental commercials: "We're No. 2, so we have to try harder." That's positioning against a specific competitor. In local markets, you're likely to see groceries and discount stores choose specific competitors to position against. The more like a commodity your product is—with no inherent difference from the products carried by your competition—the more appropriate this strategy might be for you.

In this strategy, you position yourself not just in terms of the product itself, but in terms of services, convenience, or some other enhancement that will attract customers to you rather than to some specific competitor. One consumer electronics store has the tagline "Can we really beat the giant? You bet!" to position itself against its largest competitor in the same city.

Sometimes a positioning strategy breaks new ground by positioning against an entire category. The way Miller Brewing created the light beer market by introducing Miller Lite is a classic example. This strategy is to create a niche market and then seek to become its leader. In doing this, consider more than your direct competitors. For example, in the entertainment business, sporting events compete with movies, video rentals, plays, and similar activities. Whatever your field, consider all the alternatives to your offering. J. Kinney, Florist, for example, competes not only with other florists but also with gift shops and candy stores.

By choosing this strategy, you position yourself as an alternative to a competitor or a whole category of products or services.

3. By Problem

In some categories, particularly within the service industry, the challenge is not so much fighting your competition as building a market for what you sell. This means calling attention to the problem you help customers solve.

Suppose your business is a nonprofit agency that makes assessments and refers clients to alcohol and other drug treatment programs. You may not have any competition at all—or want to steal market share from them, if they exist. What you *do* want is for those affected by these problems to be aware that solutions exist. Some examples of positioning by problem might be:

- Lawn fertilization. Problem solved: A troubled lawn becomes green and weed-free.
- Copy shop. Problem solved: Documents are copied and back in your hands with minimum delay.

You could consider this type of positioning to be the flip side of positioning by key benefit. They both deal with problems and solutions. But here, you would choose to dramatize the problem to a greater extent than the solution.

Now we'll talk about positioning strategies that blend two components (Template 2-5B).

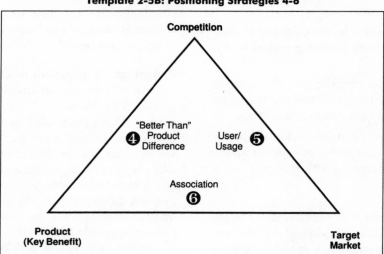

Template 2-5B: Positioning Strategies 4-6

4. Product Difference — "We're Better than the Others"

A cat litter manufacturer adds a disposable litter-box liner to each package, and advertises that its product is more convenient. That's positioning on product difference. It's not truly great positioning, however—it's too easy for the competition to duplicate. Notice how laundry detergents play that catch-up game. As soon as one came out with refill cartons, so did each of the others.

If your product or service has an inherent drama to its unique qualities, your difference will be an easy position for you to claim. Our florist, with her prairie flowers, could use product difference as a positioning strategy. The difference between this strategy and key benefit positioning is this: You acknowledge that there are other products that deliver the same benefit as your offering. Your positioning is that you deliver *more* or *better* value.

5. Users and Product Usage

This positioning encourages the consumer to use a product or service, then encourages him or her to select the product or service you sell—not your competitor's.

Many businesses grow by the "80/20 rule"—anticipating that 80 percent of the business comes from 20 percent of the customers. Take a look again at your best customers. If you know how and when they use your product, you can choose a position that plays to their usage habits. Think about "The night belongs to Michelob" or International Coffees' "Celebrate the moments of your life." These are ways to associate your product with special uses. Are there special uses for what you sell? Perhaps you run a hair salon. You might decide to target wedding business by offering group rates on styling for all members of the wedding party. This would be positioning on users and usage.

If your media plan is likely to involve television, this could be a very good positioning strategy for you. The emotional involvement of television lends itself well to users and usage positioning.

6. By Association

Positioning by association uses the beliefs of the target market to extend credibility to your product or service offering. In this approach, you associate your offering with someone or something your target customer already believes in. It is highly appropriate for the service firm. A simple example: A Hollywood hair salon advertises itself as "hairdresser to the stars."

This type of positioning doesn't take a big budget, and can directly challenge a competitor's position. You'll often see it used in political campaigns, where a successful official endorses an unknown candidate, who benefits from the endorser's reputation. Another example would be local companies in a college town using the head football or basketball coach as a product or service endorser.

Choosing the Right Position for Your Business

Let's look at our natural foods store again. Looking at the positioning statement made earlier, we can take what we know now and develop it into a tagline that captures the store's position vis-à-vis its competitors and the needs of its customers. Suppose the store developed a slogan, "We're Naturally Better." We'd know it has chosen to position on product difference, the strategy we call *better than*. The rationale: It carries better-quality products than the regular commercial groceries.

How about J. Kinney, Florist? She's using the user/usage positioning strategy, as demonstrated by her tagline, "European-style flowers by the stem." She has chosen to cultivate her clients' self-image through their flower-buying habits. She recognized how the 80/20 rule applied to her business. Rather than competing head-on with other florists offering predictable traditional bouquets, she appealed to more sophisticated flower buyers, and offered them a desirable alternative.

We've talked about claiming that space in the prospect's head and holding it. You might have differentiated yourself by offering the lowest price with high quality, or high price with high quality and superb service (as in an elegant restaurant or boutique), or best selection, or most convenient.

But is this a niche you deserve? Does it properly position you and bring out the best you have to offer? By your experience or talent, is this a statement you've earned the right to make? To succeed, positioning must be con-

sistently supported in every aspect of your business. If you've made a claim you can't support, you'll alienate your customers because you have violated their expectations. Conversely, by delivering what you promise and even exceeding your customers' expectations, you are doing exactly the right things to stay in business a long time.

Now use Template 2-5C to apply positioning strategy to your world. Think about your three closest competitors. Review their advertising, especially the taglines they use, and their scores on Template 2-4C. You should be able to place them on this map.

Template 2-5C: Positioning Strategies

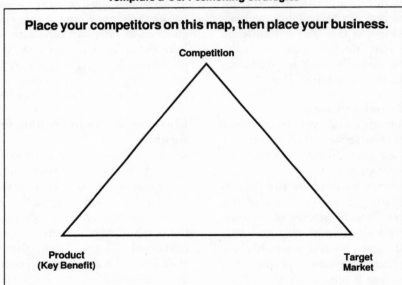

Place your competitors on this map, then place your business.

Competition

Product
(Key Benefit)

Target
Market

You now know what positions are left uncovered, or whether your competitors are fighting each other head to head. Are there any blank positions on your map? If there are, you have discovered an opening that you might be able to use to your advantage.

Review the Components of Positioning

Positioning shapes perceptions. Once perceptions have been set, changing them is difficult, so you must be careful about how you

proceed. Do not let people get a negative opinion of your business, as difficult as that can be. One rude interaction with a customer can undo months of advertising your friendly customer service.

Positioning is powerful. It can help you attract customers from your competition or build a market where there was none. It's the best tool you have for maximizing your advertising's effectiveness.

At its heart, positioning is simple. You can reduce the whole process to these three steps:

1. Start with the market. What benefit do customers seek? Think about the four aspects of value: form/function, time, place, and ease of possession.

    Says our florist: "We serve two markets: the walk-in traffic from within a few blocks, and the phone orders. Both types of customers seek a gift of flowers that will be beautiful, unique, convenient, and not too expensive."

2. Match these to the benefits you offer, to create a short list of key benefits. "Customers get:
    a. Unique and beautiful flowers
    b. Convenience, since we're either physically close or a phone call away
    c. Value: something pretty, delivered, for an affordable price."

3. Match this short list against your competitors' benefits. What is on your list that isn't on theirs? That's your unique selling proposition.
    "Customers receive a gift of flowers that are beautiful and truly unique."

J. Kinney, Florist's positioning claims the User/Usage position. The uniqueness of her product line and the unique way she sells it (by the stem or in custom arrangements) differentiates her from other florists and appeals to her customers' self-image.

Write Your Positioning Statement—Then Use It

Now it's time to compare and evaluate the different alternatives you've developed. Writing the tagline is the test that tells you when you've arrived at a solid positioning statement. Condense the components above into one sentence. It might not be "zippy" at first—it might read something like, "For natural foods consumers, Whole Earth Market is the store that provides the widest selection of highest-quality products." Brainstorm to shorten and brighten the sentence into a tagline.

Dos:
- Go with the flow—don't try to change consumer behavior too radically or too fast. Look for advantages among the current usage patterns.

- Always think in terms of your *best* current customer—remember the 80/20 rule.

- If you and your competition are fairly similar, you have two alternatives: Either consider a preemptive strategy, where you take a feature that's generic to the category and claim it as yours, or look for the gaps—something the competition has overlooked.

- Make sure everything you do reinforces your positioning, from your advertising to your building maintenance. You can't succeed by claiming to be upscale and then allowing your store to look tacky. The location of your storefront, the furniture you choose, and the way you display your goods all combine to support your positioning. Law firms recognize the importance of this, and accept paying higher rents to do business at a prestigious address.

Don'ts
- Don't forget the importance of focus. You can never be all things to all people.

- While positioning is for the long term, refinements will be needed as your marketplace evolves. Don't stop reviewing and revising your strategy as the components change.

- Don't position yourself too directly against a competitor. You're giving that competitor an unreasonable amount of control over your future.

- Don't position on price if you can't come through on the claim consistently. It's amazing what people remember about money.

- Don't promise what you can't deliver. I met a sign maker at a trade fair who grumbled about customers never giving him enough lead time. The name of his business: "Signs by Tomorrow." I say he has no right to complain! He's chosen to promote a benefit that's important to his customers. The problem is, delivering on it is putting stress on his business.

- Don't choose a strategy without doing some kind of market research and comparing several alternatives.

The Big Picture: Putting Your Positioning to Use

What you've learned as you've worked on positioning may have important ramifications for your marketing plan. Does your product need refinement to offer a benefit the market is asking for? Is this a need the competition has overlooked? If you're selling wallpaper, and people want matching flooring, it might make sense for you to expand your product line. Is your price point suitable for your position, as it relates to quality and value? Is your packaging consistent with your positioning? Does it look as valuable as it should?

It's easy—but unfortunate—to rush forward with a positioning campaign before all the components of support are in place.

Once you begin to use positioning, test how you're doing. Have you chosen the right position? Is it appealing to your best customers, and more prospects like them? You can research this through telephone surveys or a written questionnaire or a focus group. Investing in a survey by a marketing research firm could give you an important edge at this point. That survey should examine:

- Buying habits. When, where, and how often do customers purchase this product or service? How loyal are they to a particular brand or supplier?

- Media habits. Where did they learn about the product?

- Perceived benefits. Open-ended questions. Let your customers tell you what benefits they've discovered, and find valuable.

- Satisfaction. Are your customers satisfied with the value received for price paid, the performance of the product, and the emotional needs it may have met.

- Demographics/lifestyle. Questions that can help you refine your marketing plan.

Beyond Positioning—To the Advertising Strategy

Your positioning affects your advertising choices in several ways. You've defined and prioritized your key benefits; that gives you a hierarchy of what you want your target to absorb first, second, and so on. Sticking to these priorities will keep your ads simple and focused.

You know more about your target market, and where and how to reach it. You've given some thought to what your customers hold important, which helps you understand how to motivate them.

The next logical step seems to be determining your creative approach. You might jump forward to Chapter 5, "The Creative Approach," at this point, and begin to apply what you know.

Stop! There are two chapters in the way, and for good reason. In my business, in creating promotional plans for my clients, we use the motto "analyze, strategize, create." Positioning is part of the "analyze" phase of the process. Before you create, you need a good strategy that will carefully lay out how you will effectively communicate who you are and what you offer to your prospective customers.

Therefore, read in Chapter 3 about sales promotions, to study whether they have a place in your plan. You should decide before you begin how to concoct your creative approach, as it will clearly have an impact on what you communicate, and how.

Then read in Chapter 4 about writing a media plan. Right now you may have a good idea what media reach your target, but which will you use and what might the mix be? Answering these questions involves making quantitative and qualitative comparisons, as well as budget calculations. The media plan you develop is going to have an impact on your creative approach. What works in newsprint might have no application at all on cable TV.

You're ready for the "strategize" phase of the process. Before you begin to shape a creative approach, take time to learn about what you might offer, how, and where. That's what the next chapters are about.

Chapter 3

Promotions: Do They Have a Place in Your Plan?

When your mechanic sends you a coupon for a discount on an oil change, or your local coffee shop rewards you with a free cup of coffee every tenth time you buy, you're seeing a promotional program at work.

A promotion is a planned strategy for increasing sales over a short period. A promotion adds value to the product or service offered. It stimulates sales for reasons *other than* the product's inherent benefits.

We call those reasons *incentives*. Sometimes the incentive is designed to specifically make a sale, as in "$2.00 off medium pizza with this coupon." Other times the incentive is planned simply to expose the customer to the product—to break down preliminary barriers that are roadblocks to a future sale. Suppose you manage a dress store, and you're perceived as pricey. A good discount sale—as much as 20 percent off—will bring new people into your store, who before saw price as a barrier. Now that they're in your store, they may purchase something. Even if they don't, they've had a chance to become familiar with your store. They are more likely to come again.

That's the type of goal you can accomplish with a promotional program. You can persuade people to try your product, to experiment with new beliefs about your service; you can shift buying habits so that light users find reasons to buy more.

Who uses promotions? There are business-to-business promotional programs, and there are consumer programs. We'll talk mainly about the latter; the concepts we'll discuss are really about the same for both. Remember, people do business with people. It's just a matter of what market you're trying to influence—end users or intermediaries.

Different businesses are drawn to different styles of promotion. The most frequent users of promotional programs are the retail services, like car care, hair care, and restaurants. Coupons are the most common promotion for these types of businesses; dry cleaners use coupons extensively, and so do groceries. It's the ability to track results, as well as their proven effectiveness, that makes coupon offers so popular.

In the business-to-business world, suppliers frequently engage in promotions by offering sale prices. You are less likely to see coupons here, because the patterns of purchasing are a little different. The person making the decision to buy may not be the same person who is writing the check, so requiring the physical coupon to be used would be an unnecessary barrier to the desired sale.

Promotions work because people like something for nothing. They respond to two-for-one offers, and they love a good deal or free extras with their purchases. Special promotions help lots of businesses achieve their marketing objectives, such as combating seasonal cycles or stealing attention from the competition.

Objectives and Strategies

Promotions are a *short-term* marketing tool. That's one of the best things about them: You can see quick results from your efforts. In some business categories, such as medical practices, law firms, and funeral homes, promotions seem inappropriate for reasons of professional dignity. If you're in one of these fields, skip this chapter. If not, read on—you're about to discover your most powerful short-term sales-building tool.

To understand a promotional program, start by looking at the *objectives* you have designed it to accomplish. A promotional objective is a quantifiable goal statement that defines

1. What action will be encouraged (for example, first-time trial of product)

2. How much sales will be generated (dollar volume)

3. How many responses will ensue

Without goals, one never knows whether the promotion should be tried again.

The other half of a promotional program is the *strategy*, the plan of attack you choose to accomplish the objective. The strategy defines how you'll combine the elements of a promotional program: the incentive, the promotional vehicle, the timing, and the delivery method.

We'll talk more about choosing your objectives and strategies in a moment. And then we'll spend most of the chapter dis-

cussing the elements of a promotional program in detail.

Promotions are very flexible in terms of the offer you make, the method by which you follow through, and the time period you select.

There are three steps to your promotions plan:

1. Setting the objective

2. Deciding the strategy

3. Executing the strategy

We'll talk about the first two steps in detail in this chapter. The third step, execution, is covered in the various chapters of this book dealing with producing advertising for print, radio, TV, and direct mail.

As I mentioned earlier, a promotion can be aimed at the end user of your product (consumers), or it can be a business-to-business (trade) promotion, aimed at the intermediaries who influence purchase decisions, or it can be a combination of both. A hair salon that mails a discount offer for color treatments to its cut-and-style customers is using a consumer promotion to increase purchases from current customers. .

A manufacturer might be more likely to engage in a business-to-business (trade) promotion. Take for example, a manufacturer that makes a home-remodeling kit, distributed through hardware stores. To influence purchases, this company might offer a special price rebate to the store owners in return for more shelf space for the product and placement of a point-of-purchase informational display. This is much easier and much more cost-efficient for this company than finding and making an offer to the home-remodeling public nationwide.

Surma's Restaurant: A Grand Opening Promotion

Here's another example, combining both a consumer promotion and a trade promotion, that is more small-business-oriented. Surma's is a family-style restaurant in south suburban

Chicago. It's been around for forty years, but management had just passed from the father to the son. The dining room had been completely renovated, and the carry-out service area had been expanded. Now it was time to generate some excitement about the changes.

The *promotional objective:* Get people back in the restaurant—encourage trial.

The *promotional strategy:* Start with a trade promotion, which paves the way for the next step, a large-scale consumer promotion.

The first move was to host a grand opening event. Surma's invited representatives from the local newspapers, dignitaries from the surrounding communities, writers, and publicists who might help spread the word. It served them wonderful food—of course—and gave each a tote bag imprinted with the Surma's logo and stuffed with goodies from sausage to cheese to fresh bread made on-premises. Included also were imprinted coffee mugs, a menu, and coupons good for two-for-one meals. A photographer was hired to cover the event, and photos were sent with press releases to the local papers afterward. Surma's got maximum public relations value and earned a lot of goodwill with the media.

The two-for-one meal coupons in that bag were part of the larger plan: the consumer promotion. Remember, Surma's promotional goal was to use promotions to increase trial, since it was expected that once patrons experienced the rejuvenated atmosphere of the restaurant, repeat sales would take care of themselves. To achieve that goal, a two-meals-for-the-price-of-one incentive seemed like an obvious choice. Surma's chose coupons as the vehicle, and planned to distribute the message through print and broadcast advertising. The time period would be the month of May, when people dine out frequently for both Mother's Day and graduations. Surma's rightly assumed that the appeal of a two-for-one special would be very high during this family-dining season.

The management calculated the cost and payback of this plan, and decided that it made sense to continue. And that sums up the promotional strategy.

Surma's timed the grand opening event so that the resulting publicity would augment the paid advertising promoting the two-for-one meal special. Cable TV advertising was a major component of the media plan, because of its ability to target specific households in Surma's market area. (More about this in Chapter 4, "Writing a Media Plan.")

Before we go any further, let me point out that you must not confuse your promotional advertising with your regular advertising plan. Promotional advertising is geared to a short-term value-added plan. Don't confuse that with other image or product advertising you do with longer-range goals in mind.

Surma's had already begun to use cable TV with a strong ad agency-produced commercial filmed in the new dining room. (You can read more about this commercial in Chapter 8.) For the length of this promotion, it added a "crawler"—the term for type that passes by on the screen superimposed on the image—that announced the offer.

Keep in mind that the cost (minimal) of adding the crawler must be accounted for in the promotional budget, as must the cost of additional spots purchased during the promotion's time period. But the already-planned-for media costs and the cost of producing the TV commercial itself must not be considered a part of this promotion. We'll talk more about calculating cost and payback later in this chapter.

Elements of the Promotional Program: Incentives, Vehicles, Timing, and Delivery

To understand a promotional program, you need to see how it is shaped by each of the elements in Template 3-1. You could consider this template a multiple-choice test. You will choose one possibility for each element and craft a promotional program from those choices.

Template 3-1: Elements of the Promotional Program

Your promotional program will be the result of choices regarding each of these elements.
Your answers form your *promotional strategy*.

Incentives	Promotional Vehicles	Timing of Incentive	Delivery
☐ Price savings	☐ Sale pricing	☐ Immediate	☐ Advertising
☐ Product samples	☐ Coupons	☐ Delayed	☐ Coupon books
☐ Gifts	☐ Samples		☐ Newspapers
☐ Experiences	☐ Refunds		☐ Magazines
☐ Immediate	☐ Premiums		☐ Radio
☐ Delayed	☐ Games/contests		☐ TV: Cable
	☐ Events		☐ TV: Broadcast
			☐ On package/P.O.P.
			☐ Direct mail
			☐ In person

Look around you at who uses coupons in your community, or business arena. Describe their strategy in terms of these dimensions. Let's look at each of the areas.

Incentives

Incentives are the value offered in the promotion. An incentive might be an offer or a premium. Incentives fall into four categories. They are all ways of adding value.

1. Price savings (20 percent off, buy one get one free, etc.).

2. Product samples (for example, food tasting in the grocery aisles).

3. Gifts (coffee mugs, etc.). These should be thematically related to your product, of course—for example, giving away a key chain shaped like a sneaker, if you're an athletic-shoe store. Gifts range from modest advertising specialty "gimme's" to handsome rewards.

4. Experiences. This might be a party, like Surma's grand opening, or a contest or drawing. The experience might reflect *immediate* timing (a celebration at which the drawing takes place and the reward is distributed) or *delayed* timing (the prize in

the drawing is itself an experience, to be collected later, like a night for two on the town).

How will you decide what incentive to use? That's part creativity and part math. You must choose not just what you'll offer, but also how much it will cost you. Develop several scenarios, based on what you'd like to do and what you think your competitors are up to. Run cost and payback calculations on each. We'll look at how to do that a little later in this chapter.

Promotional Vehicles

The type of promotion you choose—what the ad industry calls the *promotional vehicle*—is the method you use to package the incentive. Types of promotion vehicles include

- Sale pricing
- Coupons
- Samples
- Refunds
- Premiums
- Games, contests, sweepstakes
- Events

Does this list seem to overlap with the list of types of incentives? There is some overlap, but these examples will show you how one concept flows into the other.

A grocery manager might want to promote a certain brand of frozen pizza. He might decide to use a food *sample* as an *incentive*. But he might choose to use a *coupon* as the *promotional vehicle*, requiring a person to make a purchase to receive the reward. The coupon might read, "Good for one free (brand name) pizza with any purchase." Alternatively, the grocer could stick with the food *sample* for an *incentive* and also choose a *sample* for the *promotional vehicle* by giving away small pizza samples in the frozen food aisle.

The Surma's grand opening trade promotion shows an *incentive* blending product samples, gifts, and an experience. The attendees of the grand opening received both samples of Surma's products and some logo-imprinted merchandise. The *promotional vehicle* in this case was the grand opening event.

Timing of Incentive

Once you've decided on the incentive, you must choose the timing of the delivery of the incentive.

Timing can be either *immediate* or *delayed*, or a combination of the two. With an immediate-timing incentive, the targeted customer gets the reward just for showing up. There's no requirement that he or she purchase the product or associate with it at all. No commitment is required. The advantage: Your customers' greater willingness to participate in the promotion. The risk: It will fail to generate the sales you need to make the program worthwhile. There will be increased costs associated with the promotion. What if there is no increase in sales as a result? Disaster. Your projections must be realistic. Some programs will be deemed successful even if only a fraction of the participants actually become purchasers. Others need higher levels of conversion from participant to cus-

tomer to break even. It's all a matter of calculating cost and payback.

When your grocery store is giving away free hot pizza snacks in the frozen-pizza aisle, that's an immediate-timing promotion. And enough of your customers are buying pizzas after that taste to make it a successful technique.

With a delayed-timing incentive, the target audience must make some move toward affiliating with the product to receive the reward. This is pure behavioral science at work. A typical delayed incentive might be to require customers to buy one product in order to get another one free. They must buy their nine coffees with a coffee card to get that free tenth cup. They have to show up at your open house to enter your drawing. It's important to note that a purchase is not necessarily required—just some commitment on the part of the prospect, some indication that he or she is willing to affiliate with the product.

Whether to require a purchase is a component of your promotional strategy, related to your cost projections and the rest of your marketing plan. This decision depends on the purchasing behavior that's typical with the product or service you are selling. When the cost of purchase is low, the strategy should be to require multiple purchases before delivering the incentive. This is the logic behind multiple-purchase devices like coffee cards, where a total of so many purchases might qualify you for a free item of similar value. This is used frequently by video stores as well; note that we are talking about items of similar (low) price point that are frequently purchased. With big-ticket items, durable goods, you are more likely to see discounts or rebates offered on the first purchase. A car purchase will often qualify you for a significant cash rebate.

You can blend immediate and delayed timing strategies. An example: Two banks have merged, and hold an open house to familiarize customers with the new combined identity. An announcement is mailed to current customers of both (Example 3-1). Each announcement is individually numbered. For each day of the event, the bank pulls a winning number, and posts it. The customer may be an instant winner—immediate timing—but he or she must come in to the bank to find out if he or she holds a winning number. That commitment of visiting the bank is required, a feature of a delayed timing strategy.

Example 3-1: Entry Coupon from M&I/Valley Merger
Used by permission of M&I Bank.

MERGER CELEBRATION DRAWING ENTRY

Must be 18 or older to enter.
One entry per person. Enter any time up until Saturday, September 17.
– please print –

Name _____

Street _____

City _____

State _____ Zip _____

Day Phone _____

M&I Bank

Mi LINE (608) 222-5169
24-hour Automated Customer Service Line
Personal Representatives Available 7am to 10pm

Member FDIC

YOU MAY ALREADY BE AN INSTANT WINNER

Just stop by any M&I location with this entry blank. Compare your entry blank number to the winning numbers posted at the bank...you could be one of 75 Dane County residents to win a crisp $20 bill.

After you've checked to see if you are an instant winner, drop your completed entry blank into the box. You will be eligible for the Grand Prize drawing. With so much to celebrate, everybody wins!

Employees of M&I Bank and its affiliates and their immediate families are not eligible for prizes.

Whether you choose immediate or delayed timing will depend on your predictions about rate of response. Cost and payback projections will guide you to the right decision.

Delivery Methods

The type of promotional vehicle you choose—coupons, free samples, a contest, or whatever—is going to suggest the appropriate delivery method to you.

- *Advertising media.* Will you use advertising media? Print or broadcast? That will depend on whether there are good media available. You judge that by looking at *penetration* (a term used in broadcast media to describe the potential viewing audience) and *circulation* (in print media, the number of subscribers plus newsstand copies circulated, and so the potential audience for the ad). Look for media where the demographics are a reasonable match to the market you're trying to attract. Then estimate the number of people in the audience you're reaching. This is done by calculating CPM, or cost per thousand. See Chapter 4, "Writing a Media Plan," for more about this aspect of advertising.

  Don't neglect the power of coupon books! There are probably several in your community—magazines with names like "Dollars and Sense" filled with nothing but ads, most of them with coupons. These are generally a good way to reach a communitywide market; they have mass distribution and are surprisingly well used. If you're looking for a *broad* advertising medium at low cost, make sure you talk to the coupon book salespeople in your community.

- *On package or at point of sale.* You might choose to use a coupon on your package instead of in the advertising. Maybe a point-of-purchase display with a pad of coupons might serve you better. These are both ways of delivering a purchase incentive while the product is right there for purchasing.

- *Direct mail.* The beauty of direct mail is that you can deliver your message very precisely, and calculate return on investment to the penny. See Chapter 9 for more about using direct mail.

- *In-person sales.* If you are selling through an intermediary—a wholesaler using distributors, like our home-remodeling kit example—you can communicate your business-to-business offer directly to your distributors. Or, as another alternative, you can reward your representatives for making a promotion to the end consumer.

The Promotional Program: A Summary

A promotional program is made up of an objective, a strategy, and a plan for execution. We've looked at the elements of a promotional strategy—the components you will need to choose as you develop your specific program.

You should be able to describe an incentive, choose a promotional vehicle, decide the timing, and select a delivery method, for any number of possible scenarios. Which is the right one depends on your objectives. We'll talk about that in a later section.

We've covered timing as it relates to the incentive. There's another concept related to time that you should consider.

Any promotion, no matter what the type of incentive, should have a specific *duration period* stated. A promotion is by definition a short-term strategy for increasing sales. You won't want to keep your offer going forever. If you're using a price savings incentive, give it an effective date. If you're giving away a sample, gift, or experience, make sure it's clear during what time period your audience can respond and be eligible to win. Otherwise you'll run the risk of disappointing someone.

But there's another important reason to limit the time period of your incentive.

Remember the advice in Chapter 1 on marketing objectives and measurable results. Without a time period, you will never be able to judge the success of your effort.

I'm not going to go on at length about testing your results, but I'm not going to leave it unsaid. Most successful promotional marketers design ways to test their programs. Then they diligently measure results the first few times they run the promotion. If they find that it brings predictable success, they become less stringent about tracking results. They simply repeat the successful elements of the program.

Tracking consists of quantifying the number of responses to the program and the dollar volume of sales generated from those responses, then comparing those results to earlier projections. If you don't track performance, you'll have no way of knowing if your program met your goals. You're not doing what we humans do so well—learning from our experiences.

Defining Your Promotional Objectives

You won't know what you're doing, whether it was successful, or when you're done if you don't apply your analytical skills before you plunge ahead.

The simple journalists' questions will lead you to sound thinking about objectives. Answer the questions why, what, how much and how many, when, and to whom, and you've got an objective (see Template 3-2A).

- *Why.* Relate your company's overall marketing objectives to your campaign goal. For example, if seasonality is a problem in

your business, responding to that is a marketing objective that lends itself to promotion.

- *What.* Be specific. What customer response are you looking for? It might be an increase in sales overall, an increase in purchases from current customers, or an increase in repeat sales after the first trial by a new customer. These are not all the response possibilities, just a list to start you thinking.

- *How much/How many.* If you're in business you should be able to state your gross sales, your cost of goods sold, your overhead—and therefore your profit margin. Some portion of that profit margin is the dollar amount you have to play with to seed your promotional program. State your budget constraints and profit parameters—the minimum and maximum dollars you are willing to spend, and the profit you would like to realize from that expense.

That answers "how much." To answer "how many," state the response you want *in numbers*. Both measures are important in understanding exactly what behaviors you want to stimulate with your promotional program.

- *When.* State the time period during which you will promote your offer and during which you will redeem it.

- *To whom.* Describe the demographics, including geographical area and purchasing habits, of the customers to whom you are targeting your promotion.

Template 3-2A: Promotional Objectives

Statement of Promotional Objectives

1. **Why? What marketing problem is this program designed to address?**

   _____

   _____

2. **What? Customer response we want to stimulate:**

   _____

3. **How Much/How Many?**

   Budget Constraints:

   Lowest budget _____

   Highest budget _____

   Profit Parameters

   Minimum acceptable results $ _____

4. **When? Time period during which offer will be redeemed**

   _____

   _____

   _____

   _____

5. **To Whom? Describe target market for this promotion**

   Demographics _____

   Geographical distribution _____

   Purchasing habits _____

   Other _____

   _____

   _____

Examples of Promotional Objectives

The Lincolnshire is a 200-unit apartment building in near-downtown Chicago. With a 12 percent vacancy rate projected for the upcoming slow season (late winter/early spring), it needed to do combat in a highly competitive renters' market. The management responded with a promotional program. Here it is, described in the same way you would describe a promotion using Template 3-2:

- *Why?* For the Lincolnshire, the primary market objective was to keep vacancies at two to five percent. Too high a vacancy rate could erase the profitability of the property. A strategy of fighting back against slow seasons had been agreed upon. This explains the timing and the budget for this promotion.

- *What?* Stimulate visits by prospects to see the apartment units; sign leases with a percentage of those visitors.

- *How much/How many?* Fill sixteen vacant apartments through response to the offer. That answered "how many."

For the Lincolnshire, the answer to "how much" required figuring out what it would cost if an apartment stayed vacant for a year. That included property taxes, utilities, and marketing expenses, including classified and display ads in local newspapers, real estate listings, and a share of the rental agents' fees.

This was balanced against the income that apartment could bring in during a year. For the Lincolnshire, the cost of an unused apartment was steep enough to justify making a deep discount offer to fill those units, and committing a hefty advertising budget to promoting the offer. The management decided on a tiered discount program: Respondents in January would receive three months' free rent (a 25 percent discount over the course of a year), February's respondents would receive two months free (a 16 percent savings), and those who responded in March would receive one month free (8 percent, still an attractive offer for these $1,000 to $1,700 units).

The Lincolnshire planned to make this offer contingent on signing a lease—a *big* commitment earning the buyer a big discount (a good example of delayed tim-

ing). To quantify the answer to the questions how much and how many, the managers needed to project not just the number of responses the promotion would bring in, but also the number of respondents who would become buyers.

- *When?* The Lincolnshire chose a time period beginning in January and extending through March.

- *To whom?* The Lincolnshire is situated in a residential area containing seven other large multi-unit apartment buildings, with smaller five-unit buildings filling the space between. Any tenant of these buildings whose lease was expiring might be a likely candidate to fill an apartment in the Lincolnshire. These were likely to be early-career professionals who aspired to owning a home and who, in the meantime, were influenced in their purchase decisions by the amenities, prestige, and convenience of the apartment, probably in that order.

Template 3-2B shows another example, the M&I-Valley Bank merger event described in Example 3-1.

Template 3-2B: M&I Bank Merger

Statement of Promotional Objectives

1. Why? What marketing problem is this program designed to address?

Merger of two banks has left customers and prospects confused about

which branches are going to remain open.

2. What? Customer response we want to stimulate:

Stimulate customer and prospect visits to branch offices.

3. How Much/How Many?

Budget Constraints:

Lowest budget $15,000

Highest budget $35,000

Profit Parameters

Minimum acceptable results $ 0. Goal is not to open new accounts, but to earn goodwill.

4. When? Time period during which offer will be redeemed

10 days, September 7 through September 17

5. To Whom? Describe target market for this promotion

Demographics   Adults & their children

Geographical distribution   Central and western Dane County

Purchasing habits   Have savings in CDs and money markets

Other   Potential customers for mortgages and home equity loans

---

Now try working through this planning process to set your own objectives, using Template 3-2A.

Developing a Promotional Strategy

Your promotional strategy is the scenario you choose, the story you're about to tell. The choice of elements for the story is designed to respond to the challenges set in the statement of objectives. It's the one journalists' question we haven't discussed: *How?*

Your promotional strategy describes who is going to get what incentive, how, and when. Like storytelling, this is an opportunity to demonstrate your creativity. The way you mix the promotional elements—the incentive, the vehicle, the timing, and the delivery—to meet the objectives you've set will give your promotional strategy its unique twist.

Time for some brainstorming. Review the elements of promotion. What type of incentive will you offer? What promotional vehicle will you use?

Start where your customers are: Think about their needs, and use your creativity to present them with a desirable offer in a way that's unique or entertaining enough to hold their attention.

A Closer Look at Incentives

We talked briefly about the types of incentives at the beginning of this chapter. Here I'll define the options in greater detail.

Price Savings. In general terms, the broader the offer the better—15 percent off everything in the store works better than 30 percent off one item. The exception to this rule is the "loss leader"—when you offer a price discount so deep that it may pass breakeven on an item you *know* is in hot demand. Here your strategy is to make a profit on other purchases made while the customer is in your store. Maybe you've heard the joke about "losing money on every sale, but making it up on the volume." Be very careful playing with the "loss leader" strategy.

Coupons and discount offers are both price savings incentives. One sales representative from a coupon publication said to me, "Coupons are just a price offer with a dashed line around it." It's true—asking someone to bring you the physical coupon may do a couple

of things for you, but to the customers it's just another price offer. It's the savings that encourages them to act.

Here's what the coupon does for you: It helps you track responses to the offer, and it limits the number of responses requiring payback, which helps you control the costs of the promotion. Here's how that works. I recently placed an order with a printer. A few days earlier, I had received a promotional mailing from that printer that included a coupon, which said "Get an additional 10% free!... Must present this card when placing order" (Example 3-2). Unfortunately, I didn't remember that when I placed my order, and so I got only the quantity I ordered. (I didn't whine about it because I had done some stiff price negotiating before I placed my order.) If the offer had been less specific—say, "10 percent additional copies on all orders in October"—the printer would have had to give the discount on all orders during that time period, including mine. Since it had already discounted the price to me, it would have been in the position of possibly selling below cost—or appearing to renege on an offer.

Example 3-2: Heartland Litho Coupon
Used by permission of Heartland Litho.

Product Samples. Letting prospects experience your product will increase its value in their eyes if they find they like it. It's a way to break down barriers of habit. The sample might be a service, too—the vacuum cleaner salesman who offers you a free demonstration cleaning in your home is giving you a sample of the vacuum cleaner's performance.

Gifts. A gift increases the value of the product or service. Sometimes the gift is completely unrelated to the product being promoted—it might relate to seasonality instead. Example 3-3 shows a gift promotion tied to seasonality.

Example 3-3

Toe Room
COMFORT FOOTWEAR

626 S. COURTNEY WAY, 288-7759
(Next to Stop 'n' Shop)
M-F 9-0, Sat 9-5, Sun 11-5

COUPON
FREE TURKEY
Gift Certificate
With Any Purchase
over
$**50**
(Not valid with any other offer or closeout)
Valid through 11/19

Experiences. An experience might be an immediate-timing incentive, such as a promotional event, or it might be a delayed-timing incentive, where an experience replaces the gift as a reward for participating in the promotion. Use your creativity in matching an experience incentive to your product or service offering, and you have the makings of a breakthrough promotional program. If you sell sporting goods, your experience incentive might be a weekend getaway at a ski lodge. If you sell cosmetics, you could offer a beauty makeover, combining an experience with a product sample incentive.

A Closer Look at Promotional Vehicles

Here are some of the options, so that you can get an idea of what might work for you.

- *Sale pricing.* This can take the form of advertised sale prices, or goods with prices marked down on the package, or labels on the product that flag the amount of price reduction. The point is how you *communicate* that the item is on sale.

- *Coupons.* Coupons have value only on redemption. Using coupons lets you keep precise track of your results. Coupons work especially well to encourage first-time trial, or to promote larger purchases from current customers.

- *Samples.* Sampling involves free trial of the product. Offering free samples is a very appropriate way to increase initial trial by new customers. It's a good way to build excitement when the sampling is timed to coincide with other promotional elements, such as an open house event.

- *Premiums.* Using premiums as a promotional vehicle means giving away a gift with perceived value in exchange for the desired behavior (not necessarily a purchase). The image of your product may be enhanced by the quality of the gift you are giving away. One of the commonest uses of premiums is the multiple-purchase vehicle—you encourage repeat purchases by requiring multiple purchases to receive the premium (see Example 3-4).

Example 3-4
Used by permission of Espresso Royale Caffe.

- *Games/contests.* Customers participate in order to become eligible for prizes. This is a great vehicle to choose because it enhances the product or service's image through the excitement generated. Developing a contest that dramatizes your unique selling proposition can be a good way to introduce new positioning. (See Chapter 2, "Positioning.")

- *Events.* These are like games and contests, but simpler. The only customer participation required is showing up. Events can capture attention for new products or features—this is a good way to dramatize new innovations.

This is certainly not a comprehensive list of all the types of promotional vehicles marketers use—it's just a quick survey to stimulate your thinking. If you are in a business arena where promotions are common, you ought to think about educating yourself further on the subject. Look for books and seminars specifically on the topic, or visit with an ad agency in your area and ask about its experience with promotions.

One More Time: Timing

We've talked about two different timing issues in this chapter. Both are important, but don't confuse them.

Timing as *duration of the promotion* is a decision you make when you establish your promotional objective. It answers the question, "When does the promotional program begin and end?" On the other hand, timing as an *element of the promotional program* is a feature of your strategy. It describes when the customer receives the incentive. An immediate-timing incentive does not require any commitment to your product—handing out product samples is an example. The customer who finds a free product sample on the doorstep has not even made any commitment to take it inside and try it. Delayed-timing incentives require commitment on the part of the prospect—some move toward affiliation with your product, which is rewarded. A repeat-purchase device like a coffee card is an example of a delayed-timing element.

Strategy: A Summary

A promotional strategy is a story describing what promotional offer you want to communicate, and to whom. It defines your promotion's timing, whether immediate or delayed. It specifies the delivery method you'll use to convey it. That about covers your promotional strategy, except for one thing: the cost. Setting budget parameters is part of setting objectives. Defining the costs and payback associated with a particular strategy is a subject we're finally about to discuss.

Calculating Costs and Payback

How can you tell if you can afford to make an offer? Finding a price point for a discount, for example, requires making financial projections to analyze breakeven costs and potential sales volume.

Consider the promotion *by itself* as you calculate the costs associated with it. Consider only the costs that are outside your regular advertising budget. If you had been planning to advertise in the newspaper anyway, but now find that you need to create an ad about your promotion, consider only the production costs for the ad, not the ad space—that's already accounted for in your regular advertising budget.

Project the sales you'll generate with the promotion. Subtract the associated costs from the sales. The balance is the profit, or *contribution to overhead*, that will be generated by the plan.

Estimating Your Costs

Your costs for a promotional program will fall into the categories of producing the elements (direct mail pieces, newspaper ads, coupon flyers, or whatever), delivering the message (media or mailing costs), and the cost of the incentive. Let's look at each of these cost areas more closely.

- *Production expenses.* Calculate the cost to design an advertisement or a direct mail piece, the cost of printing, and the cost of staff time in support of the promotion—planning the strategy, administering the execution, or whatever. In the chapters on print advertising, radio, TV, and direct mail, you will find worksheets that will help you estimate these costs.

- *Delivering the promotion.* Figure the cost of mailing lists, postage, media placements, etc. Chapter 4, "Writing a Media Plan," and Chapter 9, "Direct Mail Advertising," will help you estimate these costs.

- *Cost of the incentive.* If it's a $0.50 coupon, note that here. If it's a free apartment for three months, state that value in dollars. If you are buying coffee cups to give away, state the estimated cost here.

Incentive costs might be out-of-pocket, like having 500 mugs silkscreened with your logo, or might be tied to fulfilling responses to the promotion. An example of this would be the cost to you of discounting a product by 10 percent. If you ordinarily charge $10 and will now only make $9 on that sale, you need to account for that dollar forgone as a cost of your promotional program.

State any costs as a cost per piece, then state the number of responses you anticipate; multiply the cost by the response rate and you'll calculate the cost of your incentive.

Projected Response

How many responses will you get? If I could tell you the answer to that, I could charge a lot more for this book! Projecting response is a leap of faith; you can do research to ground your estimates in the real-world experience of others, but every situation is unique. Only by executing and then measuring will you know how well your own program performs. This is why tracking results is so important. Your own experiences with promotional programs will quickly teach you what you should and shouldn't do, if you take the time to measure results and study what that information reveals.

Whenever financial projections are concerned, always do a worst-case, a most-probable, and a best-case scenario.

If you're working with a good sales rep from the medium in which you plan to advertise, ask that person to help you estimate probable response. Of course, you can contact other advertisers in that medium and ask how their promotions have performed. Explain that you are not a competitor, and ask if you can pick their brains. I've found that people are very willing to share their experiences. The problem with this: Each promotion is unique. You will learn only what worked for them—not what will work for you.

A number of factors affect response. Does your product or service lend itself to promotions? (They are common in some industries, ineffective in others.) Check with your trade association or your banker for examples and response averages for your field. The purchase cost of your product is significant; is it an impulse buy or a studied decision? A rule of thumb is that the higher the cost of the product, the lower the probable response will be—no matter how attractive you make your offer.

To find the cost to you for each response, go back to your timing. If you've chosen a promotional strategy with immediate timing, every response will cost you. If you've chosen a strategy with delayed timing, you'll be paying out on only a projected percentage of the responses.

You'll arrive at the anticipated number of payouts by estimating a response rate as a percentage of the audience for the delivery method you've chosen. If the medium reaches 100,000 people, and you expect a 5 percent response rate, you are planning on 500 responses.

If the offer is contingent upon purchase, you must estimate the number of respondents who will actually purchase. Of those 500 respondents, you might get 10 percent, or fifty people, to become buyers because of your promotion. This is called the *conversion rate*.

Different delivery methods have their own predictable response rates. You might expect a newspaper ad to pull somewhere between 0.5 and 3.5 percent response. A direct mail campaign, because it can be more tightly targeted, might pull closer to 5 percent. A coupon or offer delivered on the product itself (or at the point of sale) has proven to be very effective; a 7 to 15 percent response rate might be expected.

Template 3-3A: Breakeven Analysis for Promotion

Date:
    Description:
Media used:
Total audience circulation reached:
If mail program:
        List used:
        Number of pieces sent:
Time period of offer:
Assumptions:

Description	Worst Case	Most Likely	Best Case
Fixed Costs			
1. Production Expenses			
Creative fees	$	$	$
Printing			
2. Delivering the Promotion			
Advertising space/time			
Mail handling			
Postage			
Other			
Subtotal: Fixed Costs	$	$	$
Variable Expenses			
3. Cost of Incentive			
Response percentage	0.0%	0.0%	0
Number of responses	0	0	0
Conversion rate			
Number of sales resulting	0	0	0
Cost for response postage	$	$	$
Redemption cost			
Cost of discount on average sale	$0	$0	0
Total sales forgone:	$	$	$
Other			
Subtotal: Variable Costs	$	$	$
Cost of Promotion	$	$	$
(Add fixed and variable subtotals)			
4. Payback			
Average sale:	$ $	$	
Sales generated	$	$	$
Contribution to Overhead:	$	$	$
(Subtract cost of promotion from payback sales generated)			

To fill out Template 3-3A, you will need to know some of the information about budgeting for production, media placements, and direct mail distribution that will be covered in the subsequent chapters of this book. For item 1, production expenses, see these budget worksheets elsewhere in this book:

- Print ads: Templates 6-9 and 6-12
- Radio: Template 7-6
- TV: Template 8-3
- Direct mail: Template 9-11

For item 2, delivering the promotion, you will estimate the cost of distributing the message through either advertising media or direct mail. See the worksheet on media budgets in Chapter 4, (Template 4-6). If you will be using the mail to distribute your offer, Template 9-3, Mailing List Cost Estimate, will be useful to you.

Production and delivery expenses are the fixed costs related to your program. The cost of the incentive (item 3 on the worksheet) is related to the number of responses your program generates. It is a variable cost, fluctuating with your projected response and conversion rates.

When you add the fixed and variable costs together, you have the total cost of your promotion. Calculate the payback (the following section tells you how) and subtract your promotional costs from the payback sales generated. The result will be the contribution to overhead, or profitability of the program.

Payback

The last issue on this worksheet is item 4, Payback. The object in calculating payback is to find the dollars this promotion will contribute to your operation. It's much easier than calculating cost. Simply estimate the sales your promotion will generate. If you are offering a sale price on a specific item, multiply the purchase price by the response and conversion rates you projected as you looked at costs. If you are offering an open-ended discount—20 percent off anything in the store—you will need to make a projection about what the average sale is likely to be. Check statistics for your industry to verify that your projections are realistic.

Weigh the projected sales against costs. Even at its highest estimated costs and its worst-case projections for payback, does your promotional program generate sufficient profits to be worth doing? Adjust your program by changing the incentive or the distribution plan until your scenario makes sense. Here is an example of a breakeven analysis for a music instrument retailer.

Template 3-3B: Breakeven Analysis Worksheet for a Promotional Program

Date: 3-15-95
Description: Free tuning for 1 year offer
Media used: Radio, newspaper, direct mail
Total audience circulation reached: 123,000
If mail program:
    List used: Current customers and inquiries
    Number of pieces sent: 10,000
        No reply card (simple "come in & buy" copy)
Time period of offer: 30 days
Assumptions: Radio audience 17,000
    Run 20 spots per week for 2 weeks in 3 day-part TAP plan
    Rate varies in projection: might be able to negotiate some free spots
    Newspaper audience (Sunday entertainment section) circ. 123,000
    Run ads 2 col x 10" for 2 Sundays
    Offer: Free piano tuning for one year if buy during sale period ($120 value)
    Ads run for first 2 weeks of sale period

Description		Worst Case		Most Likely		Best Case
Fixed Costs						
1. Production Expenses						
Creative fees		$1,960		$1,260		$980
Printing		2550		2550		2550
2. Delivering the Promotion						
Advertising space/time						
Radio:		2880		2400		2160
Newspaper:		728		728		728
Mail handling		185		185		185
Postage		2000		2000		2000
Other						
Subtotal: Fixed Costs		$10,303		$9,123		$8,603
Variable Expenses						
3. Cost of Incentive						
Response percentage		0.5%		0.7%	1.0%	
Number of responses		627		861	1230	
Conversion ate		3.0%		5.0%	7.0%	
Number of sales resulting		18.8		43.1	86.1	
Cost for response postage		$0		$0		$0
Redemption cost		$2,258		$5,166		$10,332
Cost of discount on average sale	$0		$0		0	
Total sales forgone:		$		$		$
Other						
Subtotal: Variable Costs		$2,258		$5,166		$10,332
Cost of Promotion		$12,561		$14,289		$18,935
(Add fixed and variable subtotals)						
4. Payback						
Average sale:	$2,000		$2,750		3500	
Sales generated		$35,756		$49,077		$70,110
Contribution to Overhead:		$23,195		$34,788		$51,175

For a different example of a breakeven analysis, see Template 9-10B. You'll find an example of a budget for a promotional program for Bi-Folkal Productions, a case study described in that chapter.

Conclusion: How to Write Your Promotional Strategy

Review the objectives you've established for your promotion, using Template 3-2A.

Then take a moment to review Template 3-1. Now it's time to take that "multiple choice" test. Template 3-4 will guide you to a statement of promotional strategy.

Template 3-4: Statement of Promotional Strategy

Statement of Promotional Strategy

Date: _____   Prepared by:_____

Incentives   **Describe Offer:**
- ☐ Price savings   _____
- ☐ Product samples   _____
- ☐ Gifts   _____
- ☐ Experiences   _____
  - ☐ Immediate   _____
  - ☐ Delayed   _____
                                            _____

Promotional Vehicles   **Describe Use:**
- ☐ Sale pricing   _____
- ☐ Coupons   _____
- ☐ Samples   _____
- ☐ Premiums   _____
- ☐ Games/contests   _____
- ☐ Events   _____
- ☐ Refunds   _____

Timing of Incentive
- ☐ Immediate
- ☐ Delayed

Delivery   **Describe Media Plan:**
- ☐ Advertising   _____
  - ☐ Coupon books   _____
  - ☐ Newspapers   _____
  - ☐ Magazines   _____
  - ☐ Radio   _____
  - ☐ TV: Cable   _____
  - ☐ TV: Broadcast   _____
- ☐ On package/P.O.P.   _____
- ☐ Direct mail   _____
- ☐ In person   _____

Budget for Promotion

Component (mailer, newspaper ad, etc.)   **Cost (see templates, Chapters 6 to 9)**

_____   _____
_____   _____
_____   _____
_____   _____

                TOTAL BUDGET: _____

The Simpler Side of Promotions

Not every promotional program is as complex as some of these programs I've described as examples. You can motivate action by simple rewards; we've all seen the coffee mugs and key chains, ad specialties used as thank-you's, and memory gimmicks. Your goal might be to reward a prospect—like leaving a candy jar full of jelly beans with your prospect after your sales presentation—or you might choose to mail prospects a gift simply to remind them you exist.

Here's another example from Surma's restaurant. The owners purchased napkin holders imprinted with the restaurant's logo and phone number. When customers ordered carry-out for large parties, the imprinted napkin holder was included in the box, along with other eating and serving utensils and, of course, napkins. Customers used the napkin holder because it was in the right place at the right time. The useful little item was kept around the home, and provided a reminder to visit Surma's again.

If you decide promotional incentives have a place in your plan, follow these guidelines:

- Have a logical plan for how you intend to use the incentive to increase sales. Don't print T-shirts just because your ego wants to see your name splashed across customers' chests.

- Pick the right incentive. Use your creativity! While coffee mugs are a perennial favorite, and economically priced, look a little further. You might find something with a unique tie-in to your business. Start with "Ad specialties" in the Yellow Pages if you don't know someone in the business. You'll soon be inundated with trinkets of every description. Then look beyond this—there might be a local product that fits your need even better. Vermont maple syrup, Wisconsin cheese, or a bottle of California wine might fit your unique personality.

- Purchase wisely. The discipline of your cost projections will enable you to predict the quantity you need to buy. It never hurts to try negotiating price. Ask your specialty vendor, "Can you do any better than that?"

Promotional Programs: A Summary

We've talked about objectives and strategies for promotion. We haven't talked much about execution. The whole rest of this book deals with executing everything from a media plan to a TV commercial. Templates in the later chapters will help you develop a detailed promotion strategy.

Template 3-5 is a calendar to help you plan the execution of your program. You must coordinate the production of each of your program's components in order to unfold the story the way you planned. Template 3-5B, showing the plan for Surma's restaurant, will help you understand how execution timing works.

Template 3-5A: Surma's Calendar

Surma's Grand Opening
Promotion Execution Calendar

Months across: February | March | April | May

Chart labels: Grand Opening Event · coupon promotion

Duration of Promotion	May 1-31
Plan	
Print: Newspaper ads	
TV: Cable crawler	
Radio: 60 spot	
Mail: Event announcement, press open house, April 21	
Menu & other giveaways	
Press release	
Reservations & First Use Dates	
Print: Reserve by April 21, appear May 1-31	
TV: Reserve by March 25, appear April 25-May 21	
Radio: Reserve by March 25, appear May 1-31	
Hire photographer for event April 21	
Catering reservation (house) for April 21	
Mail drop date for Open House announcement April 6	
Execute	
Produce newspaper ad	
Produce radio commercial	
Produce Open House announcement	
Gifts for Open House	
Produce tote bag	
Produce coffee mug	
Gather/produce other products, print menu	
Redeem	
Collect results	
Analyze	
Summarize	

Callout boxes:

- Planning should be a comprehensive process involving all components of the plan.
- Detail for this section of the execution calendar will come from your media plan.
- Worksheets in the appropriate chapters will help you plan your execution schedule.
- Ad specialties often take a long time to produce. Allow plenty of time.

Template 3-5B: Blank Calendar

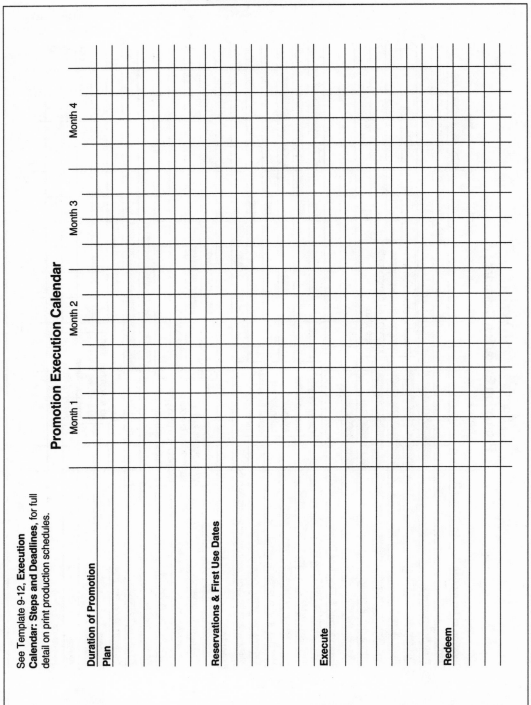

Promotion Execution Calendar

See Template 9-12, **Execution Calendar: Steps and Deadlines**, for full detail on print production schedules.

Month 1   Month 2   Month 3   Month 4

Duration of Promotion
Plan

Reservations & First Use Dates

Execute

Redeem

The last template will help you track your promotional program. Template 3-6 is a worksheet for summarizing your promotional program. It draws together the decisions you reached as you filled out Templates 3-2 through 3-5.

Template 3-6: Promotional Program Planning Worksheet

Promotional Program Planning Worksheet

Date: _____ Prepared by: _____

Title of Program _____

Statement of Objective
    Attach Template 3-2

Statement of Strategy
    Attach Template 3-4

Due Dates ◄————————————

  Production

    Concept decided

    Begin art/photography

    Begin production

    Finish production

  Distribution

    First air date (if broadcast media)

    First ad insertion (if print media)

    First mail drop (if direct mail)

    First use (on package/P.O.P./in person)

Breakeven Analysis
    Attach Template 3-3

Program Execution Calendar
    Attach Template 3-5

> Repeat the Due Dates section for each component of the program, including newspaper ads, radio and/or TV commercials, and each printed piece (on package, P.O.P., direct mail), and any ad specialties, gifts, or premiums to be purchased.

Remember: Set objectives, choose strategies, create excellent executions. You'll be rewarded with quick, on-target results.

Case Study: Coupon Promotion

The coupon promotion from a Sunday newspaper shown in Example 3-6 gives you a quick snapshot of the ways coupons are used—and misused. Which of these retailers have missed the boat on some of my suggestions?

Example 3-5: Coupon Ads

Paddy's Shamrock Room

Introducing: New Grill Menu!

Located on College Ave. at Fork Street. 836-7337

One Sandwich or Dinner Entree 1/2 Price

(with purchase of greater or equal value)

Bring In This Coupon For 1 FREE Drink
(I Mean Any Drink)
(1 coupon per table per visit)

Toe Room
COMFORT FOOTWEAR

626 S. COURTNEY WAY, 288-7759
(Next to Stop 'n' Shop)
M-F 9-0, Sat 9-5, Sun 11-5

COUPON

FREE TURKEY
Gift Certificate
With Any Purchase
over
$50

(Not valid with any other offer or closeout)
Valid through 11/19

Get A Bear-Sized Value!

Come to any Burger Bear location:
2700 South Beltline, 3700 Mankato Drive
Hwy 12 in Barabault

Bear-Sized Value Meals

Baby Burger, Small Fries, Small Drink **$1.99**

Momma Burger, Med. Fries, Med. Drink **$2.99**

Poppa Burger, Large Fries, Large Drink **$3.99**

Save-Rite

2151 Massachusetts Ave.
4629 Sienna Blvd.

OPEN 24 HOURS

COUPON

Save-Rite Coupon
Boneless
PORK LOIN
$2.⁴⁸

5-7 Lb Average

No Coupon Needed

Expires Saturday, Nov. 12th, 1994

It's a crisp Sunday in late fall when this ad appears in your Sunday paper. Here's the story behind it. An advertising representative from the newspaper created this advertising format to deliver coupons for multiple advertisers, then approached potential advertisers with the package deal. Each advertiser paid only a portion of the ad cost—and gained impact from being part of one uniform theme piece. They share the common elements of using *coupons* as a promotional vehicle, with *newspaper advertising* as the delivery strategy. Their choice of incentives and their timing strategies differ. Let's look at each one to learn more about promotions.

Paddy's Shamrock Room is offering a combination of price savings and a free sample. The free sample is an immediate-timing incentive: The offer is "1 FREE Drink (I Mean any Drink)." A person could conceivably come in with a coupon, order a free drink, and leave with no more affiliation with Paddy's than that.

In this same coupon is also a price savings incentive with a delayed timing; it says, "One Sandwich or Dinner Entree 1/2 Price (with purchase of greater or equal value)." What this coupon suggests is that if you buy one meal at regular price, you will get a second of equal or less value for half price. However, the wording on the coupon is somewhat ambiguous, and that could affect response. Here is an important warning: Be sure the wording of your offer on the coupon is clear and concrete. You don't want any misunderstandings. Notice also that there is no limit to this offer's duration. Both the poor wording and the lack of time limitation indicate that this businessperson might benefit from this book.

Toe Room is offering a gift incentive with delayed timing. When you make a purchase over $50, you receive a gift certificate good for a free turkey; you must then take the gift certificate to a food store to actually receive your reward. The value is a good one, equal to about 35 percent of the purchase price if the customer purchases the minimum $50 item to qualify. But shoe purchases frequently surpass $100, and so this is a canny offer—high perceived value, especially because of pre-Thanksgiving timing, and low out-of-pocket cost to the retailer.

Burger Bear is simply offering a price savings with delayed timing—you must make a purchase to receive the sale price. The "Bear-Sized Value Meals" are designed to increase the average purchase from customers by encouraging the purchase of prearranged menu combinations. Note that here, as in the first coupon, there is no duration of offer mentioned. However, this is less of a problem for Burger Bear, which is making special offers all the time, than it could be for a small business like Paddy's Shamrock Room.

Save-Rite is a grocery store offering a simple price discount incentive with delayed timing—you must purchase the pork loin to receive the discount. While the offer appears in a coupon format, it is really a sale pricing vehicle—note the words "No Coupon Needed."

What conclusions can you draw from these advertisers? Some use promotional programs with more savvy than others. None are likely to fail at what they've set out to accomplish—stimulate sales—but some will learn more from the outcome of their program than others. Toe Room is doing an excellent job. Save-Rite is doing all right as well. However, the restaurants—Burger Bear and Paddy's Shamrock Room—are participating without maximizing their potential benefit, since neither of them has included a duration period that would allow the restaurant to track specific results.

Next, in Chapter 4, we'll take up media planning, which is about understanding how to use different media to execute your marketing and advertising strategy.

Chapter 4

Writing a Media Plan

The largest category in your advertising budget is likely to be your media costs—the dollars you spend for air time on radio or TV, or for ad space in newspapers, magazines, and more. Because of this, it makes sense to have a sound plan to manage that investment. You'll want to set goals. You'll want to describe strategies for achieving them. You'll have to organize the day-to-day tasks of carrying out the strategies. The tool you'll need to do this is a media plan that begins with an overview and works its way down to the details. It will help you with every phase of your advertising.

Here's how many businesses manage their media buying. The person in charge of the budget starts saying yes to the salespeople who call. Advertising appears here and there as a result. When the budget's gone, the person in charge starts saying no, and the ad campaign is over. It's a method, but you wouldn't call it a media plan. And if that approach sounds familiar, you can bet you're passing up opportunities to maximize your return on investment.

Media planning is the process of choosing a course of action. Media planners develop yearly plans that list each media outlet—print, broadcast, direct mail, or outdoor—where ads will be placed. Planning then gives way to buy-ing, as each separate contract is negotiated, then finalized.

The media plan is a document in sections. A ring binder notebook is a good way to keep a media plan, because it's easy to update and easy to refer to. Or if you prefer to work on comput-er, simply think in terms of folders and files.

The sections in your notebook will be:

- *Media outlets (TV, newspapers, etc.).* This section lists all of the media in which advertising will be placed.

- *Goals.* This section describes the goals of the advertising, and explains why and how this plan meets these goals.

- *Audience.* In this section, collect all the information you can about your target audience. You will want statistics by demographics or lifestyle; your profession-al association can help you find this infor-mation, as can trade journals or your banker. Look for any relevant articles or information about your potential buyers. Pay attention to everything that helps you imagine an individual buyer who is typical of the whole.

- *Strategy.* You will write a statement of strategy backed up by a rationale. The action steps you describe here will guide a year's activity.

- *Budget and calendar.* Your media plan will outline what money is to be spent where, and when.

The document you've compiled in this notebook guides you in the execution of the plan throughout the year. The rest of this chapter deals with the specifics of each area.

Over time, these plans provide a history of your advertising. If you make alterations to the schedule in the course of the year, be sure to record those decisions in your notebook. Ring binders make it easy to update your plan as it evolves.

When you've finished this chapter, you will have an overview and the tools you need to create a media plan for your business. Let's start with basic vocabulary. The term you'll hear most often is *CPM,* or *cost per thousand.* CPM analysis is the method media buyers use to convert various rate and circulation options to relative terms. CPM represents the cost of reaching one thousand people via different types of media. To calculate CPM, you find the cost for an ad, then divide it by the total circulation the ad reaches (in thousands). By finding this information and calculating this cost for each of your options, you can give them a numerical ranking for comparison (see Template 4-1). CPM is a basic media concept, and we'll talk about it again later in this chapter and in detail in the upcoming chapters on the different media.

Template 4-1: CPM Worksheet

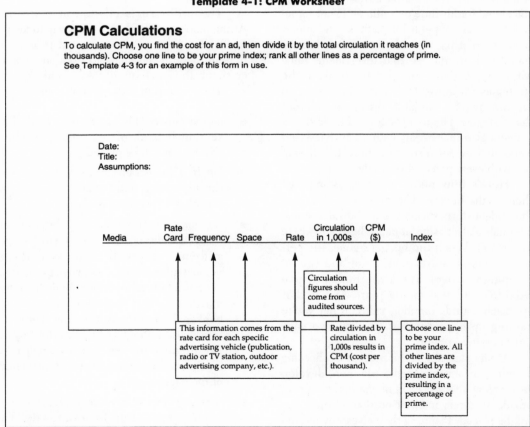

CPM Calculations

To calculate CPM, you find the cost for an ad, then divide it by the total circulation it reaches (in thousands). Choose one line to be your prime index; rank all other lines as a percentage of prime. See Template 4-3 for an example of this form in use.

Date:
Title:
Assumptions:

Media	Rate Card	Frequency	Space	Rate	Circulation in 1,000s	CPM ($)	Index

This information comes from the rate card for each specific advertising vehicle (publication, radio or TV station, outdoor advertising company, etc.).

Circulation figures should come from audited sources.

Rate divided by circulation in 1,000s results in CPM (cost per thousand).

Choose one line to be your prime index. All other lines are divided by the prime index, resulting in a percentage of prime.

Print advertising prices are based on the circulation of the publication in question. Publications will quote you a circulation figure based on paid subscribers. The *audited circulation* figures are verified by monitoring organizations. The publications will try to convince you that actual circulation is higher by including the free copies they distribute and the pass-along readership they claim. Sometimes these claims of "bonus" circulation are valid—for example, magazines distributed on airlines get at least eight readers per copy. Still, you should be wary of inflated circulation figures.

Audience is the equivalent of circulation

you depends on whether your strategy is to dominate the market or to reach a certain niche within that market.

Reach and *frequency* are key media terms used more in broadcast than in print. *Reach* is the total number of people exposed to a message at least once in a set time period, usually four weeks. (Reach is the broadcast equivalent of circulation, for print advertising.) *Frequency* is the average number of times those people are exposed during that time period. To make reach go up, you buy a wider market area. To make frequency go up, you buy more ads during the time period. Usually, when reach goes

up, you have to compromise and let frequency go down. You could spend a lot of money trying to achieve a high reach and a high frequency. The creative part of media planning comes in balancing reach, frequency, and budget constraints to find the best combination in view of your marketing goals.

In developing your media plan, you will:

- Review your marketing objectives through the "lens" of media planning.
- Review the options available.
- Evaluate them against your objectives.
- Set your minimum and maximum budget straints.

ate alternative scenarios until you over the strategy that accomplishes r objectives within those constraints.

elop a schedule describing ad appear-es in each medium.

nmarize your plan in the form of a cal-ar and a budget.

gotiate with media representatives to cute your plan.

Your Media Objectives

dia planning notebook begins with a detailing the media you'll use. To vhat goes in there, you'll need to know something about each of the media that apply in your situation. We're about to look at each category close up. As you read about each medium, think about your overall marketing objectives. You've decided to use advertising for some reason—there is some goal you think it will accomplish for you. How is this medium supposed to help?

Here's how to create a statement of your media objectives. You do this by answering each of the questions in Template 4-2 and explaining your rationale for each answer. (Here's a hint: Look back at your business review from Chapter 1. If you took the time to write out your answers then, you have a jump on the work ahead of you now.) Again, we use the journalists' questions to guide our thinking. As I explain each point, I'll give you an example from a client of mine, First Business Bank. This bank focuses on attracting and serving business accounts only—an unusual but effective niche. In Chapter 6 you'll read more about this bank's advertising. Here's some of the background that went into creating that story.

- *Who?* Write a statement about your customers. Knowing your customers' buying patterns and lifestyle demographics is critical to selecting the best medium to reach them. You must advertise at a time and in a way that will encourage prospects to buy. Who are you advertising to? What do you know about them? I'm hoping you took me seriously in Chapters 1 and 2 when I talked about knowing your customers in relation to marketing objectives and positioning. You will select media based on the match between their audience and your customer profile. Obviously, the more you know about your customers, the more accurate this selection will be.

    First Business Bank's customers are owners and chief financial officers of businesses with typically $4 million or more in sales per year. Most are between thirty-five and fifty-five, conservative in their tastes, well educated—I could go on with demographic and lifestyle descriptions, but you get the idea.

- *Where?* Describe the geographic distribution of your customers. You will use this to find the best match in terms of reach or circulation from among the media options available. State where the advertising should go geographically.

    First Business Bank's customers are located within a twenty-mile radius of the bank. Distribution around town is quite even; there are no real "hot spots."

- *What?* What market position are you claiming? What is the benefit you've got to sell? Take a look at your business review, particularly your self-concept and plans for growth, from the exercises in Chapter 1.

    Look at your results from Chapter 2's exercises on positioning. What about special promotions? After reading Chapter 3, do you have an idea for a special event or a sale? Reflect on these factors, then describe a communication goal.

    Make a statement regarding the attitude your advertising will project and the message you intend to communicate. It bears repeating: What is the key benefit you offer to your customer?

    First Business Bank is innovative in its services and offers an excellent track record in financial performance. Specializing in serving the business customer makes this bank stand out from its competition. Advertising should project an attitude of bold originality, but should not rely on humor (generally inappropriate for banking).

- *When?* State the seasonality and timing that affect your plan. Timing is driven by your goals. Are you planning a quick-in-and-quick-out media blitz to get last year's merchandise off your showroom floor? That's a timing strategy. Seasonality is the way time of year affects your business— the annual holiday season, beach season, Spring Break. Some people advertise specifically to fill in slow times; others advertise at their busiest seasons, to maximize that opportunity. State the timing and seasonality affecting you, and how you intend to exploit them.

    First Business Bank is planning a specific campaign to take advantage of a merger between two large commercial banks. The timing of the media plan will reflect the two "waves" in which the merger will be in the public eye: We anticipate an initial shock wave when the announce-ment is made, and a second large wave when the actual rearrangements of per-sonnel, branch locations, and services take place. We will advertise in sync with those waves.

- *How much?* State the dollar amount you're budgeting for advertising. How do you arrive at that budget? One method is to use the "task approach"—estimating the cost of producing and placing advertising in fulfill-ment of a set schedule, as defined by the strategy you propose. If the bottom line you calculate is beyond your means, you move to the other approach: compromise. Work backward, removing the lowest priority ele-ments from your plan until the balance of budget and projected reach and frequency meet your needs.

  You don't have to complete the entire budget calculations now—just state your parameters, minimum and maximum, and the method you intend to use to establish the budget.

  For First Business Bank, we choose a task approach: The strategy will dictate the budget. We anticipate that the first wave will cost approximately $2,500 (mostly radio commercials) and the sec-ond wave $5,000 (newspaper advertising).

- *How many?* State your objective regarding results. How many new customers would represent success? What sales goals have you set that you expect this media plan to accomplish? If you're introducing a new product, the sales generated might be as little as half or less of the media budget. If you're an established player with a prod-uct at a mature stage in its cycle, your fig-ures should run close to your industry's averages.

Template 4-2: Statement of Media Objectives

Statement of Media Objectives

Who? Describe your customers.

_____

_____

Where? Describe the geographic distribution of your customers.

_____

_____

What? What is your positioning? What key benefit are you selling?

_____

_____

When? State the timing and seasonality affecting you, and how you will exploit them.

_____

_____

_____

_____

How Much? State your budget parameters, minimum and maximum.

_____

How Many? State your sales goals.

_____

_____

Know Your Options: What's Right and Wrong with Each Medium?

You have an array of media to choose from. The trick is finding the right combination to reach your objectives.

Your media plan will probably rely on a combination of several media, perhaps using radio to build awareness of a coupon promotion and using newspapers to deliver the coupon and the details. Or you might be a business-to-business advertiser. In this case, it might be more practical to rely on trade journal advertising combined with targeted direct mail to reach your customer.

To find out what media are available in your market, your source will be the SRDS books, which provide an exhaustive list of periodicals and broadcast outlets. The listing includes all pertinent information, including circulation, rates, and contact address and phone (see Example 4-1). Separate editions cover trade journals, consumer magazines, newspapers, radio, broadcast and cable TV, direct mail, and outdoor/transit advertising. Special books cover Canada and the Hispanic market. These books are a wonderful resource, and highly accurate. SRDS books should be available at your public library; if not, contact the publisher at 3004 Glenview Rd., Wilmette, IL 60091.

Example 4-1: SRDS
Used by permission of SRDS.

The Print Media

Magazines and newspapers produce sales kits containing rate cards and other helpful information describing audience characteristics, buying habits, lifestyles, and so on. These publications usually have representatives, or "reps," who will help you in your media decisions. They are, of course, salespeople who will do their best to match you with their publication. We will talk more about working with these reps at the end of this chapter.

Magazines

Because of their timing, magazines perform slowly. You can wait months between the time you decide to place an ad and the time it actually comes out. Another month or two might go by before your business sees the response to that ad. A media strategy featuring magazine ad placement will work better for building long-term sales than for the quick fix, where newspapers or direct mail might work better. Most companies who use magazine advertising are using it to build awareness and to educate potential customers regarding complex or high-investment products, such as business computers or industrial equipment. If you are a manufacturer or distributor selling to businesses nationwide, you are likely to advertise in your industry's trade journals. If, on the other hand, you are selling to a local consumer market, there may be no magazine appropriate for you.

Consumer magazines. This term covers every mass-circulation publication, from *Vogue* to *Sports Illustrated*. Ads in regional editions of some magazines, like *Time* and *Sports Illustrated*, are available at comparatively low cost. Media brokers, like 3M Media Network, offer packages of several magazines by geographic area, down to a three-digit Zip code. That means that a car dealership in Royal Oaks, Michigan, could have a black-and-white ad appearing in *Newsweek, Sports Illustrated, Time,* and *U.S. News & World Report*—but only in those issues delivered to the northwest Detroit zip codes. He would pay about $5,660 for one month's schedule, reaching 72,550 paid subscribers. Each is located within driving distance and is, according to the magazines' demographics, the type of person who might buy a car from this dealership.

If your strategy is to dominate in a geographic area, you might want to look into this. But for the smaller business, with limited resources or a less focused market, large-circulation consumer magazines are not a cost-effective option. And there really aren't very many small-circulation consumer magazines. If you're a smaller advertiser wanting to reach consumers, the only magazine option available to you might be your city magazine.

Newspapers or radio might be better choices, unless your product is a large-ticket item requiring the upscale presentation of a magazine. It's hard to sell furs in newsprint.

Business magazines. Business magazines come in two flavors. One is the regional business publications, such as the weekly *Crain's Chicago Business* or *Corporate Report Wisconsin*, which, as their names imply, provide news strictly on business topics. The other business alternative is trade journals, which serve vertical markets by industry type. An example would be *Wood Products Today*, which addresses an audience of manufacturers, distributors, and service providers within the lumber industry. You are probably aware of such magazines in your industry.

Because these journals serve a specific industry, you can pinpoint types of buyers with little waste compared to most other media. Lots of small businesses cope with vertical markets. I've done advertising for distributors of everything from cheese to T-shirts—all selling to retailers that re-sell the products to an end user.

Manufacturers need to advertise in a vertical marketplace too. In industrial parks all over America, people are creating products and selling them to one another. The publications they advertise in range from newsprint glorified price lists to glossy four-color magazines.

If you do sell business-to-business to a national market, trade journals are probably your most cost-effective way to reach your customers—if the journal is well targeted.

What will you pay for advertising space in a national trade magazine? The rate cards will tell you—but don't be afraid to ask if you can do better. There is an increasing trend toward rate negotiation in specialized business publications, which you may be able to take advantage of. Also, these types of publications often provide special editorial sections that improve your chance of directing a message precisely to select readers interested in the topics covered in these sections.

Your research may uncover drawbacks in your industry, however. Some business publications are not targeted well enough to serve your objective. For example, suppose you sell inks for silkscreen printing to the imprinted-activewear industry. The trade journals available, however, are not segmented to silkscreen only, but address the embroidery and iron-on transfer segments as well. And these people don't buy inks at all.

These businesses are related enough to have many common interests, so it's not surprising that the publishers have found it more profitable to address the aggregate market, rather than spin off separate publications for each subindustry. But for you, some of their readers are wasted circulation. The media kit from the publication should give you a breakdown of readers by type of business, or by job description. Look for the details that tell you whether these people buy what you sell. If half the readers are categorized as "embroidery managers" and you sell to "silkscreen production supervisors," discount the circulation figures by half when you do your CPM calculations.

To get better results, you must either rely on the publication to provide special editorial sections, improving your chance of getting to your customers, or look at other media strategies, perhaps direct mail.

Whatever type of magazine you are considering, you face these advantages: Your cost per thousand is comparatively low, and your readership is relatively high, provided the magazine you choose delivers good editorial content. Many buyers will read a magazine (and notice a good percentage of the advertising) but will throw away direct mail solicitations unopened.

A disadvantage you must take into account is the wasted circulation, however. If your choice of magazine is not narrowly targeted, you will want to subtract some percentage of the circulation when you calculate the CPM ranking. Study the media kit until you feel you really know who's reading the magazine.

Newspapers

Who should use newspaper advertising? If your market is a broad general consumer base in a defined geographical area, newspaper advertising is for you. It's a primary focus of most retail business advertising. It's quick and flexible; you can be in or out in a matter of days, and you can change your ad copy up to the last minute, sometimes literally the evening before the ad appears.

You can specify placement in a certain section, such as the lifestyle, sports, or money section, to target your customer more directly. The audience for the sports section is predominantly male, as you'd expect, making it an ideal place to advertise not just sporting goods but tires, suits, and sporty cars. Luxury cars might go for the business section instead, where you'll find banks advertising their CD rates, too. Entertainment events crowd the lifestyle section of most papers. Look closely at the demographics for each section and place your bet, then produce an ad that speaks to that demographic group.

Production costs are inexpensive, and timing is fast. And usually, there will not be too many newspapers competing in one geographic area. This simplifies your decision process.

Newspaper advertising can include a lot of information. Your reader can take as much time as necessary to absorb your message. At relatively low cost ($25 to $50 per column inch in most markets, depending on circulation and section) you can buy enough space to include maps, directions, multiple addresses and phone numbers, or promotional coupons. This is not true of broadcast media.

What about disadvantages? Newspaper ads are easy to ignore. There is a great deal of clutter in newspapers. It is difficult to stand out on the page; it takes space and frequency to achieve dominance, and that means you'd better have a serious budget.

The printing quality of newspapers is typically poor. Because of the high speed at which they're produced and the low quality of the newsprint paper, ink density goes all over the place. Your ad can look washed out in some copies and overinked in others. This means that creative concepts have to rely on simple visual power.

A big disadvantage of newspapers is their short shelf life. You've heard the saying, "Today's news, tomorrow's fish wrapper." If people don't read your ad the first time they look at the paper, you're very unlikely to get another shot at them. An ad in a magazine has a longer functional life, since the magazine usually gets picked up a number of times before it's tossed. With some magazines there's reason to count pass-along readership as well. A newspaper ad, however, is in the public eye for only a few hours at most.

People spend less time with newspapers today; your ad may have about five minutes to attract the reader's attention. You may be getting less circulation than you're paying for.

Yellow Pages and Industry Directories

The Yellow Pages are a "must," because in them you reach people when they are ready to buy. People don't browse the Yellow Pages for entertainment. They need a widget, and they don't have a referral in mind, and they don't remember driving past a widget store on the way to work, so they don't have a clue as to where to go to buy one. But boy, do they need that widget. So they pick up the Yellow Pages, or the *Thomas Register*, or whatever equivalent is at hand. They start dialing around. Your phone rings.

There used to be just one phone book to think about, but it's more complicated than that today, as competing directories proliferate. You have many choices, with regional and business-to-business directories offered as well as your local phone company's directory. Do you advertise in one, some, or all?

Industrial directories, like the *Thomas Register*, offer business-to-business advertisers a similar environment. These can be an important part of your media mix: Statistics show that they are very successful at generating industrial purchases. They have a long shelf life; they typically get passed around and can stay in circulation for several years.

There are drawbacks to directories, whether industrial or geographical. You must consider the number of categories you need to be listed under in the directory. Because these directories are divided into so many sections, staying visible can be a costly proposition. In Chapter 6, on print advertising, you'll find Template 6-14 useful in preparing your directory advertising plan and seeing that it stays within budget.

Because directories require ad materials well in advance and stay in circulation for several years, you are committing for a several-year span when you place advertising. Even though new directories are delivered to replace the old ones, it's true that in both businesses and homes the old directories stay in use for up to four years or even more. If you are anticipating a business move or change of phone number when the directory deadlines come, you are in a pickle. Planning well ahead is your best defense.

Print Collateral

Print collateral is a term advertising agencies use to describe any printed pieces you create and distribute yourself, as opposed to ads that you place in publications for them to distribute. Print collateral includes direct mail, point of purchase displays (P.O.P.), billboards, and transit and out-of-home advertising.

Direct Mail

Effective direct mail starts with a good mailing list. Shopping for the right list is the equivalent of choosing the right magazine or radio station for your message. You may have a good customer and prospect list that you've built as part of your ongoing operations. Good for you! It could turn out to be your most valuable sales-generating asset. If you've got a database that tracks customer purchase behavior, such as seasonality and trends in repeat purchases, you should put it to use in direct mail. Create a promotional incentive program tailored to your marketing objectives, perhaps using coupons to stimulate add-on sales. Since these are your customers, you have a good idea what type of offer will push their buttons. You've got a money-making machine ready to roll.

If you have no list of your own, you will be dealing with list brokers to find a set of available names that matches your target market. You will describe a set of selection criteria—say, women between forty-five and fifty-five living in a four-county region who hold a driver's license and have a college degree—and your list broker will do a trial sort and tell you that, for example, 9,720 names match that description. He will then quote you a price per thousand, and you can negotiate to arrive at a number of pieces and a cost per thousand that fits your budget. (Read more about this in Chapter 9.)

Questions of the list aside, there are advantages and disadvantages to direct mail.

Direct mail produces easily measured results, since you know precisely how many pieces were mailed and how many people responded. Unlike print and broadcast media, with their general circulation figures, direct mail delivers no wasted circulation when you've properly selected your list.

Direct mail can create quick sales boosts by delivering an "urgent" message. Coupons in the mail pull even better than coupons in newspaper ads. Scheduling ads in print or broadcast media to coincide with your direct mail promotion, when done right, can produce a real powerhouse campaign.

You can control the cost of direct mail, but you can't do it for nothing. When the costs of design, printing, lists, and postage are added, direct mail can be tough to justify for the smaller business. Direct mail for a bank in a midsize community—mailing to 100,000 prospects—might cost $9,000 to $17,000, depending on the "look" desired—low cost or upscale.

Timing can be a problem with direct mail. Lead time from plan to mailbox can be substantial—ten to twelve weeks, and longer if you are mailing at bulk rates. Clutter in that mailbox once you reach it is a problem, too. "Junk mail" angers some recipients; growing concern over the environment means that the piece you send had better bring something of real value into the recipient's life. Information with news value—describing a product benefit in detail, for instance—will be welcomed, as will a promotional offer with a promise of real savings. Sometimes an amusing or beautiful piece will satisfy the recipient's need for value—it all depends on the type of business you're in. Chapter 9 covers the subject in detail.

Point-of-Purchase Materials

Point-of-purchase (P.O.P.) materials go anywhere customers can buy your product or service. Everyone is familiar with the P.O.P. displays in grocery and liquor stores. Sometimes the retailers create them for their own use, but more often they are created by manufacturers for the retail selling site. Suppose you're a specialty food manufacturer— you make a line of all-natural fruit dessert toppings, sold in the freezer case. You distribute through a nationwide natural food distributor. You and that distributor might work out a deal to produce and distribute an attention-getting P.O.P. display that attaches to the shelf of the freezer. If you and the distributor share the cost of the program, that's *co-op*.

Here are some types of P.O.P.:

- Table tents (heavy paper, used in restaurants and bars)

- Shelf-talkers (small cards that attach to store shelving and project into the aisle)
- Counter cards (free-standing cards with cardboard easel backs, often up to $8^1/_2$ x 11 inches in size)
- Display racks (metal, plastic, or even heavy cardboard systems that typically hold two or three shelves of merchandise and feature a head piece with an attention-getting message)

All types of P.O.P. will have these elements in common: The message will be extremely simple, just a few strong words, and the color will be overpoweringly bright. There's no room for subtlety in this medium.

Specialized vendors, printers, and ad agencies produce P.O.P. displays. Make sure to get several bids, and samples of quality, before you proceed, as these items are purposely one-of-a-kind. This is not an area to attempt on your own; you will spend too much time learning the ins and outs of specialty printing.

Point of purchase is a visible, effective sales motivator, ideal for introducing a new product or presenting a contest or promotion. However, you're subject to the clutter of competing displays. Study what competitors are doing in your market before you decide that P.O.P. is right for you.

For the retailer with only one or two locations, it's usually not cost-effective to custom-print P.O.P. displays. This is too bad, because their effect on sales is noticeable. Look into co-op programs with your vendors, and explore one-of-a-kind displays you may be able to make yourself, before you give up on P.O.P. Do not rule out hand-done signs, like those you often see in grocery stores. Just be sure that the person doing them has distinctive and clear handwriting so that the signs don't appear amateurish.

Outdoor and Transit Advertising

Billboards and bus cards are *the* truly local advertising. If you're trying to reach an audience on a geographic basis, you should include outdoor in your plan. You get good repeated exposure. The same people will tend to pass your billboard daily. Billboards can convey your message powerfully and creatively, although they must be simple. You have only a few seconds while a driver passes.

But don't let that stop you from using your ingenuity. Klinke Cleaners, a dry cleaner in Madison, Wisconsin, created a billboard with a giant hanger protruding from the boundaries of the board. Then the board was wrapped in a giant, billowing clear plastic bag. The name and address "inside" were clearly visible, and the flapping plastic proved to be a real attention-getter. (You'll read more about their advertising in upcoming chapters.)

Whatever your message, you will probably have to commit to a fairly long time frame—several months to several years—because production costs are high. But the basic cost of outdoor media can be very reasonable when production costs and space rental are prorated over the life of the board.

There are other types of outdoor advertising besides the billboard. A branch called "out-of-home advertising" is rapidly developing in urban centers. It presents some interesting options: posters displayed in bus stops, train stations, and airports. These can be an effective way to reach business travelers.

Every city offers types of transit advertising—buses, taxis, any fleet that moves may offer advertising. These options reach geographically targeted markets with high impact and high exposure rates—after all, the fleets are on the road twelve to eighteen hours a day.

The Broadcast Media

The basic value of broadcast media is measured in ratings and share. These provide the basis on which networks price programs, and on which advertisers compare their value. Ratings are established primarily by two national research companies, which are neutral "third parties" observing and monitoring the broadcast media. Local radio and television stations subscribe to the Arbitron rating service, and state their ratings in Arbitron points. Network television relies on the famous Nielsen ratings, based on the people meters the company has placed in homes since the 1950s. A rating point represents 1 percent of all households with television. These rating points tell you how big an audience is watching the program, just as circulation figures indicate how big the readership of a magazine might be.

"Share" is shorthand for "share of audience." This is a competitive evaluation that shows how one program performs against others airing at the same time. It is stated as a percentage of the total television audience.

But don't choose broadcast media solely on the basis of ratings and share points. The composition of the audience is equally impor-

tant. A lower-rated show might deliver a selected target audience that fits your market objective better. For example, a cooking program might not earn high enough ratings or share to compare favorably with a situation comedy. But if you're selling a gourmet kitchen gadget, the cooking program will deliver the better audience for you—at lower cost.

Broadcast media are priced differently at different times of day, based on the estimated size of the audience. The day is divided into day-parts, which are a little different from radio to television. As you might expect, in radio the drive-time hours are the most popular; in television, it's the evening viewing hours that earn the highest fees. In Chapters 7, "All About Radio Advertising," and 8, "Television," you'll find more information on how broadcast time is sold.

Example 4-2: Arbitron Reports
Used by permission of Results Radio.

```
                TAPSCAN ReachMaster 2 WEEK SCHEDULE ANALYSIS
                            ADULTS 35-64
                       MADISON METRO SURVEY AREA
                        SUMMER 1994 ARBITRON
SCHEDULE DESCRIPTION

                              SPOTS #  TOTAL  AVG   CUME   AVERAGE   CUME            GROSS
STATION       DAYPART         /WK WKS SPOTS  RTG.   RTG.   PERSONS  PERSONS  GRP's IMPRESSIONS  RATE   CPP

WTDY.........
WEEK 1        M-W 5:30A-10A.... 13   1   13   1.9%   7.7%   2,600   10,200   25.1   33,400     $24   $12.41
              M-W 10A-3P....... 13   1   13   2.5%  10.4%   3,300   13,800   32.3   42,900     $24   $9.65
              M-W 3P-8P........ 12   1   12   0.6%   4.4%    800     5,900    7.6   10,100     $24   $37.91
              M-W 8P-12M....... 12   1   12   0.3%   1.4%    400     1,900    3.2    4,200     $24   $90.99

WEEK 2        M-W 5:30A-10A.... 13   1   13   1.9%   7.7%   2,600   10,200   25.1   33,400     $24   $12.41
              M-W 10A-3P....... 13   1   13   2.5%  10.4%   3,300   13,800   32.3   42,900     $24   $9.65
              M-W 3P-8P........ 12   1   12   0.6%   4.4%    800     5,900    7.6   10,100     $24   $37.91
              M-W 8P-12M....... 12   1   12   0.3%   1.4%    400     1,900    3.2    4,200     $24   $90.99
                                                                                   ----------------------------
  TOTALS FOR WTDY:             50   2  100   1.4%  13.9%   1,800   18,400  136.5   181,100     $24   $17.59


SCHEDULE COMPUTATIONS   2 WEEKS
ADULTS 35-64   (POPULATION -     132,700)

                         NET                    EFF            GROSS    TOTAL                          AVG
STATION       SPOTS     REACH  = REACH  FREQ.   REACH  GRP's  IMPRESS   COST       CPP       CPM       RATE
------------------------------------------------------------------------------------------------------------
WTDY.........   100    16,900 =  12.7%  10.7   10.7%  136.5  181,100   $2,400    $17.59    $13.25    $24

TOTALS:         100    16,900 =  12.7%  10.7   10.7%  136.5  181,100   $2,400    $17.59    $13.25    $24

====> THE COST OF REACHING EACH TARGET PERSON AN AVERAGE OF 10.7 TIMES IS 14.2 CENTS.

*****************************************************************************************
                      <==== QUICK-SCAN SUMMARY ====>

              TOTAL SPOTS:      100       REACH:     12.7%    COST:    $2,400
              AVERAGE RATE:      $24       FREQ:     10.7     CPP:     $17.59
                                       EFF REACH:    10.7%    GRPs:    136.5
*****************************************************************************************

PREPARED WITH THE TAPSCAN RATINGS ANALYSIS SYSTEM.  REPORT DESIGNS AND CONTENTS (C) COPYRIGHT 1994 TAPSCAN, INC. (205) 987-7456.
DATA (C) COPYRIGHT THE ARBITRON COMPANY.  SUBJECT TO LIMITATIONS AND RESTRICTIONS STATED IN ORIGINAL REPORT.
```

Example 4-2 shows some reports generated from Arbitron data. These were the result of my inquiry about a schedule of radio commercials for First Business Bank. My radio sales rep drew up this potential schedule, then calculated the reach and frequency it would deliver. Audience demographics helped me decide whether this was the right plan to recommend to my client. The first page describes the schedule and computes its reach, frequency, CPM, and ratings points. The second page shows the audience for one of the day-parts described in the schedule. (The rep's proposal went on for many pages, with demographic profiles for each day-part in the schedule.) This demographic report describes the A.M. drive-time audience for Mondays and Wednesdays between 5:30 A.M. and 10 A.M. The first block reports the audience among men, broken down by age groups. The second block reports the audience among women in the same age groups. Note how many more women than men in the older age groups are listening. This is the kind of information that can help you decide when and where to advertise, and then help you shape an appropriate creative message.

Radio

Radio is a strong alternative to newspaper. Like newspaper advertising, it serves a broad market, is defined geographically, and is similarly low-cost and flexible.

Because radio is where people go first for news, you can schedule messages around news updates. Because radio stations choose certain formats, such as All Oldies or Easy Listening, you can narrow your choice to stations whose audience demographics match your target. This ability to target an audience is a big advantage of radio.

Radio is intrusive, unlike print. A listener can't skip past your ad on the radio. It's one of the most involving of all media, through the power of the script, the sound effects, and the other production values of the commercial. Radio is great for conveying urgency. With a strong commercial, you can pull customers right out of their cars and into your store.

Radio tends to appeal to a somewhat younger audience than newspaper; this is good to keep in mind as you decide whether to use radio, and then as you create your spots.

Creating radio spots can be very inexpensive. The stations will work with you to produce commercials at little or no cost. If you feel you need higher production value, you can choose to work with an ad agency.

Radio does have its disadvantages. Your rep will try to steer you toward package buying plans that force you to accept advertisements at odd times of day in order to get the in-demand time slots you want.

The market you're reaching is tough to get a fix on. That younger audience is notoriously fickle, changing its loyalties faster than the ratings services can keep up. The stations' sales reps typically present ratings to you in ways

that are designed to highlight the station's best features. It can be difficult for the neophyte to make fair comparisons between stations.

Different radio stations set different limits on how many minutes of commercials they'll mix into each hour. A very crowded station might sell as much as twenty-two minutes out of every hour, meaning that your ad is in danger of getting lost in the barrage. Be sure to ask your rep about this before you commit to a plan. You would prefer to hear that less than sixteen minutes an hour goes to advertising.

Television

Television is a powerful medium, with its combination of sight, sound, and motion. It has an unequaled ability to stimulate emotions. The power of TV can make your business seem larger and more successful. TV viewers are generally in a relaxed state of mind, and open to suggestion. You can use TV to create image, or to motivate action. A shot of a juicy pizza followed by a home-delivery number really makes the phone ring.

With the arrival of cable TV, some very efficient media buying is possible. Special-interest networks, like Lifetime or MTV, let you aim for a very specific target market. And as with direct mail, you can make geographical buys with pinpoint precision.

The most obvious drawback: Expense. Producing a commercial for television will take more of your time, energy, and money than any other form of advertising. While the creative potential is tremendous, the pressure to outspend your resources will be intense. Your mistakes will be expensive. Most spots produced by the TV studios will look low-budget compared to agency-produced commercials. Your image may not be able to afford the damage done by taking the least expensive route. Expect to pay from $1,000 to $8,000, depending on the complexity of your creative idea.

The cost of airtime on TV is more expensive than other media, although cable offers some real bargains. Spots are almost always sold in a unit of 30 seconds, called a :30. Network television :30s might cost $60 to $120 in a small market, and up to $1,000 or more in a large market. The only way to buy network time for less is to purchase "avails"— last-minute openings that become available because of other advertisers' changes of plans or a shift in network programming. You purchase at a discounted rate, and you give up control of precisely when the commercial runs. This can work to your advantage— sometimes a real gem of a spot becomes available. However, if you've ever seen a commercial advertising an event that just passed, you know the advertiser bought avails.

Meanwhile, cable channels can offer you a cost much closer to that of radio time. A targeted area in a large market can be bought for $10 to $15 a :30. Cable channels (such as CNN, ESPN, or Lifetime) sell some of the available commercial time to national advertisers. The balance goes to the local cable companies to fill with local advertisers. Because the viewership is much lower than for network shows, the cost is also much less.

Rates change frequently, as does the programming on most TV stations. Relying heavily on television in your media mix means that you must continually monitor and revise your media schedule. That's a time commitment you want to make sure you're ready to make.

There's much more to know about television, both network and cable—you can read about it in Chapter 8.

Evaluating Media Options: Ranking Apples and Oranges

We've looked at the options available to you: print media (magazines, newspapers, and directories), broadcast media (radio and TV, both network and cable), and the collateral category (P.O.P., outdoor, and transit advertising). How do you evaluate these against one another? Unfortunately, at this point it becomes more art than science. This will always be a matter of ranking apples against oranges. There is no easy way to do a numerical calculation of precisely which media, in what mix, will deliver the results you want. However, let's look at some techniques for making decisions about your media plan.

Quantitative Ranking

Media planners use spreadsheet comparisons a great deal. CPM, the cost per thousand ranking based on circulation, helps you compare print media. Arbitron ratings help you with radio. Nielsen ratings likewise help you rank television options. Collateral has its own performance ratings, from store traffic for P.O.P. to commuter traffic counts for an outdoor board, usually calculated against a cost per piece.

Use these quantitative statistics to help you compare options within a media category— to compare one magazine with another, or one radio station with another station. Ask yourself, "All other things being equal, should it be this one or that one?" If you're comparing print, make sure you're comparing the same size ad and the same frequency—full-page black-and-white, one-time rate, for example. If you're comparing radio or TV buys, make sure you're comparing the same number of spots, same schedule, over the same time period. You can also use CPM calculations to compare apples to oranges—to see whether you reach people more efficiently via newspaper than via TV, for example. But the answer is less clear, since the media are inherently different in many more ways than just their cost per thousand.

Some media will not match your marketing objectives closely enough. Others will come at a cost that is simply not justifiable in relation to your resources. Some will be viable competitors for your advertising dollar.

Template 4-3 shows the quantitative analysis I did as I examined media recommendations for First Business Bank. It shows comparisons of both apples to apples (the two radio stations being ranked) and apples to oranges (radio compared to outdoor and two kinds of print).

Template 4-3: Quantitative Ranking

Date: 10-26-94
Title: Media Comparisons, First Business Bank
Assumptions: In Business: no change from current plan.
State Journal: Plan on 4/month. $10,000 contract
WIBA: 5 spots/week 6 am / 6 pm
WTDY: 5 spots/week 6 am / 6 pm
Outdoor: Billboards @ U.S. 51 north of 12/18

Media		Rate Card	Frequency /year	Space	Monthly Rate	Circulation in 1,000s	CPM ($)	Index
Print:	*In Business*	1995	12x	2/3 Page	$970	13	$74.62	100%
	(city business magazine)							
	Wisc State Journal	1995	10,000	20"	$1,804	123	$14.67	186%
	(city newspaper)							
Radio:	WIBA	10/26	260	On air :60s	$884	40	$22.10	91%
	(A.M. CBS affiliate)							
	WTDY	10/19	260	On air :60s	$600	28.4	$21.13	62%
	(A.M. local station)							
Outdoor:	Adams Outdoor	1995	3x	12 x 25 panel	$800	22.8	$35.09	82%

Qualitative Ranking

Next, look at your options from a qualitative perspective. Does this medium have the ability to enhance your advertising message? Is the editorial value strong? Does your gut tell you that this magazine is being read by the customers you want to reach? Is the other advertising in it attractive, and can you afford to create equally compelling ads? What are your competitors doing? Which media do they favor, and are you more likely to be successful approaching them head-on in their main medium or doing an end run to dominate in a secondary niche they've left uncovered? So many questions. Take some time to think about each. The worksheets in Template 4-4 will help you make your decision. Use Template 4-4A to summarize the qualitative aspects of each medium under consideration. Then use Template 4-4B to compare the qualitative performance of each.

Template 4-4A: Qualitative Media Ranking

Qualitative Media Ranking
Answer these questions for each medium under consideration.

1. Creative implications: If you choose this medium, can you afford to do a good job?

_____

_____

2. Editorial environment: Does this medium offer good news value? Is the editorial voice generally supportive of your product/service?

_____

_____

3. Are your competitors advertising in this medium?

_____

_____

4. Is the audience delivered by this medium generally interested in what you sell?

_____

_____

Template 4-4B: Qualitative Ranking Comparison

Qualititative Ranking Comparison

	Bad	Poor	Neutral	Good	Excellent
1. Creative implications					
_____	☐	☐	☐	☐	☐
_____	☐	☐	☐	☐	☐
_____	☐	☐	☐	☐	☐
2. Editorial environment					
_____	☐	☐	☐	☐	☐
_____	☐	☐	☐	☐	☐
_____	☐	☐	☐	☐	☐
3. Competitors					
_____	☐	☐	☐	☐	☐
_____	☐	☐	☐	☐	☐
_____	☐	☐	☐	☐	☐
4. Audience interest					
_____	☐	☐	☐	☐	☐
_____	☐	☐	☐	☐	☐
_____	☐	☐	☐	☐	☐

For each medium you are comparing, place an "x" in the appropriate square. Add up the scores for each medium, using "1" for "bad" through "5" for "excellent." The medium with the highest score is your best candidate from a qualitative perspective.

The winners of your quantitative and qualitative analysis will make your "short list" of potential media options. You've weeded out any clearly inappropriate media. From here, your decision process comes down to balancing reach, frequency, and timing against your budget.

We've talked about the different types of media, how they might be useful to you, and how to evaluate your options. You are beginning to see, I hope, that this is as much art as science. Numerical calculations can help you predict the audience you'll reach and the cost of reaching them. What advertising scenario is right for you? That you'll have to decide based on your own gut instinct—after you do your homework. Your ultimate decisions will become your media plan.

Choosing Your Media Strategy: Comparing Potential Scenarios

When you've studied the media options available (and these are discussed in much detail in the chapters to come), met with the reps, and reviewed the information in the appropriate chapters of this book, you have the raw ingredients for a media plan. What's left is for you to create the recipe: In what proportion, and with what timing, will these elements be blended?

You must balance your desires for reach, frequency, and continuity of timing, since almost no one can afford to reach an ideally broad market with maximum frequency and with never a break in the schedule. Your creative moments lie just ahead, as you move from analysis into action, matching strategies to your goals. Using spreadsheets, you can outline a scenario for action by mapping out a potential calendar, then calculating the costs based on these decisions. You can then revise until you reach a combination that fits your budget. As you do so, you will be balancing these components: reach, frequency, and timing.

Reach

As I mentioned at the start of this chapter, reach defines how many (unduplicated) people are exposed to your message within a designated time period. Most media planners use a period of four weeks for defining reach. Reach and circulation are used interchangeably when talking about print media.

Example 4-3, from an outdoor advertising company, shows how reach and frequency are different.

Example 4-3: Adams Outdoor Advertising "Big Hit" Program
Used by permission of Adams Outdoor Advertising.

The Big Hit is a **one-week** poster campaign specifically designed for highly focused, short-term promotions. With nearly 350,000 daily exposures, your message will definitely be seen.

The Big Hit gives you:

20 poster panels throughout the market
344,900 exposures daily (adults 18+)
$1.35 CPM
78.7% weekly reach
9.4 x weekly frequency
2,414,300 total circulation

The Big Hit is designed for:

- Important Sales Periods

- Short-term Promotions

- Retail Sales Promotions

- Special Events

- Any advertiser that wants immediate market penetration and high impact for a limited time at a great value.

The Big Hit delivers **immediate** awareness of your message in a one-week period.

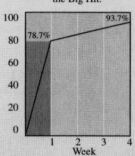

Outdoor Reach
Percentage of total adults reached in one week by the Big Hit.

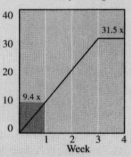

Outdoor Frequency
Average number of times each adult is reached in one week by the Big Hit.

Frequency

How many times is your message seen or heard by one person during the designated time period? Answer that question and you have frequency, one person's average number of exposures to your ad during the designated time period. In broadcast advertising, frequency is very important, since a person can't review your ad if he or she missed part of the information. We generally say that people need to hear or see an ad three to five times before they even begin to remember the advertiser or the message.

In print advertising, frequency is a slightly different concept, because the ad is not so ephemeral. The frequency for a magazine ad might be twelve times a year as opposed to thirty times a week for a radio ad.

When you're buying broadcast advertising, be sure to invest in sufficient frequency to get past that initial three- to five-repetition phase with your listeners or viewers. Take another look at Example 4-2, the schedule for First Business Bank. This schedule proposes fifty spots a week, concentrated on Mondays and Wednesdays, airing between 5:30 in the morning and 12:00 midnight. This averages out to 0.7 spot per hour, or 12.5 spots per day-part. This schedule reflects a strategy of clustering the fifty spots on two days out of the week, so as to be a dominant presence on the days we choose to advertise.

Timing

A component of frequency is the element of timing: On what schedule will your message appear? For each medium in which your ads appear, you will need to address the question of timing. There are a number of strategic approaches (see Template 4-5A):

- *Continuity.* You could set a schedule for advertisements and run it continuously into the future, with no variation in timing. But this is uncommon, because of the expense. More probably, you will plan to run ads using one of these other approaches.

- *Heavy-up.* You run a light continuous schedule of ads, with occasional increases in frequency ("heavying up") to support your seasonality goals, or new product introductions, or promotions like special events.

- *Flighting.* You appear in your chosen medium for a set period—say eight weeks—then disappear entirely for another period—say two weeks—and then reappear. This is similar to heavy-up except that you leave the medium entirely at times. This works because of the inertia inherent in the customers' perception. You will hear, "I saw your ad in today's newspaper" when you know perfectly well you weren't there. Just as it takes multiple appearances before the audience notices you've begun to advertise, it also takes time before they realize you've quit. You can take advantage of this lag to "rest" your ad budget between flights. This works well for short-term promotions and events.

- *Pulsing.* With pulsing, you reduce or increase your advertising in a continuous pattern; for example, the ad runs two weeks, is off two weeks, and then is on two, off two, on a regular basis. The predictability is easy to administer, and the benefits of flighting still accrue. This works well to cut through clutter without increasing your ad space budget.

Note that you could be flighting in one medium while pulsing in another and appearing continuously in a third. Also note that you can use timing to increase sales in already-busy peaks, working with the flow, or you can work against the flow to counteract slow times. The creative approach you choose would probably be different, but the concept of timing applies either way.

Template 4-5A: Media Calendar Showing Timing Strategies

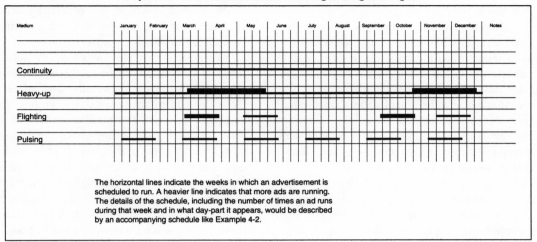

The horizontal lines indicate the weeks in which an advertisement is scheduled to run. A heavier line indicates that more ads are running. The details of the schedule, including the number of times an ad runs during that week and in what day-part it appears, would be described by an accompanying schedule like Example 4-2.

When you've proposed a scenario regarding reach, frequency, and timing for a specific medium, you can calculate approximately how many viewers will receive your message how often. Media departments of the larger ad agencies use formulas to reduce media variables to a numerical score. This is beyond the need—or patience—of most do-it-yourself advertisers.

You will use your quantitative analysis (comparing the alternative scenarios you've projected) and your qualitative analysis (your gut instincts evaluating the intangibles) to decide your media strategy.

How Your Marketing Plan Affects Your Media Strategy

Creating a strategy is simply a process of matching what you know about the available media with the objectives you'd like to accomplish. Those objectives are defined by your marketing plan. Your answers to the Objectives exercise at the beginning of this chapter (Template 4-2) will prepare you to create a media strategy. Your answers to who, what, when, where, how much, and how many are the summation of how your marketing plan affects your media strategy.

Without a marketing plan, you can't have media objectives. Without media objectives, you can't have a strategy—just an assortment of stabs in the dark.

How Your Promotions Plan Affects Your Media Strategy

The focus of a specific promotional plan will be very helpful to you in deciding on your media strategy. It will specify how each medium is involved in communicating the promotion. If you've read Chapter 3, you remember Surma's restaurant and its plans for a grand opening event. The promotion called for newspaper ads, a crawler added to the restaurant's regular commercial on cable TV, a radio spot, and mailing of an invitation. This media strategy described print, broadcast, and direct mail components.

If you have chosen not to run a specific promotion, but are planning to advertise in the media, you will be doing image advertising instead. The results will be more difficult to measure, and the shift in customer attitudes and behavior will take place over a longer period of time.

Your Media Mix: Deciding Which Ads Go Where

If you serve more than one market, you must decide what relative emphasis to give each segment, as it competes for your overall advertising dollar. Very probably you'll use more than one of the possible media.

It is better to be a big fish in a small pond than lost at sea. You want to achieve recall in the minds of your audience. You want to buy enough frequency to get past their initial resistant phase. If your competitors are on the air six or seven times a day, you might want to be on at least that often. If you're advertising in print, you want your ads to be bigger than your competition's. You have to allot enough of your budget to your first choice to allow you to dominate in that medium. Then if you can afford to, add another ... and another.

When you use a broad mix of media, there's a synergy that starts to happen. Each medium has something that it does particularly well. With radio, it's frequency, with TV, it's reach. Print is the place to convey complex information. Your job as planner is to get each of these to complement the others. By using all types of media in your mix, you're getting the maximum possible exposure.

To summarize: Review your options, in terms of both which media to choose and how to use them. (How many ads, how often?) Consider the quantitative data—your CPM comparisons—and the qualitative factors as well. Research your competition's media mix. Check in with your gut instincts. Then evolve a plan of your own, describing the media to be used, the goals to be accomplished, your target audience, and a strategy for reaching them. Add a calendar and budget to these statements, and you have a complete media plan.

The Calendar and the Budget

If you're tackling this subject thoroughly, you've probably created a number of alternative scenario spreadsheets. It's time to review these projections and schedules, and decide on your chosen plan.

Template 4-5B: Blank Media Calendar Form

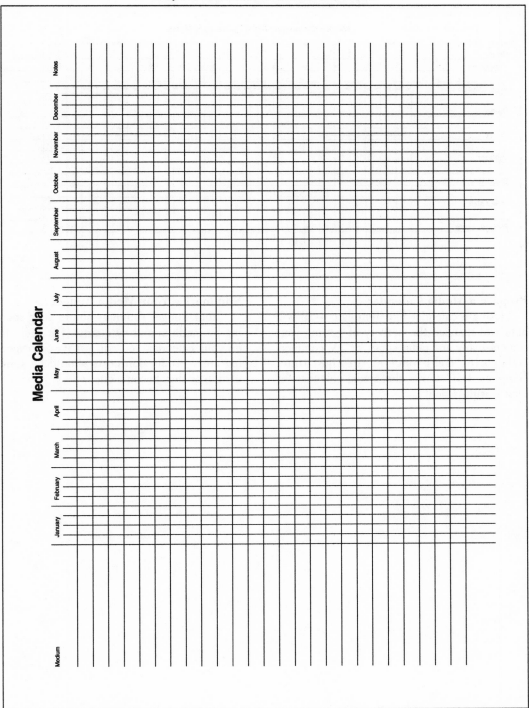

Template 4-5C: Media Calendar for FBB

Media Calendar: First Business Bank

Prepare a Media Calendar

Using a calendar like Template 4-5B will help you manage the activity of getting your camera-ready art, radio spots, or TV commercials to the right place at the right time. Template 4-5C shows the media calendar for First Business Bank.

Summarize Your Media Budget

Your budget summary shows your spending by medium and by quarter. For each item on your calendar, you will list its corresponding cost. Production costs should be scheduled in as they become due.

Template 4-6A: Blank Media Budget

Media Budget
Spending by Medium and Quarter

Date:
Title:
Assumptions:
Prepared by:

Medium	1st Quarter	2nd Quarter	3rd Quarter	4th Quarter	Total ($)	Total (%)
Print						
Radio						
TV						
Outdoor						
Direct Mail						
Total by Quarter:						
Percent of Total:						

Template 4-6B: Media Budget For FBB

Media Budget
Spending by Medium and Quarter

Date: 11-22-94
Title: First Business Bank Media Budget by Quarter
Assumptions: See media calendar
Prepared by: SW

Medium	1st Quarter	2nd Quarter	3rd Quarter	4th Quarter	Total ($)	Total (%)
Print						
In Business	$2,910	$2,910	$2,910	$2,910	$11,640	25%
Wisc. State Journal	$5,625	$5,625	$5,625	$5,265	$22,140	48%
Radio						
WTDY	$2,400		$2,400		$4,800	10%
Outdoor						
Adams Outdoor	$2,000				$2,000	4%
Direct Mail						
Business Briefs	$2,000		$2,000	$2,000	$6,000	13%
Total by Quarter:	$14,935	$8,535	$12,935	$10,175	$46,580	100%
Percent of Total:	32%	18%	28%	22%	100%	

You'll use the budget calendar in Template 4-6A to plan your cash flow to fund your advertising program. Template 4-6B shows the budget calendar for First Business Bank. Obviously a good budget is an important business management tool.

Co-Op Advertising Programs

Many manufacturers offer co-op advertising programs, which will help you by subsidizing your ad budget or providing materials that cut your production costs. If you are in a distribution or retail business, ask your suppliers about co-op programs. Their contributions can be significant—in the thousands of dollars—so don't overlook this possibility.

Working with the Media

Tips on Negotiating Rates

Prices for print advertising are fixed, as the print media can be flexible in matching supply with demand. They have expandable space; if they sell more advertising than usual, they can print more pages.

Your negotiations with print media will revolve around what other services they can offer you, such as reader response cards, additional ads in a special issue, special position, free color, and so on. You will probably not be able to negotiate an actual discount off the rate card.

Prices for television and radio are negotiable, because the amount of inventory is fixed. There are only so many minutes between the programs themselves that can be sold. If there is competition for those minutes, the price goes up. The effect is really noticeable when there's a sudden surge in demand for commercials. The perfect example is the election season. I'm sure you've seen this in your community: Each competing politician buys time on local TV and radio. Regular advertisers are pushed right off the air, or pay big bucks to hang on to just a portion of the air time they would like to buy.

Spring is the beginning of the broadcast media buying season, since networks issue their fall schedules in May. Networks like to get money early, so to encourage you, they will usually offer attractive package deals at this time. This is the best time to negotiate for overall lowest cost. See Example 4-4.

Example 4-4: Bronze/Silver/Gold plan from MAGIC 98
Used by permission of Results Radio.

1ST QUARTER BONUS BUYS!

	:60 second	:30 seconds
GOLD PACKAGE	**$12,000**	**$10,200**
* 300 Paid TAP announcements	$40	$34
* 30 Weekday ROS bonus announcements	No Charge!	
* 30 Weekend BTA bonus announcements	No Charge!	
* 30 Free overnight bonus announcements	No Charge!	
* Three free prize pool tickets	No Charge!	
SILVER PACKAGE	**$8,800**	**$7,600**
* 200 Paid TAP announcements	$44	$38
* 20 Weekday ROS bonus announcements	No Charge!	
* 20 Weekend BTA bonus announcements	No Charge!	
* 20 Free overnight bonus announcements	No Charge!	
* Two free prize pool tickets	No Charge!	
BRONZE PACKAGE	**$4,800**	**$4,200**
* 100 Paid TAP announcements	$48	$42
* 10 Weekday ROS bonus announcements	No Charge!	
* 10 Weekend BTA bonus announcements	No Charge!	
* 10 Free overnight bonus announcements	No Charge!	
* One free prize pool ticket	No Charge!	

GOLD _____   SILVER _____   BRONZE _____

CLIENT _____   ACCEPTED BY _____

SIGNATURE _____   DATE _____

Average unit rate after No Charge Bonus Announcement _____.

1. All paid announcements will be scheduled in a four daypart TAP plan with equal distribution: 5:30a-10a, 10a-3p, 3p-8p, 8p-1a.

2. All no charge weekday ROS bonus announcements will be scheduled pre-emptible 12mid to 12mid.

3. All no charge weekend BTA bonus announcements will be scheduled pre-emptilbe 5:30a-12mid.

4. All no charge overnight announcements will be scheduled 1a-5:30a.

5. Prize pool drawing will be conducted Monday, April 10th. Prize pool includes over $1,000 dollars in prizes. One prize maximum per client.

6. All announcements must air between 12/26/94 - 3/31/95. Failure to fulfill the terms of this agreement shall result in the use of the applicable short rate.

Opportunities come up throughout the year as other advertisers change their plans. You can make good buys at any time, but the deal might be structured differently. If you got a call from a radio station tomorrow saying that it has a highly prized time slot available during the morning newscast, and it will cost only $22 per spot, but you've got to decide fast, would you have an answer ready? A good media plan can help keep you focused on how that deal fits into your overall strategy. If it delivers an audience you want, and if it's available at a price that fits your budget, you're in business. It helps to have a well-documented plan to assist in these fast-breaking decisions.

If you plan to use broadcast media heavily, I recommend that you work with an agency or media service. Those who know the territory thoroughly and are working on your behalf will be better able to find the best buys.

If you are buying your media time and space yourself, here are some tips:

- Be sure your chosen medium delivers your target market. The media sales reps are expert at putting their offerings in the best light. Everybody can find something to claim "We're Number One" about. You don't care. Does the medium deliver the audience you want to reach? That's the key question.

- Beware of bringing your personal biases to your media decisions. Don't buy a certain radio station just because you listen to it—ask instead if your potential customers do. And it works the other way, too. Don't *not* advertise in a certain newspaper just because you hate one of its reporters.

- Look for verifiable information from your sales reps. Audience size, share, gross rating points—these calculations should be based on information from third-party ratings sources. Beware of any statistic described as "estimated"—ask about the source for that information.

- Representatives from the various media will call on you; no matter what the title on their business cards, they are salespeople. Do not allow them to make your decisions for you. High-pressure sales techniques are fairly common. Rely on these people for information, but do your own calculations, and make the decisions that are right for *you*.

Myths of Ad Agency Discounts

Accredited ad agencies receive a 15 percent commission on all advertising they place. This discount is not available to businesses that purchase advertising for themselves. The 15 percent commission almost always represents the largest source of agency revenues. The entire media planning function described in this chapter is typically provided free of charge by an agency, in return for those commissions. However, the small advertiser (with a media budget under, say, $100,000) might have to negotiate a fee for planning functions provided by the agency. Unless you have a truly huge media budget, the agency will bill you for the cost of producing ads for print, broadcast, or outdoor advertising.

Media planning is a business of details, and it requires a considerable amount of time. Just meeting with the sales representatives from the different media and hearing their proposals can be time-consuming. My feeling is that you should have an ad agency work with you on a media plan if your market requires more than local newspapers, radio, or local TV. The expertise the agency applies to your case earns it the commission it receives from the media in which it places your advertising.

Everything on earth is negotiable. In recent years, ad agencies have agreed to various splits of that commission, rebating some proportion to the advertiser. Remember that any good business relationship is based on the mutual benefit of both parties; you must look for a deal that fairly compensates the agency for the work you expect it to perform. A workable arrangement might be to pay a fee for the agency's planning services, then have the agency place the media, earn the 15 percent discount, and rebate 5 to 7 percent to you. (The exact percentage would depend on the total dollar volume of the budget and the amount of the original planning fee.)

For more on this subject, see Chapter 12, which discusses working with ad agencies.

Summary: Writing Your Media Plan

At the beginning of this chapter, I promised I would give you the tools to develop a media plan. I've guided you through a process of reviewing your objectives, choosing from the options available to create a strategy, and negotiating and developing schedules and budgets to execute that strategy. Often I referred you to the upcoming chapters, where I get specific about each different medium. Before you move on to these chapters, summarize your media plan.

Use the journalists' questions again to describe your strategy. How will you achieve the objectives you've set?

- *What?* State your thinking regarding creative strategy. If this advertising is planned in support of a promotion, state that now.

- *When?* Choose and state your timing strategy—flights, or pulses, or front-loading, or whatever. Explain your rationale. Follow this with a calendar of advertising, filling in each detail of timing. (Use Template 4-5.)

- *Where?* Match your target market to your short list of media options. State the specific media you have chosen, and your rationale.

- *How?* Make a tactical statement describing how each medium will be used. For example, a bank might use the local newspaper to promote specials and attractive rates, use a regional (citywide) business publication to do image advertising, and use radio as a way to augment newspaper specials to counteract slow cycles.

- *How much?* Summarize your cost scenario. Use Template 4-6.

If you've put this material in a notebook as I described early in the chapter, you're seriously ready to manage a whole year's media. Don't forget to record changes to the plan as you go along, so that each year's plan becomes an accurate historical record of your advertising. You'll find this very useful year after year, as you evaluate and alter your plans.

In the subsequent chapters on print advertising, radio, TV, and direct mail, I will go into detail about who should use each medium, how each is packaged for sale, how to negotiate the deal, and how to create high-impact advertising in each medium. I'd recommend that you familiarize yourself with those chapters before you carve your media plan in stone. Read on, then find your way back to this chapter and use the guidelines presented here to write a plan that works for you.

Chapter 5

The Creative Approach: Taking Aim at Great Advertising

You're a bow hunter, up in a tree in your deer stand. It's a beautiful fall morning, and you've had plenty of time to think as you wait for that rustling in the distance to turn into a deer in your line of sight. You have two tools to make that deer yours: your bow, and your arrow.

What's this got to do with creative approach? One tool has the point; without the arrow there will be no kill. But without the bow, the arrow isn't worth much. It's the bow that gives the arrow its power and direction.

That's how the creative approach affects your advertising. Your creativity is your bow, and your resulting advertising is your arrow. You're going to take aim at a customer's perception, so use your creative muscle first. You're readying your bow to give that advertising copy its thrust.

The Ad Strategy and the Big Idea

In this chapter you'll get to know about two components of the creative approach: first the *advertising strategy* that states the criteria by which ad decisions will be made, and then the *Big Idea,* the creative hook that expresses your personality while dramatizing the benefit you offer.

Here's why you should have an advertising strategy:

- It will keep you from trying to be all things to all people.
- It will keep your advertising focused on key benefits, prioritized in a hierarchy governed by what you want the prospect to absorb first.

The net result? Advertising that is simple and focused—and therefore effective.

An advertising strategy is a plan of action that defines a goal and suggests tactics for achieving it. The original meaning of *strategy* is military: "The art of command applied to the overall planning and conduct of large-scale combat operations." It is no longer popular to use military metaphors for business, but it's not a bad framework to consider for a moment. We talk about ad campaigns. We talk about the battle for top-of-mind awareness with consumers. We use positioning like a general deciding where to send his troops. We make tactical moves by choosing to communicate in print, broadcast, or direct mail. With an advertising strategy in place, we have a "battle plan" for the marketing war.

An advertising strategy provides direction for all the advertising you'll do for the next year or longer. It saves you time by locking in decisions that you don't intend to review and rethink. At this point, when every idea seems like a possibility, choosing a strategy will be a big help in focusing your efforts. You will need it when you begin working on your Big Idea. By judging ideas against the advertising strategy, you set a challenge based on specifics, rather than trying to be creative in a "try everything" mode.

We'll talk more about developing the Big Idea later in this chapter. Then, when we've covered these two components of the creative approach, we'll explore techniques for using the approach to write ad copy. In this chapter we'll just lay in the background. I'll explain more about writing for each specific medium in Chapters 6 through 9.

The Wording of the Advertising Strategy

An advertising strategy is not a form to be filled out, but a thinking process to be followed. An advertising strategy might read like this one, developed for one of my clients (see Template 5-1A):

Advertising will convince business location decision makers that purchase of commercial real estate in Columbia County will increase their profitability. This will be attributed to low costs for land, transportation, wages, and utilities. Tone of the advertising will be informational (newsy).

That doesn't sound like hard-hitting ad copy. But it does describe criteria by which ad copy can be judged.

Here's another example. Klinke Cleaners is a dry-cleaning company with locations all over town. To outshine its competition, it installed dry-cleaning equipment at each location, so that service could be much quicker. (Others have to ship their customers' clothes to a central processing plant, then distribute them again to the proper locations.) You can see examples of the Klinke advertising in Example 6-5 in Chapter 6, "How to Create Print Ads that Sell," and Examples 8-1, 8-3, 8-4, and 8-5 in Chapter 8, "Television."

The Klinke Cleaners statement of advertising strategy might read like this (Template 5-1B):

Advertising will convince Madison-area businesspeople that quality dry cleaning from Klinke's will be fast. This will be attributed to on-site processing equipment. Tone will be humorous.

If you've read Chapter 2, "Positioning," and you look at the Klinke advertising examples, you can see that Klinke has chosen strategy 3, dramatizing a problem of the target market. Do you start to see how the pieces work together—marketing objectives, positioning, ad strategy, and the Big Idea?

Use the same structure to try your own statement of strategy, using Template 5-1C.

Template 5-1A: Columbia County Example

Statement of Advertising Strategy

Advertising will convince _____ business location decision makers _____
(target consumers)

that _____ purchase of real estate in Columbia County _____
(product)

will _____ increase their profitability _____ .
(benefit)

This will be attributed to _____ low cost for land, transportation, wages, and utilities _____ .
(feature/rationale)

Tone will be _____ informational (newsy) _____ .
(adjective)

Template 5-1B: Klinke Cleaners Example

Statement of Advertising Strategy

Advertising will convince _____ Madison-area businesspeople _____
(target consumers)

that _____ quality dry cleaning from Klinke Cleaners _____
(product)

will _____ be fast _____ .
(benefit)

This will be attributed to _____ on-site processing equipment _____ .
(feature/rationale)

Tone will be _____ humorous _____ .
(adjective)

Template 5-1C: Blank

Statement of Advertising Strategy

Advertising will convince _____
(target consumers)

that _____
(product)

will _____ .
(benefit)

This will be attributed to _____ .
(feature/rationale)

Tone will be _____ .
(adjective)

Five Dimensions of Advertising Strategy

What you want to do is learn how to take your complex story and make it simple. To fill out that simple advertising strategy template, you actually have to consider five major dimensions and reduce each one to a brief statement.

1. Identify the target *market*. We've done so much reviewing of the target market in the first chapters that by now you probably have a short phrase ready—"busy working women" or "upper management technical purchasers." Jot down a brief phrase—whatever describes your best customers quickly.

2. Define the *product* to be advertised. Are you promoting your company's overall image, your product or service offering as a whole, or a specific product or product line?

3. Make a *promise*. Define the key benefit in a simple sentence. Use a verb. Klinke Cleaners' ad copy starts with "Get Your Clothes Back While They're Still in

Style." You can see how this line of copy sprang from the promise described in the advertising strategy.

4. *Support* the promise with a feature—a rationale substantiating your claim. Tell why this product characteristic makes this key benefit possible. Dry-cleaning equipment on-site is the feature that supports Klinke Cleaners' claim of speed.

5. Describe your *tone*. State the character you'll establish, the personality of the product and of its advertising. You might say you're classy, or funny, or youth-oriented. The tone of the ad may vary from season to season, but basic character traits should deepen, not change, as your advertising matures.

Even though you choose a category of tone, like "informative" or "humorous," there's still plenty of room for variation in the execution. If you choose a tone like "fun for young children," you might express that with a cowboy theme, or you might choose circuses.

Some examples of tone adjectives:

Intrusive
Newsy
Honest
Irreverent
Empathetic
Dedicated
Rational
Emotional
Fashion-conscious
State of the art
Sophisticated
Fun (define for what age group!)
Awe-inspiring
Tough
Competitive

Want to limber up your "tone" muscle? Here's an exercise to try. Pick up two magazines; make one a business-to-business publication, like a trade journal or a regional business magazine, and make the other a consumer magazine. Choose five ads in which you feel the tone comes across well. What differences do you see between the business-to-business and consumer categories? Can you see a "pack mentality" in either category? Can you pick out an advertiser who seems to be consciously bucking the trend? How does that help or hinder the effectiveness of this advertiser's message to you? That feeling you are getting is an example of how the tone of an ad works.

If you find you can't hone in on one answer to each dimension of positioning, that's not a bad thing. Keep several alternatives in mind. You can mix and match these pieces as you brainstorm. Write several possible statements, then judge each by whether it supports your positioning. Does it make any promises you can't keep?

Background for Choosing the Advertising Strategy

Your advertising strategy will take into consideration each of the following elements. Some are sweeping statements about your business and your industry, and others are nitpicky details. What do they have in common? Without them, the advertising strategy won't work.

You will be creating advertising executions based on your conclusions in each one of these areas. If you take off without laying this groundwork, you'll find yourself hunting with an arrow but no bow.

We'll discuss each of these in detail:

- Marketing strategy
- Media plan
- The product or service
- Marketing perceptions
- Positioning strategy
- One thought to take away
- Image advertising vs. Response offers
- Your sales cycle
- The must-have list

Marketing Strategy

Review the marketing strategy you've chosen. Remember, in the business review in Chapter 1, we asked, "Where does it hurt? What can advertising do to help?" It's time to answer that question. Decide the focus of your attention. You can reasonably expect to solve only one problem at a time. Increase your likelihood of success by knowing which problem you're aiming at before you go further. Write a statement now that defines the problem your advertising will address.

You say you have no problems? There must be something motivating you to market yourself. Even maintaining a happy status quo is a perfectly reasonable marketing strategy. You wouldn't be reading this book if you didn't think there was some goal that advertising could help you accomplish. Review the templates in Chapters 1 through 3 now, so that your strategy is fresh in your mind.

Media Plan

Review your media plan. Can you reduce it to a sentence? Try filling in Template 5-2C. The examples in Templates 5-2A and 5-2B will help you get the idea.

Columbia County Economic Development Corp. will use Wood Products Today, Plastic News, *and* Plant Sites & Parks *to promote our opportunities to increase prospect businesses' profitability.*

Klinke Cleaners will use full-page ads in local magazines and 30-second TV com-

mercials to promote fast, convenient dry-cleaning services.

Ideally this statement will be backed up by a complete media calendar and budget, since ad sizes, deadlines, and so on will be critical in planning ad production. But in the real world these decisions are usually still being made while the search for the creative approach goes on. Collect what you know about your media plan, and try summarizing it in a sentence. Chapter 4, "Writing a Media Plan," will tell you what you need to know to make your media decisions. If you've completed Chapter 4, you should have no problem completing a working draft of this summary.

Template 5-2A: Columbia County Example

Summary of Media Plan

Columbia County Economic Development Corp.
(name of business)

will use   *Wood Products Today, Plastic News, and Plant Sites & Parks*
(list the specific publications or other media you have chosen)

to promote   our opportunities to increase

prospect businesses' profitability   .
(benefit)

Template 5-2B: Klinke Cleaners Example

Summary of Media Plan

_____ Klinke Cleaners _____
(name of business)

will use _____ full page ads in local magazines and 30-second TV commercials _____
(list the specific publications or other media you have chosen)

to promote _____ fast, convenient dry-cleaning services _____

_____.
(benefit)

Template 5-2C: Blank

Summary of Media Plan

_____
(name of business)

will use _____
(list the specific publications or other media you have chosen)

to promote _____

_____.
(benefit)

The Product or Service

The uniqueness of the product or service you sell will fuel your search for a creative approach.

Real news is the key to finding a persuasive creative approach. Think like a journalist going after the story. Dig for the facts. Look for interesting details in the processes, the people, the history, the environment of the product or service you'll promote. Gather performance statistics. They might support a benefit claim, or give you an idea for a dramatic creative angle.

When an advertising agency is first hired by a company, its first job is really getting to know the business. The challenge facing you is to find that outsider's fresh perspective on your firm. Probe among your staff and advisers. It will surprise you how different their points of view might be.

Here's a suggestion: Seek out an employee who has recently come to your company—maybe in the last six to eighteen months. Ask that person what he or she knew about your product or service offering before coming to work for you. Then ask how that idea has changed since. Ask this: If you had five minutes on the Late Show to talk about us, what is the one thing you'd like people to know?

Follow your nose. You might uncover memorable characters like Juan Valdez hand-picking only the best coffee beans, or Bartles and James out on their porch chatting. Of course, these advertising icons aren't actual people—just caricatures created to give product attributes a human face. This technique works so well that we see it all the time. You can be sure that these examples were born of a research process that turned up a story about somebody, somewhere, associated with the product.

You can uncover all kinds of useful management information from an interview process, but for your purposes now, focus on the product or service you want to advertise. Looking at facts about the product accomplishes two goals. First, it helps to spell out what the product is and does, and even its shortcomings, if any. Second, it can help you find a dramatic selling slant. Where do you think "two scoops of raisins in a package of Kellogg's Raisin Bran" came from? Some ad guy looking for ideas spilled the cereal out on his desk and counted.

Creativity is mostly a matter of looking at the ordinary from an unusual angle. So in coming up with a creative slant on what you offer, look at what you do from "out of the box." You might surprise yourself with what you come up with.

Market Perceptions

Perception *is* reality in advertising. You have to start from where your customers are, then move them toward where you want them to be.

Probe your market's perceptions. Will you be building on a positive perception, or trying to turn a negative perception around? For Columbia County, probing revealed that most of the market had no knowledge of that county, but had generally favorable impressions of Wisconsin. Prospects tended to think of Wisconsin in personal terms—great vacations,

nice place to raise a family—rather than business terms. So the challenge for Columbia County was to connect these good impressions to good business sense.

Positioning Strategy

Review your positioning statement from Chapter 2, where you summarized your strategy with regard to target market, key benefits, and competition.

If you're not all that different from your competition, you still must choose a key benefit to promote. For you the challenge is to find a significant rationale to support that claim. The answer? A creative approach that accents your sincerity, believability, and creativity. Find your USP and keep accentuating it in every ad you do. Make your ad break through the claims of your competitors.

One Thought to Take Away

What is the one thought you want the prospect to take away from your ad? You want to change perception toward what? Finish this sentence: "I should buy this product because...." Make sure the ad communicates the key benefit. You will probably find it incredibly hard to boil down your offering's many dimensions of greatness to one thought to remember. You'll need to list all the possibilities, then ruthlessly rank them in order of priority. Talk to your customers—they know which benefit really trips their triggers.

Notice that I said "benefit." I hope you've been paying attention to turning features into benefits. Features have no place on your list—the thought your customers take away must be a benefit they anticipate from purchasing your offering.

Image Advertising vs. Response Offers

Advertising falls into two general categories or approaches: ads that communicate a feeling about your company, and ads that convey specific news followed by a call for a specific action. We refer to the first category as *image advertising*. The second we call *response advertising*. (We'll talk more about these two approaches in the upcoming chapters when we discuss print, radio, TV, and direct mail individually.)

Image advertising is aimed solely at creating a shift in perception, rather than at motivating a specific action. When you see this type of advertising, it's usually used as part of a larger campaign, in conjunction with other advertising and publicity efforts, and aimed at long-term results rather than immediate measurable response. It's an expensive strategy, and it requires a budget to match your ambitions. If you have few dollars, and you want to track whether you're spending them successfully, stick to response advertising.

Response advertising (also called *item* or *order request* advertising, or the *news approach*) poses the question: What exactly do you want your prospect to do? Pick up a phone, stop in, return a coupon? Response ads close with a *call to action*. Often that call is sweetened with a specific promise of reward, called the *offer*. "Call before midnight and receive an additional 10 percent discount" is a response offer.

What do your customers want that would motivate them to take action? You've got to find a desirable offer that you can afford to make and that plays off the benefit you've chosen to promote. Often this involves a specific limited-term offer called a *sales promotion*. In Chapter 3 you'll find much more information on choosing the offer your advertising will make.

If you have no specific sales promotion or incentive like a coupon or a discount sale, your response advertising still closes with a call to action. This phrase states very specifically what you would like your prospect to do next. It might be "call this toll-free number today" or "visit the location nearest you."

Take a look at the first examples (6-1 and 6-2) in Chapter 6. Both of these ads are for banks, and they ran during the same time period in response to the same marketing challenge. (You'll learn all about this interesting

marketing case when you get to Chapter 6.) The first ad, for Anchor Bank, is image advertising. Look for the call to action—you won't find any. The second ad, for Firstar, fits our definition of response advertising. While it doesn't have a sales promotion as such, it does end with a specific call to action. Read it, and you will know how to act on the desire it creates.

Want more examples? Try this: Look through a newspaper or magazine and make a list of call to action statements. Which seem most effective to you? Which might be appropriate for your situation?

Look at your competitors' advertising. Are they taking the image or the response approach? Note carefully where and when their ads appeared. Analyze their benefit statements and their offers. Take note of whether they use toll-free numbers, coupons, or other incentives to encourage their prospects to act.

Your Sales Cycle

Your advertising is just one arc of a great circle that leads customers to your store, fulfills their desire for what you're selling, sends them away happy, and then brings them back for more. You can't start that wheel in motion without at least roughing out a plan for every phase. You'll ask for an action, and then what? How will you track leads and sales? How will you keep up with the orders? Know what you want your sales cycle to be, from first lead to repeat sales.

Here's an example.

Remember J. Kinney, the European-style florist we discussed in Chapter 2? She wanted to increase flower purchases during the slow time between Valentine's Day and Mother's Day. We're in Wisconsin, and many people dream about heading south for a getaway as winter drags on into March and April. I helped Kinney develop an ad (Example 5-1) with this headline: "When Your Heart Says Hawaii But Your Wallet Says Waunakee..." The call to action: "Let J. Kinney Florist bring the tropics to you."

Do You Need a Toll-Free Number?

If you draw business from anywhere outside your immediate community, chances are the answer is yes. You must do everything you can to remove the barriers from the road that connects a customer to you. If the cost of a phone call might keep customers from contacting you, then you should invite them to call by offering to pay the cost. Toll-free or 800 numbers are flexible and not that expensive. Rates vary from carrier to carrier but are generally lower than regular business long-distance rates.

Your 800 number can be regional, multiregional, or national. You will pay a service fee each time you change the region your number covers, so look ahead to your future needs as you examine this decision. Maybe all you need is a LATA 800 number, which covers local communities in your LATA (local access transport area). If you do business in several area codes, you will pick a long-distance carrier and arrange a regional or national 800 number through that company.

These LATA regions were created (when the phone company was split up in the early 80s) to determine what local companies would provide signal transport service where. Long-distance carriers provide calling service outside the LATA through arrangements with the local companies and their customers.

Billing is based on an initial fee for the first hour of 800 number use, then a charge per minute for all time used over that first hour. You will want to be a careful consumer, and compare different long-distance carriers' offers. The way they structure their billing, down to the way they slice the increments of use, will affect your bill.

With regulation of the telecommunications industry changing rapidly, there's little I can tell you except to call your local telephone company and ask about business 800 service. I encourage you to look into this. If you consider yourself a customer-driven company, offering an 800 number is a good way to show it.

Example 5-1: J. Kinney Florist ad
Used by permission of J. Kinney Florist.

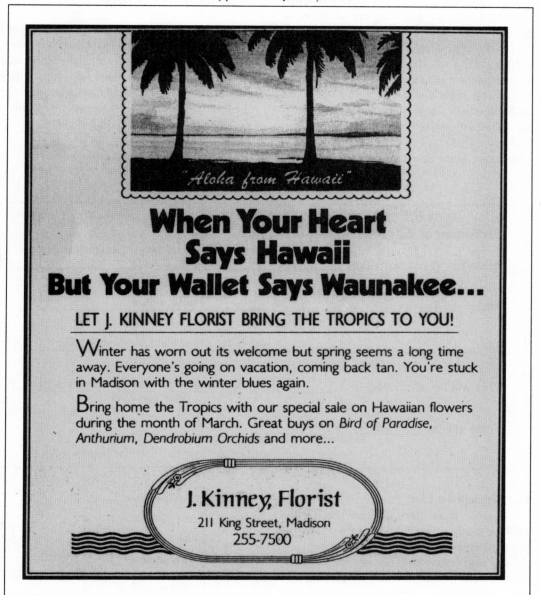

Here is the plan of action behind this simple ad: She places the ad in our alternative newsweekly, a good choice for reaching young professionals who don't quite have the earnings to match their fantasies. She plans to track results by the simple method of comparing monthly sales figures with the previous year's, when she did no special advertising.

Keeping up with the orders will be easy— she knows her staff has time to do the custom arrangements, since it's a slow time of year. This is important. She hopes that satisfaction with the first order will bring repeat business, perhaps even large party and wedding orders, later in the year. Good planning helps her avoid a drop in the quality of either her flower arrangements or her customer service.

In this story you can see that the sales cycle describes a goal and a tactic for achieving it—increase sales by tickling a funny bone. Make sure that you can define your sales cycle specifically, as we have in this example.

J. Kinney's advertising strategy statement might go like this (Template 5-1D):

Advertising will convince consumers with sophisticated tastes but limited disposable time or money that exotic flowers will make them feel better about life. This will be attributed to the joy of having unusual tropical flowers around. Tone will be tongue-in-cheek.

Template 5-1D: Florist Example

Statement of Advertising Strategy

Advertising will convince _consumers with sophisticated tastes but limited disposable time or money_
(target consumers)

that _exotic flowers_
(product)

will _will make them feel better about life_.
(benefit)

This will be attributed to _the joy of having unusual tropical flowers around_.
(feature/rationale)

Tone will be _tongue-in-cheek_.
(adjective)

The Must-Have List

Just one more piece of housekeeping and we'll be ready to start looking for those Big Ideas to express our advertising strategy.

On your "must-have" list are the elements that must be included in all advertising: the nuts and bolts that are so obvious that it's easy to overlook them—and it's so embarrassing (or expensive!) when you do.

A summary of the must-haves in your advertising:

- How company and product names are used

- How tagline is used
- Contact information
- Legalities
- Ad requirements

Let's review each of these.

Company and Product Names. State how your company and product names and/or logos must be used in the advertising. If one should take precedence over the other, say so—"Pink Lemonade from Snapple" as opposed to "Snapple brings you Pink Lemonade." Your advertising *must* be consistent to be its most effective, and consistency is at its most important when your name is concerned.

Tagline. If you use a tagline or slogan with your company name, state how it is to be used and precisely what the wording is to be. Repetition is the best tool you have to build yourself a position in a prospect's mind. The tagline pounds home your USP.

Contact Information. Be specific. Decide what locations and phone numbers need to be included, and exactly how each must be worded.

Legalities. If you have made product claims that need disclosures or disclaimers, make sure you have the legal niceties taken care of. Get the exact wording approved by your lawyer if you have contest rules in your ad. If you are in a regulated industry, such as banking, airlines, or telecommunications, you should be familiar with the disclosure regulations that apply to you.

Permissions are another legal issue. Have you considered questions of copyright? You cannot borrow excitement from public personalities, or use certain images or songs, without paying for permission. It might surprise you to know that the "Hollywood" sign—the giant letters on the side of a hill outside Los Angeles—is protected by copyright. The Hollywood Chamber of Commerce receives a fee each time you see that image. Most famous personalities, from Babe Ruth to James Dean, are also covered by "personality rights." You can certainly arrange to use almost any image you desire, but you should take into account that this will be expensive. Use rights for famous personalities usually begin at $700 per appearance (for example, one radio commercial, or one ad in a magazine) in a limited-circulation market.

If you use an illustration or photograph, make sure you and the creator have an understanding about what rights you have purchased, and get it in writing. You might contract for unlimited use rights, one-time use in a specific medium, or any variation in between. The exclusivity you purchase will probably be negotiated on the basis of whether the artist could re-sell that image elsewhere. A specific photo of your product, for instance, has very little intrinsic value to a photographer, and so he or she will probably grant you unlimited rights with the basic cost of the shot. But suppose you commission a painting of a rural landscape to illustrate a brochure describing your subdivision's quiet country atmosphere. Your artist may feel that he or she can resell that image, or perhaps exhibit it as fine art. You would probably want to negotiate an agreement giving you all reproduction rights, to keep other clients from using your painting. Your agreement might state that the artist retains all rights to exhibit the piece, and if you're feeling kind, you could grant the right to reproduce the painting in the catalog of any exhibition. Don't forget that who owns the actual painting is part of the negotiation, too. Will it hang in your real estate office or remain in the artist's possession?

This may seem like too much detail to worry about now. You don't even have the Big Idea yet—how do you know if you'll need copyright permission? The reason to think about it now is this: If you're not willing to pay for copyright permissions, you should admit that before you begin your idea process. You won't waste time reviewing ideas that are financially impractical. Even stock photo use starts at around $100 and goes up quickly. If you're on a tight budget, admit it and put your time into brainstorming great *simple* ideas.

Ad Requirements. From your media plan, describe the advertising placements you will contract for. We want to know the ad dimensions (height and width for print; run time for broadcast), deadlines, and other production specs from each magazine, newspaper, radio station, etc. This is the blank canvas for your creative approach to fill.

Are You Ready to Begin Creating Your Ad?

If you have made decisions as you read through the first part of this chapter, you are ready to begin the creative phase of the process: looking for the Big Idea that dramatizes your advertising strategy. Together these will become your creative approach.

Have you completed each of these elements of your ad strategy?

____ Key benefit defined.
____ Supporting rationale defined.
____ Tone defined.
____ Media plan summarized (Template 5-2).
____ Product or service attributes described.
____ Attach a description of anything unusual you've uncovered—a performance statistic, a personality, a unique process, a historical tidbit.
____ Market perceptions probed.

____ Positioning strategy completed (Template 2-5C).
____ One thought to take away defined.
____ Image or response ad? Have you defined your offer?
____ Sales cycle considered; response logistics worked out.
____ Must-have list completed.
____ Company name.
____ Tagline use.
____ Contact information.
____ Legalities and permissions.
____ Ad requirements.

How Do Ads Sell Your Products or Services?

The fundamental way ads sell is by *dramatizing the benefit*. That's why people respond: The drama makes the benefit real to them in a way that creates desire. There are a number of ways to create that drama: using product demonstrations, for instance, or humor, or unusual visual approaches, or personalities with whom your audience will identify. We're about to talk about this in detail.

How Will You Judge Your Ideas?

How will you know when you've hit on an idea that can fuel a successful ad campaign? Hard-hitting ads combine strategy, substance, structure, and style. We'll talk about each, and how you can make sure your ad idea measures up.

Strategy. A successful creative approach is consistent with the company's vision, marketing objectives, and strategic thinking. Is your idea faithful to the advertising strategy you've just defined? If not, ask yourself why. Sometimes a creative mind introduces new elements at this stage that are so compelling that they demand an alteration of previous strategy decisions. But in general, if it isn't consistent with your advertising strategy, there's a good reason why it's a bad idea.

Substance. Your message *must* have news value. Your challenge is to find an idea with substance. Is it believable? Is it exciting? Look around you and you'll find plenty of examples of ads that clamor for attention without communicating anything real. Overheated adjectives or too much reliance on flashy special effects are not an adequate substitute for substance.

Structure. Look for the bone structure. A good idea will be easy to understand, because it begins with establishing context, then delivers content, and ends with a logical conclusion. You should be able to summarize your idea in this structure—context, content, conclusion. If you can, you've got a jump on the task of copywriting that lies ahead.

Style. Good ad ideas have a personality that's distinctive. It might be a sense of place. It might be an attitude. It could be an original visual style. The personality projects the tone prescribed by the ad strategy. Does your idea project a tone that will make your company liked, respected, and admired?

Strategy, substance, structure, and style. Now you know what's on the test. That makes it a lot easier to get started. So—it's time for you to get creative.

How to Have the Big Idea

In the first half of this chapter, we've been talking about the advertising strategy—the component of your creative approach that provides the focus for your advertising by defining the market, the product, the promise, the support, and the tone it will communicate. Now it's time to work on the second component of the creative approach. The *Big Idea* is the hook that brings the benefit you promise to life in a unique and memorable way. Finding the creative approach is the test of your creativity. You may not have thought of yourself as "creative" before this; don't let that stop you. We're not talking about whether you can draw or not. We're talking about whether you can think with originality. Most people—especially those with the drive and vision to run businesses and make advertising decisions—do have this capability.

What makes creativity? Often it's a matter of finding new combinations of old elements. In other words, you're uncovering what's always been there.

Some people believe that creativity takes a flash of inspiration, and that there's no way to predict or control when that inspiration arrives. But those of us who work with deadlines have had to develop a different attitude.

You *can* jump-start the creative process. To do this, it helps to know the stages you'll go through:

- Preparation
- Incubation
- Frustration
- Illumination
- Evaluation

As we examine each of these stages, remember that creativity doesn't run in a straight line; you may loop back and forth through these stages. Don't give up if you start to feel stuck. Keep at it until you pass through these stages and feel satisfied with the result. You'll be ready to choose an idea and execute it in any and all media.

You'll be scribbling lots of notes as you pass through these stages. Don't expect to write the actual wording of your advertising yet; we'll talk more about that in subsequent chapters as we address writing for each medium. Right now, just try to come up with phrases or images that capture your idea and make it more tangible. Don't get hung up on this. You're looking for ideas, not executions, at this point.

Now, let's take a closer look at each step.

Preparation

To begin, do warm-ups. Write out a vocabulary for your product or service. List nouns, verbs, adjectives you've used in selling situations. Look for the positive, active words. Review facts and figures that demonstrate benefits (largest distribution area, over 10,000 sold, etc.). Remember, from earlier in this chapter, the probing you've done with your staff and advisers. Get it all swirling around in your mind.

Think about your unique selling proposition. Jot down any phrases that cross your mind. If you use a tagline, write it down now.

Think about a certain prospect or customer, and a selling conversation you've had. Something he or she said is about to strike you in a new way.

A client of mine recently started a company to sell a foundation coating material called Thermal-Cote™. It's a dry powder that homeowners can mix with water and apply to their exposed foundation walls. It has a variety of benefits, from being flame-retardant to adding a thermal barrier, and we listed them all on the package.

My client went to work persuading stores to place the product on their shelves—and he quickly got a surprise. Customers in Florida loved the product, not because of its thermal properties but because it worked very well as a moisture barrier. In the Florida humidity, to be waterproof is definitely a key benefit. What we had seen as just one more product feature turned out to be a benefit that lends itself to a creative visual representation and speaks to a genuine customer need. It's the customers who told us this. If we wanted to do an ad campaign in Florida, we'd know our Big Idea should promote the waterproof benefit.

Incubation

Your intuition will kick in as the thoughts you've prepared start bouncing off each other. New ways of looking at your customers should start to occur to you. Or you'll see your product in a new light. Start matching words and images in your head. Look for startling combinations. A pun might come to you, or a dramatic visual idea. Write down key words or sketch images to remind you of these ideas, but don't get bogged down in descriptions. Keep your thoughts moving.

Look at unrelated advertising. Leaf through a magazine or newspaper, pick an example, and twist it to fit your service or product. Look at a car ad, and see if you can twist it to sell your product. A map of Columbia County in the center spotlight like the Lexus in a magazine ad doesn't make much sense—but the thought might lead you to an idea that does. You could think about how that car company uses visual style to communicate prestige and desirability, and find ideas to give your offering those attributes. You are benefiting from the experience of the ad team whose work inspires you.

Another idea is to think in terms of opposites—for example, what are five reasons *not* to buy your offering? By thinking about what your offering *isn't*, you can help stimulate your thinking about what it *is*.

I find that these techniques will nearly always jump-start my thinking if my ideas aren't coming fast enough. They may not lead you to the final idea you'll choose, but they will help you see your situation in a new light.

Frustration

The ideas aren't coming, or they're not good enough. At some point, you'll start to feel frustration. Expect it. It's normal and helpful. Allow time for it in the process. Frustration is your mind helping you not to settle for a mediocre thought. Frustration can be an important step on the path to the Big Idea.

In the preparation phase, your rational left brain began working on the problem; in the incubation phase, your right brain got a chance to play with it. Now you need to give the two time to work up some ideas together. You—the director of the process—need to take a break. A short burst of physical exercise will do. Or sleep on it. Sometimes just a change of scene will break the barrier and lead you to the next step.

If the words aren't coming, try being a different kind of thinker. Consider your product in a nonverbal way. What images come to mind? Sketch them. Is it sounds you hear? You could be on your way to an effective radio campaign. Whatever comes to mind, capture your ideas on paper. The seed of your Big Idea might be there.

Illumination

Think of times you've felt that click—times you've suddenly found the creative answer you've been seeking. It might be finding the right gift for an unusual client. Maybe it's imagining the right location for a staff retreat. Your intuition told you that this idea isn't just right, it's got pizzazz. By thinking of these times, you warm up your belief that you *can* do this.

Let yourself ramble. Your ideas should start bubbling to the surface. Just sit with a blank pad, hold your calls, and get those ideas down on paper. That might mean sketches, if your ideas are visual, or sentences starting to resemble advertising copy.

Since we're talking about illumination, it's time for a light bulb joke.

Q. How many art directors does it take to change a light bulb?

A. Does it have to be a light bulb?

The ideas you bring out may redefine your whole advertising strategy. You may have been planning on a print campaign in your local newspaper. If your "light bulb" of illumination reveals a great auditory pun, it's time to consider a radio campaign instead. Your idea will be judged against the predetermined strategy, but in advertising nothing is an unbreakable rule. If your idea is that good, a compelling rationale for the change of strategy will appear.

A technical note: Be generous with your supplies as you brainstorm. I find it helpful to write each idea on a separate sheet of paper or an index card. I like to come back, write more thoughts around them, maybe match one against another in different combinations. Now is no time to scrimp on paper.

Evaluation

Go back to your notes from the preparation stage. Match your good ideas against your key benefit. If you can't find an idea that speaks eloquently about your benefit, you're not done yet. You need that connection between creative hook and benefit. Ads that don't connect the two can be very creative but miss the boat when it comes to producing results. You can't afford that. Keep your creative message centered on the benefit.

Judge your ideas now. Summarize each Big Idea by describing first its context, then its content, then its conclusion. Which idea stands out in relation to your strategy? Which has substance? Which will be easy to express with structure and style?

Here's an example of a Big Idea that passed the test. For Columbia County, my economic development client, our idea process produced a creative approach tying the county's key benefit—great transportation access—to a memory device we hoped would build name recognition. Playing off the universal recognition of Christopher Columbus the discoverer, we developed a theme: "Discover a new world of business opportunity in Columbia County." This theme gave us a palette of visual images to use—a compass, a passport, maps, and other icons of discovery. We designed a new logo combining a map of the county with a compass (Example 5-2), and the creative approach was ready for execution (Examples 5-3 and 5-4). This is not a wildly creative Big Idea, but it's solid, functional, appropriate to the market, and open-ended enough to offer potential for further creative development as it's applied to advertising, print collateral, and other components of marketing.

Example 5-2
Used by permission of Columbia County Economic Development Corp.

Example 5-3
Used by permission of Columbia County Economic Development Corp.

*Discover a New World
Of Business Opportunity—*

COLUMBIA
COUNTY

ECONOMIC DEVELOPMENT CORP.

**STRONG BUSINESS ENVIRONMENT
PRODUCTIVE WORK FORCE
EDUCATION WITH BUSINESS SAVVY
EXCEPTIONAL "QUALITY OF LIFE"
GREAT TRANSPORTATION ACCESS**

It's no wonder nationally-known
corporations like **Penda, Stokely,
Del Monte** and **Rayovac** have
facilities in Columbia County.

Call or write for a brochure and
discover our world of opportunity!

1-800-842-2524

Columbia County Economic Development Corp.
P.O. Box 134, Portage, Wisconsin 53901

Example 5-4
Used by permission of Columbia County Economic Development Corp.

PASSPORT

COLUMBIA COUNTY
ECONOMIC DEVELOPMENT CORP.

*Discover
a new world of
business opportunity.*

Your Big Idea may not necessarily be "imaginative." Actually, you can be very successful with an "unimaginative" ad. Prospects appreciate the straightforward approach. It will work for you if you are offering a value that's above average.

If you created the idea, it's almost impossible for you to judge it. So go back to your advisers—your business associates or key staff people. Get their opinion on whether your Big Idea *sells*.

Having a good idea is easier than making it work. You've got some hard work ahead of you, turning your creative approach into successful ad copy. In a few hundred words—at most—you've got to get attention, build interest, create desire, motivate action, make sales. It takes discipline.

Using the Creative Approach to Write Ad Copy

The creative approach directs you as a copywriter. Before we get specific about writing for each particular medium, here are some tips that apply to all.

Dos

- Keep the message simple and the voice direct. Give your copy single-minded focus.

- Develop several alternatives and then determine the best approach.

- Be specific. State facts plainly. Pin things down.

- Speak person to person. Copy should sound natural when read out loud.

- Emphasize the service, not the source. An ad should make readers *want* to buy before telling them *where* to buy.

- Do something unusual, uncommon, unexpected. Be bold. If it makes someone nervous, then your idea has power. That's how you break through the clutter.

- Look for a tagline. Pare down your benefit statement to a simple dramatic phrase, like "Same day service, same great price." Then use it whenever the product or company is mentioned.

Don'ts

- Don't make promises you can't keep.

- Don't let pleasing a committee take the guts out of your idea.

- Don't accept ideas that are off strategy without a compelling rationale for changing that strategy.

- Don't start your copy with "We." Beware of arrogance!

- Don't exaggerate claims. You'll lose your credibility.

- Don't be too hard-sell. Beating on your audience with boastful rhetoric can't hide a lack of real information.

Summary

That's all the advice I can give you without getting specific to one medium or another.

You've learned to think of your creative approach in terms of four dimensions: the market, the promise, the support, and the tone. You've placed it in the context of your marketing strategy, positioning, and media plan. You've probed for information on the product and the market, and refined the offer and the details until you have a checklist to judge each idea against.

You know how ideas sell, and how to judge whether your ideas have selling power. And you've picked up some tips on the idea process. Maybe you have some Big Ideas taking shape; survey your alternatives and choose the leader.

If you've been following my suggestions and worksheets, your desk is now a mess! It's covered with strategy templates and idea scribbles. Now it's time to choose the components of your final creative approach. Make your decisions and "hand in your papers." Tidy up your desk—but don't throw away all the notes and scribbles that didn't make the final cut. When you sit down to prepare for your next Big Idea, you'll want to review these notes.

As you finish this chapter, you should finalize your statement of advertising strategy. You should also briefly outline the marketing objective and the media plan. Templates 5-1 and 5-2 are tools to help you. Now all you need to do is summarize your Big Idea and you're ready to proceed.

You'll put these elements to use as you work toward executing your ideas for whatever media you've chosen. Read on.

Chapter 6

How to Create Print Ads that Sell

The announcement hit the papers on a Monday: The two largest banks in town were merging. Back in the boardrooms, every banker in town had heard it was coming. Their ad agencies were already working on counter-strategies. In a matter of days, the newspaper fattened with bank ads. The shark. The donut. The dog biscuit. Each bank knew that there were going to be disgruntled customers out there, ready to be persuaded to take their business elsewhere. Each bank chose an angle and hit it hard (Examples 6-1 to 6-3).

Example 6-1: Anchor Bank Ad
Used by permission of Anchor Bank S.S.B.

Example 6-2: Firstar Bank Ad
Used by permission of Firstar Bank.

You Might Call it Donuts with Your Banker.
We Call it a New Vision.

A father meets his banker to talk over college investment plans for his kids. Nothing remarkable. Except that it's 7 a.m. And they're at a coffee shop.

A woman rolls over a maturing CD into a money-market account. On the phone, at 9:30 on a Friday night – talking to a real live banker.

A small business owner needs a loan to open a second location; one phone call gets him in touch with an Economic Development Specialist, expert at obtaining government guaranteed small business loans.

All over Madison incidents like these are adding up to a picture of a different kind of bank – Firstar Bank Madison. A bank that's applying new ideas about quality and service to its operations.

You can see it in full-service nighttime phone banking. In banking teams dedicated to the needs of small business owners. And in personal bankers who meet their clients' needs in new and better ways – *including* meeting them for coffee and donuts at 7 a.m.

Nothing earthshaking. Just a different way of thinking about banking. From a different kind of bank – Firstar Bank Madison. Call Firstar at **252-4300**.

FIRSTAR
BANK MADISON

Member FDIC © 1994 Firstar

EQUAL HOUSING LENDER

Example 6-3: Park Bank Ad
Used by permission of The Park Bank.

Most Big Banks Offer Just As Many Products And Services As We Do.

(Unless the free dog biscuits count.)

You may think of us as a small community bank in your neighborhood. But don't let the free dog biscuits we give at our drive-through service fool you.

We have the full array of sophisticated bank products and services found at the big banks. Our bankers have the knowledge and expertise needed to help you get ahead. And we offer a level of personal attention uncommon in any bank today.

In other words, as the oldest independent community bank in the Madison area, we offer the kind of banking that can make a wealth of difference to you.

Just look at all you get when you do your banking in The Park.
Now, banking at The Park is even more like a picnic in the park. Open an account and receive a special Park "Picnic Prize." And don't forget to enter The Park "Picnic Raffle." There's no

purchase necessary and you could win a deluxe, fully stocked, family picnic basket.

For details, stop by The Park Bank nearest you or call Mollie at 278-2801.

Pick-A-Park Service	Get-A-Park Prize*
Park Bank Credit Card Approval	Park Bank Apron
Checking or Savings Account	Park Bank Flying Disk
CD (minimum $5,000)	Set of Barbecue Accessories
Direct Deposit (with free checking)	Park Bank Thermal Jug
Loan (minimum $5,000)	14-1/2" Barbecue Grill

Hurry, each offer is good only while supplies last.

Only In The Park

Park Bank

Cub Foods East	**Cub Foods West**	**Fitchburg Store**	**Park Street Store**	**Raymond Road Store**
4141 Nakoosa Trail	7455 Mineral Point Road	2802 Fish Hatchery Road	2401 South Park Street	6701 Raymond Road
Madison, WI 53714	Madison, WI 53717	Madison, WI 53713	Madison, WI 53713	Madison, WI 53719
608/283-6835	608/283-6892	608/278-2840	608/283-6800	608/278-2880

Member FDIC

© 1994, Park Bank

The daily newspaper got the bulk of the new ads, but the city's monthly business magazine picked up some pages too. A few of the banks backed up their print with radio commercials, and there was even a TV spot or two from the competitors with the deeper pockets. But by and large, the battle was fought in print.

Why? Print is an inexpensive, efficient way to reach a broad, general consumer base in a defined geographical area. That describes the market for most banks.

For the banks in our example, each of the ad messages was a variation on claims of service quality. This makes an interesting case study in positioning, so let's review the strategies we discussed in Chapter 2. Can you place these ads on the triangle in Template 2-5C?

Here's my analysis. Strategists for each of these three banks are assuming that the merged banks' service level will suffer. Each bank is choosing a strategy to take advantage of this opportunity. Each is attempting to win customers away from the merged bank by promoting a better level of service. How they do that varies—and that's where you see their different positioning strategies.

Anchor Bank is challenging the competitor directly, which would be the *against a competitor* strategy we discussed in Chapter 2. Firstar is choosing to emphasize service without mentioning competitors; that's a *key benefit* positioning strategy. Park Bank falls between these two, emphasizing its superiority over unnamed big banks. This is an example of the *product difference,* or *"better than,"* strategy.

Why did the banks choose print? Because print reaches a lot of people and delivers a lot of information. That makes it a good medium to choose if you have a complex message to get across. These banks are selling an intangible: warm and friendly service. That message has to be delivered with credibility. To do that, the copy (supported by the art or photo) has to set up a believable context, describe benefits, and create a desire to take action. That's why the banks chose print—to reach that broad consumer base, and get there first with the most.

Notice how the banks used visual metaphors to engage the reader's imagination. As your brain tries to connect these seemingly unrelated images to the banks whose logos you recognize, you become involved with these ads as a participant. Now you're likely to pay attention to—and accept—their claims and calls to action.

That's a crash course in how print works. When you finish this chapter, you'll be able to

1. Use print strategically to accomplish marketing goals.

2. Calculate budgets and make media calendars.

3. Negotiate with advertising sales reps to your advantage.

4. Write and produce print advertising for
   - Magazines.
   - Newspapers.
   - Yellow Pages and industry directories.
   - Outdoor and transit ads.

Why Print?

Print ads convey information. Print is the only medium we as prospects can *study*—the page is there, and we can refer to it as often as we like. We can compare features in one ad with those described in a competitor's. We can pick up a sense of the style of the company from the way it chooses to look in print.

Radio and TV commercials are here for a few seconds, and then they're gone. While they can convey style and emotional appeal, they lag way behind print as a medium for communicating substantive information. That's one reason why such ads must be repeated frequently to have any impact.

Do print media make sense for you? Let's look at them by category. One or more of these media will almost certainly have a place in your plan. (For more about the different print media and how to use them, see Chapter 4, "Writing a Media Plan.")

Your Options in Print

Here we'll describe the general categories of print media. Later in this chapter we'll talk in much more detail about how to plan budgets, project schedules, and create ads specifically for each of these categories.

Magazines

Glossy magazines are the top of the heap in print media. Here the quality of reproduction is finest, and the shelf life is longest. If you sell business-to-business, sooner or later you're likely to use magazine advertising. Whether it's a regional business magazine like *Crain's Chicago Week* or a trade industry publication like *Paper Trades Journal*, you'll want to reach decision makers with the informative power of print.

What about consumer magazines? Mass-circulation magazines rarely make sense for small advertisers. They are expensive, and only a small fraction of their readership may be interested in what you have to offer. However, before you rule them out, look at whether a regional edition puts their rates in line with your pocketbook. If you sell high-ticket items, like jewelry or cars, and you're near a large metropolitan area, you might find a good fit with a local edition. See the section on magazines in Chapter 4 for more information on regional editions of national magazines.

The other niches using mass-circulation magazines are the craft, hobby, and upscale leisure industries. You might sell figurines, or cross-stitch kits, or replica toys—or books on tape, or a catalog listing bed-and-breakfasts. In this case, a small (one- or two-inch) display ad in magazines like *Atlantic, Yankee,* or *Modern Maturity* might be the most direct path from you to your customer. Check those magazines, and you will see these kinds of ads.

Newspapers

When most of us think of print, we think of newspapers. If you're a retailer serving a broad consumer base, I don't have to tell you about the importance of newspaper advertising; you are probably already using it daily.

Newspaper advertising has its pros and cons. On the up side, it is comparatively inexpensive, and the timing is fast. You can see your ad in the paper just days after you decide to advertise. You can see results, like more traffic in your store, just as fast. Another advantage: In the newspaper you can convey a lot of information, including specific prices, location maps, and coupons. You can change ads frequently, and often the newspaper will help you design the ad and do the production at little or no charge. That's the good news.

The bad news with newspaper advertising is that the quality of reproduction is often poor, and the competition for attention is fierce. And newspaper advertising has a limited life—a new edition comes out every day. Unless you buy dominant ad sizes, you are sharing the page with many other advertisers and the news stories themselves, all competing for the reader's attention. You have to use repetition and size to combat the clutter. Don't underestimate the budget you'll need to be effective.

To illustrate my point, I'll tell you about my entry in the bank wars we discussed at the beginning of this chapter. I handle the advertising for yet another local bank. (I'll go into more detail about this a little later). We target ourselves at a different niche, and ordinarily we don't advertise in the newspaper at all. But we didn't want to be missing in action during the fray, so I proposed a modest calendar of newspaper advertising. Template 6-1 gives the schedule.

Template 6-1: Advertising Calendar, FBB Example

Date: 6-16-94
Title: Advertising Calendar, First Business Bank
Wisconsin State Journal

Ad rotation: two product ads, two image ads

Date:	Ad Art:	Size (Inches)	Rate:
6-19 Sun	Certificate of Deposit	11	$393.25
6-22 Wed	When Banks Change . . . Jerry	20	526.00
6-26 Sun	Money Market Rate	11	393.25
6-29 Wed	When Banks Change . . . Diana	20	526.00
7-3 Sun	Certificate of Deposit	11	393.25
7-6 Wed	When Banks Change . . . Jerry	20	526.00
7-10 Sun	Money Market Rate	11	393.25
7-13 Wed	When Banks Change . . . Diana	20	526.00
Total:		124	3677

The total cost was $3,677 for eight ads, all smaller than the examples from the other banks. I estimate that the other banks were spending between $7,500 and $15,000 on their newspaper ad space. (That shows how the cost of newspaper advertising can add up fast. But it's money well spent if it achieves your goals.)

Yellow Pages and Industry Directories

The one thing to remember about directories is that they reach people *when they are ready to buy*. People use directories for one specific purpose: to find vendors. You can't afford not to be listed. The tough part is deciding how. Choosing which categories to list under and how big an ad to place can require a compromise between your budget and your ambition. To solve this problem, you may want to consider working with a directory advertising consultant if a majority of your traffic comes from the Yellow Pages.

Yellow Pages directories are going through dramatic changes as I write this. Competing directories are appearing, and the old standbys are redefining themselves. The trend is to split the "big book" into targeted Yellow Pages publications that reach certain markets more efficiently. In my area in the Midwest, we now have three types of Yellow Pages: a Business-to-Business directory, an Industrial Purchasing Guide, and a consumer Yellow Pages. Other regions are changing along similar lines.

The Business-to-Business directory serves users seeking commercial office products and services, professional services, and advertising and promotional services. This book is distributed beyond the metro area into related commercial markets. For instance, here in Wisconsin, the same directory serves Milwaukee and Madison, seventy miles apart.

The Industrial Purchasing Guide lists products and services related to manufacturing processes, process materials, and plant maintenance. It is distributed to related industrial markets in multistate regions. The original Yellow Pages is now a consumer-oriented directory that lists personal products and services for each local metro area.

The dilemma, of course, is that some businesses sell in more than one category, and now must devote more of their advertising budget to cover all the bases in directory advertising.

You should establish a budget and a plan for directory advertising along with the rest of your media plan—don't take it for granted. Make sure your accounting system tracks your directory advertising costs to the advertising category of operating expenses, not the telephone category.

Directory advertising is the most long-range of the print media. For example, with the Yellow Pages, you contract for your ads three to six months before the directory is published, and then your ad is out there—and appearing on your monthly bill—for the next one or two years. You can't cut back if you feel like tightening your belt. You can't change the copy if your phone number or address changes.

Industry directories, like *Thomas Register,* are a standard tool in business-to-business marketing. Your state may have an association of manufacturers and businesses; such statewide directories can be very important if you market to industry. Planning and budgeting for industry directories is no different from coordinating your Yellow Pages advertising, and the timing is just as long-range.

Outdoor and Transit Advertising

Billboards, bus cards, and other local "out of home" advertising round out your options in print media. This category can be used ingeniously to reach geographically targeted markets with a high number of repeat exposures.

Production is similar to that for other print ads—basically, you assemble words and images into camera-ready art—but crafting the message is a little different. From a creative standpoint, treat outdoor advertising as you would radio. You have only a few seconds with your viewers, and they're doing something else—driving, probably—while you're together. Your ad message must be direct. Keep the copy short—just a sentence. Print may be the medium of choice for complex messages, but not on billboards. Save your long explanations for your newspaper and magazine ads.

Does Print Make Sense for You?
Yes, if ...

- You have a limited budget—print is almost always your least expensive option.

- You sell a product that changes often—perhaps the price or the product line. Restaurants use print to advertise menu changes. Department stores use print to announce new product selections and sales.

- Your product requires detailed information to be understood. Computers are sold by print ads that contain a lot of details. So are technical products in the business-to-business market.

How Print Advertising is Sold

Print advertising, whether magazine or newspaper, is sold on a basis of *ad size* and *frequency of appearance*. The publication sets a value on the circulation it offers, then creates a rate card listing prices for various ad sizes and frequencies of appearance, or insertion (Example 6-4). Special positions that are more likely to command reader attention (back cover, inside front cover, center spread) add a premium to the rate.

Example 6-4: Rate Card
Used by permission of In Business/Magna Publications.

Issue & Space Reservation Dates

	Insertion Orders	Camera Ready Material
1992 Issues		
September	July 22	July 29
October	August 26	September 2
November	September 23	September 30
December	October 21	October 28
1993 Issues		
January	November 23	November 30
February	December 22	December 30
March	January 20	January 27
April	February 24	March 3
May	March 24	March 31
June	April 21	April 28
July	May 19	May 26
August	June 23	June 30
September	July 21	July 28
October	August 25	September 1
November	September 22	September 29
December	October 20	October 27

Published Monthly : On sale by first of the month.
Cancellations : Must be submitted in writing and received by the insertion order date for the applicable issue.

Editorial Features

Regular Columns : ShopTalk, Interiors, Gardening, Business, Peoplescene, Politics, Education, Arts, Restaurant Reviews, Dining Out listings and a monthly Calendar of Events.
These Special Editorial Opportunities are Planned :

1992
September : Health Care / Fall Fashion Advertorial
October : Home & Garden / Smart Money
November : Winter Travel / Gift Guide
December : Christmas Entertaining / Holiday Shopping Directory insert

1993
January : Business Forecast/ Readers' Choice Dining Guide
February : Connecticut Bride / 1993 Health Care Resource Guide
March : Home & Garden / Fashion

April : Vacation New England / Real Estate Report
May : 1993 Homeowners Resource Guide / Health Care & Fitness
June : Summer Fun Guide
July : Great Bargains / Summer Entertaining
August : Directory Dining Out Guide / Kids!

Reader Response Cards :
Connecticut Bride September.
February
Health & Fitness September, February, May
Personal Finance October
Travel November, April
Retirement Living November, April
Business Products & Services
January
Education January, July
50+ Marketing July

Mechanical Requirements

Ad Sizes / Specs (in inches)	Width		Depth
Full Page	7	x	10
Bleed Full Page	8-3/8	x	11
2/3 page (Vertical)	4-5/8	x	10
2/3 page (Square)	7	x	7-3/8
1/2 page (Vertical)	4-5/8	x	7-3/8
1/2 page (Horizontal)	7	x	4-7/8
1/3 page (Vertical)	2-1/4	x	10
1/3 page (Square)	4-5/8	x	4-7/8
1/6 page (Vertical)	2-1/4	x	4-7/8
1/6 page (Horizontal)	4-5/8	x	2-3/8
1/12 page	2-1/4	x	2-3/8

Printing Process : Web offset; saddle-stitched.
Trim Size : 8-1/4" wide x 10-3/4" deep.
Safety Margin : Keep all live matter 3/8" from outer trim edges and gutter.

Black & White : One piece offset negatives preferred, right-reading emulsion side down. 110-120 line screen. Negative should allow for 7 to 8% dot gain. Tone density of halftones must not exceed 85%. Velox-110 line screen maximum.

Black & 1 Color : Process inks are used to approximate the specified PMS color (not applicable to metallic inks). It is recommended that negatives be furnished at the specified percentages for each process color with a Cromalin proof or matchprint for press guidance. Film negatives not accompanied by color guidance will require color proof.

4-Color Process : 4 colors printed wet at high speed. For best results, provide right-reading, emulsion side down, 133-line screen negatives with register marks. Maximum density in any one area all colors, 320%. Film should be accompanied by Progressive proof, Matchprint or Cromalin.

Production/Prep Work : Due by insertion order date. Production/ film/proofing services provided by publisher are non-commissionable and will be billed at prevailing rates to the client or its agency. Film will be held by publisher for one year, and disposed of unless return requested.

Circulation

Connecticut Magazine bases its current rates on an average 12-month circulation of 85,000 copies per issue.
Connecticut Magazine's circulation is audited by the Audit Bureau of Circulations.

CONNECTICUT
M A G A Z I N E

789 Reservoir Avenue
Bridgeport, CT 06606
(203) 374-3388
FAX (203) 371-6561

Retail Rate Card 22 (Effective September 1992 Issue)

Black & White	1-2x	3x	6x	12x
Full	$3525	$3355	$3250	$2995
2/3	2650	2515	2440	2250
1/2	2085	1980	1920	1770
1/3	1340	1275	1230	1140
1/6	775	735	710	660
1/12	495	470	455	420

Black & 1 Color (Process Inks)	1-2x	3x	6x	12x
Full	$4270	$4055	$3930	$3630
2/3	3205	3045	2950	2725
1/2	2535	2410	2330	2155
1/3	1715	1630	1580	1460

PMS Color $1295 / insertion

Four Color	1-2x	3x	6x	12x
Full	$4975	$4725	$4575	$4230
2/3	3730	3545	3430	3170
1/2	2935	2790	2695	2495
1/3	2085	1980	1920	1770

Covers	1-2x	3x	6x	12x
2	$6465	$6150	$5950	$5495
3	5970	5670	5490	5075
4	6915	6570	6360	5880

Agency Commission : 15% of gross to recognized agencies.
Preferred Position : 10% premium.
Bleed : 10% premium.
Pre-Printed Inserts, Consecutive Pages : Rates on request
Frequency Rates : Based on number of insertions in a 12 month contract year. If the number of insertions is not specified on order or contract, each insertion will be billed at the one-time rate until a

frequency rate is earned. Advertising ordered at a frequency discount rate which is not earned within one year of first insertion will be charged a short rate reflecting the correct frequency discount. Credits earned by increasing frequency during a contract year will be applied toward future billing for space.
Display Classified : $150.00 / inch. Check or money order must accompany copy.

Payment Terms

Net 30 Days : Payment with order is required until credit is approved.
Finance Charge : Accounts outstanding more than 30 days incur a 1-1/2% per month finance charge. Any invoice outstanding 60 days will result in interruption of scheduled advertising.

Most advertising in magazines is sold by sales representatives (ad reps). The rep for a magazine in which you have an interest will bring you a media kit that describes that magazine's costs, advertising production requirements, editorial policies, and audience analysis. You can also call or write to receive these kits. Once you request a media kit, you are likely to be made part of a regular program of follow-up by an ad rep. This is especially true with magazines. You will receive mailings about upcoming editorial features and advantages of advertising in certain issues. A good sales rep can really help you plan your program. Take advantage of his or her expertise.

The media kit you receive will be a folder and will typically include:

- *An editorial calendar.* This describes editorial features planned for issues up to a year in advance. This helps you decide when to place ads, and what message to convey. For instance, an upcoming issue of your city magazine that features a special section on home products would be a good place to advertise your lawn care service or your furniture showroom.

- *The rate card.* This is the most important piece of information in the kit. This information changes often, and each change renders the previous rate card obsolete. You will always want to make sure you're working with a current rate card. It will have a date on it, or a key number. Call to see what the current effective date or key number is if you've had your kit longer than a few months.

- *Self-promotion.* The media kit will include a variety of pieces that describe audience statistics, readership profiles, and editorial feature promotions. You will find readership broken down by demographics like age, income, occupation, and education.

Publications use surveys to draw a picture of their typical readers. For a consumer publication, you might find information on grocery expenditures, average trips to shopping malls, vacation patterns, sports participation, and so on. For a business publication, the information might reflect influence on company purchase decisions, types of computer hardware/software owned, etc. In either case, the goal is to let you know who is reading the publication, and what products and services they might be shopping for. The kit might contain an insert with a corporate mission statement, or helpful advertising tips, or promotions of upcoming special sections. The media kit will usually include sample copies of the publication as well.

Circulation Figures and Cost per Thousand

Somewhere in the media kit should be the publication's circulation figures; these may be on the rate card or on another insert. If you can't find them, ask your rep. You need circulation figures to compute your CPM, or the cost for reaching 1,000 readers. This can help you compare the expense and economy of advertising in one publication with those of advertising in another.

Be sure to ask whether the circulation figures the publication quotes you are *paid subscribers.* Some publications will inflate their circulation figures by as much as five times by including all free copies distributed in the count as if they were of the same value as subscriber-requested copies. Don't accept that. Free copies are often less likely to be read than those that are paid for. Use only paid subscriber figures when you compare CPM. Several organizations monitor the publishing industry and provide third-party audited circulation figures. Ask whether the numbers you are given are *audited* circulation.

The media kit for a trade journal or business magazine will be quite straightforward. To use it, you simply pull the rate card, decide which sizes and frequencies interest you, and plug the numbers into your ad scenarios, along with the circulation figures. The rest of the material in the media kit is often "fluff" (although there can be useful information there). You'll usually learn more from looking through several issues, seeing who's advertising and how, than you will from studying the publication's self-promotion.

The rate cards for local newspapers will be more complicated. Newspapers offer advertising by the inch, rather than by the fraction of a page, as magazines do. Therefore the size variable is much more flexible. Newspapers also offer various contract rates based on how many inches you commit to using in a time period, usually a year. You can use the inches any way you want—big ads some times of the year, small ads at other times. But you must keep track as the year goes by, and see that you are fulfilling your contract. If you use fewer inches than you contracted for, you will pay a *short rate adjustment* that bumps you up to a lower-volume price. Make sure your newspaper's sales rep explains the newspaper's rates

and policies clearly to you. Often newspaper sales reps are busier, and less helpful, than the sales reps for magazines.

You will need to work harder to get what you need from your newspaper reps. Outline a scenario and ask them to calculate the costs— they're more familiar with the various discount programs they offer than you are, and they should be happy to prepare a proposal for you.

Once you understand the circulation figures and rate cards for the publications you're considering, you can prepare a CPM analysis. This is a method for converting various rate and circulation options to relative terms, so that you can compare apples to apples. In doing this, you express each rate as a cost per thousand by dividing the total circulation in thousands by the cost of one advertisement. (Chapter 4 includes more about this.)

Templates 6-2A and 6-2B show a CPM analysis done on four trade journals from the screen-printing industry.

Templates 6-2A: Media Efficiencies Comparison

Date: 11-23-94
Title: Media Efficiencies Comparison
Assumptions: Full Page with Spot Color
See rate cards for spot color charges

Medium	Rate Card	Frequency	Space	Rate	Circulation in 1,000s	CPM ($)	Index
Impressions	#31	6x	Full page	$3,815	30	$127	1.00
Screen Play	1994	6x	Full page	$2,145	15	143	1.12
Press	9/93	6x	Full page	$3,200	27	119	0.93
Stitches	#14	6x	Full page	$1,715	9	191	1.50

Templates 6-2B: Media Efficiencies Comparison with Explanations

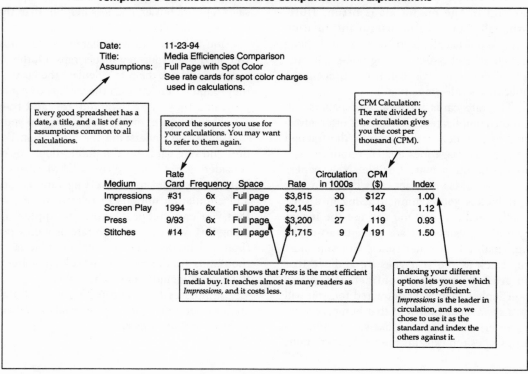

Date: 11-23-94
Title: Media Efficiencies Comparison
Assumptions: Full Page with Spot Color
See rate cards for spot color charges used in calculations.

Every good spreadsheet has a date, a title, and a list of any assumptions common to all calculations.

Record the sources you use for your calculations. You may want to refer to them again.

CPM Calculation: The rate divided by the circulation gives you the cost per thousand (CPM).

Medium	Rate Card	Frequency	Space	Rate	Circulation in 1000s	CPM ($)	Index
Impressions	#31	6x	Full page	$3,815	30	$127	1.00
Screen Play	1994	6x	Full page	$2,145	15	143	1.12
Press	9/93	6x	Full page	$3,200	27	119	0.93
Stitches	#14	6x	Full page	$1,715	9	191	1.50

This calculation shows that *Press* is the most efficient media buy. It reaches almost as many readers as *Impressions*, and it costs less.

Indexing your different options lets you see which is most cost-efficient. *Impressions* is the leader in circulation, and so we chose to use it as the standard and index the others against it.

Using a template like this, you can compare your media options. If you have a computer, set up a spreadsheet program and save it as a blank template. You will use this tool frequently to analyze media efficiency.

Template 6-2C: CPM Calculation Blank

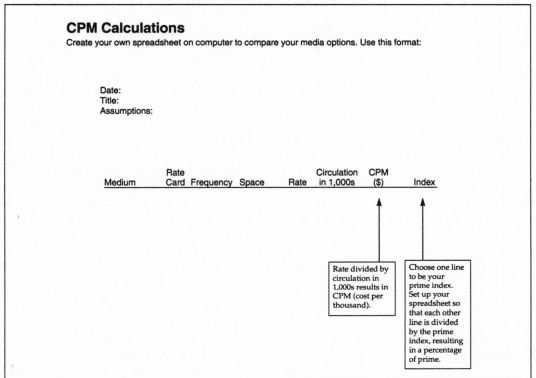

CPM Calculations
Create your own spreadsheet on computer to compare your media options. Use this format:

Date:
Title:
Assumptions:

Medium	Rate Card	Frequency	Space	Rate	Circulation in 1,000s	CPM ($)	Index

Rate divided by circulation in 1,000s results in CPM (cost per thousand).

Choose one line to be your prime index. Set up your spreadsheet so that each other line is divided by the prime index, resulting in a percentage of prime.

Negotiating the Deal

Your sales reps will bring you proposals summarizing the rates, frequency discounts, and bonuses they can offer you. Print advertising rates are not as negotiable as those for broadcast media; you are unlikely to be offered discounts off the published rates. What your reps *can* offer you are bonuses and incentives of all kinds. For example, in trade publications, almost every advertiser gets in on the "bingo" card—that reply card with lots of code numbers that prospects circle and return to the publication. The magazine then collects and distributes these leads to the various advertisers. While you should use them if offered, bingo cards are of limited value, in my opinion. I've heard stories that lead me to believe that some magazines cheat. To make you think their bingo cards are working, they will send you leads that are not actually responders, but random names drawn from their mailing list. I can't prove this is true—but I wouldn't be surprised if it were. In general, well-established national magazines will not engage in this practice. You should be aware of the possibility, though.

Many trade magazines also host industry conventions. They'll offer you all kinds of freebies, from literature distribution to booth space at trade shows, as part of their negotiation if they want your advertising account. If you've been to one of these trade magazine-hosted shows, you've seen this in action. The same advertiser you've seen in premium positions in the magazine—back cover, or center spread—will have the choice floor spot in the convention hall. You too can negotiate for this kind of special treatment, if you have some dollars to spend.

Rates for advertising get lower as the quantity of advertising purchased goes up. This is expressed as *frequency*. Frequency means the number of times your ad appears in the publication—how many days it's in the newspaper, or how many months it appears in the magazine. We call this the number of *insertions*. Most rate cards will state this as a number followed by an "x"; for example, "3x" translates as "three insertions" or "a frequency of 3," meaning that the ad appears three times.

Many magazines and newspapers are willing to extend frequency discounts to new advertisers. You might only need to sign a 3x contract to receive a 12x rate, if you play hard to get. You might also ask about free ad production, or get the two-color rate for a four-color ad. Like any negotiation, this is a business of offers and counteroffers. Never forget to ask, "Is that the best you can do?"

Case Study: Planning a Print Advertising Campaign

You have two tools for building your advertising campaign: calendars and budgets. Using those tools, you can develop a hypothetical advertising plan detailing how many ads will appear, where, and when. Then you can calculate the costs associated with that plan. This includes both the production costs and the advertising space costs. When you see the bottom line, you may decide to go back and start over. Or you might decide to research co-op support programs that might subsidize your plan. (Read more about this at the end of this chapter.) In the end, you might create three to five alternative scenarios for evaluation. Never stop at just one. The following case study will show you how to prepare and evaluate different advertising scenarios.

In 1992 I was invited to submit a proposal for advertising services to First Business Bank. This bank focuses on attracting and serving business accounts only, an example of a niche marketing strategy that is unusual but very effective in banking. I wanted this local success story on my client list!

Here's how I went about preparing my proposal. I wanted to create several scenarios for advertising plans, because I wasn't sure how much the bank was ready to increase its budget. The bank was gearing up for aggressive growth, but how aggressive? I wanted to present two options, a conservative proposal and an ambitious one.

First, I got rate cards from the two magazines that I felt were the best potential media for the bank to use. *In Business*, as its name implies, is a local publication with a strictly-business focus. For a bank with a strictly-business niche, it's the obvious first choice for advertising.

Madison Magazine is more oriented toward a consumer market, but still very focused in its geographic distribution. If you compare the two magazines' circulation figures, you'll see why I wanted to include *Madison* in the media schedule if the bank could afford it. *Madison* has 17,500 readers, compared to *In Business*'s 13,000. Who are those other 4,500 people? Could the bank afford the extra advertising budget to reach them? Could we afford to miss them entirely in our campaign? How much overlap might there be?

I ruled out our local newspapers for strategic reasons: I wanted to recommend image advertising, and I felt achieving the needed size and frequency of advertising using newspapers would cost too much, and too much of that cost would be wasted on the newspapers' broad consumer readership.

To start an advertising cost scenario, you need some ideas about your advertising strategy.

I knew that the bank had been running full-page ads in *In Business* occasionally, but not very frequently. I had a hunch that smaller ads run with greater frequency would make more of an impression on the target market. To examine that idea, I prepared a CPM analysis spreadsheet based on the appropriate rate cards.

I wanted to know rates for different sizes of ads and different frequencies of appearance, so that I could calculate alternative scenarios. I thought I would recommend either half-page or full-page ads, depending on how the cost scenarios worked out, so I ruled out all the other possibilities and just compared those sizes.

Keep these assumptions in mind as you study Template 6-2D.

Here's how I use indexing to guide my decisions.

Somewhat arbitrarily, I decide which line will be indexed as 100%, the prime index. All other lines will be judged against that standard and assigned a relative index, expressed as a percentage of the prime index.

In this example, I indexed all the lines against the first line, "*In Business* full-page 3x rate," because that was the bank's current contract rate.

The CPM, or cost per thousand, calculation puts each of our options in relative perspective. Now we can make apples-to-apples comparisons. No matter what the size of the ad, or the number of subscribers, we know what it costs us to reach one thousand of them one time.

To calculate the index, I take each line's CPM and divide it by the prime index, which in this case is $101.54. The resulting percentage tells us immediately, by whether it is below or above 100 percent, whether that line is better or worse than the prime index.

Indexing doesn't tell you which option to choose, but it does help you see how your options relate to one another in terms of the cost of exposing your ad to the widest possible audience.

Template 6-2D: Media Comparisons, FBB

Date: 1-8-92
Title: Media Comparisons, First Business Bank
Assumptions: All rates are from 1992 rate cards.
The variables are the size of the ad and the frequency of appearance.
All rates are indexed against In Business full page 3x because
that is the bank's current contract rate.

Medium	Rate Card	Frequency	Space	Rate	Circulation in 1,000s	CPM ($)	Index
In Business	1992	3x	Full page b/w	$1,320	13	$101.54	100%
In Business	1992	6x	Full page b/w	$1,175	13	$90.38	89%
In Business	1992	9x	Full page b/w	$1,045	13	$80.38	79%
In Business	1992	6x	Half page b/w	$695	13	$53.46	53%
In Business	1992	9x	Half page b/w	$635	13	$48.85	48%
In Business	1992	12x	Half page b/w	$560	13	$43.08	42%
Madison Magazine	1992	3x	Full page b/w	$1,710	17.5	$97.71	130%
Madison Magazine	1992	3x	Half page b/w	$1,085	17.5	$62.00	82%

You will see that the first grouping concerns full-page ads in *In Business*, with the variable being the frequency discount offered. The rate drops about 12 percent as we move from three insertions (3x) to six insertions (6x), and again as we move to nine insertions (9x). The second grouping compares half-page ads in the same magazine. Again, the variable is the frequency of insertions. The last two lines give rates for *Madison*, half-page and full-page ads, on a 3x frequency. Because of its higher cost, I knew *Madison Magazine* would be at most a distant second in my recommended schedule, so I didn't even bother to calculate higher frequencies.

With Template 6-2D I created a tool kit. Now I had the full complement of rate calcu-

lations I might need to explore different calendars. (I'm using the word *calendar* to mean a schedule of insertions over a period of time—in this example, one year.) I will refer back to the frequencies, rates, and circulations shown here as I prepare calendars and a final comparison between scenarios. What is obvious from this spreadsheet, from the index numbers, is the cost savings in running smaller ads more frequently. (The sidebar near Template 6-2D gives an explanation of using indexes to analyze relative costs.)

To start my explorations, I prepared a calculation of First Business Bank's current advertising plan, and I called it Scenario 1 (Template 6-3A). It totaled $4,700 for four ads.

Template 6-3A: Advertising Calendar, FBB Scenario #1

Date: 1-8-92
Title: Advertising Calendar, Continue Current Plan
Scenario #1
Assumptions: Continue to advertise in the same pattern as before.
Rate is based on 3x frequency.

Month	In Business Size	Rate	Madison Size	Rate
January February March	Full page	$1,175		
April May June	Full page	$1,175		
July August September	Full page	$1,175		
October November December	Full page	$1,175		
		$4,700		Grand Total: $4,700

Then I prepared a calculation for my idea of using smaller ads at greater frequency. I wanted to keep the budget within sight of the bank's current expenditures, and so I decided that nine insertions was a good compromise between overall cost savings and total dollars required. This plan, called Scenario 2, totaled $5,715 for nine ads (Template 6-3B). This recommends a 21 percent increase in the bank's ad space budget. But it didn't address the concern of reaching beyond the 13,000 subscribers to *In Business*.

Template 6-3B: Advertising Calendar, FBB Scenario #2

Date: 1-8-92
Title: Advertising Calendar, Proposed
Scenario #2
Assumptions: Decrease size of ad but increase frequency.
In Business ad rates are based on 9x frequency.

Month	In Business Size	Rate	Madison Size	Rate
January	Half page	$635		
February	Half page	$635		
March				
April	Half page	$635		
May	Half page	$635		
June	Half page	$635		
July	Half page	$635		
August				
September	Half page	$635		
October	Half page	$635		
November	Half page	$635		
December				
		$5,715	Grand Total:	$5,715

Then I prepared a "blue-sky" calculation that brought *Madison Magazine* into the mix (Template 6-3C). The result: a plan that spends $10,040 of the bank's money, but reaches a wider circulation.

Template 6-3C: Advertising Calendar, FBB Scenario #3

Date: 1-8-92
Title: Advertising Calendar, Proposed
Scenario #3
Assumptions: Use Madison Magazine to reach additional audience.
In Business ad rates are based on 6x frequency.
(Size of ad does not affect frequency determination.)
Madison Magazine ad rates are based on 3x frequency.

Month	In Business Size	Rate	Madison Size	Rate	
January	Full page	$1,175			
February	Half page	$695			
March			Half page	$1,085	
April	Full page	$1,175			
May	Half page	$695			
June			Half page	$1,085	
July	Full page	$1,175			
August					
September			Half page	$1,085	
October	Full page	$1,175			
November	Half page	$695			
December					
					Grand Total:
		$6,785		$3,255	$10,040

Which plan is the right one? That depends on many factors beyond the answers spreadsheets can give us. But spreadsheets help, and so I prepared a numerical analysis comparing the total cost and the total circulation achieved by each plan (Template 6-4). Again using CPM and indexing helps us see the trade-offs.

Template 6-4: Evaluation of 3 Scenarios by CPM

1-8-92
Evaluation of Three Scenarios for First Business Bank
All rates are from 1992 rate cards.
Total cost taken from "Grand Total" field of each scenario.
CPM calculation: Divide Total Cost by Total Circulation.
See scenarios for breakdown of what size ad runs when and where.

Total Cost	Total # of Appearances	Monthly Circulation	Total Circulation	CPM ($)	Index
$4,700	4	13	52	$90.38	100%
$5,715	9	13	117	$48.85	54%
$6,785	7	13	91		
$3,255	3	17.5	52.5		
$10,040			143.5	$69.97	77%

In Scenario 1, the CPM is $90.38. In Scenario 2, it drops to $48.85. In Scenario 3, it comes to $66.97, a better investment than what the bank is currently spending. However, the total cost, which is an increase of 221 percent, argues against this scenario.

What did the bank decide to do? I made my presentation and got the account, in part based on my media analysis and recommendations. The advertising calendar we implemented was Scenario 2.

You can use the blank Template 6-2C to prepare your CPM analysis. Then, using blank Template 6-3D, you will be able to develop different scenarios for your situation to figure out which is likely to generate the best return for your advertising dollars. If you use spreadsheets on your computer, create these and save them as blank templates. You'll use them frequently and appreciate the convenience of instant calculations.

Template 6-3D: Advertising Calendar, Blank

Date:
Title:

Assumptions:

Month	Magazine Size	Rate	Magazine Size	Rate
January				
February				
March				
April				
May				
June				
July				
August				
September				
October				
November				
December				
	$		$	Grand Total: $

When you've chosen your scenario, use Templates 6-5 and 6-6 to describe the cost and timing of your print advertising. Using this format will make your plans consistent with your media calendar, Template 4-5, and your media budget, Template 4-6. Production estimates will come later in this chapter.

Template 6-5A: Print Media Calendar, Example

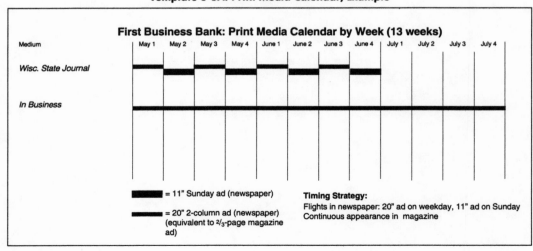

First Business Bank: Print Media Calendar by Week (13 weeks)

Medium: Wisc. State Journal, In Business
May 1, May 2, May 3, May 4, June 1, June 2, June 3, June 4, July 1, July 2, July 3, July 4

■■■■ = 11" Sunday ad (newspaper)

■■■■ = 20" 2-column ad (newspaper) (equivalent to 2/3-page magazine ad)

Timing Strategy:
Flights in newspaper: 20" ad on weekday, 11" ad on Sunday
Continuous appearance in magazine

Template 6-5B: Print Media Calendar, Blank

Print Media Calendar

Medium	Week 1	Week 2	Week 3	Week 4	Week 1	Week 2	Week 3	Week 4	Week 1	Week 2	Week 3	Week 4

Template 6-6A: Print Media Budget, Example

Spending by Vehicle and Week

Date: 3-22-94
Title: First Business Bank Print Media by Week
Assumptions: See Media Calendar
Costs based on rate cards 1/94
Wisc. State Journal Sunday $35.75/inch
Wisc. State Journal Daily $26.30/inch
In Business $695 (contract negotiable rate)
Prepared by: SW

Medium	May Week1	Week 2	Week 3	Week 4	June Week1	Week 2	Week 3	Week 4	July Week1	Week 2	Week 3	Week 4	Total ($)	Total (%)
WSJ	526	393	526	393	526	393	526	393					$3,677	64%
In Business	695				695				695				$2,085	36%
Total by Week	$1,221	$393	$526	$393	$1,221	$393	$526	$393	$695				$5,762	100%
Percent of Total	21%	7%	9%	7%	21%	7%	9%	7%	12%	0%	0%	0%	100%	

Template 6-6B: Print Media Budget, Blank

Spending by Vehicle and Week

Date:
Title:
Assumptions:

Prepared by:

Medium	Week1	Week 2	Week 3	Week 4	Week1	Week 2	Week 3	Week 4	Week1	Week 2	Week 3	Week 4	Total ($)	Total (%)

Total by Week

Percent of Total

Crafting the Print Ad: Writing Copy

Ads sell by persuading, informing, even begging for action. With a well-written headline, clear body copy, your offer, and a closing identification, you are going to take aim, pitch, follow through, and hit the target where you intended.

Now is a good time to review your *positioning* from Chapter 2 and your *creative approach* from Chapter 5. Crafting an ad is a matter of building on this foundation.

Structure and Style

The structure of an ad follows a proven outline. The style is up to you. Your personality will tell you what's appropriate; the visual design of your ad as well as the copy will express that style. But first let's talk about structure.

An effective print ad will

1. Get attention.
2. Build interest.
3. Create desire.
4. Motivate action.
5. Make sales.

You will see this abbreviated more concisely as the "AIDA" formula—Attention, Interest, Desire, Action.

The beginning of your ad will establish the context; are you selling cremation urns or potato chips? You've got to get the attention of the person who's looking for what you sell. By establishing context, you say, "This ad is for *you.*"

In that critical first paragraph, you start from what your customers know. Then you build interest in the benefit your product or service offers. Remember, people are motivated by the benefit—what the product will do for them. This means that your copy has to start with a promise, not a claim. If you're writing sentences that start with "we," stop and start over.

Take a look at the Klinke Cleaners ad in Example 6-5. We're going to take it apart to discover its structure and how it works to sell this service.

Example 6-5: Klinke Cleaners Ad
Used by permission of Klinke Cleaners.

First the headline: Get Your Clothes Back While They're Still In Style

Then the art: Photo of a couple in seventies attire—platform shoes and a minidress for her; bell bottoms and nehru jacket for him.

Next the copy: If you're tired of waiting for dry cleaning or to have shirts laundered, come to Klinke Cleaners. When it's in by 11:00, it'll be ready at 4:00 any day, Monday through Saturday. And with over a dozen Madison area locations, we're right on your way to looking good.

Next the tagline: Same Day Service. Same Great Price.

And last, the closing: Logo. Address location/street address list.

The headline *gets attention* by stating the key benefit. It dramatizes the problem—waiting too long for your clothes to come back from the laundry. (Remember positioning strategies from Chapter 2? This is an example of a *problem* strategy, focusing on the target customer's frustrations, then offering a solution.)

The first sentence establishes context, which *builds interest*. Then the ad describes what the benefit does for the reader, which *creates desire*. The tagline *motivates action*. The closing copy *makes the sale* by delivering the address information, enabling the readers to act on their desire. This is a simple and very effective ad.

Let's take another example, this time a much longer ad (Example 6-6). We'll analyze the copy line by line.

Example 6-6: KMS Ad, page 1
Used by permission of KMS.

Example 6-6: KMS Ad, page 2
Used by permission of KMS

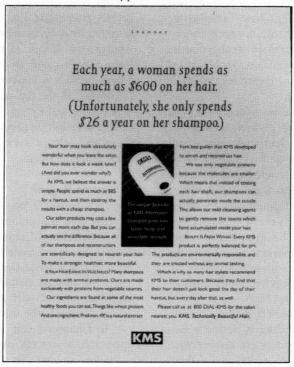

Headline: Each year, a woman spends as much as $600 on her hair. (Unfortunately, she only spends $26 a year on her shampoo.)

Product photo caption: The unique formula of KMS Alternative shampoo gives hair luster, body, and incredible strength. [This caption states the key benefit and connects it to a product feature—its unique formula. From this we know that the company has chosen a "key benefit" positioning strategy.]

First paragraph: Your hair may look absolutely wonderful when you leave the salon. But how does it look a week later? (And did you ever wonder why?) At KMS, we believe the answer is simple. People spend as much as $85 for a haircut, and then destroy the results with a cheap shampoo.

The following paragraphs unfold the story. Watch as this ad copy supports its promise: Our salon products may cost a few pennies more each day. But you can actually see the difference. [Notice how the promise of value is delivered; this builds interest]. Because all of our shampoos and reconstructors are scientifically designed to nourish your hair. To make it stronger, healthier, more beautiful.

Now the copywriter begins to connect the benefit to a product feature: the scientific design of its composition. Note the subhead: Is Your Hair Eating Its Vegetables? Many shampoos are made with animal proteins. Ours are made exclusively with proteins from vegetable sources. [This copywriter is educating you about shampoo technology. It may be more than you want to know—but it sure builds credibility for the claim.] Our ingredients are found in some of the most healthy foods you can eat. Things like wheat protein.

And one ingredient, Prolimin-49, is a natural extract from bee pollen that KMS developed to enrich and reconstruct hair. [The writer found an appealing way to talk about chemicals, by connecting them to health foods. Note the active verbs (enrich, reconstruct) he's chosen. He's creating desire for the product in you.]

We use only vegetable proteins because the molecules are smaller. Which means that instead of coating each hair shaft, our shampoos can actually penetrate inside the cuticle. This allows our mild cleansing agents to gently remove the toxins which have accumulated inside your hair. [You're practically an expert on shampoo chemistry now. The writer has indulged in long copy because the product positioning needs explanations to support the claim. Note the choice of adjectives: mild, gentle—and also the negative word "toxins." We don't want those in our hair!]

Note the second subhead: Beauty Is From Within. Every KMS product is perfectly balanced for pH. The products are environmentally responsible, and they are created without any animal testing. [The writer is now moving on to other product attributes, but to keep the ad focused, he has not elaborated on the benefit of each.]

Which is why so many hair stylists recommend KMS to their customers. Because they find that their hair doesn't just look good the day of their haircut, but every day after that, as well. [This is the offer that motivates you to action. The writer promises you that your hair will look better for a longer time after using this product.]

The close: Please call us at 800-DIAL-KMS for the salon nearest you. [This is the *call to action*: the specific step the advertiser wants you to take, in hope of turning your interest into a sale.]

Tagline: KMS. Technically Beautiful Hair. [The writer has restated the positioning strategy in language that sells.]

The tone, in both copy and visual style, is elegant without being overly formal. The copy breaks grammatical rules, occasionally using sentence fragments. The style of the layout is what we would call "editorial," meaning that it looks as if it could be an article in the magazine in which it appeared. The tiny heading "shampoo" at the top contributes to that look. The copy is quite long—which works just fine in this very informational ad. We'll talk about these and other aspects of print ads in much more detail as we go.

Where to Begin?

In Chapter 2 you created a positioning strategy that has defined and prioritized your key benefits and helped you find your USP. Look back at the benefits you listed. The priority you gave those benefits will guide you as you write your ad, helping you to keep focused on what your benefit is and how you distinguish yourself in the minds of customers.

In Chapter 5 you developed your creative approach, a strategy defining tone and audience, and an idea that dramatizes the key benefit with a creative "hook." Keep those thoughts handy now, so that the copy you write will be on target strategically. Especially important to you as copywriter are these elements of the ad strategy:

- One thought to take away
- Response offers (have you decided whether this is call-to-action or image advertising?)
- The must-have list

If you're not familiar with these elements, you'd better go back and read Chapter 5!

Skillful writing adds credibility, shifts attitudes, educates, informs, persuades. When you write an ad, follow the five-point structure outline—get attention, build interest, create desire, motivate action, make sales.

Keep checking your draft against the outline, to keep your copywriting on track. Soon you'll find yourself ready to write the call to action, make your offer, and close.

How Long Should the Ad Be?

There's no one right answer. Your choice of media, the size of your ad, and the product or service you are offering will all affect your decision. Print is certainly the only medium that allows you to go into great detail. Long copy has one advantage: It tends to appeal to the prospects who are likely to take action. (Who else would read through all that?)

Newspapers, in particular, are sources that people look to for information. Informative advertising placed in a well-respected local newspaper is very effective. Someone suffering from back pain will read every word of an ad that offers relief. So long copy is not a problem in newspaper advertising.

See Example 6-7. We won't reproduce the text here—it would go on for pages! We'll discuss the marketing strategy behind it, and why it made long copy OK.

Example 6-7: Leisure Concepts Ad
Used by permission of Leisure Concepts.

The Truth About
SOFTUBS!

Until 1985 portable spas and hot tubs were all made the same way. A hard fiberglass shell with a smooth inner surface made first from gel-coat, and since the early 1980's acrylic. All these types of spas use a conventional heating element to keep the water at the normal operating temperature of 100 to 104 degrees. Almost every spa that operates at 110 volts heats with a 1500 watt heating element.

It's Totally Different

The softub is totally different from all other conventional hot tubs or spas. Softubs are made from a unique process of laminating polyolefin foam until it is 25 or more layers thick. The 6 inch thick hard cover, the walls, and the floor of the tub are all made from this special foam. Polyolefin is a closed cell "memory foam". It will return to it's natural shape if it gets pushed or squeezed. That factor allows Softubs to be squashed down to fit through a doorway that is actually quite a bit smaller than the tub itself. Polyolefin foam also happens to be insulation, so the entire spa structure is made from insulation.

All the plumbing lines that feed water to the jets are located just inside the foam walls in a carefully carved out tunnel close to the inside of the tub, so heat loss from the pipes is cut to almost 0. These pipes, like the tub itself, are also flexible.

It's Very Durable

This foam structure with the whirlpool system installed is then covered with a very high quality marine grade vinyl. This vinyl is manufactured by Softub, and has ultra violet and mildew inhibitors right in the material. This vinyl also covers the 6 inch thick hard cover, the power pack, and the connecting pipes from the tub to the power pack. The tub's interior is made from a special heat resistant, 20ml. thick virgin vinyl that is very similar to a high quality in-ground swimming pool liner. Most pool liners will last 10 years with a little care, and they have to spend all winter frozen outside! After 5 or 6 years of use outdoors, even the best materials in the world will show signs of age. Softubs are no different, but unlike our own skin, the vinyl skin of a Softub can be easily removed, and for around $300.00 on the medium size, all the vinyl can be replaced! This will make your Softub like a brand new tub again. You can even change the color, there are 31 to choose from. You will save more money on electricity over a 5 or 6 year period, than you would spend if you decided to give your softub a new skin.

FREE HEAT!

Now the really interesting part of the Softub story is that they have NO HEATER! The powerpack houses all the equipment for the Softub, and is also made of, what else, foam. When you get your Softub home, you roll it to the desired location, connect the two power pack hoses to the tub using the two supplied stainless steel clamps, and the supplied wrench. (We'll do all that for you.) You throw

Softubs for as little as
$59⁰⁰
Per Month
No payments until Nov. '94

the garden hose into it and fill it up. Once the Softub is full, plug it into any standard 15 amp 110 volt outlet and turn the thermostat up. As the pump runs, a small amount of water is circulated around the motor, and two good things happen. First, the motor is cooled by having coils filled with water circulating around it, this will prolong the life of the motor. Second the heat from the motor is transferred in to the tub.

Ready When You Are

When the medium size Softub is filled with cold water from your hose, it will initially take about 24 hours to reach 100 degrees, then the pump will automatically shut off. The pump will stay off until the thermostat senses the need for more heat, it will then come back on and run, heating and filtering, until the desired temperature is reached again. The Softub is always heated to your desired temperature and ready to use any time you want. Just remove the cover, get in, and press the "jet" button. The "jet" button turns the pump on and starts a 10 minute timer at times when the thermostat isn't calling for heat, but you want the jet action. After 10 minutes the jets will turn back off. If you want another 10 minutes, just push the jet button again, it's that simple.

You've Never Felt Like This!

The interior seating area of a softub is completely open and unobstructed. When you submerge yourself down into the hot water, you experience something that most people have never felt. You are totally submerged in hot turbulent water, but the surface that you're sitting on is soft! Everything is soft, padded, and really comfortable. The fact that there are no designated seats inside a Softub allows for totally free movement, and there is always room for one more person. That's another Softub secret!

All the components that make up a Softub are as high in quality as the components that make up the most expensive conventional spas. Softub has just found a way to manufacture spas much faster with less manual labor required, and because they use a totally different group of materials for the actual structure, they can do it for much less money too!

Nearly 40,000 In Use Today!

Leisure Concepts has sold nearly 200 Softubs in the first year that we've carried the line, and the Softub owners are nearly 100% satisfied. Softub Inc. will sell nearly 15,000 Softubs in 1994 alone. We at Leisure Concepts demand quality out of all of our suppliers, and Softubs meet our demands every day.

Don't put off owning a Softub! Right now is the best time of the year to buy, prices will never be lower.

LEISURE CONCEPTS

2480 Perry St., Madison • M-W 9-8, T_TH 9-6, F 9-5, Sat. 9-4, Sun 11-4
Call For Free Brochure 257-4200 in Madison • 1-800-809-9111 in WI

The Leisure Concepts ad is nearly a brochure. Point by point it delivers the whole story on portable spas. The subheads lead you through the copy, and the photo gives you an idea of the product in use. My only quibble with this copy is that it could use a stronger call to action at the end. As a marketing strategy for a company introducing a high-ticket, complex, and innovative product, this ad is on target. Long copy telling the whole story is going to generate interest and bring better-qualified prospects into the store.

Should you try this approach with your advertising? The Softub example is an extreme one. It is an excellent example of a long copy ad that works—for its particular purpose. However, you will probably not choose to put quite this much copy in your ad. Ask yourself this: Do your customers need to be educated to know that they need your product? Your advertisements should give them all the information they need, in as much detail as necessary. Don't prejudge the length of what you've written. Judge its effectiveness at getting attention, building interest, and calling for action.

Finding Your Copy Approach

The first you thing you need to do is *find your verb*. Action is the heart of any good story, and that's what you're aiming to tell. Think about the key benefit you are offering to your customers, and match it to a verb.

Good Verbs

Make
Buy
Change
Win
Get
Includes
See
Say yes to...
Find out about...
Jump

Then think about adjectives. Look for adjectives that clarify, inform, or intensify your message. But beware of hyperbole—an unbelievable claim just undermines your credibility. Your best discoveries will be colorful adjectives that support your creative hook.

Good Adjectives

Revolutionary
Absolute
Right
Hot
Tender
Good
Beautiful
Smooth
Hand-crafted
Well-made

Now you're on your way to a headline, and it's time to establish style. Here are several tried-and-true advertising copy approaches.

Seven Reasons Why

This style of advertising is the simplest to write: Ask yourself (adopt a stern tone as you do this), "Why would I want what you sell?" Now start writing out the answers. You don't need to be "the creative type" to write a compelling, fact-based ad. Write as many simple explanations of customer benefits as come to you in about ten minutes. If you get stuck, reflect on comments you've heard from your customers, or questions you've heard as you've tried to close sales.

You are angling to change perception here. How persuasive are the answers you've written to the question, "Why should I try it?" Work a little harder now and edit your first draft. Look for your action verbs. Critique your benefit statements; rank them in priority. Then arrange them to follow the outline we discussed before: get attention/build interest/create desire/motivate action. (Remember AIDA.)

Suppose you're selling a camping lantern that competes with a better-known national brand. Your answers might read like this:

1. Bright light without excessive heat or noise (performance).

2. No-mess fuel comes in plug-in cartridges (convenience).

3. Electronic automatic lighter is easy to use (convenience).

4. Sturdy molded plastic carrying case makes it easy to transport and store (convenience).

5. Company guarantees performance for five years or money back (value).

6. Efficient fuel use gives more hours per canister than the competition (value).

7. Adjustable carrying handle doubles as a hanging device or stable stand (convenience).

I wrote these down in the order they came to me. Then I reviewed each point, adding the word in parentheses to define the benefit this fact delivers. Once we shuffled the order so that it matches our target market's needs and desires regarding camping equipment, we'd be ready to write the ad copy. Here's a start:

Headline:

We'll Give You Seven Reasons to Buy a Coolight—But We Think You'll See the Light After the First Two.

Try completing this ad. Start with the promise of value, then move on to performance and then to convenience. Use a subhead for each benefit promise. Start each supporting claim with a number. There you have it—a persuasive fact-based ad.

"Seven Reasons Why" ads work because readers knows what to expect. The informational tone inspires confidence. We've all seen variations, from three reasons to one hundred and one; the principle is the same. When the product is complex and the benefits are compelling, the "seven reasons" approach is a favorite—because it works.

Demonstration Ads

A demonstration ad takes a benefit statement and uses an example to dramatize that claim. This might be a straightforward comparison: A bank could advertise its checking account by comparing fees and services with what other banks are offering. It might be an idea that demonstrates a product feature, like clarity (in glass) or lack of distortion (in mirrors). You get the idea.

You don't have to demonstrate the solution—you might choose instead to demonstrate the problem dramatically. A public service campaign developed by the Madison Advertising Federation, a chapter of the American Advertising Federation, included a series of ads in which the headlines were a meaningless mix of letters. Seeing it, you instantly knew what it felt like to be unable to read. That quick demonstration packed a punch (Example 6-8).

Example 6-8: Literacy Ad
Used by permission of Madison Advertising Federation.

You're doing a good deed when you bring valuable information to your customers. Look for the action verb again. Tell real news and you've got an ad that will motivate action.

Humor

Humor is popular in advertising but dangerous in the wrong hands. Humor can help a small budget make a big impact. If you have a hunch for an advertising angle that might be hilarious, explore it.

There are several different ways to make ads funny:

- *Use a pun*: a double meaning or verbal misunderstanding that makes us laugh.

Funny one-liners, often combining a headline and a photo, have been making waves in advertising for the last decade.

- *Exaggerate*: overstate or understate the truth; exploit a contrast to create humor. (This can lead to dramatic visual solutions like the Klinke Cleaner ad, Example 6-5.)

- *Use incongruity*: try juxtaposing unrelated elements for a "sneak attack" on your funny bone.

The Midelfort Clinic ad (Example 6-9) shows the effective use of humor to sell its services.

Example 6-9: Midelfort Clinic Ad
Used by permission of Valley Health Plan and Fallon McElligott.

Storytelling

"They laughed when I sat down at the piano, but when I started to play..." People have enjoyed the story-telling advertising style for a century. With today's "grazing" patterns of reading, this approach isn't wise for most situations. But sometimes the exception proves the rule. Banana Republic made storytelling a distinctive company style, in its catalogs as well as its ads.

Sometimes the story-telling technique is less obvious. A case history or a testimonial will often take a story approach, setting a scene and establishing characters, to dramatize a benefit (Example 6-10).

Example 6-10: Jim Beam Distillery Ad
Used by permission of Jim Beam Brands Co.

Summary: The Copy Approach

If there's real news about your product, even if it's important to only a narrow target market, this might be for you. Choose your publication carefully and give it a try.

Whatever approach you choose, keep it simple. As you write, look for familiar combinations of words. Avoid jargon. When you've written a few sentences, review them for phrases that can be shortened or deleted. Keep it simple, and keep it brief. Try reading it out loud. Does it sound conversational? Rewrite any awkward phrases or transitions. Remember, much of good writing comes from the rewriting. The more you hone and tighten your copy, the better it is likely to be.

Choose the style you feel is appropriate for your ad—or try several! Write a draft. Refine it by comparing it to our five-point structure outline. Then critique it. It's a good ad if, sentence by sentence, your story unfolds as follows:

- Targets your consumer.
- States your benefit to that consumer.
- Relates that benefit to a specific product feature.
- Repeats this cycle through each feature you want to discuss.
- Mentions your product or service by name.
- Makes a call to action.

Style of Language

Advertising and poetry have more in common than you think. The tools of the poet—alliteration, assonance, and rhyme—can help you write a powerful headline and copy that flows gracefully from point to point.

- *Style.* Keep your style as quietly correct as you can. Good grammar is unobtrusive, but advertising shouldn't read like a school text, either. The most common grammatical liberty in ad copy is the sentence fragment. Used for drama. For punch. For brevity. You get the point.

- *Verbs.* Keep an ear out for bad verbs. Hunt down the passive verbs and translate them into active ones. Change "Forty patients were cured by Brandex" to "Brandex cured forty patients." These translations will shorten and brighten your copy.

- *Adjectives.* Check your adjectives. Are you adding clarity or excitement, or just making claims? You can't force a prospect to believe you by piling on more superlatives.

- *Pronouns.* Pronouns should be consistent. You'll make a decision early on: Is it "we," "you," or "they"? I prefer "you." Choose the second person whenever possible. Every rule has its exceptions: The storytelling approach lends itself to first- or third-person writing. Use whichever works for your approach, then make sure your voice is consistent.

- *Parallel construction.* Parallel construction builds good ad copy. If your thinking is logical, your ad should come out that way, too. Some examples: "When you're out of Schlitz, you're out of beer." "You're not getting older, you're getting better." "Same day service, same great price."

Look back at the "donut" ad for Firstar Bank shown at the beginning of this chapter (Example 6-2). This is a great example of straightforward copywriting. Here is the copy from that ad:

Headline: You Might Call it Donuts with Your Banker. We Call it a New Vision.

Copy: A father meets his banker to talk over college investment plans for his kids. Nothing remarkable. Except that it's 7 A.M. And they're at a coffee shop.

A woman rolls over a maturing CD into a money-market

account. On the phone, at 9:30 on a Friday night—talking to a real live banker.

A small business owner needs a loan to open a second location; one phone call gets him in touch with an Economic Development Specialist, expert at obtaining government guaranteed small business loans.

All over Madison incidents like these are adding up to a picture of a different kind of bank— Firstar Bank Madison. A bank that's applying new ideas about quality and service to its operation.

You can see it in full-service nighttime phone banking. In banking teams dedicated to the needs of small business owners. And in personal bankers who meet their clients' needs in new and better ways—*including* meeting them for coffee and donuts at 7 A.M.

Nothing earthshaking. Just a different way of thinking about banking. From a different kind of bank—Firstar Bank Madison. Call Firstar at 252-4300.

Closing: Logo.

Note how this copy flows along; there are many sentence fragments, but they help keep the rhythm, not break it. Notice how the voice gracefully shifts from third person to second, as the examples are brought home to a key benefit and its supporting claim. There's nice parallel construction here, too. The three examples from the opening paragraphs are referred to again later in the copy.

If your copy reads this naturally, you've got a talent for copywriting. And even if you can't come up with copy like this on your first try, you can find other ads you like and use them as models or benchmarks for your own efforts.

Layout and Design

Most advertising you see has been crafted with care by someone, usually a professional with a background in art and on-the-job experience in salesmanship, reading dynamics, and technical execution skills. You could hire such a person to get your ad idea ready to print. Or production services may be available through the publication the ad is going in. Or you could do it yourself. But whether you take on the job or direct someone else, you need to know how you want your ad to look. Here are some basic design principles to help you figure this out.

The Overview

There are specific techniques for laying out newspaper ads, magazine ads, and billboards. But before we get specific, we'll talk about the general processes and techniques that apply to all print advertising. Then we'll get to advice on creating ads for newspapers, magazines, directories, and outdoor advertising.

Unless you're very familiar with computer illustration and page layout software, you'll probably need outside help in creating the actual printer's negatives that you send to your publication. My goal is to help you understand the process, and the underlying issues of layout and design. With this background, you can do as much as possible yourself, and be clear in the direction you give your outside professionals when you get to that stage. You'll save time and money by being prepared.

Layout: The Grid

Experience from previous advertising prescribes fairly rigid guidelines for the layout of advertisements. There's a classic approach that functions beautifully and dominates most advertising you see. It's derived from scientific research into how people look at ads. Your natural inclination is to look at the upper left, then sweep in an S curve, ending down at the lower right. Ad designers take advantage of this. You've probably noticed that most ads have the logo and address in the lower right, where the reader's eye comes to rest.

How the elements come together on the page is called a *layout*. The underlying logic that gives those elements a feeling of order is called a *grid*. Think of a grid as a tool for guiding placement decisions. You wouldn't build a house and hang all the windows at different heights—you would position the windows the same distance from the ground, so that the appearance from the street was one of harmonious symmetry. That's the grid applied to architectural design. The same desire for harmony applies to placing elements in a print ad, or any piece of graphic design.

The grid helps to establish margins, space between elements, and where various elements align. Even the simplest headline/visual/copy/logo ad is governed by a classic symmetry that constitutes a grid. Chaotic page design is tension-producing, and unless you're selling excitement, you're wiser to look for order. Develop a grid as you begin to design your ad.

The first step in the design process is to create a "thumbnail" sketch of your ad. This is a kind of model that helps you see alternative designs quickly. Graphic artists draw thumbnails at very small scale—two or three inches wide—but maintaining the height-to-width proportion of the ad at its true size. The whole point is to work fast—you'll notice we don't use rulers when we draw lines or try to be too careful as we sketch. Ideas, not neatness, are what counts at this stage.

Try drawing a thumbnail sketch of a simple ad. Place your elements in this sequence: headline, visual, copy, logo. Now try this variation: Put the headline after the visual. That's your big creative decision. Your copy might look best in one, two, or three columns; legibility should guide this decision. Your logo, tied to its signature address and phone, cannot stray from the bottom.

Example 6-11: Royle ad
Used by permission of The Royle Group.

Our Group Concept Works
To Provide Balanced Printing Services.

With technology so rapidly changing the printing industry, you need a printer who is equipped to handle your needs and can push new levels of performance.

At the Royle Group, we have the combined resources and state-of-the-art technology that only a printing group can offer. Through the dedication of over 200 skilled professionals and with an investment in some of the most advanced equipment in North America, we're earning a national reputation for the kind of quality and efficiency that is setting new standards.

If your print suppliers are limited in their view of what's possible, give us a call. We'll provide you with a more balanced perspective.

A Breakthrough Printing Performance

Royle Printing   Artcraft Press   Graphic Image   Royle Publishing   112 Market Street   Sun Prairie, WI 53590   (608)837-5161   1-800-728-7768

Example 6-12: Thumbnail sketch for the same ad

Pay attention to where things align in the Royle ad (Example 6-11), and you will see how the thumbnail sketch (Example 6-12) reveals the grid that will be used when the ad is designed at full scale. You can sense an invisible center line down the middle, on which the logo, the headline, and even the very symmetrical photo are aligned. You can see that the address line at the bottom has been spaced to correspond to the width of the columns of body copy, giving the ad a balanced margin around the four sides.

There's a grace to the simplicity of the headline/visual/copy/logo approach, and if you page through a consumer magazine, you'll see the pattern repeated often. Try drawing thumbnail sketches of several of the ads shown in this chapter. Then imagine the elements of your ad in the same layout.

Now you've written your copy, you have an idea for the visual style of your ad, and maybe you have some thoughts on photography or illustration.

If your ad copy and concept lend themselves to one of the thumbnails you've sketched, you don't need a big creative budget to execute it. Most magazines and newspapers will help you lay out your ad for free or at low cost. If you have written your ad copy and developed a rough sketch of the ad that pleases you, ask your publication about production services. That's probably the best place to start.

Magazines and newspapers won't be able to help you much with the visual, however. So, if your layout calls for a dramatic visual or a more complex page design, you will probably need the help of a graphic artist. Freelancers are available who will help you; typical rates range from $25 to $50 an hour, depending on the skill and equipment the person has. You might talk to a photographer, or you might talk to a graphic design firm about your ideas. Explain the image you have in mind, and focus on what you're willing to do and pay to get it. Keep meeting and talking with people until you have a good understanding of what's involved and who brings the right skills to the table.

Bringing the Page Together

Three elements come together to make a page: art, copy, and white space. How you choose to combine them establishes your style. Look at examples in publications like those you intend to advertise in, and get a sense for what style the ones you like are using. As you see the types of photos they use—stark or lush, soft or hard focus, abstract or concrete in their imagery—you'll start to understand style.

What are your competitors doing? What about companies that you know are successful? There are plenty of ads that are exciting visually but do not produce results. If you think you might be admiring an ad that's more flash than pull, look for its AIDA structure (attention, interest, desire, action). Does it pass the test?

Using Photographs in Your Ads

Be prepared to invest in creating a great photo. There may be props to build, locations to research, models to choose, and even more details. If this seems too complicated, maybe you should look for a simpler idea.

Several of the ads we've talked about in this chapter are good examples of effective ads that were inexpensive to produce. The Royle ad we just discussed (Example 6-11) used a historical photo from a stock agency and built a concept around it. The only cost was a small use fee for the stock photo.

The Klinke Cleaners ad discussed earlier (Example 6-5) is another example of inexpensive production. This photo did not require complex sets or props; the clothing was from resale shops, and the models were local talent being paid for one simple pose. The photo shoot probably didn't take much longer than an hour. It's good concept and copy that make this ad work.

These are examples of ads that use photos to illustrate concepts. You might also consider using a photo of the product itself, a photo of your store, or a testimonial photo of a satisfied user. These would relate more directly to your offering, but might not have the same power to get attention.

My feeling is this: The more consumer-oriented your media strategy, the more important the concept of your photo becomes. In an industrial directory, a photo of your product might be perfectly appropriate. In the daily newspaper, you'll have to try a little harder than that to make your prospects sit up and take notice.

Using Illustrations

Illustrations are another universe of style. Advertisers choose cartoons, paintings, montages, even technical cutaway views for specific reasons that are then translated into style. Cartoons communicate with humor and get a point across very quickly. They can be great in small-space advertising. Paintings and drawings are an alternative to photography; they are sometimes chosen because of the variations in mood they can project, but also sometimes for budget reasons. Don't get me wrong. An original illustration is not inexpensive—don't expect to commission a professional-caliber illustration for much under $1,000. But illustration is a great way to execute a concept that would be difficult to photograph. The shark ad from Anchor Bank (Example 6-1) is a good example. Illustrations project a very distinctive sense of style.

When should you use illustrations? If your competitors are using photos, illustrations might be a way to give your ads a unique look.

If your product is intangible, illustrations are a good way to connect your offering to something tangible through a visual metaphor. If you deal in high-style products, like fashion apparel or home furnishings, illustrations can lift your ads into a dreamy imaginary world— one that's very stylish. Consider illustrations an option.

Using Type

Next, look at typography. The way you use type projects an attitude in subtler ways than a photo or illustration, but the effect is significant. Classify styles of type in the ads you admire (whimsical, solid, celebratory...) and see if the mood fits your concept. Take the examples in Template 6-7A along when you talk with your graphic artist.

Template 6-7A: Font Styles

Times
The quick brown fox jumped over the lazy dog.
ABCDEFGHIJKLMNOPQRSTUVWXYZ
abcdefghijklmnopqrstuvwxyz

Times is the most popular serif typeface in the world. It has excellent legibility at all sizes, and its compact proportion makes it a good choice for tight spots.

Serifa
The quick brown fox jumped over the lazy dog.
ABCDEFGHIJKLMNOPQRSTUVWXYZ
abcdefghijklmnopqrstuvwxyz

This square-serif font offers an alternative to old-fashioned looking type. It is popular for ads and promotions. Very readable.

Souvenir
The quick brown fox jumped over the lazy dog.
ABCDEFGHIJKLMNOPQRSTUVWXYZ
abcdefghijklmnopqrstuvwxyz

Souvenir has a relaxed, informal feeling. The uncommon design of some letters makes it an attention-getter. Good for headlines.

Helvetica
The quick brown fox jumped over the lazy dog.
ABCDEFGHIJKLMNOPQRSTUVWXYZ
abcdefghijklmnopqrstuvwxyz

The most popular sans-serif typeface in the world. Gives anything a clean, modern look. Many weights available. Mixes well with other fonts.

Gill Sans
The quick brown fox jumped over the lazy dog.
ABCDEFGHIJKLMNOPQRSTUVWXYZ
abcdefghijklmnopqrstuvwxyz

Gill Sans has a quirky personality. Rounded letter shapes make it informal and friendly. Very legible without being a bore.

Talking about Type

Terminology is important if you want to be precise about type. A *typeface*, or *type family*, is the name for an entire complement of weights and styles; for example, Garamond Light, Garamond Light Italic, Garamond Book, Garamond Book Italic, Garamond Bold, and Garamond Bold Italic are a type family. A *font* consists of all the characters of one particular typeface. Garamond Book would be one font, and Garamond Book Italic would be a different font. Template 6-7B shows the names for the parts of characters that distinguish one font from another.

Template 6-7B: Names for Parts of Type

Names for the parts of type:

Terminology

SERIF
ASCENDER
X-HEIGHT
BASELINE
SERIFS
DESCENDERS

If your copy is long, legibility is important. If you are producing the ad yourself, follow these guidelines and you'll stay out of trouble. Choose a tried-and-true typeface, such as Times Roman, Helvetica, Palatino, or something similar, and stay away from columns of type that are too wide. To judge how wide to make your columns, simply type an alphabet twice in the size and font you've chosen. Then measure the width of the line. Set your columns no wider than this.

In ad copy, don't hyphenate words if you can avoid it. Look for beauty in the type: There shouldn't be any "rivers" of white running down the column when you squint at it (caused by words breaking at similar places down the column), or any uneven color as the letters blur. If you see these problems, your word spacing and tracking settings need to be fine-tuned. Check the manual for the software you're using.

We'll talk more about legibility and other graphic design issues in Chapter 9, "Direct Mail Advertising," and Chapter 11, "Your Corporate Image."

The Design Process: Steps to Completion

You have to get your ad idea out of your head and into physical form, known as camera-ready art. We've been talking about how your layout might begin to take shape, how you decide whether to use a photograph or an illustration, and how you will use type. But that's not really the beginning of the process.

Before we talk more about producing ads for one medium or another, let's review the steps you will go through.

The process really begins with planning. Assess your budget for ad production and review the deadlines. Review your creative approach from Chapter 5, especially your must-haves list.

Start with thumbnails. Create a layout showing art concepts, estimated length and placement of copy, logos, etc. Review services that may be required, such as photography or illustration, and consider who your suppliers might be.

Show this initial work to your advisers and friends, consider their comments, and then revise your work if necessary. When you feel confident that the design is good, proceed to the next step: ad production.

Production begins with creating the necessary elements, then arranging them into their final form for printing. The publication may handle production for you. You may be able to do everything yourself, if you have a computer with desktop-publishing software and a good artistic eye. If not, you might talk to ad agencies, or graphic designers, or free-lancers who list under "Commercial art" or "Desktop publishing" in the Yellow Pages. Your best bet is to ask your business associates for referrals.

Take your examples, and have a good long conversation with these professionals about what you like and don't like, what you can afford and what you can't. Allow your potential collaborators enough time to respond with a creative services and cost proposal.

If you like what you see, select your partner and ask for a "comp," or comprehensive mock-up, of the final ad, using the copy you've written. If you are getting co-op support from any manufacturers, they will want to see the mock-up and the ad copy, to give their approval. (A more detailed explanation of co-op comes later in this chapter.) Now for the specifics of actually producing the ad.

- *Art direction.* If photos are in the plan, arrange a photo session. Don't forget the advance work of finding props, procuring (or mocking up) your product, selecting models, etc. Either you or the supplier you work with will need to take responsibility for each detail. Typically a planning session called a preproduction meeting is scheduled, at which the plan is finalized and responsibilities assigned.

- *Copy preparation.* Now it's time to finalize your copy. Get final approval from any decision makers at this stage, so that you won't be delayed by alterations later. These can cost extra money if you're working with an outside supplier. The frustration of small changes late in the game is costly whether you're doing the work in-house or out.

- *Preparing the plate-ready films.* Most graphic artists use Quark XPress or other software to prepare page layouts. Using this program, the artist scans the photos, separates them into printing colors, and places them on the page. The final copy will be typeset according to the design layouts, and electronic manipulation will bring the elements together into final pages. At this time it's a good idea to check in with the publications where you intend to run the ad. Your graphic artist will need to know their mechanical specs (exact size, maximum line screens acceptable, and dot grain—there's a sidebar later in this chapter that explains these terms in detail). *Always* work to the publication's specifications, rather than taking a one-size-fits-all approach. When you are designing an ad for placement in several different publications, it's not uncommon for each of them to require a slightly different page size. You can set up one ad with different trim marks to accommodate the different sizes. It's very important that you be aware of this before you get too far in designing the ad!

- *Checking proofs.* After you have approved a final proof from your graphic artist, the electronic file will be turned into plate-ready film. A last proof is made from the negatives. If your ad contains process color (the four inks used in printing to simulate the full spectrum of visible color), this proof will be a *matchprint* (a proof made from the four negatives that shows exactly how the final ad will look). If your ad is black and white, your proof will be a *contact print*, which is a photographic print made directly from the negative. If your ad has black plus a spot color, your proof will be a *color key*. This proof uses acetate layers, one made from each negative, to show what color appears where. Each of these proofs looks as close to the final result as current printing technology can get.

  Proofs made from the negatives are your last chance to catch errors before ink is applied to paper. Look this over carefully, then make a photocopy for your files, and ship the plate-ready films and proof to your publication.

Tips and Tools for Planning, Producing, and Placing Your Ads

How is your print advertising campaign shaping up? Which media are the most appealing? In this section you'll find specific advice for each category of print media. We'll review calendar and budget planning for each medium, using examples. I'll give you some specific tips on copy and layout for each medium. The templates will help you put my advice to use. Follow the case histories, and you'll learn from other people's experiences. Let's get started!

Creating Ads for Newspaper

Use the calendar in Template 6-8 to track the deadlines for each ad you place. Check with your newspaper ad rep to find out how far in advance of the publication date the newspaper will need your space reservation, and how far in advance it will need your artwork. Usually newspaper deadlines run about three days prior to the publication date.

Template 6-8: Newspaper Advertising Schedule

Date Prepared:
Prepared by:

Day and Date Ad Appears	Art Due to Newspaper (Date)	Ad Art (Name of Ad)	Size (Inches)
		Total Inches:	"

(Total number of inches is important in keeping track of your contract rate fulfillment.)

Template 6-9 gives an example of a budget for producing a two-part series of simple newspaper ads (Example 6-13). This is what you might pay a freelancer or a graphic design firm to prepare artwork for you. The newspaper might produce your ad for a somewhat lower fee.

Example 6-13-A
Used by permission of First Business Bank.

Example 6-13-B
Used by permission of First Business Bank.

When banks change...

It may be smart to change banks.

It's easy when Diana Brockway helps you begin your new relationship with First Business Bank.

Diana will come out to your office and help select a starting date for your transfer of funds and courier service. She's helped hundreds of businesses make this a smooth transition.

First Business Bank: the simplest, most cost-effective way for your business to do its banking.

First Business Bank
Of Madison

University
Research Park
(608) 238-8008

*Member FDIC
A locally-owned,
independent bank*

Diana Brockway
*Helping clients for
First Business Bank
since 1990.*

When banks change...

It may be smart to change banks.

Personal attention. Timely response. Entrepreneurial thinking. When we asked businesses what they'd like to see in a dream bank for business, this is what we heard. And what we've delivered... consistently, since 1990.

First Business Bank: the simplest, most cost-effective way for your business to do its banking.

First Business Bank
Of Madison

University
Research Park
(608) 238-8008

*Member FDIC
A locally-owned,
independent bank*

Jerry Smith
*President
30 years in banking*

Template 6-9: Cost Estimate: Simple Print Ad Production

Job Description: 2 ads in series, black & white
2 photos in studio, nonprofessional talent (no model fees)

Fees:		Expenses:	
Meetings & Administration	$120	Scans:	50
Copy Writing	60	Deliveries:	33
Art Direction	100	Misc. Materials:	7
Graphic Design	200	Photographer:	270
Production	35	Pre-press:	26
Typesetting	55		
		Total Fees:	$570
		Total Expenses:	$386
		Estimated Job Total:	$956

Copy Advice for Newspaper Ads

Use a lot of copy or very little; don't fall in between. A lot of copy makes an ad look informative, and that appeals to prospects who are seriously considering a purchase. Your ad will draw well-qualified inquiries. On the other hand, using just a little copy leaves room for a dramatic visual. Either is good. Fall in the middle, and you will lose pulling power.

Layout Advice for Newspaper Ads

Ads that work well in newspapers are usually simple in concept and visually bold. Often you'll see two-thirds or more of the ad space devoted to a photo. The reason: Newspapers are crowded-looking, with their multiple columns of small type. If you're buying a half-page ad (that's *big*!), the big picture in your ad will become the dominant element on the page, no matter what. Take advantage of this

and go for a dramatic shot. The Captain's Chair ad (Example 6-16) takes this concept to the extreme.

If you're like many advertisers, you're trying to stand out with an ad a fraction of that size. My best recommendation is to *get color into your ad*—in black and white. Even if you don't have a picture to dramatize your benefit, find a way to add shades of gray to your ad, so that it isn't just another mass of little words next to the news stories. You might use a light gray background behind everything. You could use a decorative border. Or use the white space in your ad creatively, so that it creates a "color" in comparison to the gray columns of type around it.

The ad for a musical performance in Example 6-14 pushes the "black and white in color" principle so far that you can practically hear the music.

Example 6-14: Cloud 9 Ad
Used by permission of Ron Paskin.

Many retailers have found catalog-style ads to be successful (see Example 6-15). These show as many as six or eight products accompanied by descriptions and prices. Because buyers look to the newspaper for information, these informative ads work well.

Example 6-15: Workbench Ad
Used by permission of Workbench.

Our Annual Storewide
Summer Sale
Save 20% - 40% on Almost Everything

Announcing our storewide Summer Sale. Where you can save 20%-40% on our timeless collections of modern classic furniture. You'll find great prices on exciting new upholstery, innovative storage systems, dining tables, chairs, desks, bedroom chests, butcher block, lamps and accessories. The list goes on and on but the sale doesn't.

Techline 3 pc. Desk System
Constructed with heavy 1 1/4" panels and durable melamine laminate. As shown 60" x 30" desk reg. $280 Sale $252; typing return reg. $189 Sale $170; 3 drawer pedestal reg. $254 Sale $228.

Our Big Bench Collection
Aptly named. Each oversized piece in natural cotton fabric features big, squishy loose-pillow styles for super-sized comfort reg. $1,375 Sale $1,099. Optional slipcover also available.

Colette Arm Chair
French Art Nouveau design in rich chenille fabric reg. $809 Sale $649.

Shaker Style Cherry Bedroom
New Shaker bedroom in cherrywood is as functional as it is beautiful. Queen Spindle Bedframe reg. $1,000 Sale $799. Horizontal Wardrobe reg. $1,435 Sale $1,149.

Classic Dining
Our classic dining table is available in teak and oak and has 2 hidden panels that extend to seat 8 reg. $560 Sale $439. Windsor chair reg. $165 Sale $129.

Soft Edge Bookcases
Work well in any room. Choose from 4 sizes, all with shaped edges in teak or oak veneer. Individual units reg. $215 - $300 Sale $169 - $239. Optional doors and extra shelves.

Shaker Wall System
Crafted in cherry solids and veneers our Shaker entertainment center combines bookcases flanking a deep TV cabinet. Optional doors and pull-out swivel shelf. System as shown reg. $3,615 Sale $2,887.

Drop Leaf Table
Fits in small places on small budgets. It features easy-clean white melamine top and sturdy beechwood base reg. $290 Sale $229. Solid beechwood chair reg. $100 Sale $79.

Madison • 414 N. Midvale Blvd. • 608-231-3711

workbench

Getting Started with Your Newspaper Ads

Template 6-10 shows some thumbnail sketches for newspaper ads. Note how many rely on symmetrical positioning of elements. There's a reason: The editorial part of the newspaper page is often laid out in a cluttered jumble. Orderly layout in the advertising makes it appealing by comparison.

These thumbnails are derived from the examples that appear throughout this chapter—can you match up the thumbnail with the ad?

Template 6-10: Thumbnails

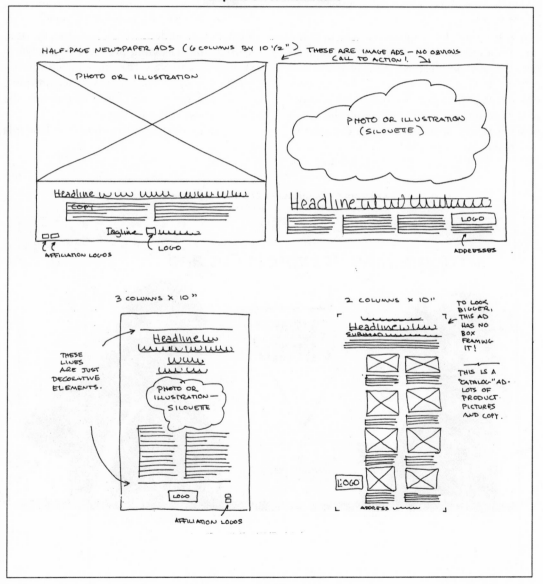

Now let's look at some case studies of companies using newspaper ads and how they went about it.

Case Study 1: Captain's Chair

What do you do when someone comes into town and starts selling what you sell at half the price and twice the convenience? Find a way to fight back, or run for cover. This kind of marketing threat requires a dramatic solution.

When bargain hair-care chains came into being, traditional styling salons had to come up with a quick response or start losing business. Some chose to stress the quality and skill of their service and stay out of the fast-and-cheap category. Captain's Chair chose to compete head-on. Its strategy: Revamp the menu of services so that it could offer a competitive low-price, no-appointment-necessary cut. How to do this? Eliminate the shampoo and blow-dry steps, but maintain the premium quality of the cut itself, and thus keep Captain's Chair positioned above the new walk-in services.

Captain's Chair planned a local media blitz to introduce the $8 no-appointment package, an aggressive campaign to outshine the bargain competitors. The media plan called for newspaper ads, billboards, and bus cards. The launch began with an orientation for the staff: Stylists from all Captain's Chair locations attended a training presentation, learned the reasoning behind the change in services, and saw the new ad campaign revealed. Later, phone surveys and individual store sales figures were used to measure the effectiveness of this campaign.

The newspaper ad is shown in Example 6-16.

Example 6-16: Captain's Chair Newspaper Ad
Used by permission of Captain's Chair Salons.

Dramatic, yes—the flirtatious play between the people pulls you in; the road sign drives home the benefit of the offering. This ad would be effective as a half-page ad; the visual and the white space around it would draw attention from the news stories around it. But Captain's Chair went further. It conquered space! This ad ran as a full page, at right angles to the normal orientation of the newspaper. Now the phrase "TURN A HEAD" took on double meaning. Play value like this—causing you to turn your head, or your newspaper, to look at the ad—makes for breakthrough advertising, whether in print or in direct mail. Boost that breakthrough power with the support of repetition in outdoor advertising, and you've got a campaign that makes news.

The downside? Cost, if you're not ready for it. The newspaper ad cost over $3,000 each time it ran. But here's why it made sense for Captain's Chair: The strategy—combining newspaper advertising with highly visible outdoor boards—built memorability fast. The trick was to get in, make an impact, and get out before the tab got too high. This makes sense only if you're selling a service or product that naturally builds loyalty, so that customers don't need your advertising to remind them to return. That describes hair care; if it describes your category of business, give this case study some thought. Maybe you should develop an ad campaign that comes on strong, makes news, then lets you take your new customers back to business as usual.

Case Study 2: Ginza (Japanese Cuisine)

Suppose your ad budget isn't equal to a short run of full-page ads. Even quarter-page ads are out of your league. Are you out of luck? Not at all. Take a look at Example 6-17.

Example 6-17A
Used by permission of Ginza of Tokyo.

Example 6-17B
Used by permission of Ginza of Tokyo.

Example 6-17C
Used by permission of Ginza of Tokyo.

Example 6-17D
Used by permission of Ginza of Tokyo.

GET SCALLOPED!

And enjoy it, at our new Sushi bar. Choose
from Scallops or any of 27 varieties of fresh or
cooked specialties from the sea uniquely prepared and served in the Sushi tradition.

HIBACHI TABLES   PRIVATE TEA ROOMS   SUSHI BAR

GINZA
J A P A N E S E
C U I S I N E

6734 Odana Road, Madison 833-8282
Open for lunch Mon.-Fri. 11-2, dinner served 7 days from 5 p.m.

Example 6-17E
Used by permission of Ginza of Tokyo.

ITCHIN' FOR URCHINS?

You'll find relief at our new Sushi bar. Choose
from Sea Urchins or any of 27 varieties of fresh or
cooked specialties from the sea uniquely prepared and served in the Sushi tradition.

HIBACHI TABLES   PRIVATE TEA ROOMS   SUSHI BAR

GINZA
J A P A N E S E
C U I S I N E

6734 Odana Road, Madison 833-8282
Open for lunch Mon.-Fri. 11-2, dinner served 7 days from 5 p.m.

Example 6-17F
Used by permission of Ginza of Tokyo.

FEEL LIKE EEL?

You can get your hands on some at our new
Sushi bar. Choose from Eel or any of 27
varieties of fresh or cooked specialties from
the sea uniquely prepared and served in the
Sushi tradition.

HIBACHI TABLES   PRIVATE TEA ROOMS   SUSHI BAR

GINZA
J A P A N E S E
C U I S I N E

6734 Odana Road, Madison 833-8282
Open for lunch Mon.-Fri. 11-2, dinner served 7 days from 5 p.m.

You're in the heart of the Midwest, it's the mid-1980s, and you want to sell raw fish to farmers. That's right, you're about to introduce sushi to Madison, Wisconsin. While we might take exception to being called "farmers," the truth is, people in this part of the world are pretty unadventurous about what they eat. So for Ginza the challenge is to reassure the public: This new kind of Japanese-style dining will be fun and tasty. Here's a series of small-space print ads designed to tickle the curiosity of consumers and create a desire to try unusual food. See how the short and silly headlines get your attention. Notice how the copy repeats one consistent thought with slight variations in each ad. Consistency in size and type style helps the individual ads to add up to a unified whole. The public soon started watching and wondering what the next silly seafood ad would say.

These are examples of ads that are very inexpensive to produce, but only if you're the type of creative writer who can give your copy this kind of punch. Otherwise you'll be investing in someone else's creative work. But after that, these ads can be produced on a tiny budget. There's no photo or illustration to pay for, and one layout works for all. The size of the ads is fairly small: these are "2x4s," or two-column by four-inch ads. They might cost about $225 to run in a daily paper in a mid-size community.

These ads are hard workers. They get attention by offering a little humor; they educate about a new way to dine; they create desire by positioning the restaurant as sophisticated and fun. Could this approach work for you?

Tips on Creating Ads for Magazines

Use the schedule in Template 6-11 to track the deadlines for each ad you place. Monthly magazines will typically "close" (stop accepting ad space reservations) on the twenty-fifth of the month for the issue coming up two months ahead. In other words, on the twenty-fifth of July, the September issue will close; on the twenty-fifth of August, the October issue will stop accepting space reservations, and so on. Your magazine ad reps will tell you how far in advance they will need your artwork. You usually have another week or two after you've reserved your space. If an ad rep mentions a "drop-dead" deadline, pay attention; this means what it says. Blow this deadline and you will pay for a blank space with no ad in it!

Template 6-11: Magazine Advertising Schedule

Date Prepared:					
Prepared by:					
		Magazine Name:		Magazine Name:	Magazine Name:
Cover Date	Art Due				
Month	To Magazine (Date)	Ad Size		Ad Size	Ad Size
January					
February					
March					
April					
May					
June					
July					
August					
September					
October					
November					
December					

If your magazine is not local, with ad reps who call on you in person, you will probably want to have a local freelance artist, graphic design firm, or ad agency prepare your artwork. Even if the magazine has an art department, I think it's just too hard to achieve good creative results long distance. Template 6-12 gives an example of a complex budget for using professionals to help in producing a series of magazine ads.

Template 6-12: Cost Estimate, Complex Print Ad Production

Job Description: 4 ads in series, full process color
5 duplicate sets of each for multiple publications
4 photos requiring special effects and props

Fees:		Expenses:	
Meetings & Administration	$240	Scans:	720
Copy Writing	700	Deliveries:	125
Art Direction	850	Misc. Materials:	55
Graphic Design	510	Props:	235
Production	400	Photographer:	1990
Typesetting	380	Pre-press:	1950
		Total Fees:	$3,080
		Total Expenses:	$5,075
		Estimated Job Total:	$8,155

Copy Advice for Magazine Ads

Tone and style are very important in magazine ads. The higher quality of printing means that you can convey tone more precisely than you can in newspapers. Mostly you will do that through layout decisions, but take advantage of it in your copywriting as well! Push your language to make it more colorful. Use more story-telling techniques than you would in the newspaper. Create characters, and write dialogue. Capture a sense of place. Evoke a mood. People read magazines for entertainment—and that includes the advertisements.

Layout Advice for Magazine Ads

Magazines have the highest quality of printing, and they pay more attention to graphic design than newspapers. Successful advertisers realize the advantage of looking as sharp as the surrounding editorial pages. Design your ad in the context of the specific magazines you will use. Study the editorial style: Is it upbeat? Chaotic? Zany? Does it have type on angles, different type styles on every page, bright colors and zig-zag borders? Or does it fall at the other end of the spectrum: conservative, traditional, spare? Compare an issue of *Outside* with *The New Yorker*. The style of the ads is very different for these two publications.

Colors reproduce well in magazines. Use bold, bright colors with confidence—if they help get your message across. Or you can use colors in more sophisticated ways. But remember, a little goes a long way—undisciplined use of color is distracting. Photographs convey mood or ambiance very well in magazines. If you have chosen a positioning strategy of product usage, this is your perfect opportunity to illustrate the product in use in a story-telling way. Hiking boots seen from a worm's-eye view after finally reaching the mountaintop, herbal tea enjoyed under a warm coverlet by a mother reading to her child—these are examples of product usage translated into emotive visual images.

A word of advice for advertising in trade journals: Don't waste your ad space restating the obvious. If your ad is in *T-Shirt Retailer,* your headline doesn't have to say "New Product for T-Shirt Retailers!" Start from where your audience is, and take them further. An image that communicates a key benefit will be more effective than a picture of someone in a T-shirt.

Getting Started with Your Magazine Ads

Template 6-13 shows some thumbnails to help you visualize your magazine ad. Because the visual (whether it is a photo or an illustra-tion) is so important, the placement of other elements is kept very simple. Review your creative approach and look for the Big Visual Idea!

Template 6-13: Thumbnails

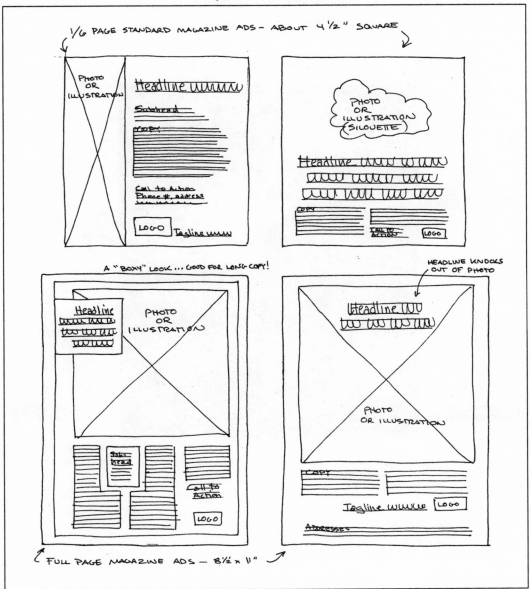

Now, let's review a case study of successful magazine advertising.

Magazine Case Study: Stardust

A booming industry exists around the imprinting of T-shirts and other activewear for teams, clubs, events, and the retail market. The shirts, sweatpants, and sweatshirts are basically commodity products; most brands are nearly identical, and buyers make their decisions more on the basis of availability and price. Distributors operate on narrow margins, and each is making basically the same promise—we've got it in stock, we'll get it to you fast, and you'll pay a low price. How is one distributor to stand out in the crowd?

The series of ads in Example 6-18 answered that question for a client of mine. We used an unexpected image—the archery target—to visually illustrate our metaphor: Stardust is on target.

Example 6-18A and B
Used by permission of Stardust Corp.

Example 6-18C and D
Used by permission of Stardust Corp.

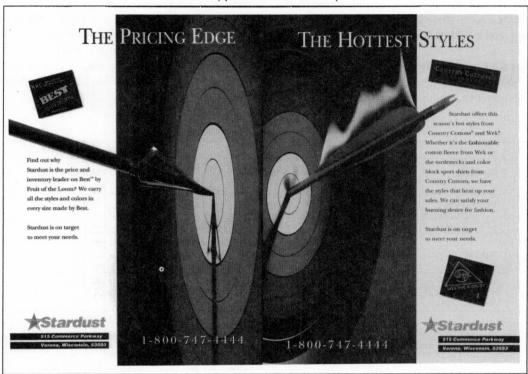

How did we come up with that idea? I hate to admit it, but the client handed it to us. We'd been trying for weeks to come up with something breakthrough that wouldn't break his bank. Everything we presented smelled like stale fish to him. Then he brought out an ad he'd seen in a different industry's trade journal. Anyone could see how the idea could work for this market. (Note an important point here: You can get ideas for your ad from others who are not necessarily in the same business as you.)

The bright primary colors related to popular product colors. The big, simple image had dramatic visual impact. There wasn't a T-shirt in sight. We had to admit the concept was good.

We massaged the idea a little, trying different ways to show the arrow hitting the target and different points for the copy (excuse the pun). We worked our different manufacturers' brand names into the copy and showed their logos, so that we could earn co-op support. (We used the product tags rather than the actual company logos, to avoid visual competition with the Stardust logo.) The co-op rules required that the manufacturers' logos be as big as ours, and so we kept ours fairly small. The big photos gave the ads more power than big logos would, and kept the ads focused on the benefit to the customer. Throughout the series, Stardust comes across as confident and powerful.

The ads ran in several trade journals, frequently with several per issue, on consecutive pages. The net result: a satisfying increase in response over previous years' advertising. The message for you: Good ideas can come from anywhere. Don't get me wrong—I'm not recommending that you steal someone else's creative work. But if you look around, you're likely to find ideas that you can adapt to your situation, while adding your own unique twist.

Tips on Creating Directory Ads

Start with a worksheet to project your directory placement costs. Template 6-14A gives an example of such a sheet for my business, and Template 6-14B is a blank that you can use for your analysis. Check with your Yellow Pages or other directory representative to find out when your deadlines fall. Directories come out only once a year or even once every two years, so don't let those deadlines slip by!

Template 6-14A: Directory Advertising Analysis Example

Ad Copy	Directory	Headings	Size	Monthly Rate
WHITE SPACE DESIGN — Free Initial Meeting & Estimate Direct Mail · Corp ID · Packaging Annual Reports · Brochures · Ads 849 E Wash Av ———— 251-7329	Madison Yellow Pages	Advertising Agencies	1/2" (in-column)	$33.50
WHITE SPACE DESIGN 849 E Wash Av ———— 251-7329	Yellow Pages	Desktop Publishing	Standard Free Listing	$0
WHITE SPACE DESIGN — Free Initial Meeting & Estimate Direct Mail · Corp ID · Packaging Annual Reports · Brochures · Ads 849 E Wash Av ———— 251-7329	Yellow Pages	Graphic Designers	1/2"	$33.50
WHITE SPACE DESIGN — Free Initial Meeting & Estimate Direct Mail · Corp ID · Packaging Annual Reports · Brochures · Ads 849 E Wash Av ———— 251-7329	Southern Wisconsin Business-to-Business	Advertising Agencies	1/2"	$48.00
WHITE SPACE DESIGN — Free Initial Meeting & Estimate Direct Mail · Corp ID · Packaging Annual Reports · Brochures · Ads 849 E Wash Av ———— 251-7329	So. Wisc. Business-to-Business	Graphic Designers	1/2"	$48.00
Total Investment				$163.00

Template 6-14B: Directory Analysis Blank

Ad Copy	Directory	Headings	Size	Monthly Rate
Total Investment				

A worksheet like this can help you see "the big picture" in your directory advertising. First assemble your current directory advertising in this format. Then try some variations and see what objectives you can achieve.

How about production costs? If your directory ad is straightforward—just type, and maybe a logo—let the directory produce it for you. If you would like to provide camera-ready art, look back to the budget for newspaper ads. There's really no difference between producing an ad for one and for the other.

Copy and Layout Advice for Directory Advertising

People look at directories *when they're ready to buy*. Prospects will be making comparisons between you and your competitors when they look you up in the Yellow Pages or your trade directory. In this category more than any other, it makes sense to start by studying your competition.

Think of your three closest competitors. Look at the size of the ads they are placing and the categories they choose to list under. You will want to make your ad of equal size (not larger unless you have aggressive growth goals and your budget can stand it). Look at the benefit statements they are making and the enticements they offer. You will want your copy to be equally compelling. If you can make a statement using the word *free*, this is the place to do it! "Free Estimates" or "Free Initial Consultation" is a good way to get your phone to ring.

Getting Started with Your Directory Ads

I don't need to do thumbnails for directory ads for you: you have a whole book on the subject close by. Leaf through your industry directory or Yellow Pages and you will pretty quickly get a sense for what works well.

For a crash course in using Yellow Pages advertising, turn to the category "Florists" in your local book. Note what benefit statements the advertisers make, and how they use positioning to differentiate themselves. Some might emphasize service— "Deliveries Citywide" or "Same Day Delivery Anywhere"— while others emphasize product— "The Rose Specialists" or "Everything but the Ordinary." What advertising strategies do you see here that you could apply to your own directory ad? Besides florists, check other categories, including the one for your business. You'll see lots of ways you might create your ad. And your directory advertising rep will assist you in creating your ad, as well.

Outdoor and Transit Advertising

Billboards, bus cards, and other local "out of home" advertising round out your options in print media. This category's special power is that it reaches geographically targeted markets without the fragmentation of radio. It reaches everybody in a car, not just those tuned to one particular station. If you truly want to reach nearly everybody in town and you want to make a big impression, think outdoor.

The cost per thousand works out to be very attractive, because outdoor media reach so many people so often. Both the circulation and the frequency (number of repeat exposures) are great—within an extremely specific geographic area. Outdoor advertising can be quite inexpensive in comparison with other media. Production is easy compared with other types of print ads. The sign company does all the work to assemble words and images into giant art—at little or no charge.

Advertising on billboards might be the breakthrough you've been looking for, if your market is concentrated in one area.

Look at your mass transit options as well. Buses offer display space on the sides, rear, and interior surfaces (see Example 6-19). The artwork can tie in to themes in your print or radio advertising, for an effective, well-rounded campaign. Costs for transit advertising will be similar to those for billboards.

Transit ads reach people when they are out during the daytime and are not where they can be reached by radio or TV commercials. Like all outdoor advertising, they can be located close to where the shopper buys the product. That means that if you use transit ads, people are likely to see your ad one moment and be ready to make a purchase the next. I've seen retail businesses that anticipate spur-of-the-moment purchases, such as fast-food restaurants and quick-cut hair salons, target the bus routes that bring customers past their stores.

Example 6-19: Milan's Bus Card
Used by permission of Milan's.

Tips on Creating Ads for Billboards and Other Out-of-Home Media

In most midsize cities, one company usually owns most of the billboards in town. Therefore, you will probably need to contact only one firm to get the scoop on outdoor advertising in your area. Negotiating your schedule and locations will be simple. Be aware that in larger cities there are more likely to be several companies, and so putting together a really high-impact campaign will be harder.

Meet with the outdoor advertising sales reps who cover your area. (Look at the bottom of a billboard in a location that interests you, where you'll find a company name, or check your phone directory.) Sales reps for these companies can be very helpful in preparing

your calendar and budget. They will show you maps with locations and routes where advertising is available, and explain the programs offered.

Keep in mind that demand exceeds supply, so plan ahead if you want specific times and places. It's a fact of life that in outdoor advertising, you have to take some "bad" locations to get the "good" ones. An outdoor program will rotate your ad from one position to another. In a midsize suburban community, a billboard program might cost from $4,000 to upwards of $20,000 monthly, so it's not inexpensive. But done right, it can get you a lot of exposure. The map in Example 6-20 shows the Adams Company billboard locations in Madison, Wisconsin.

Example 6-20: Adams Billboard location map
Used by permission of Adams Outdoor Advertising.

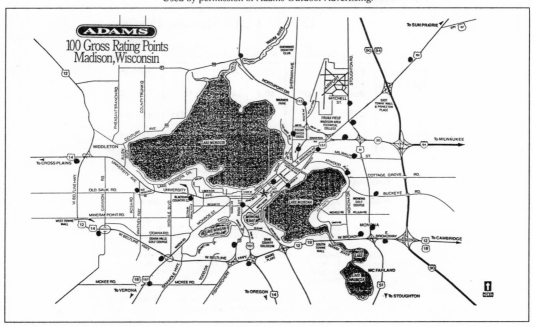

Billboards come in two sizes; these are industry standards that have evolved over the years. The smaller size is the *poster panel*, which is 12 by 24 feet, or about 300 square feet. Posters are usually printed by a press on

squares of paper that are then pasted in position on the billboard. These last about thirty days before needing to be replaced. A process for developing near photographic quality for billboards has become popular lately, and computer-driven painting on vinyl is another option. Poster panel-type billboards are usually located on main streets (not freeways) in town. They are often found in older parts of town.

Over the past several years, a new, larger-size billboard, the *Bulletin*, which is 14 by 48 feet, has become popular. These are high-impact signs that present a premium image. They are usually either painted or produced by computer-driven painting machines, often with very striking and realistic results. These kinds of billboards frequently feature images that extend beyond the square surface. These cutouts, or extensions, are not that expensive—typically, about $20 to $50 per square foot.

Production costs are relatively inexpensive, about $150 to $200 per poster for printing up the panels. Outdoor advertising companies often have in-house design departments to help you come up with an appropriate design for your ad. You simply need to provide them with a layout, or ask for their creative help.

The Costs of Outdoor Advertising

The costs for outdoor advertising, like those for magazines, are given on a rate card. Example 6-21 shows a rate card for a poster panel program. This program allows you to choose from a menu the plan that fits your budget. Here's what the columns on the card mean:

Example 6-21: Adams 1994 Poster Rates
Used by permission of Adams Outdoor Advertising.

ADAMS — 1994 Rates

12' x 24' Poster Showing Program

Market	Showing	# Of Panels	Reach	Freq.	Monthly Space Cost	Guaranteed Daily Impressions
Madison/ Core	#25	8	76.2	8.4	$4,000	62,500
	#50	16	86.4	14.75	$8,000	125,000
	#75	20	90.6	21.1	$10,000	187,500
	#100	26	96.7	27.5	$13,000	250,000

Post Dates: Posting takes place every Monday.

Production: Approximate cost per poster is $85-$130 for flat color. No additional charge for assistance with art and layout.

Allow at least 2 weeks for printing. Posters must be delivered to Adams by the Friday preceding the post date.

Suburban Towns Available:
Belleville   Blue Mounds   Cambridge   Cross Plains
Deerfield   Lodi   Mt. Horeb   North Leeds
Oregon   Stoughton   Sun Prairie   Verona
Waunakee

Illuminated: Approximately 50% of locations per showing are illuminated. These locations are illuminated until midnight.

* Suburban towns can be added individually.

Rates are subject to change without notice.

L/94

Adams Outdoor Advertising
102 East Badger Road, Madison, Wisconsin 53713. (608) 271-7900. (608) 271-4253 (FAX)

- *Market*: This is the geographical area covered. The company will provide you with a map of this.

- *Showing*: This is the percent of saturation of the market that you are buying. A "#50 showing" means that you're getting seen by half the available market on any one day. A "#100 showing" tells you that you have the maximum coverage available—a 100 percent saturation.

- *Number of panels*: This is the amount of space you'll be contracting for. You might compare this to the number of insertions on a magazine rate card. For example, "8" means that your artwork is physically on eight different billboards throughout a thirty-day period. For CPM calculations, use this number in the frequency column (see Template 6-2C).

- *Reach*: This cumulative total measures the percentage of the total market that you've gotten in front of during those thirty days. In other words, for a #25 from this card, you will reach at least 76.2 percent of the total population of the area at least once during the month. This percentage figure is based on traffic counts and statistical calculations. It is different from showings, which is the number of guaranteed daily impressions.

- *Frequency*: This calculation tells you how many times on average one person will see one billboard in one month. This is different from what we've been calling frequency with magazine rate cards (which has to do with the number of insertions of your ad in different issues), so don't get the two concepts confused.

- *Guaranteed daily impressions*: This is just another way of expressing the showings. This example tells you that the total population of Madison is 250,000 people; choosing #75 or #50 or #25 delivers a corresponding percentage of that population.

The rate card for bulletins or for bus cards will be structured just the same. Only the rates and sizes will change.

Using Outdoor Advertising

It's this ability to deliver almost all of a city's population that makes outdoor media so appealing. Outdoor advertising is great if you want to build name awareness or if you are introducing a new product or if your business has changed its name or location. If you want to make a splash, publicize an event, or launch some sort of program, think outdoor.

Here's a plan for you to consider: The outdoor advertising company may offer short-term programs for one or two weeks that are very affordable. Tie one of those in with some newspaper advertising, as Captain's Chair did (see the newspaper case study), and you'll see a dramatic impact in a hurry.

Negotiating your contract is simple: Since the outdoor company has only a limited number of posters, bulletins, and buses to fill, the law of supply and demand is in force. Working with your rep, you'll figure out a schedule and rotation, and a monthly cost. Don't expect a lot of negotiating in your rates. You may be able to pick up bonus showings, but basically there are more buyers than there are locations to sell. So plan ahead if you want to be choosy about precise locations. Some high-visibility boards have waiting lists as long as a year.

Copy and Layout Advice for Outdoor Advertising

From a creative standpoint, treat outdoor advertising the way you would radio. You have only a few seconds with your viewers, and they're doing something else—driving, probably—while you're together. Your ad message must be direct. Keep the copy short—just a sentence. Print may be the medium of choice for complex messages, but not on billboards. Save your long explanations for your newspaper or magazine ads.

Humor is a good choice for billboards. It's easier to write a funny billboard than a funny ad. Look at Example 6-22. This Greyhound Racing billboard works purely on wordplay. This board won awards in local and regional advertising competitions.

Example 6-22: Geneva Lakes Greyhound Racing Billboard
Used by permission of Abbey Group.

The Schoep's billboard (Example 6-23) was an award winner as well. Why is the Schoep's billboard appealing? There is humor in both the style of the cartoon and the way it works with the headline. The whole idea is colorful, and consistent with our belief in ice cream as a fun treat.

Example 6-23: Schoep's Sundae Driver Billboard
Used by permission of Schoep's Ice Cream.

Successful outdoor advertising relies on creativity, and you must express your ideas with brevity and visual drama. Your sales rep can show you examples that prove this point. Note how parts of the Schoep's ad extend over the top of the billboard. This is an excellent way to "push the creative envelope."

Getting Started with Outdoor Advertising

Ask your outdoor rep for samples of the company's work. Pay attention to the quality of the execution. Don't be too concerned about how to produce the billboard. The company you contract with will guide you. Focus your attention on what the creative message should be. Even though you're only looking for five to ten words, it might make sense to hire a free-lance copywriter to help you. That's how critical finding the *right* words is.

You've probably noticed "teaser" campaigns in your community. First part of an image is displayed, then, after two weeks go by, the "answer" is added. These campaigns get great results. Any idea that works on scale seems to work very well on billboards. Taking small images, like a mosquito or a paper clip, and blowing them up to 25 feet across just naturally appeals to people's sense of humor. Puns are well loved for the same reason. Check out billboards around your town for the use of these two devices.

You may find some excellent creative talent on the outdoor company's staff. Bring them any ideas you have, and ask for a proposal. It's the quality of the *creative* work that makes a billboard campaign stand out. And it's not that expensive to produce a breakthrough idea.

I could tell you case studies about billboards in my city, but I recommend that you talk to a rep from your own community. That won't cost you anything except an hour or two. You'll be surprised how familiar you are with companies that have successfully used outdoor advertising (and that use may be one reason you are so familiar with them). And that proves my point: Good outdoor advertising gets remembered. If your prospective customers are driving around your city daily, reach out and grab them with outdoor media. Outdoor advertising is affordable, it's fun, and it gets noticed.

If You Decide to Take on Your Advertising Program All by Yourself

I have seen entrepreneurs take on every stage of the marketing/advertising cycle, right up to producing full-color product catalogs from home on their Macs. It didn't happen without a *lot* of sweat and excellent coaching. And that's my point: Creating your own print ads is relatively simple by comparison. Just make sure you have adequate time to learn as you go along, and line up your teachers. This book can get you started, and the production staff at the publication you're advertising in can help you along the way.

Some Technical Terms for Print Production

Silhouettes. These are photos that have the background removed. People or objects stand alone in the white space around them. Finding the edge and removing the unwanted image area requires handwork, and whether this is done mechanically or on computer, there will be a charge for doing it.

Knockouts. This refers to making type or artwork "knock out" of a photo or field of color. The body of the type or art shows through as the color of the paper "underneath" the photo. This is also called "reversing out." Computers make this effect simple to achieve, and so there should be no extra charge.

Halftones and screens. Shades of gray in print are called "screens" because they're made up of a mesh of halftone dots that are printed solid black but give the illusion of a smooth gray surface. Photos are screened, or "half-toned," to translate them into dots for printing.

Color separations. Color pictures are scanned and separated into four separate screened images, which print in the standard process colors of cyan, magenta, yellow, and black. As these colors lay their patterns of dots one on top of the other, the illusion of a full-color image is created on paper.

Flat colors (also called tints). These are created out of combinations of screens. Computers make it easy to add these screens, but there's one detail you need to know if you use them. Each publication will have a preferred line screen frequency which you must use in your ad negative. This frequency will probably be

- 85-line screen for newspapers
- 100-line screen for newsletters and directories on uncoated (not glossy) paper
- 133-line screen for most magazines

When you sign your advertising contract, ask for the mechanical specifications for advertising. These will tell you the screen to use. Provide this information to the service that makes the negatives you send to the magazine.

Dot gain. This is another measure that will affect print reproduction. When those printed dots hit paper, each one spreads slightly as the ink is absorbed by the paper. On highly absorbent paper, like that on which most newspapers and directories are printed, the degree of dot gain can be as much as 5 or 10 percent. To compensate for this, you will want to make your screens lighter by that amount. A glossy magazine might have dot gain of 2 percent. Again, you should talk directly with your publication's production department to find out the best settings for the publication's reproduction process.

The Budget for the Print Ad

How tightly do you want to control the process? How much are you planning to spend? To answer these questions, you'll need to prepare a budget. These items should appear on your worksheet for estimating the cost of creating a print ad:

Creative fees: If you are working with an agency, you might be billed for services related to administering the project, art direction (working with photographers and illustrators), writing, graphic design, and production and typesetting. Be sure you and your account rep are clear about which services you have requested, so that you know what you will be billed for.

Production expenses: Included here are

- Scans (process color separations or gray-scale scans, which convert the photo or illustration into an electronic file)
- Deliveries (around town, or shipping to final destinations)
- Illustrations (the creation of original art, or use or permission fees for using existing art)
- Models and stylists (personnel who assist at photo shoots)
- Photography (typically time and materials will be broken out on the photographer's estimate)
- Pre-press services (creation of the actual plate-ready films and their accompanying proofs)
- Miscellaneous expenses (if this area of the estimate is over $100, ask for a breakdown or "guesstimate" of what it might cover.)

For an example of a complex budget, see the tips for magazine ads (Template 6-12). For an example of a simpler budget, see the tips for newspaper ads (Template 6-9).

What Do You Send to the Media?

Each publication will have guidelines regarding how materials should be submitted. Your advertising rep or the publication's production manager will tell you exactly what the publication needs. Do not guess on this point! Your ad's appearance may suffer. Make the phone calls to find out what you should provide.

Everyone wants "camera-ready art." For a newspaper or directory, this will usually mean reflective copy (black type and artwork on high-resolution white paper), with any screens at a frequency of 85 lines or coarser. (See the sidebar on technical terms for print production for an explanation of screen frequencies.) For magazines, the artwork should be negatives, accompanied by a contact print if the ad is black and white, or a color proof if the ad is four-color. Magazines will usually request screens at a 133-line frequency.

For billboards, your artwork will be a layout for the company's painters and artists to follow. Again, I would emphasize that you should let the advertising vehicle specify exactly how it wants the artwork prepared, then follow these specifications to the letter.

What's the Story on Co-op?

Co-op means that your suppliers will share your advertising expenses if you feature their products as part of your ad. The Stardust ads shown in Example 6-18 mentioned various T-shirt companies so that the Stardust company could get part of its costs reimbursed by the likes of Hanes and Fruit of the Loom. Manufacturers may not promote their co-op programs, but almost every product for sale has some version of co-op support behind it. If you distribute or retail a product, you can probably find a co-op program that will help

pay for your advertising—it's worth doing some research to find out.

A co-op program will have restrictions covering how the manufacturer's product is to be shown, how it is to be referred to in copy, and how the manufacturer's logo is to be used. There are usually guidelines like "our logo must be the same size as your logo, and 50 percent larger than any competing brand's logo." The manufacturer's goal is to dominate your ad, and its rules may be too restricting for you. On the other hand, the dollars the manufacturer will rebate to you might be worth the compromise.

To qualify for a co-op program, you submit your ad layout and copy for approval before the ad appears, then file tearsheets and receipts after the ad appears. The rules can be complicated, but don't be put off by them. The money you save is worth the effort of compliance.

Testing Your Ads

The big players in the advertising game do some very refined research on their ads. Focus groups help shape their messages before we ever see them. Then ads are run in test markets, and statistical analyses of responses suggest further refinements in the ad schedule or message. Big corporations aren't known for taking chances. They've done what they can to make advertising a science, where results can be predicted and success can be measured in dollars.

Just because you can't afford to approach testing your ads in the same way they do doesn't mean that you shouldn't learn from their example. And remember, you use testing to confirm your hunches. You'll start to get a sense for what kind of ads work for you. Don't expect testing to yield competitive scores; just remember that your goal is to create better and better advertising. Now let's talk a little more about how to do that.

Inquiry Tests

Your goal in doing an inquiry test is to be able to track how many inquiries resulted from each advertisement you ran and each publication it appeared in. You'll use this information to guide future decisions about where to advertise, and also about what message pulls the most response.

Put a code in the coupon or paragraph in which you state your offer. It might be a post office box, a department number, or simply a code you make up that is printed on the card that is returned. For call-in responses, you can arrange for a special phone number if you expect a large response.

This would be a good time for you to review the sales promotion strategies from Chapter 3. We discussed several techniques for increasing response by making short-term special offers.

You can speed up your learning curve if you do A/B splits. This refers to changing one factor at a time as you proceed. For example, you might place two ads with different copy in the same periodical; the first ad might appear in June, the second ad in July, and so on. The differences between the two ads being tested might be differences in copy approach, visual style, or offer. You might raise or lower a price; test a funny headline against a straightforward one; change a picture or a typeface. The trick is to stop at changing only one thing.

By changing one factor at a time, keeping careful records about what works when, and allowing a broad enough frame of data collection (sometimes this takes years, if your ad budget and market are small), over time, you will craft an advertisement that works well for you. Because people and situations are always evolving, you will never arrive at the ultimate perfect ad. Times change, and so will your ads—and, indeed, what you offer. Keep altering and testing, and yours will be a smooth evolution.

Are You Measuring Inquiries or Sales?

It takes a little more thoroughness to track inquiries through to the resulting sales. What you learn may be invaluable, though. If you

track both inquiries and orders, you can begin to test which ads pull *sales*.

This isn't science. Several factors you can't control can skew your test results. Your slight tweak in the ad copy might have coincided with a general shift in the public's taste. Popular taste is a swiftly moving target!

If your offerings are radically different, you're testing apples against oranges. A change in the value of your offer is not fair unless you're testing specific price points to find that comfortable place where the offer is attractive, but you're not giving away the store. Test other variables first if you're fairly confident that your price offer is what it should be. Maybe a simple change to a more legible type will boost sales for you. Why discount your price before you test the other possibilities?

Page sequence—where your ad gets placed in the magazine—has a lot to do with how well your ad will pull responses. You can control where the newspaper or magazine places your ad, but you should be prepared to pay a premium for this. Your A/B split test can be nullified by placements that are too dissimilar. If the magazine you choose accepts heavy-paper inserts or catalogs as bind-in advertising, the "flippability" of the magazine changes radically. If your ad is a couple of pages from one of these heavy inserts, it might as well not be there at all. But if it lands on the facing page, you've gotten a windfall.

How Frequently Do You Advertise?

Sometimes timing alone will act as a variable in your ad response. If you're a retail business with a style niche or a quick-turning inventory, you're probably in the local newspapers on a nearly daily basis. You can tinker with your ad message and see results quickly, without fear that a change of seasons has skewed your response. But if you're a provider of professional services—a lawyer, architect, or insurance professional, for example—you face a tougher challenge in testing. You probably have fewer media outlets to choose from: perhaps a city magazine or the weekly business section of the local paper. Since consistency of image is important in selling these types of services, tinkering with the components of your ad strategy will be a much subtler, more long-term activity for you.

And finally, there's the sheer randomness of life to take into account. People selling loans and building supplies experience booms after natural disasters. It has very little to do with their advertising.

Summary: Print Advertising that Sells

Almost every business will use print advertising at some point in its advertising cycle. Whether it's magazines, newspapers, directo-ries, or outdoor boards, the print ad is a key tool for accomplishing marketing goals. Using what you've learned in this chapter, you should be able to decide where to advertise, and you should be able to negotiate a fair price for the ads you place.

As you craft your ads, make sure the copy follows the five-point structure we've discussed. Then critique the layout: Is it a skillful combination of art, copy, and white space?

Produce and run your ads (and use co-op support from manufacturers to offset your costs). Test your ads, and make refinements until you're satisfied with the results you're getting.

Sound like a lot of work? Of course it is. That's how you create print ads that sell.

Chapter 7

All about Radio Advertising

Birds are chirping. Someone is sawing wood; the rhythmic scraping disturbs the calm.

"Hey, should you be sitting up on that branch?"

"Dad's showing us how to trim our trees."

"But if he cuts the branch he's sitting on he'll fall …"

Your hand was moving toward the dash to change the station, but you stop. What's going on here? You've created a mental picture, and now it won't let you leave the scene. Is Dad going to wind up in the hospital? What could this possibly be about?

An independent community bank is running a radio commercial touting its stability. This aired in 1992, when failures in the savings and loan industry were stirring up distrust of banks in general. The big financial institutions were rapidly expanding into small towns, coming on strong with marketing campaigns from the home office. Independent banks were feeling the heat. The Independent Bankers Association of Wisconsin produced a marketing kit its members could purchase. The kit included everything from camera-ready art for newspaper ads to radio commercials, prerecorded and ready to run. Example 7-1 gives the scripts for two of these commercials.

Example 7-1A: Radio Commercial 1

Used by permission of Independent Bankers Association of Wisconsin.

Independent Bankers Association of Wisconsin
Independently Healthy Promotion

Sixty Second Radio Commercial #1, "Mattress"

SFX:	*Off key bugle call.*
Dad:	Family! Atten. . . shun!
SFX:	*Feet shuffling together.*
Anncr:	Why do you have your family standing at attention on a mattress?
Dad:	It's top secret.
Anncr:	Oh?
Dad:	We could tell you, but then we'd have to shoot you.
Anncr:	With broomstick handles?
Mom:	We don't believe in guns.
Anncr:	You aren't by any chance hiding money in there are you?
Dad:	Family! Prepare arms!
SFX:	*Sticks and feet shuffling.*
Anncr:	Don't you know about your independent community bank?
Kid:	Dad says, "today's financial institutions lack the safety and security of the modern box spring."
Dad:	No talking in the ranks.
Anncr:	But your independent community bank is different. It's independent of the outside controls and risky investments that are hurting some institutions and it's community owned and operated so your money goes to work right here.
Mom:	Will they take queen-size deposits?
Anncr:	If you take it out of the mattress first.
Dad:	How about king-sized loans?
Anncr:	Your independent community bank knows you and will always be there to help.
Dad:	Family! Atten. . . shun! Forward march!
SFX:	*Marching feet (fades to end).*
Anncr:	Where are you going?
Dad:	Our independent community bank. I'm going to put this family at ease.
Family:	Hooray!
SFX:	*Dog barks*
	(Insert local announcer tag here)
Tag:	Your independent community bank in (*City or Town*) is the (*Bank Name*). Independently Healthy. Member F.D.I.C.

Example 7-1B: Radio Commercial 2
Used by permission of Independent Bankers Association of Wisconsin.

Independent Bankers Association of Wisconsin
Independently Healthy Promotion

Sixty Second Radio Commercial #2, "Branch"

SFX:	*Birds chirping. Sawing wood by hand.*
Anncr:	Hey, should you be sitting up on that branch?
Kid:	Dad's showing us how to trim trees.
Anncr:	But if he cuts the branch he's sitting on he'll fall. . .
Dad:	Just a few more strokes and. . .
Anncr:	Shouldn't this be left to professionals?
Mom:	Let's just say our financial institution saw it another way.
Anncr:	They wouldn't trim your trees?
Mom:	No, they wouldn't give us the home improvement loan that would've paid for it.
Anncr:	Was this the independent community bank?
Mom:	No, it was that big financial branch.
Anncr:	No wonder.
Mom:	There's a difference?
Anncr:	You bet. Unlike the branch of mega money center, your independent bank is deeply rooted in the community. It's independent of the outside control and risky investments that make some institutions shaky. And it's community owned and operated so all decisions are made right here.
Mom:	Like who gets loans.
Anncr:	Exactly. Rely on someone else's financial branch and you could find yourself out on a limb.
Mom:	Honey, I think you should come down and listen to. . . oh, hi.
Dad:	What were you saying about big financial branches?
Kid:	Timber!
SFX:	*Branch crackles and limb comes crashing down.*
Anncr:	I think you just illustrated my point.
	(Insert local announcer tag here)
Tag:	Your independent community bank in (*City or Town*) is the (*Bank Name*). Independently Healthy. Member F.D.I.C.

Why were these commercials successful? Partly because they were part of larger campaigns, involving print media and public relations as well. This is important, because you should remember the context of the whole advertising plan when you look at the individual components like radio.

The campaign had timing going for it: It addressed a topic that was on people's minds, and did it in a friendly, reassuring way.

But mostly, it succeeded because it did what radio is good at: It involved the listener creatively, and prompted a positive perception about the advertiser.

How did it do this? By sound effects—the creator has instantly given us a sense of place.

By techniques of storytelling—the script unfolds like a play, introducing characters, showing action. The imagery is poetic—the tree and its branches. And most of all, it's relevant to the point of the commercial—that branches are unstable. The play on words linking tree branches to bank branches gives the commercial a memorable hook. And that's why it's good advertising.

This chapter will cover what you need to know to advertise on the radio. We'll talk about why you might want to; how to choose which radio station to advertise on, how to budget your production costs, and how to craft the radio commercial. In Chapter 4, "Writing a Media Plan," we introduced some ideas about radio, how the ratings work, and how to compare radio with other options in your media mix. Now it's time to go into detail. Let's start with a review: What are the particular strengths of radio?

Why Radio?

The radio is a trusted friend. It's the voice that keeps us company through the night on a long drive. It's the man we love to hate on the talk station. It's the hushed voice of the ballgame announcer when we surreptitiously listen at our desks. The same box that brought us rock 'n' roll songs in high school brings us news as it happens today. It's the sound track of many people's day. From wake-up call on through the day, the radio is playing in the workplace, the car, and the kitchen.

Radio is habit-forming. People will choose three or four stations that suit their tastes and then flip between them, and they'll usually listen at the same time every day.

The great thing about radio, if you're an advertiser, is that you have a captive audience. Your listener can't skip past the ads back to the programs. That gives you a golden opportunity to grab interest, convey excitement, and deliver information. How you do that we'll discuss in detail later in this chapter.

The intrusiveness of radio can be very involving. If your commercial asks a question and leaves a dramatic pause, you can bet that the listener will be involved with you in a way that's unique to radio. If your commercial yells, "Hey, Dad" and it's playing at the beach, watch all the fathers look around.

Radio can be very intimate, speaking one-on-one, announcer and listener.

Radio invokes the imagination of listeners, who have to create the "picture" for themselves. That's why radio attracts such great creative work. Through the tools of production—the voices, the music, the sound effects—you can project a whole movie in the listener's head. See the scripts in Example 7-1.

Radio has attributes that will please the bean counters as well as the creative minds in your organization. Radio stations deliver a specific geographic market, well targeted to certain demographics and lifestyles. Radio reaches a highly mobile group of people; they take radio with them wherever they go, listening in their cars, around their yards, and at the beach.

Statistics

61 percent of adults have radios at work.

99 percent of all homes have radios (with an average of 5.6 per home!).

95 percent of all cars have radio.

Source: Radio Advertising Bureau, Inc.

Air time is available at comparatively low cost. That makes radio an excellent medium for the budget-conscious media planner. Creating radio spots doesn't cost a lot of money either. You can get into radio for less than $500 if you produce one commercial and run it a dozen times or more.

Radio is a newsy, urgent medium. Last-minute changes are easy to make, so radio conveys a sense of immediacy that other media lack.

As listeners, most people don't draw too fine a distinction between the programs and the commercials. It's all just "the radio" to us. If we feel a sense of confidence in the accuracy and immediacy of the news programming, we extend that confidence to the news sponsors. If we identify with the entertainment programs, we tend to identify with the advertisers on those programs. Radio listeners are very loyal that way.

Who Should Use Radio?

Banks. Car dealers. Consumer brands. Restaurants and cafes. Retail stores. OK, the answer isn't quite as simple as that—but if you're on this list, don't skip this chapter. Radio is as good a value as newspaper advertising for small business, in terms of response generated per dollar spent. Retailers of every description find that radio makes their cash registers ring.

Look at the radio stations available in your market. Look at their statistics regarding audience demographics, and compare them with your average customer. If you get a good fit, buy radio.

Are you doing a sales promotion? (If that doesn't ring a bell, take a look at Chapter 3.) To boost short-term sales, radio can be very effective. For a one-two punch, advertisers use a radio ad to build awareness of a promotion, then deliver a coupon by newspaper or direct mail.

Today's radio gurus are suggesting that you emphasize direct offers if you plan to use radio. It's generally a very hard-sell medium; most advertisers use radio commercials to deliver a specific call to action. Listen carefully to the commercials on the stations in your area and you'll see what I mean. How many are image ads (communicating a general feeling about the advertiser) compared to how many are response ads (conveying a call to

action)? We'll talk more about these two approaches to radio advertising later in this chapter, when we get to crafting the commercial. If you've read the previous chapters of this book, you are already used to thinking of advertising in these categories.

Does your marketing objective call for image advertising? Look at your options in television before you settle on radio as the way to go. Radio can be good at image advertising, but it works more slowly when used to build image. Make sure your plan includes more than just a few weeks in the schedule.

If you decide to use radio, you'll want to take advantage of its special characteristics. Listeners feel loyalty to certain stations, and they'll extend that to your company if you consistently sponsor certain programs. Be very predictable about when and how you advertise.

The quality of imagination in radio advertising means that listeners build their own mental picture of you, and since this picture is their own creation, they're likely to remember it. You can make this work to your advantage by producing a creative commercial that maximizes the suggestive power of sound.

If you plan to use radio for image advertising, consider hiring professional help with your script. A high quality of production will be important to your credibility. (We'll talk more about production later in this chapter.)

Whether you're using radio to build image or to induce actions, make your message memorable, and take advantage of radio's niche audiences.

You're Not Buying a Commercial, You're Buying an Audience

Radio stations sell time, and they sell access to markets. The key feature of a radio station is its format—the type of programming it features and the style of the announcers in between. The format determines the audience the station appeals to, and the audience it delivers to advertisers. Some of the most common descriptions are

- Top 40
- All talk
- Progressive rock
- Golden oldies
- All news
- Classical
- Adult contemporary
- Beautiful (easy listening)

Some local stations will be affiliated with the national broadcast networks like CBS. These stations have more credibility as a news source, and consequently will be able to charge higher rates.

> You may have public radio available in your area as well. "Advertising" on public radio usually goes by the name of sponsorship. You can arrange to underwrite certain programs or to contribute to a general fund. Your support will be recognized with an announcement of your company's name and perhaps a brief nonpromotional description. Many service and professional businesses, such as law and medical practices, find this a tasteful way to stay visible without appearing too self-promotional.

Buying Radio Time: Pick Your Day-Parts

Radio stations design their programming to attract certain listeners, then sell those listeners to advertisers in tiny increments. A radio station has an ad time inventory of about eighteen minutes per hour, which it sells in increments of fifteen seconds, thirty seconds, and sixty seconds (:15s, :30s, and :60s). But not all minutes are valued equally. Audience size shifts dramatically throughout the day, and radio rates vary to reflect the change in the estimated number of listeners you are reaching.

The day is divided not into hours but into day-parts. *A.M. drive time,* 6 A.M. to 10 A.M., has the most listeners. They are at their most receptive, too—ready for the news of the day, and the news of your product as well.

Midday, 10 A.M. to 3 P.M., will have considerably fewer listeners, but they are often very loyal to a certain station. These people are listening to the radio while they work, and they follow very predictable habits in their listening. If you do too, advertising at the same time daily with the same message, you will build awareness quickly with these people.

P.M. drive time, 3 P.M. to 7 P.M., will have almost as big an audience as the morning drive time. These people may be in more of a buying mood than those rushing to work in the morning.

Radio listenership drops off rapidly once people get home and out of their cars. The evening belongs to television—unless you're in a "shift town." If you are buying radio time in a city where factories run around the clock, pay more attention to your local station's Arbitron ratings than to these generalizations. Radio in the workplace is a powerful influence.

The *Evening* day-part lasts from 7 P.M. to midnight, and *Late night* from midnight to 6 A.M. At these times you'll find fewer, but fanatically loyal, listeners. These listeners have made a conscious decision to listen to radio rather than watch TV. With the right creative approach and the right match of station format to product, the evening hours can lend themselves to breakthrough advertising. If evening gives you access to the right market, it could be your best time to buy.

Radio prices are based on the day-part, the length of the spot you run, and the frequency, or the number of times your ad will air over the course of a certain period. If you're comparing radio to advertising in the newspaper, you might say that the day-part is analogous to what section of the newspaper you appear in, the length is equivalent to the size of the ad, and the frequency is to how many days your ad appears in the paper.

Reach and Frequency

You look at two factors when you propose a schedule of ads: reach and frequency. Reach is the total number of listeners who hear your commercial once. Frequency is the number of times one of those listeners hears your commercial repeated. Usually the period of time compared will be one week.

You can't assume that listeners pay attention the first time they hear your ad. The second time they might pay more attention, if they're looking for what you're selling, or if your ad has that breakthrough kind of creativity. The third time, they might actually tune in and get your call to action. The "magic number" in radio advertising is a frequency of at least three to five airings per week. Buy less than that and you're throwing your money away. Buy more than that and you start to get somewhere. Thirty airings a week would make you a dominant presence on the air.

One of the advantages of advertising on the radio is that rates are much more negotiable than those for print. It's the law of supply and demand. The newspaper can add more pages if it sells more advertising, but the radio station only has so many commercial slots available in each day. Once they're sold, they're gone—unless an advertiser backs out.

Popular highly rated stations find themselves in a "sold out" position some of the time. In that situation, prices will climb higher until the demand and supply are in balance. On the other hand, many radio stations will find themselves with unsold time on their hands part of the year, and that time is as perishable as produce. If the station has a time slot open at 7:00 A.M. Tuesday and it is not sold, once Tuesday comes, it's gone. That time slot can't be kept in inventory until a buyer is found.

You can negotiate your best radio advertising rates by projecting a schedule that looks far ahead. Buy key parts of the year well in advance, so that the law of supply and demand works in your favor. The "hot" times in radio are the Thanksgiving-to-New Year's holiday season and the summer months. At these times, people are more active than during the rest of the year. They are out in their cars or beyond, away from television but usually still near a radio. Wait too late to book these seasons, and you'll be lucky to get on the air at any price. At other times of the year, you will be in a stronger negotiating position for short-term planning. Sometimes, though, an advertiser backs out or a station makes a scheduling change. If that happens, your radio sales rep might approach you with an extremely favorable offering—but you must decide quickly.

Throughout the broadcast media, you'll find that the basic unit of measure is the thirteen-week contract. This is one quarter of a year. That makes it an easy administrative unit, in terms of budgeting and scheduling, for both advertisers and stations.

You can get time on many stations with a few days' notice, and you can run a single ad or just a few in a short flight. But thirteen weeks is about the shortest period over which it is reasonable to expect advertising to have an effect. Your ad needs repetition to be effective. Your sales rep will try to convince you to contract for a longer period, not just because the sales rep wants the commission, but because he or she wants your experiment to be successful. It's not in the sales rep's best interest to leave you saying, "I tried radio once and it didn't work."

If you're willing to sign a contract that extends for a longer period, you can negotiate even better rates for your spots. Stations thrive on these long-term contracts, and they'll reward you.

Stations' advertising rates vary wildly, and not just by day-part and contract length. Even their methods for pricing the spots vary. Some will lump thirty-second spots together with sixty-second spots and just charge you for a "unit," letting you decide the length. Listeners usually don't distinguish between :30s and :60s, so to keep down the audio clutter, stations commit to airing only so many units per hour. On FM stations, sixty-second commercials are popular, with :30s just behind. AM stations tend toward shorter commercials, mostly :30s and :15s.

Some radio stations may give discounts to ad agencies; others may give discounts to local direct buyers like yourself and charge more to agencies that are buying on a national level. In other words, deals are made in a variety of ways, and you should be aware of this.

Packages and Sponsorships

You have several options in buying air time. Before you decide to buy a certain day-part, ask your sales rep for a proposal on a package plan or a sponsorship. Most stations make available special packages that give you a combination of spots covering different time periods. These packages are often called *TAPs,* or *total audience plans* (see Example 7-2). These plans allow the station some latitude in deciding when your ad will run. A "Rotator" is the same as a "TAP."

A TAP contract will give you the best average cost per spot. Selling TAPs is to the station's advantage, because it gives it flexibility. The disadvantage for you is that you broaden your focus from specific audiences during specific day-parts. Whether a TAP is the best buy for you depends on how well the station's overall listener demographics match your target market.

Example 7-2: TAP Plan
Used by permission of Q106FM.

MADISON'S COUNTRY
Q106FM
WWQM

Results With Adults©

RATE CARD # 36

WWQM-FM/WHIT-AM

WEEKDAY DAYPARTS

Mon–Fri 5:30a–10a	Mon–Fri 10a–3p	Mon–Fri 3p–8p	Mon–Fri 8p–1a	Overnite 1a–5:30a
78	72	68	30	15

WEEKEND DAYPARTS

Saturday 5:30a–3p	Saturday 3p–12mid	Sunday 5:30a–3p	Sunday 3p–12mid
55	41	44	32

TOTAL AUDIENCE PLANS

PLAN	Mon–Fri	Saturday	Sunday
TAP I (5:30a – 8p) _3 DAY PARTS_	68	50	40
TAP II (5:30a – 1a) _4 DAY PARTS_	62	46	36
TAP III (12mid – 12mid)	56	42	32

Q106-FM broadcasts 24 hours a day, and simulcasts on WHIT-AM during daylight hours.
Consult station for details.

T.A.P. spots are guaranteed to be scheduled equally within applicable dayparts, as inventory permits.

✱ For specified times add 20%

Maximum spot length: 60 seconds

Effective March 7, 1994

WHIT / WWQM-FM RADIO • P.O. BOX 44408 • MADISON, WI 53744-4408 • 608-271-6611

Certain types of stations, like country-and-western or oldies formats, attract a fairly homogeneous audience all day. TAP plans are a great buy on these stations.

Although a TAP contract allows the station to run your ad at a time of its choosing, it will certainly try to honor your requests for when you want your ad to play. If you'd like all your spots to run between Wednesday and Sunday, or before 4 P.M., ask for it. Because of its inherent flexibility, radio is one of the most accommodating media you'll find. But if you want to be *certain* your ad runs at a specific time, expect to pay for it. A 20 percent surcharge is typical. Again, it's supply and demand at work.

The most expensive option in radio is to buy sponsorship of a certain program segment, such as news, weather, or sports. Spots during these segments are more valuable because they have larger audiences. The station promotes these programs on the air, and it will often mention the sponsoring advertiser: "Stay tuned to the news on the half hour, brought to you by McCann's Motors."

Sponsorships associate the advertiser's name with a specific program; over the long term, this can be an extremely effective image-building tool. Think of the obvious possibilities—an auto repair service buys sponsorship of a call-in car show; a pet store buys time on "All About Pets." It can take a long time for the sponsorship you want even to become available, because of that law of supply and demand. But here's the bottom line: Your spot is heard day in and day out by the same very highly targeted audience. Sponsorships are a good value, especially for image advertising.

If you've read the previous chapters, you are starting to get familiar with a client of mine, First Business Bank. Here's the story of how we first tried radio. The bank wanted to reach business decision makers with a mes-sage about specialized commercial banking services. To generate some excitement, we wanted to try radio in addition to our local print advertising. We quickly honed in on WTDY as the right station for us; that left the decision as to when and how to buy time on WTDY. We felt that there were three options we should consider: buying a TAP plan, sponsoring a program segment, or buying specific times of day at the peak commuter time.

A quick look at how narrowly the target market is defined showed us that it wouldn't make sense to buy a TAP plan. We briefly looked at buying commercials at the open rate in just the A.M. drive time day-part, to reach decision makers while they were commuting. But that's four hours long—buying sufficient frequency was still too costly in our projections.

We also looked at buying sponsorships—either the hourly news breaks, or possibly sports. This option offered us a narrower, more targeted market, but the station charged a lot for that.

We decided to stay away from sponsorships, not only because they cost too much but because we didn't want to wait for the right sponsorship to become available. We were reacting to changes on the local banking scene, and we wanted to act fast. So we chose to buy a specific time instead. We zeroed in on a certain type of commuter. Using a form like Template 7-1A, we found that buying a specific time gave us the best-targeted audience for our ads at an affordable cost. We calculated back from the customary start of the local business day to find the peak executive drive time, and paid a premium to run a commercial at precisely that time each day. We ran only twenty commercials, cutting our reach but keeping our frequency high enough in our very narrow market.

Template 7-1A: Media Comparisons

Date: 12-6-93
Title: Media Comparisons, First Business Bank
Assumptions: Comparison of different plans
All on WTDY
All are 60 seconds.
TAP plan runs at best time available, 6 a.m. - 7 p.m.
News sponsorships are at 5:30, 6:00, 6:30, 7:00, 7:30, 8:00, and 8:30 a.m.
Specific time purchase: 6:31 a.m.

Media		Rate Card	Frequency /year	Space	Open Rate	Circulation in 1,000s		CPM ($)	Index
WTDY	TAP plan (3 part)	10/26/93	20	3 day-parts, BTA	$26	12.6	AM drive time		
						21.4	Midday		
						13.8	PM drive time		
						15.9	average audience	$1.63	100%
	News sponsorship	10/26/93	20	News/sports sponsorship	$35	12.6		$2.78	170%
	Specific time	10/26/93	20	Specific spot	$31	12.6		$2.46	151%

You can use Template 7-1B to create your own radio cost comparisons.

Template 7-1B: Media Comparisons

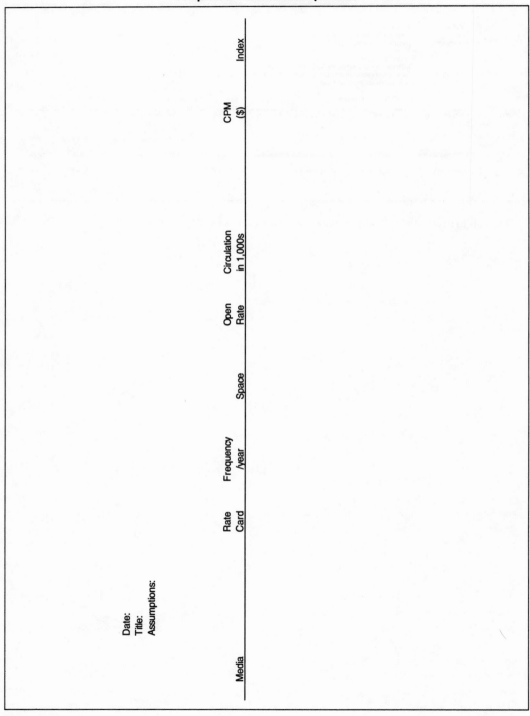

As you can see, buying radio time is a matter of negotiating the length, the price, and the frequency you commit to. By understanding what's in the station's best interest, you can make a deal that's good for both of you.

Promote Special Events with Live Remote Broadcasts

Retailers—this one's for you! Many stations have vans and other equipment that allow them to broadcast directly from your place of business or your special event. It's the perfect marketing device for grand openings, special sales, and promotional events. You can use the station to add "showbiz" excitement to your event. Ask your radio sales reps whether they offer a live remote broadcast package.

A three-hour live remote package might include these elements:

- Thirty promotional announcements prior to the event
- Twenty-five commercial announcements in a TAP plan
- Ten live cut-ins within the remote broadcast (that's where the announcer does "man on the street" interviews live from the event)
- Engineering, promotions, and talent for three hours
- Extras, including a lighted marquee sign and giveaways

In a midsize market, this package sells for around $2,500. What kind of effect would this have on your next sidewalk sale?

What Length of Spot Is Right for You?

Thirty seconds may sound like an impossibly short time in which to get a message across. But you'd be surprised how much can be communicated! Glance at your watch next time you're listening through a commercial break on the radio. Pay attention to how much gets said in thirty seconds. You may clock some fifteen-second commercials too—smaller time splits have become popular in both radio and television. These shorter commercials have appeal for budget reasons, and occasionally for creative reasons as well. You might consider buying fifteen-second commercials in "donuts," airing one at the beginning and one at the end of a commercial break (the hole in the donut). You might pose a question, then answer it—or come up with your own variation on the "Energizer Bunny...still going."

Thirty-second spots are by far the most common. They give you an opportunity to speak 80 to 100 words. If that's not enough to communicate, you can look into :60s. If you've been paying attention to :30s, a sixty-second commercial will suddenly seem very long! The longer format does allow you more variety in music and sound effects. If you're announcing a new product or explaining a confusing topic, you might need a :60 just to get the facts across. If you have multiple locations or complicated response instructions, as for a contest, you may need a :60 just to accommodate the air time you'll burn through asking for the next action.

But I'd recommend that you begin with a schedule of :30s. Unless you can afford professional studio production, a :60 sounds long and, if the seams are showing, amateurish. A thirty-second commercial is best, so get focused on what you want to say, and do it right. We'll talk more about how to create ads later in this chapter.

But first: You have an idea now how radio is sold; do you know how radio *sells*?

How Radio Sells

How is radio advertising unique in motivating action? It can be very direct—you can practically pull someone off the highway, out of his or her car, and into your restaurant with a well-placed, well-produced commercial. The key to radio selling is frequency. Repetition. Recurrence. Reiteration. Radio ads work by working over and over and over. If you can only afford to broadcast your message once or twice, don't do it at all.

As a rule of thumb, don't consider running less than twenty spots per week. People need to hear your message at least three to five times to have any recollection of it at all. The next three to five times will build recognition of your key sales message, and the next three might just drive home your call to action. You know each prospect isn't going to be present for each airing of your commercial, so buy enough spots to give yourself favorable odds.

There are lots of ways to be smart about timing your ads. In Chapter 4 we talked about timing strategies:

- Continuity—no variation in timing

- Heavy-up—occasional increases in a generally light schedule

- Flighting and pulsing—strategies that use a rhythmic schedule to stretch ad dollars and take advantage of the inertia of listener perception

In talking with radio sales reps, you may hear the word *flight* used interchangeably with the word *schedule*. This is because flighting is so very common in radio. You might opt for a schedule of flights, such as two weeks on, one week off. You'll be amused at how often your customers say, "I heard your ad today" when you know you haven't been on the air all week.

Templates 7-2A and 7-3A describe a campaign for "Medic Now!," a walk-in emergency-care clinic. This media plan places advertising on two radio stations; the goal is to reach mothers who are decision makers about health care for their families.

Template 7-2A: Media Calendar for Medic Now!

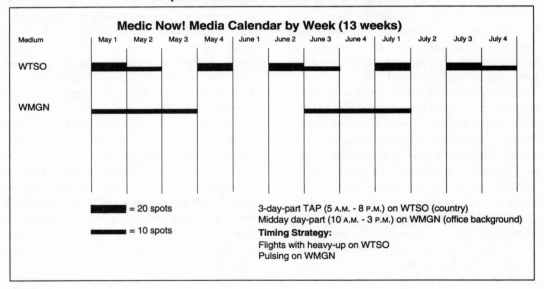

224

Template 7-3A: Budget by Week for Medic Now!

Media Budget
Spending by Station and Week

Date: 11-22-94
Title: Medic Now! Media Budget by Week
Assumptions: See media calendar
Costs based on rate cards 10/26/94.
WTSO 30-second spots, $22/spot, three-day-part TAP
WMGN 30-second spots, $27/spot, midday day-part
Prepared by: SW

Medium	May Week 1	Week 2	Week 3	Week 4	June Week 1	Week 2	Week 3	Week 4	July Week 1	Week 2	Week 3	Week 4	Total ($)	Total (%)
Radio														
WTDY	$440	$220		$440		$440	$220		$440		$440	$220	$2,860	64%
WMGN	$270	$270	$270				$270	$270	$270				$1,620	36%
Total by Week:	$710	$490	$270	$440	$0	$440	$490	$270	$710	$0	$440	$220	$4,480	100%
Percent of Total:	16%	11%	6%	10%	0%	10%	11%	6%	16%	0%	10%	5%	100%	

The plan calls for a three-day-part TAP plan on a country radio station; here the TAP plan makes sense because of the loyalty of the listeners, as demonstrated by their Arbitron ratings. (We'll talk about that just ahead.) We know this plan will build frequency in a hurry, as these listeners stay tuned throughout their days.

The plan also calls for commercials during the midday day-part on an adult contemporary station. We've chosen this because the station is often listened to as background music in offices and homes. Again, we know this from the ratings and demographics the station has shown us.

Study the templates, and you'll see how they illustrate the media plan. Use Templates 7-2B and 7-3B to work out cost and timing scenarios for your radio advertising.

Template 7-2B: Media Calendar (blank)

Medium	Week 1	Week 2	Week 3	Week 4	Week 1	Week 2	Week 3	Week 4	Week 1	Week 2	Week 3	Week 4

Template 7-3B: Media Budget by Week (blank)

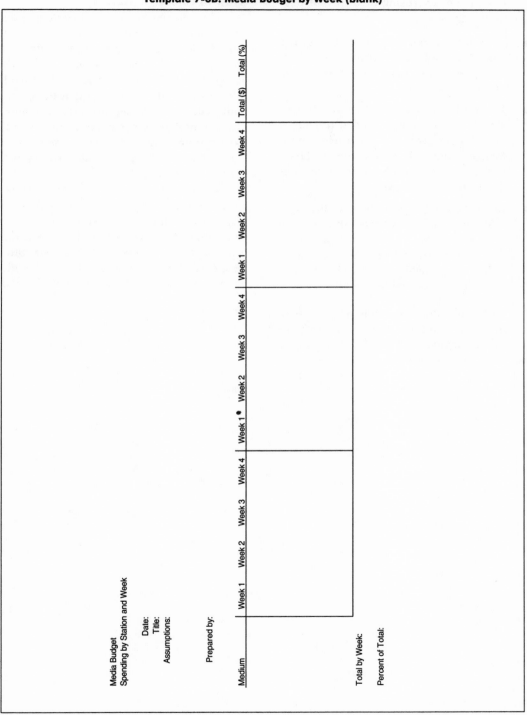

Does radio advertising fit with your marketing objectives? Yes, if

- You want to increase customer traffic. The immediacy and credibility of radio make it very effective at motivating this type of action.

- You need to reach a local consumer market. Radio can be very good at reaching a broad geographic distribution with focused audience demographics. That's why you'll hear your bigger local retailers dominating the airwaves.

- You sell a product repeatedly to the same customers. Radio listeners are loyal, and often extend that loyalty to the advertisers as well. For personal services where loyalty becomes a habit, like dry cleaners and hair salons, radio will be effective.

Using radio to its maximum potential is all a matter of reading the audience demographics and responding in a way that's appropriate *and* has creative appeal.

How to Choose a Station

How do you know which stations to buy, and how many? How do you compare what each station offers? Radio reps are some of the most persistent in the sales game, and so they are probably not the best source of advice for you to start with. Statistics are at the heart of radio sales, and any rep can present numbers that position his or her station's offering in the best possible light. Statistics for radio are based on some very unreliable survey techniques, however.

I recommend that you perform a survey of your own. Start with your customers. Ask them what stations they listen to, and when. Where are they when they listen? In their cars, or at their desks? As always, your current best customers can give you most of the information you need to find more just like them (Template 7-4).

Template 7-4: Advertising Listening Habits Questionnaire

Advertising Listening Habits Questionnaire

About you:

Your age: (range) 0–18 18–25 25–35 35–45 45–55 55–65 65+

Your gender: M F

Your family size: _____

Your occupation: _____

Your degree of influence on decisions to purchase
(name your product or service here) at work? Little Some Sole Decision Maker

Do you read the daily newspaper on weekdays? Yes No

On Sundays? Yes No

Do you open direct mail you receive? 0–25% 25–50% 50–75% 75–100%

Do you watch television news? Yes No

Do you subscribe to cable TV? Yes No

About your radio listening habits:

At work:

Is the radio on? Yes No

What station is on the most? _____

How is the choice of station made? _____

How often is the station changed throughout the day? 1–3 times 4–6 times More

What stations are on most frequently? _____

In the car:

Do you listen to the radio? Yes No

Most listeners choose 3 or 4 stations and cycle between those throughout their drive. What stations make

your "short list"? _____

(continued on next page)

Advertising Listening Habits Questionnaire (continued)

At play:
Are there other places where you hear the radio? (In the weight room at the health club, your portable radio at the beach, etc.) If you hear the radio in such a place often (more than three days a week), let's look at it more closely. Describe the setting. Who chooses the station, and why? Do you remember any advertisers from that station?

      (We ask this question to find out how closely the listeners pay attention in this setting. Radio over the loudspeakers at the swimming pool gets a very different quality of attention from radio piped in to a tanning booth.)

_____

_____

_____

_____

At home:
Where are radios located in your home? _____

Of the two most frequently used, answer:

How often is it on?   1x/week   3x/week   5x/week   more

What time of day is it on? (from _____ to _____)

About radio ads in general:
What commercial do you remember best right now? _____

Why? Was it because it was advertising something in which you had an interest?

_____

Was it something about the creative approach that stuck in your mind?

_____

Do you remember what action that advertiser wanted you to take?

_____

_____

_____

This is an informal survey, and I don't expect you to derive hard quantitative data from it. But as you compile the results, certain patterns will start to emerge. From what your customers tell you, what radio stations should make your "short list"? Did you get any clues as to what day-part commands the most attention with your customers?

Meet with each station's sales rep, and ask for ratings and demographics on the day-parts that interest you.

Reviewing the Rate Kits

Your reps will bring you folders full of information about each station's audience and ratings.

The ratings information comes from national companies, like The Media Audit, that come into a market and do phone surveys. These services ask questions about listening habits, spending power, employment, and lifestyle and demographics. They sell that information to individual stations, which get a database of results on disk. Each station subscribes to one or more rating services, and from these impartial sources the stations compile statistics that make the station look attractive.

Example 7-3: Q106 Results with Adults
Used by permission of Media Audit, Inc.

Results With Adults©

Q106-FM LISTENERS
RETAIL SPENDING POWER

Over 57% of Q106-FM listeners
own their own home.

Almost 35,000 of these listeners have an
annual household income of $35,000 plus!!

34.6% earn more than $50,000.00.

In the next twelve (12) months, Q106-FM listeners plan to purchase these household items:

12,630	New furniture.
11,000	Personal Computer / Software.
8,900	Stereo Equipment.
6,800	Major Home Appliance.
6,700	New TV.
5,600	Video Equipment.

Source: The Media Audit; Madison, Wisconsin   September - October, 1993

MADISON'S COUNTRY

Media kit inserts like Example 7-3 tell you who is listening to this particular station. They describe the audience by demographics, purchasing traits, and other statistical profiles. You will also receive customized printouts showing the actual ratings points each station earns.

Arbitron, the main source for ratings, publishes scores for "AQH" and "CUM." Here is what these terms mean:

- *AQH.* What is one station's share of the total audience available in one geographic region? If you ask this question every quarter of an hour, the answer is the station's AQH, or average quarter hour share.

- *CUM.* How many listeners have tuned in to one station during one quarter hour? That's a slightly different question, and the answer is that station's CUM, or cumulative rating.

Confused? Think of a radio station as your store. The CUM is the average number of people who come in your door in fifteen minutes. The AQH is the number of people who *stay* in the store during those fifteen minutes. AQH is measuring loyalty and consistency in the audience. CUM is measuring reach. Radio stations will present their scores in each category. Ask to see "rankers"—comparisons of how one station ranks against the competition, in terms of a target audience described by age and gender. Many stations will invite you to come in and use their computers to access the Arbitron database and explore the data yourself. The time you spend exploring rankings for different day-parts will help you decide when and where to place your ads. See Example 4-2 for an Arbitron printout showing CUM and AQH ratings. To understand more about this, work with a rep from a radio station in your area.

Arbitron Ratings

Arbitron publishes ratings, available as both printed books and more frequently updated databases. There will be four books a year in big markets (where a dozen or more radio stations compete in the same area); smaller markets might have only one or two books a year. The method employed to gather these statistics is to send out diaries and pay people to fill them out. This information is then grouped by geographic areas called "metro areas" and wider "total service areas" (TSA). (Radio is full of acronyms. Some stations use the term ADI, or area of dominant influence, instead of TSA. The meaning is the same.)

Please be aware that Arbitron and other rankings are just a tool! Arbitron states up front that there can be a 50 percent margin of error in its statistics. Arbitron suffers from this because of its unscientific method of data collection. There is nothing you can do about that. However, when you compare statistics, make sure you are comparing like time periods and data sources. If one station bases its proposal on Arbitrons from spring 1994, ask that other proposals use Arbitron spring 1994 as well. Even then, use these statistics as a guide to a station's popularity, not a guarantee.

Calculating CPM

You have two factors to keep in mind as you rank stations: You want to know how many people you are reaching for the dollars you spend—your cost per thousand (CPM)—and you want to know what frequency is desirable to pound your message home.

In Chapter 4, "Writing a Media Plan," you'll find a complete explanation of CPM calculations, including how to set up your spreadsheet and use it to compare apples to apples. In Chapter 6 we again covered this in detail. To make CPM comparisons for radio, study Template 7-1A. Template 7-1B is a blank form you can use to make your own calculations. Set this up as a spreadsheet on your computer.

To keep things fair, make sure you're describing the same demographic group for each station you rank. Make sure the audiences you're comparing are within the same geographic area. Make sure the rate you're using describes the same offering—one station's three-part TAP plan against another station's similar plan, or one station's open-rate single :30 against another's. ("Open rate" is the price before any discounts, bonuses, or package deals are negotiated.) Make sure the rating information that gives you the total audience numbers is from the same source. If one station offers you Arbitron reports and another is using Pulse, you aren't making an accurate comparison.

The Other Factors

You're trying to decide which one station, or several stations, deserves your advertising dollar. By creating your short list of candidates and meeting with the reps, you've gotten data about the audience for each. Are there other factors to consider? Of course. And they're even more intangible.

Take a long, hard look at each station now (Template 7-5). How does it promote itself? How does it sound? I mean the quality of the signal itself, and also the personalities on the air. Are they professional? Are they popular? How's the quality of the commercials? Can you hear a difference between those produced by the station and those coming from outside sources?

If a lot of the commercials sound the same—the same announcer's voice, the same style of writing—you know that station's creative department is not right for you.

Does the station run a lot of contests? Some run contests all the time; others not at all. Whether this is a good thing or a bad thing depends on the audience you're trying to reach. Some types of listeners love contests; others don't. A country station might do lots of giveaways; the loyalty and sociability of the station's typical listeners make them participate. An oldies station might do fewer contests. They know that people tune in to hear their old favorites, and so an oldies format will deliver more music with less talk.

Is the station involved in the community? Does it sponsor concerts? These build loyalty, and create unique advertising opportunities as well. Judge the stations as you would any potential vendor. Do you like what you see? Then you're about to make a "sound" decision.

Template 7-5: Ranking Intangibles

Ranking the Intangibles: How to Choose a Radio Station

	Bad		OK		Great
Quality of self-promotion: How are its ...					
Printed materials?	1	2	3	4	5
Self-promotional commercials?	1	2	3	4	5
Quality of sound:					
How is their broadcast signal	1	2	3	4	5
The on-air personalities: Are they ...					
Professional?	1	2	3	4	5
Popular?	1	2	3	4	5

How many commercials on average every hour? _____

Quality of commercials	1	2	3	4	5

Ask to hear samples that were produced in-house. How do they sound?

	1	2	3	4	5

Does this station feature contests?

    Describe a typical example. _____

Does this station feature concert sponsorships?

    Describe the types of music it supports. _____

Is it a good citizen? Stable in business? Straightforward in billing? Ask for references, then call them. Ask these questions and others that concern you.

References: _____

_____

_____

Negotiating the Deal

Each radio rep will bring you a proposal, which might include a cassette with a commercial for your company created "on spec." Ask whether production is included in the proposal. Stations charge for production, but it's usually quite inexpensive, $20 to $60 a spot. To get your business, some stations are willing to waive charges for production. The voice talent will be their on-air announcers, and some stations even have writers on staff to help you.

The other possibilities are to go to a commercial production studio or an ad agency.

Because radio production is not particularly complex, most stations are perfectly capable of doing a fine job. It's the strength of your script that will make or break your production. Whether you write your own or have the station work from your instructions, critique the script severely before you record. Does it mention your name and business category often enough? A :60 should mention your name three to five times; in a :30, two or three mentions is the most you can hope for. Does it convey a benefit? If you can answer, "What's in it for me?" and "Where do I go to get it?" after hearing the commercial, it's got the key ingredients.

You might consider using an independent production company if your script idea is fairly complex. You will pay more, but you will find a higher caliber of creative talent at your disposal. If you are committing to an aggressive radio schedule, look at your commercial production costs as a percentage of your overall media expenditures. We'll talk more about budgets for radio ad production near the end of this chapter, in the section "Production Cost Alternatives."

You'll find some of the most aggressive salespeople in the world selling radio time. They make their living on commissions, and so it's a business of cold calling and following up with persistence. Some reps work hard at being good consultants. They will help you define your goals, provide you the information you need in a straightforward way, and respond to your requests with a willingness to negotiate. Other reps will badmouth the competition, badger you with special act-now offers, and drop in on you so persistently that you'll do anything to get rid of them. Don't be bullied by these hard-sell techniques.

Radio stations are known for doing a lot of trade-outs—swapping air time for services they need, like printing or temporary office staff or catering. You will find a lot of opportunities to bargain if you look for them.

No matter how good the deal looks, remember that you're buying an audience, not an ad. Don't waste advertising dollars buying an audience that doesn't fit your offering. Instead, look closely at station demographics, audience size, and rates until you negotiate a radio buy that fits your marketing objectives.

Crafting the Radio Ad

We've talked about the aspects of radio that help you decide whether or not to use it. We've talked about its price structure, and how to negotiate the best deal. If you've gotten

this far, I think you're seriously planning to use radio in your media mix. It's time to talk about how to fill the air time you're about to purchase. How will you decide the message of your ad, write the copy, and produce the actual audiotape? Experts are standing by to help you, from the radio station's production staff to independent radio producers. Who will you use, and how? What exactly takes place as you craft that commercial? That's the subject for the remainder of this chapter.

Image vs. Response Advertising

What is your advertisement's message going to be? Remember, you have to choose between two broad categories, image and response. Here's the difference:

- An image ad communicates a feeling about your company.

- A response ad conveys news about a product or a price discount, and issues a specific call to action.

In Chapter 5, "The Creative Approach," we talked about these two general groupings. You'll want to review that section for more detail on how the two are different. In general, you choose an image advertising strategy when you are planning a campaign aimed at long-term changes in consumer perceptions, rather than immediate measurable response. Image advertising can be successful in radio, but it takes a long time to work. Eventually the response becomes very strong. But how long can you wait for your cash register to ring? If you want to see more immediate results, or if your budget won't permit a long-running campaign, choose a response advertising approach.

If you decide to do image advertising, keep these factors in mind:

- Use the same tagline, or positioning slogan, in each commercial.

- Use the same wording to repeat your name in your commercial, and always mention your category with it.

"Tarantello's, the Home of Fine Meats" works; "Shop at Tarantello's" does not.

- Use music consistently. Whether it's a certain sound effect or your own jingle, always use it in the same way every time.

These elements build a specific personality for your advertisement. And that's where your image gets its strength.

If you're like most advertisers, you'll decide to do response ads instead. Response ads take a newsy approach to let customers know who, what, how, when, and why to take advantage of your offer. If your offer has real value, and you deliver the message in an entertaining way, you will see measurable results in a short time.

Co-op Support: Manufacturers Offer Free Lunch

If you are in a retail or distribution business, you are probably familiar with the idea of manufacturer co-op support programs. Gear your advertising message to these programs. Almost every product for sale has co-op dollars behind it. Manufacturers will reimburse you for 50 percent, 75 percent, even 100 percent of your media costs. The manufacturers you deal with may not publicize their co-op programs, especially if you're a smaller retailer, but that doesn't mean they don't offer them. Ask! Your radio sales reps can help you discover co-op opportunities. It's part of their job.

There are restrictions that apply when you work with co-op. The manufacturer's goal is to dominate your ad; it will require you to meet certain guidelines, and that may not fit your marketing goals. For example, you might not be able to mention a competing product in the same ad. So instead of advertising that all refrigerators are on sale, and mentioning brand names, you might have to say, "All Amanas on sale" and rely on that brand alone to draw traffic.

Do the math to figure out your best advantage. Compare your different manufacturers' offers. Usually it's worth the effort.

To qualify for a co-op program, you submit the script in advance, get approval, then file broadcast affidavits (proof describing when and where the commercial aired) within a set period (usually ninety days) after the ad is broadcast. If you work with an ad agency or media brokerage service, it will take care of this paperwork for you.

The filing rules can be complicated; too many advertisers let this money go unclaimed because of the complexities of filing for it. Don't be lazy! Suppose you negotiate for the station to pay your production fees, and you qualify for 100 percent co-op for the media you place. You just got your radio advertising absolutely free! The hidden cost? The co-op program, not you, directed the thrust of your message. If that choice fits with your overall advertising strategy, you're sitting pretty. If not, you've made some tradeoffs—and that's often the way it goes with a smart business decision.

Summary: Choosing the Radio Approach

If you're like most advertisers, you will want your commercial to be a little of both image and response advertising. You don't want to give up all your personality just to get the sale details across. Both have their advantages and drawbacks; for most advertisers, and especially those with co-op support available, response advertising focused on specific products is the leading choice. With the consistent use of a jingle or a tagline, you can get your response ad to be a little of both.

If you have chosen your media placements, try this exercise. Really tune in to the station(s) you've chosen. Pay attention to all the commercials in the day-part you've chosen. How are the current advertisers using their air time? Do you hear image or response ads? Are brand names mentioned, suggesting that this advertiser is using a co-op support program? What categories of business are advertising here—retailers, service businesses, captains of industry building their image? Are your competitors present in the mix? Take notes, and analyze what you hear. Build on what you learn from the decisions of others.

When is an image ad a good idea?

Let's say you plan to run sales in January, March, and May, and to publicize them on the radio. To get your best price per spot, you might contract for twenty-six weeks. That means you'll be on the air all of January through June. In the months when you don't have a sale running, you'll still be on the air—and that's where the *rateholder* ad comes in. This ad promotes image, and fills the time slots otherwise given to your sale ads. It keeps your contract obligation without requiring you to always have some type of sale or discount to advertise.

Writing Radio Copy

When you've decided whether your ad will promote image or ask for a specific response, you can begin to write the script. Review your positioning from Chapter 2 and the creative approach you developed in Chapter 5. Refer to these notes as you write, so that your ad stays focused and in tune with your marketing strategy. Even if you don't con-

sider yourself a great writer, you will want to skim the following points. You will need some understanding of the task when you hire someone to do it for you. The commercials that aren't written by you—the advertiser—are usually crafted by advertising agencies or freelance writers. Production studios take it from there. We'll talk about that in much more detail in the next section. Here's what you should know about writing for radio, no matter who takes on the task.

There are three ways to approach a radio commercial, and three thousand or more ways to combine them with creativity. The three ways are the pitch, the situation, and the music spot. Let's look at each approach individually.

The Pitch

The announcer reads a script. In crafting this ad, you have two tools at your disposal: the sound of the announcer's voice, and the words you give him or her to speak.

These commercials are very inexpensive to produce; your radio station will almost certainly throw in the production for free for an ad this simple. So it makes sense to study this form of writing.

Group Health Cooperative developed a "pitch" commercial to announce the opening of a new location. Example 7-4 shows how it sounded.

Example 7-4: Health Cooperative Radio Commercial
Used by permission of Group Health Cooperative.

Sixty-Second Radio Commercial, Title: "Cough Sneeze Waltz"

Up music:	Blue Danube Waltz
SFX:	Cough. Cough. Sneeze. Sneeze. Blow nose. Sneeze. Cough.

(In time with music)

Waltz continues under sound effects.

(This goes on for twenty seconds.)

Anncr:	If you're looking for quality health care, this will be music to your ears. Group Health Cooperative is pleased to announce the opening of their new Sauk Trails Health Center.
	Located just off the West Beltline, Sauk Trails gives westside members access to GHC preventive care at the drop of a Kleenex. With all the services right there, including a pharmacy, Sauk Trails Health Center is nothing to sneeze at.
SFX:	A-a-a-chu!
Anncr:	Unless, of course, you have a cold. Then, we're just a sniffle away.
	Group Health Cooperative. Opening new doors to quality health care.
Music:	Closing bars of Blue Danube waltz.

The script for a "pitch"—and all radio ads—will have a beginning portion that establishes context, a middle section that delivers the reasons to buy, and a conclusion that delivers the call to action, along with any nuts and bolts like addresses and phone numbers.

In this example, almost half the air time was devoted to establishing context—the sneezing and coughing in rhythm with the waltz. The sound was genuinely amusing, and so the producer gave it time to build to good dramatic effect. Then, the announcer moved in with the news of the new location, giving "reasons to buy" like convenience and service. (Notice the mention of the pharmacy.)

This is not a hard-sell commercial, and the conclusion is understated. The only "call to action" is the message implied by two lines: "nothing to sneeze at" and "just a sniffle away." Still you get the point: These people want you to avail yourself of their services.

The commercial closes with a tagline. This shows how a commercial can be both response and image advertising. The phrase "Opening new doors to quality health care" provides consistency with GHC's other promotions using this phrase, and serves to support the overall public image of this health care cooperative.

Here's another example: a :60 spot featuring an announcer's voice over music, promoting a hair salon. Look at the script in Example 7-5 and you'll catch the dreamy pace of the ad. Glamorous music fills the background—and the commercial works because the producer found just the right music. It was medium tempo, a little jazzy, with a touch of syncopation. It had just a touch of tropical flavor to it, like something you might hear at a fashion show. The result was inexpensive to produce—just a music fee and an announcer's voice. Effective? Very.

Example 7-5: Captain's Chair Radio Commercial
Used by permission of Captain's Chair Hair Salons.

Captain's Chair Hair Salons
:60 radio

"Glamour Wave"

Touchable texture ... radiant shine ... it's your hair in the kind of superb condition you've come to
expect when you perm your hair at Captain's Chair, with Redken! Call it a Glamour Wave ... because
when you get any perm at Captain's Chair you'll receive a glamour photo session FREE! ... from the
new Olan Mills Glamour Studio in West Towne Mall.

A glamour photo shoot with pretty clothes, hats, and even lingerie, will capture you at your best ...
and ... our Top stylists agree: Redken permanent waves perform, whatever your hair type or
condition ... there's a Redken perm that can give your hair perfect body ....

Captain's Chair stylists can give you soft, long-lasting, natural-looking waves. They rely on Redken
... it's the power behind beautiful hair. So treat *yourself* this holiday season. To a glamour wave ... a
perm from Captain's Chair ... and get a glamour photo session and an 8 by 10 photo FREE! It'll make
a great gift ... but you've got to call now ... Captain's Chair Hair Salons!

The Situation

We love to eavesdrop on the conversations
of others; we generally find it more amusing
than being "preached at" by an announcer.
The most memorable situation commercials
tend to be humorous. Often, you'll find the
same two characters interacting in a series of
commercials that explore different settings
and different reasons to buy.

Just like the pitch commercial, the situation will open with a few phrases designed to
give context, to tell you where you are and the
personalities of the people speaking. Then the

repartee begins; our characters go through
some sort of interaction that dramatizes the
advertiser's key benefits. The conclusion will
contain some sort of payoff—a punch line, or
a dramatic solution to a problem. By the end,
the product or service is shown to be a hero.

The examples from the Independent
Bankers Association of Wisconsin that opened
this chapter are excellent examples of situation
scripts. As you can see, they used the same
family of characters and took them through
several story lines. Example 7-6 shows another
from that series.

Example 7-6: IBAW Commercial #3, "Convertible"
Used by permission of Independent Bankers Association of Wisconsin.

Independent Bankers Association of Wisconsin
Independently Healthy Promotion

Sixty Second Radio Commercial #3, "Convertible"

Anncr:	Nice day for a convertible ride with your family.
Dad:	You got that right.
Anncr:	So why not put your top down before the light changes?
Kid:	Dad says we're wise to avoid gamma rays.
Dad:	Actually, the top doesn't work any more.
Anncr:	Too bad. Engine still purrs like a kitten, though—I can't even hear it running!
Mom:	That's because it's not running. We're waiting for the tow truck. . . again.
Anncr:	Sounds like you could use a new cruiser.
Dad:	But our financial institution put the skids on the old car loan.
Anncr:	Did you try the independent community bank?
Dad:	They're different?
Anncr:	You bet your fuzzy dice they are. They're independent of the outside controls and risky investments that are hurting some institutions and community owned and operated so your money goes to work right there.
Mom:	Like for car loans?
Anncr:	Whether you want to save up for the future or cruise top down today, your independent community bank can help.
SFX:	Truck honk.
Anncr:	Your tow truck's ready.
Dad:	Driver, to the independent community bank—and take the scenic route, it's the last cruise for this old boat.

(Insert local announcer tag here)

Tag:	Save for a rainy day with the bank that can help you enjoy the sunny ones. *(Bank Name)*. Independently Healthy. Member F.D.I.C.

It takes more skill to write a situation commercial than to write a pitch, but don't let that stop you from trying. If you can carry on a conversation, you can write dialogue for a situation script. Let your own experiences suggest the setup to you. Write a "slice of life" conversation between two likable people in a believable situation.

The Song

Radio is "the music medium." That's why jingles and songs have been a staple of radio since its inception. The added dimension that music gives your message may be what you need to get your name heard. People are more likely to remember an often-heard jingle long after a voice message is forgotten. In fact, most of us can still recall advertising jingles from our childhood that we haven't heard for years. Just ask anyone raised in Indiana to sing "Let's go Krogering...the happy way to shop!"

More elaborate than a jingle is a song. A song has a beginning, middle, and end just like the spoken scripts; it still needs to establish context, convey a message, and make a call to action.

The beginning is the intro, the first notes that set the tone for the piece. Will it be the sleepy country-music feel of Tom Bodett for Motel 6, or the Lone Ranger's theme from the *William Tell* Overture? With the first few notes, you establish your attitude. The middle delivers the product benefit, as smoothly as possible. With the closing notes—"the hook"—you create the part of the song that sticks in your listener's mind.

It's very rare for a whole commercial to be one song, and I don't recommend that you try it. Even if you pay $10,000 for your music, it will sound cheap compared with the $200,000+ production of the songs on the radio. Put a voice in at the beginning or end, to lift you out of competition with the songs.

It's your call whether your sound should be pretty, jazzy, or raunchy, upbeat or downtempo. There's a whole world of musical styles to choose from. When you decide what it will be, get help. In general, advertisers are unlikely to undertake creating a musical commercial without help, even for a tagline jingle just a few bars long. If you are interested in using musical advertising for your business, you will almost certainly be working with production specialists to develop your sound. Information on music production is coming up.

Combining Copy Approaches

Most ads aren't pure examples of a pitch, a situation, or a song. Instead, you'll find combinations. If you're creating a pitch commercial, read by an announcer, the most common way to pep it up is to add sound. A little music coming up behind the announcer's voice can give your ad a boost. First, the music makes the ad more distinctive, and inherently more memorable. Second, the music helps by establishing context. A Caribbean rhythm introducing an announcement for a travel agency helps you get the point more quickly, doesn't it? Prerecorded music makes it easy to produce this kind of combination ad on a low budget. We'll talk more about that when we get to production.

Sometimes the jingle can just be the tagline for a voice commercial. That can be very effective to help listeners remember your business.

Another combination is the sandwich approach. You can open with a song, have your announcer make the pitch, then close with a reprise of the song. This is a great way to stretch the investment in the jingle. Year after year you can use the middle of the sandwich to make timely announcements, and just keep on building the recognition factor of your song.

It's easy to imagine more combinations. The announcer can introduce a situation, or he can burst in on the conversation. The dialogue in the situation might end with a song, or the song might come in at the payoff. Let your sense of humor run wild when you think about radio. It's possibly the best medium for using comedy to sell.

Whatever combination of approaches you use, consider closing your commercial with a tag. This is blank space in the last few seconds of the commercial, allowing time for the station announcer to read some information. Your ad message can be as current as your latest fax to the station. This is a particularly popular technique in retail advertising.

Making Humor Work for You

People remember humor spots when they work—and when they don't. That's the problem. There are only two ways to go: Either you win or you're a flop. Go ahead and try writing a funny spot—then show it to someone who will be brutally honest. That probably rules out your employees and members of your family!

Whether you wrote the copy or someone did it for you, here's how to rule out the bad jokes. Ask yourself:

- Is there anything that offends or makes fun of my customer? Never ever make fun of the product or its buyer.

- Who's the butt of the joke? Much good humor is built around the sadsack, the fellow who suffers life's indignities. There's nothing wrong with that, but it's a fine line: Never ask your customer to identify with someone you're making fun of.

- Is your humor in good taste? Do people behave with civility to each other, and treat each other with respect?

Remember, you don't just want humor—you want likability.

Example 7-7 is a humorous ad that was a big hit in Madison, Wisconsin. Timing was one key element in its success—it made fun of an event that was currently in the news, a big debate in the legislature, where polka enthusiasts were lobbying to make polka the "official state music." The other element working for this commercial is its high production value. The script was written by an advertising agency, read by talented voice actors, and dubbed with care to create the right background ambience. This commercial succeeds at creating a visual in the mind—I wish you could hear it. You'll just have to imagine it, as we all did when we heard it.

Example 7-7, Michael's Custard Radio Commercial
Used by permission of Michael's Frozen Custard.

KITSON MARKETING/Michael's Frozen Custard
Job No: 11004 :60 Radio
April 11, 1994

LEGISLATURE

JOHN:	This legislative session will now begin.
SFX:	Gavel.
JOHN:	First the agenda is to vote on the official frozen custard flavor for the state of Wisconsin. Michael's Frozen Custard has generously prepared more than 52 flavors for your consideration. My personel favorite is Chocolate English Toffee, but please, don't let my superior status sway your vote in any way.
CONGRESSWOMAN:	I vote for Michael's Raspberry Truffle Cheeeeeeeeesecake . . . after all, this is the Dairy State.
VOICE:	WAS.
GREG:	According to the poll taken in my district, looks like a tie between Caramel Cashew and Banana Chocolate Chunk . . . so my vote goes to Bavarian Thin Mint . . . my wife's favorite.
CONGRESSMAN:	Shouldn't we be discussing the budget?
GREG 2:	You get a lot for your money at Michael's Frozen Custard. Have you seen the size of their waffle cones?
CONGRESSWOMAN:	Yeah. And have you ever tried their turtle sundae? A mountain of rich, creamy custard (voice gets dreamy) drenched in hot fudge and caramel, piled high with fresh, crunchy pecans . . .
JOHN2:	I vote for polka.
CONGRESSMAN:	You're out to lunch.
JOHN 2:	Lunch? Great idea. Let's break for Michael's.
GREG (ANNCR):	The flavors can't be beat at Michael's Frozen Custard. Atwood Avenue, Monroe Street, and Verona Road in Verona.

AGREEMENT

JOHN:	Okay, representatives, we've been over this budget a hundred times and it's getting a bit taxing.
WOMAN VOICE:	Yeah, on the property owners.
JOHN:	We haven't reached an agreement on anything yet this month and the people of this . . .
WOMAN VOICE:	Whispering.
JOHN:	What?
WOMAN VOICE:	The messenger is here with your Michael's Frozen Custard, sir.
GREG:	'Scuse me, Mr. Speaker, I took the liberty of ordering turtle sundaes from Michael's Frozen Custard. Each is a mountain of rich, creamy custard drenched in hot fudge and caramel, then piled high with fresh, crunchy pecans and topped with a cherry.
	For those who *don't agree* turtle sundaes are the best item on the menu, I had Michael's Frozen Custard deliver a sampling of their 52 mouth-watering flavors.
CONGRESSWOMAN:	Ooooh, I'll take the Triple Raspberry Truffle Cheesecake in one of Michael's homemade waffle cones.
GREG 2:	Caramel Cashew over here.
CONGRESSWOMAN:	Make that two.
JOHN:	Mmmmm. . . now back to the matters at hand. . . eliminate property taxes?
(Unanimous "Yeah.")	
JOHN:	More greenspace?
(Unanimous "Yeah.")	
JOHN:	Build the convention center?
(Silence.)	
GREG (ANNCR):	Michael's Frozen Custard. We think you'll agree it's the best frozen custard in town. Atwood Avenue, Monroe Street, and Verona Road in Verona.

Nonhumorous advertising is much safer territory. Nonhumor doesn't have the same pressure to be great or fail. Testimonials are very popular and among the easiest spots to create. The trick is to find an interesting angle or method of storytelling. Otherwise your straightforward approach might translate into a story that's simply dull.

Example 7-8 is a simple pitch script, enlivened by the use of two announcers. Tom and Linda Holmes have a tire store. They don't do a lot of advertising, but when they do, it's on the radio—they spend maybe $20,000 a year. They write their own scripts. "Sometimes it looks like Tom wrote it on his knee as he was driving over," said their audio producer.

What makes this commercial effective is that Tom and Linda don't sound like announcers. Their cozy family feel projects in the ad, positioning this third-generation family-owned business right where they want it. The introduction of the female voice is savvy, too— because fewer are heard on the radio, a woman's voice has a power to break through clutter. And women buy tires too—this commercial lets them know that their business is welcome at Holmes. Add the fact that this commercial was produced for under $50, and you see why I consider it a success.

Example 7-8: Holmes Tire Radio Commercial
Used by permission of Holmes Tire and Auto.

Client   Holmes Tire and Auto

Event   November Tires

Co-op   Dunlop

☐ 60

Length   ☒ 30   Begin 11/1/93   End 11/6/93

☐ 30

DIRECTION   AUDIO

LINDA	—	When you're talking tires for tough winter driving, you're talking Dunlop all season and snow tires...
	—	
	—	
TOM	10_	Holmes Tire and Auto has them, like the Dunlop Max Track Grips starting at _____ or for high performance or luxury cars, the Qualifier Mud and Snow starts at only _____!
	—	
	—	
LINDA	20_	And Duratread Retread snow tires with thousands of biting edges are now two for $38.38!
	—	
	—	
TOM	—	Holmes Tire has been helping Madison area drivers make it through with the right tire for their driving needs for over 60 years!
	30_	
	—	
	—	
LINDA	—	So...when you're talking tires for tough winter driving...
	40_	
TOM	—	There's no place like Holmes!
	—	
	—	
	50_	
	—	
	—	
	—	
	60_	

Reading your own scripts the way Tom and Linda did is not uncommon, but it's not always effective, either. Voice talent is a profession, and voice actors have worked to remove all unpleasant aspects from their delivery. Your style of talking might not translate well to radio. If you'd like to use yourself or your relatives on the air, audition for the job just as if you were professional talent. Let the producer of your commercial have the final say.

What about celebrity endorsements? In spite of what you might think, these tend not to work in local or regional advertising. They test lower than any other type of commercial in terms of recall. You might have the coach of a local football team pitching your product, but your prospects are too likely to remember the celebrity and miss the connection with your product. Make sure the script leaves the emphasis on you—not your spokesperson.

Should you try humor or choose another approach? Of course you should give it a try, if it appeals to you. Just make sure you listen to the advice of your critics when you try your ideas out on them.

Tempo and Sound

Tempo is the pace of your delivery, and it's a distinctive part of your commercial's overall tone. Use pauses to add importance to key concepts. Use repetition to build rhythm and emphasis. Repetition is extremely important in radio copy. Unlike with print, your audience can't look back to see what they've missed. If their attention has wandered, you want to pull them back in.

Your tempo might be fast, to convey excitement; or it might be slower, just a relaxed, friendly chat. Listen closely to the next few commercials you hear and note how they use tempo to establish mood.

Sound is the other tool you have to create mood. Your announcer's voice conveys intensity, warmth, authority, desirability—you name it. Flirtatious boy-girl conversations turn up often in situation commercials. Because

women's voices are less common on the radio, using a female announcer can be one way to make your commercial unique. Use a voice that gets attention, and one that's appropriate to your image.

But don't be irritating just to be unique! A better way to break through the clutter is to use the drama of dead air. Pauses add punctuation to your message as clearly as sound effects.

Sound effects, from echoes to spectacular crashes, help project an image between your listeners' ears. Since your listeners have to participate in creating the image, they're more likely to remember it than they would as passive viewers of the same image on television. That alone is a good reason to explore sound effects. The Group Health Cooperative commercial described earlier in this chapter is a good example of a commercial that uses creative sound effects to get its point across.

How to Get the USP Across

A thirty-second radio commercial is only 80 to 100 words long. A sixty-second commercial will seldom pass 200 words.

Whichever length you choose, you will spend about half of those words establishing context, building rapport with your listener. You'll use more of them in your closing call to action. By the time you get done with those requirements (especially if you have multiple locations to describe), you've got precious few words left for selling your offering. Yet between those opening and closing segments, you have to deliver your pitch. How are you going to get your unique selling proposition across? The answer is focus. Take your key benefit, and phrase it as simply as if you were stating it in conversation. If it's taking you too many words, ask yourself, are you stating a benefit or describing a feature? Descriptions can run on forever. A good benefit statement won't be much more than a subject, a verb, and a phrase that supports the claim. "Jack's donuts taste great because they're made fresh every hour."

That's not great advertising yet, but it will be, after you blend it with the intro and the closing of the commercial. See Chapter 2, "Positioning," for more on this subject.

Look at Example 7-6 again, the script for the Independent Bankers Association of Wisconsin called "Convertible." This is a sixty-second commercial. The first eighty-six words are spent establishing context, introducing the characters and the situation we find them in. Then comes the USP.

In 67 words we learn how independent banks are different from big institutions. "They're independent of the outside controls and risky investments that are hurting some institutions, and community owned and operated so your money goes to work right here.... Whether you want to save up for the future or cruise top down today, your independent community bank can help." That first sentence is a mouthful, but a professional voice actor handled it smoothly. I like the friendly, conversational language with which this script conveys some fairly complicated concepts.

A final 40 word segment returns us to the theme of this script—the ride in the convertible—and ties that in with the benefit, while issuing a clear call to action: "Save for a rainy day with the bank that can help you enjoy the sunny ones."

Example 7-9 is another set of commercials that demonstrate how well this three-step outline works. Watch how these commercials from the Munz Corporation establish context, deliver benefits, and make a call to action.

The Munz Corporation is a real estate group with six apartment properties to advertise. The properties are geared to different markets, from students to working women to active senior citizens. The company found an effective and cost-efficient advertising approach that reached all markets while maximizing its investment in studio production.

In each of six commercials, you hear the same opening and closing segments—owner Dick Munz speaking, with music in the background. By talking about the home he grew up in and the homes he has for rent, he establishes context.

Then, to create a middle segment for each spot, an announcer reads benefit-oriented copy describing each separate property in a way that speaks to that market's unique desires. Different background music accompanies each middle segment.

Going back to "one for all" at the end, Dick reads a closing call to action.

The studio mixed down six different versions, and the commercials ran on a variety of radio stations chosen to reach their individual audiences. By making efficient use of its production time like this, the Munz Corporation got more bang for the buck. The spots cost less than $200 each to produce.

Example 7-9A, Munz Scripts
Used by permission of The Munz Corporation.

Client ___The Munz Corporation_____

Event ___Image open/close_____

Co-op _____

☐ 60

Length ☒ 30   Begin _____ End _____

☐ 30

DIRECTION   # AUDIO

—
—
—
10_
—
—   I'm Dick Munz, I was born and raised here in Madison, in a
small home on the East side. A special place to me, clean,
and comfortable, what a home should be. For 25 years now,
I've built apartment communities that have that same
special feel, the feeling of really being at home.

*** announcer insert for each
community

***

20_
—
—
—   Call us at 255-9433 for more information on the Munz
Apartment Community that's as individual as you
are...your comfortable place where you'll really feel at
30_   home.
—
—
—
40_
—
—
50_
—
—
60_

Example 7-9B, Munz Scripts
Used by permission of The Munz Corporation.

women 35-64
WMGN
WWQM
WOLX

Client ___The Munz Corporation_____

Event ___MORNINGSIDE ON THE GREEN_____

Co-op _____

☐ 60

Length ☒ 30   Begin _____End _____

☐ 30

DIRECTION

AUDIO

Morningside On The Green is a peaceful retreat from your busy
professional world. These 1, 2 and 3 bedroom apartment homes
are across from Easte Towne and a perfect fit for the

10_ contemporary person.
Our variety of floorplans are all enhanced with full size washer
and dryer, private entrance and garage, all the amenities. Look
through any window at Morningside On The Green and see the

20_ Nature Conservancy a stone's throw away...just the place for a
walk or bike ride after a busy day ... Enjoy the pool, entertain in
the clubhouse ... .it's all yours at Morningside On The Green.
Hayes Road across from East Towne, where life is easier ...

30_

(pick up follows)

40_

50_

60_

Example 7-9C, Munz Scripts
Used by permission of The Munz Corporation.

adults 25-54

WMGN

WWQM

WIBA-FM

Client ___The Munz Corporation_____

Event ___FOREST RUN_____

Co-op _____

☐ 60

Length ☒ 30   Begin _____End _____

☐ 30

DIRECTION

AUDIO

— Forest Run ... surrounded by a Forest preserve, this East side
— apartment community has the quiet and beauty of nature
— included in the rent, yet its location lends itself to such
10_ convenience ... we've built a home for you without the hassles.
— Private garages and entryways, full size washer and dryer,
— cathedral ceilings, walk-in closets, swimming pool, sun deck ...
— look out any window at Forest Run and see Wisconsin's natural
20_ beauty ... follow the path to Forest Run, just minutes from East
— Washington Avenue. It's the East-side address where you can get
— away from it all, without leaving it all behind.

(pick up follows)   30_

40_

50_

60_

Example 7-9D, Munz Scripts
Used by permission of The Munz Corporation.

Client   The Munz Corporation

WTDY   Event   ORCHARD VILLAGE

WMGN-FM   Co-op

WWQM   ☐ 60

WIBA-FM   Length ☒ 30   Begin _____End _____

             ☐ 30

DIRECTION   AUDIO

Orchard Village, where unique becomes the perfect descriptive.
Each 2 bedroom apartment includes individual washer and dryer,
underground parking, cable TV ... so what's so unique? How
about a loft, spiral staircase, skylight, fireplace ... individual
entrance ... all available at Orchard Village ... and just 10 minutes
from the Beltline on Raymond Road on Madison's West side.
Look out any window at Orchard Village and see young
professionals climbing the corporate ladder, families, and active
seniors glad to have the freedom apartment living provides.
Orchard Village ... a very unique place to make yourself at home.

(pick up follows)

Example 7-9E, Munz Scripts
Used by permission of The Munz Corporation.

WMGN
WWQM
WOLX

Client The Munz Corporation

Event CAMELOT

Co-op

☐ 60

Length ☒ 30   Begin _____ End _____

☐ 30

DIRECTION   AUDIO

— What a wonderful place to live. Next to Lake Mendota and

— Tenney Park in your back yard … Camelot's legend of gracious

— living is, well, legendary. From efficiencies to 1, 2, and 3 bedroom

10_ floor plans, Camelot is at your service, providing washers and

— dryers, undergrouund parking, swimming pool, clubhouse for

— entertaining … ahhhh.

— The legend continues with the excitement of State Street and the

20_ Capitol just minutes away, and shopping right next door. Look

— out any window at Camelot and see everyone from students to

— active seniors enjoying the park setting and convenience that is

— Camelot, where the legend's happy ending is just for you.

(pick up follows) 30_

—

—

—

40_

—

—

—

50_

—

—

—

60_

Example 7-9F, Munz Scripts
Used by permission of The Munz Corporation.

WMGN
WWQM
WZEE

Client __The Munz Corporation_____
Event __STONEWOOD VILLAGE_____
Co-op _____
□ 60
Length ☒ 30   Begin _____ End _____
□ 30

DIRECTION

AUDIO

KIDS SFX* —

GIGGLE* —

(pick up follows)

—
—
—
10_
—
—
—
20_
—
—
30_
—
—
—
40_
—
—
—
50_
—
—
60_

Raising a family is a tough job these days, and where you raise your children is important. Stonewood Village, nestled next to a wooded park on Madison's East side, is family friendly, from our spacious closets and individual washer/dryers to the big pool and playground area. Look out any window* at Stonewood Village, and see families growing in a wonderful environment that's close to schools, shopping, everything. Right off highway 51. Stonewood Village, a blend of convenience, class and comfort, just off Milwaukee Street … it's a great place to call home.*

Example 7-9G, Munz Scripts
Used by permission of The Munz Corporation.

Client ___The Munz Corporation_____

Event ___VILLAGE GREEN EAST_____

WMAD-FM

WZEE-FM

WIBA-FM

Co-op _____

☐ 60

Length ☒ 30   Begin _____End _____

☐ 30

DIRECTION

AUDIO

—
—
—
10_
—
—
—
—
20_
—
—
—
—
30_
—
—
—
(pick up follows)   40_
—
—
—
50_
—
—
—
60_

You're going to work, going to school, going from being somebody's kid to being somebody … we've got the perfect apartment home for you. Village Green East. 1 or 2 bedrooms, with everything you want. Dishwashers, big closets, swimming pool, tennis courts … sounds expensive, but it's not. Even bike paths with 22 acres of nature nearby. But it's close to everything … it's a lot like home, without your parents! Look out any window at Village Green East, and see people just like you … making it on their own, with a terrific place of their own at Village Green East, just north of East Towne. It's what you've been looking for!

Copy Tips

So how do you *really* write a radio commercial? It's not that different from any other advertising copy. Just remember the AIDA formula.

- Get **a**ttention.
- Arouse **i**nterest.
- Create **d**esire.
- Stimulate **a**ction.

To write your opening, start by picturing someone who buys your offering. Write what you think would get that person's attention.

Now connect your opening to your key benefit. Depending on the approach of your commercial—pitch, situation, or music—how you do this will be different. Once you make that connection and unroll the story of your benefits, you simply have to close by stating the action you would like listeners to take or, if you are writing an image ad, summarizing the impression you are trying to make (like Group Health Cooperative's phrase "Opening new doors to quality health care"). If you use a tagline, state it now.

Count the words. If you are writing a :30, try to stop before you reach 100 (spoken words, not including directions like sound effects). If you are writing a :60, stop at 200 spoken words.

As far as the format goes, don't worry too much about it. As the examples in this chapter show, different people type their copy in slightly different formats as far as margins, indents, and use of capital letters go. Choose whichever's easiest for you.

I have given a lot of advice elsewhere in this book that will help you with writing radio advertising copy—see Chapter 5 on the creative approach and Chapter 6 on print advertising.

Here are some specific tips on writing for radio:

- Act fast. You have about three seconds to engage your listener. What can you open with that will establish, "This is for you, and we mean business"? Think about the Group Health commercial again. The coughing and sneezing to the Blue Danube Waltz acts fast to get the attention of cold sufferers.

- Speak fast. We are accustomed to radio announcers who are skilled at fast patter. Ordinary conversational speech sounds absurdly slow in comparison.

- Try humor. Radio is particularly suitable to all kinds of humor, whether sophisticated or folksy. Just be sure you're writing with your audience's sense of humor in mind—write to amuse them, not yourself. And get a second opinion before you assume that your copy is funny and in good taste.

- Make a list of the important points you want to make, then prioritize them. Don't be surprised if only number one and maybe—if you're lucky—number two will fit. Radio is no place for clutter, since you're working fast and without visual clues. It's more important that you communicate one point well, by establishing context and then using repetition to reinforce it. If you have too many points to fit under one umbrella thought, it's time for you to split them up and produce several commercials. This is no place for a "seven reasons why" ad. Think instead about a "seven reasons why" campaign, with seven commercials under that umbrella concept, linked by sound effects, announcer's voice, and music.

- Think of your closing call as an audio logo. Make the wording of the call to action identical in each commercial, and use music and a slogan or tagline to reinforce your identity. Repeat this over and over.

- Above all, be consistent. Radio demands frequency to work, but if the message isn't consistent, the frequency doesn't buy you the build-up effect it should. Make each ad consistent, recognizable as part of the whole. Don't adopt different styles in your radio advertising in an attempt to reach different audiences. You will never be all things to all people. Instead focus on one audience via one style of advertising, and go, go, go until they walk in your door humming your tune. Absolutely positively use your tagline in a consistent way in every commercial.

We've been talking about how to design the message you deliver, how to sculpt the listeners' experience so that it leaves them with a desire to take the action you request. You've learned how the elements of copy approach, style of delivery, music, and sound effects help to create that experience. Your task is to decide which approach is right for you, and how you're going to give it your own unique twist. When you've made these decisions and written your script, it's time to tackle radio production.

I have been writing as if I thought each of you would write all your commercials yourself. Of course there are professionals available who can do this work for you. Freelance writers and advertising agencies are just two possibilities. The reps who call on you from the radio stations and the production studios will also help. But this is a how-to book. Why not try your hand at it before you assign the task to someone else?

There is an even better reason to give the craft of writing your serious attention. When you have tried to do the job yourself, you are in a better position to judge the creative efforts of others. Whether you write the actual words or not, after studying this chapter, you know what to look for in a good radio script. If you don't find the AIDA formula at work, you know it's time to ask for a revision.

Radio Production

Carl and the three women sat huddled over their microphones. Betty drew a feather over the sensitive wire cage, blowing through her pursed lips as she did so. The sound of a cold wind whipped through the room. With a maraca she added the sound of hail against the window glass.

Up came the music track, and the women began to sing: "Jamaica, paradise, the getaway that's oh so nice..." As they drew out the last note, Carl's voice came in, deep and rich as a coconut. "Jamaica Vacation Holidays. Act before January 31 and you'll receive..."

That's how a radio commercial production looked forty years ago—but not today. Today each component of the commercial would be produced separately, sometimes on audio tape (reel to reel), but more often these days on digital media—a floppy disk. The specialists might be in different parts of the country—a sound effects library in Los Angeles supplying the storm, while Carl supplied the voice from a studio in Atlanta, and a jingle house in Chicago recorded the "Jamaica, paradise" song. A producer in yet another city would collect the elements and mix them down to the final commercial.

To produce Jamaica Vacation's thirty-second radio commercial, a half-dozen talented people orchestrated their efforts, from scriptwriting to sound mixing to special effects. Leading them was a producer, and collaborating throughout, of course, was the client.

Three elements of sound must be laid down on tape to create your commercial: voice, music, and sound effects.

Who's going to do all this for you? The producer—and the talent this person assembles.

How do you decide who will produce your commercial? You might find yourself working with your radio station's in-house producer, or with freelancers, or with a production studio. As always, I suggest you start by asking your professional associates for recommendations.

Who has provided good service on a similar project? If this fails to turn up the lead you're looking for, consult your Yellow Pages under the heading "Audio Production Services."

Production Cost Alternatives

Your least expensive option is to choose in-house production by the radio station where your commercial will run. Talk to your rep; you can probably negotiate a simple production for free or nearly free. The rep or someone on staff will write copy for you if you ask. (To judge its quality, see the copy tips above.) Your commercial will be read by one of the station's announcers, and the background music will be "needle-drop," or prerecorded licensed music. Maybe this production is just fine for your needs.

If your ideas are more elaborate, you'll find yourself working with perhaps a freelance writer or producer and an independent audio recording studio. You'll be paying more for the production—perhaps $750 to $1,000 for a spot with three voices and some background music. If you have a song in mind, expect that to go up to $4,000 or $6,000 or even $10,000. You will be paying professionals to write and produce the music, as well as the script of the commercial.

You get what you pay for. A successful spot is an equal balance of three good elements: good copy, good talent, and good production. If you compromise on any one element, you compromise your whole ad.

Listeners tune into flaws in the production like cars passing an accident scene. Your commercial has only a few seconds to set up a situation. You have to get your listeners to suspend disbelief and play along with you. If the tape warbles, or the mikes are bad, or the sound effects aren't good, you've lost them.

Your production company should provide you with an estimate broken down into categories of studio time and materials, including tape, music, voice talent, and dubs (duplicate copies for distribution). If any item is unclear to you, ask for a full explanation.

Template 7-6A shows a typical format for a radio production estimate. The invoice from a production company would look quite similar.

Template 7-6A: Jamaica Vacation Produced by Production Company

Radio Production Estimate

Client: Jamaica Vacation
Contact: Betty Hodawa
Date: 11-30-94
Project Description:

                                   :30
                                   Voice + music + sound effect, record and mix

Description	Quantity	Unit Cost	Total
Studio time			
Record voice, mix down	3	$65.00	$195.00
Tape			
3 tracks to combine	18	0.50	9.00
Music/SFX			
Jingle production	1	2,000.00	2,000.00
SFX from library	1	no charge	0.00
Voice			
Anncr only	0.5	130.00	65.00
Dubs			
4 reel-to-reels	4	26.00	104.00
1 cassette for client	1	6.00	6.00
		Subtotal	$2,379.00
		Tax	130.85
		Total	$2,509.85

This is the cost for a complex, high-quality, studio-produced commercial. Pare it down to a bare-bones budget and you might hear the owner of Jamaica Vacation reading the script, and canned music with a tropical theme taking the place of the jingle. Now the budget might look more like that in Template 7-6B.

Template 7-6B: Jamaica Vacation Produced by Radio Station

Radio Production Estimate

Client: Jamaica Vacation
Contact: Betty Hodawa
Date: 11-30-94
Project Description:

:30
Client voice + needle-drop music + sound
         effect record and mix

Description	Quantity	Unit Cost	Total
Studio time			
Record voice, mix down	1.5	$30.00	$45.00
Tape			
3 tracks to combine	18	0.50	9.00
Music/SFX			
Needle-drop	1	65.00	65.00
SFX from library	1	no charge	0.00
Dubs			
5 cassettes	5	6.00	30.00
		Subtotal	$149.00
		Tax	8.20
		Total	$157.20

Template 7-6C is a blank form you can use to keep track of your own estimates.

Template 7-6C: Production Estimate Blank

Radio Production Estimate

Client:
Contact:
Date:
Project Description:

Description	Quantity	Unit Cost	Total
Studio time			
Tape			
Music/SFX			
Voice			
Dubs			
		Subtotal	$0.00
		Tax	0.00
		Total	$0.00

Defining the Budget Line Items

There are two categories in radio production: the studio time and the materials required to complete the commercial. An estimate will typically show the unit cost for each category, and then the total projected for that job. An invoice will show similar information with the final costs. Here are the cost line items that you can expect to see.

- *Studio time.* Studio time is based on an hourly rate; the price will range from $50 to $100 per hour in a midsize market, and closer to $200 or $250 in a big city. The rate reflects a combination of factors: the technological sophistication of the facilities you use, the creative skill of the producer, and of course "what the traffic will bear." Your production company might be willing to negotiate on this line item. (On the materials, probably not.) On the estimate should be a description of how the time estimate is allotted. The description might include recording the voice track, mixing, researching sound effects and music, etc.

- *Tape.* A small amount of audio tape is consumed in mixing a commercial—usually about six times as much as the length of the final spot. In other words, a sixty-second commercial will require six minutes of tape to record, by the time the various tracks are created and then mixed down to one master. This should be a small charge—$10 or less.

- *Music fees.* In most cases this line will refer to "needle-drop" music, the prerecorded music available from libraries. When you are purchasing needle-drop music, this cost will be a dollar amount based on the length of the music used and the exposure it will receive—how widely the commercial will be distributed. These music rental fees are just a pass-through cost for the production studio or radio station. It's not a money-maker for them—they pay annual licensing fees in order to have this music in stock for you, and this is how they recoup that investment. Music use fees vary from market to market, but should not come to more than $100.

  Production of custom music—songs and jingles—is another matter; this can cost from $2,000 up. See the description in the section "Music Production."

- *Voice talent.* The talent you use will probably be members of a union, and that affects the rates you pay. Follow your producer's advice regarding sources of talent and payment terms. For a commercial that airs statewide, you might pay $150 and up. Exposure in just a local market will go for less—$75 to $100. Of course, this varies with the size of the market, as well. In Chicago these numbers might be more like $1,000.

  If it seems crazy to spend this kind of money on an hour or two of someone's time, remember that the fee is based on the skill and talent of the performer. You are hiring a specialist—maybe for his or her skill at doing character voices, or for the ability to make forty seconds of script sound good in a thirty-second commercial.

- *Duplication.* Most commercials are still being produced on reel-to-reel tape, at least by the production facilities. Radio stations that help you for next to nothing are more likely to use cassettes, a much cheaper format that delivers much poorer sound quality. These are both examples of analog sound. The industry is moving rapidly toward digital sound, created in computers during the editing process and transferred around on floppy disks.

  Once the master recording has been created, whether it's digital or analog, you will need duplicates, or dubs, to send to other stations. Even if your schedule calls for only one station, you will want to have a cassette made for your own files. There should be a line item on your budget with an explanation of how many dubs will be made, and in what format. The cost will not be more than 5 to 15 percent of the budget.

These rates are for a midsize market in a midwestern city, and are fairly close to the national averages, I believe. If you are in a larger market, you might expect to spend several times this amount on production. Of course, the price of hamburger there is probably different, too.

Rates are going up as digital editing becomes widespread. Production facilities have new equipment to pay for, but that's only part of the reason. The other half of the equation is the greater flexibility of digital editing. With so many alternatives available, decision making takes longer. And in production, time is money. (I talk more about this in Chapter 8, "Television.")

Voice Talent

Your next step, after choosing your production vendor and developing your script, is to cast your talent. The voices who will be heard in your commercial might be freelance professionals, or employees of the radio station, or you or someone you know.

If the radio station records your commercial, it's simplest to have its on-air staff read the parts. A note of caution: Pay attention to what day-part your commercial is produced for. You might want to have a different announcer read your script. You don't want your commercial to get lost in the general patter.

If you need a polished production to make your concept work, consider hiring professional voice talent. Perhaps your script calls for a character actor—a warm old grandpa, or a wisecracking "Fonzy" type. Don't let an amateur voice shoot down your idea; spring for the talent to do it right. When negotiating with professionals, be sure to make it clear that you want to pay only a one-time fee rather than residuals, which are based on how many times the commercial airs. Most actors are members of the union, and follow trade customs in their arrangements with you. As in any business deal, you will negotiate a fee before you contract for the talent.

Amateur voices, yours or those of people you know, are your third alternative. The lack of polish might just cause listeners to stop and pay attention, simply because it's not what they're used to. You be the judge whether this is appropriate to you. What's the general tone of your advertising? Does the informal "folks next door" approach fit?

If your script runs long, that's an argument in favor of professional talent. A trained actor can read more clearly than you or I

could, while still sounding perfectly natural. That's a definite advantage.

Music Production

The power of music is too important to ignore. You can have original music produced, or you can use free music from the radio station's collection. A third option is to arrange for permission to use an existing recording by a published artist, but that's a long shot. Even if your idea is to parody a popular song, not actually use it, you are infringing on that artist's rights. Permission is usually difficult and expensive to obtain. Copyright infringement is not a mistake you want to make. You might feel that your chances of getting caught are about like those of getting struck by lightning. Unfortunately, the results are about as devastating. At the least you'll get a cease-and-desist order and a bill for the cost you would have been charged. But these days there's a real likelihood that you might be hung out to dry, just to set an example. Your error in judgment could cost you your business. If you want to use someone's copyrighted material, do it. But first arrange permission and pay the money you owe them.

Any radio station or production house will provide you with canned, or "needle-drop," music for a modest access charge. Plan to spend some time with your radio rep or production house in the library, exploring sounds. Here's a tip: If you can think of a song that sounds like what you want, bring it to the session. Of course you won't be able to use that precise piece of music, but it can be worth thousands of words in trying to explain to your rep what sound you're looking for. Your rep has probably spent hundreds of hours in the library with other clients, and might know just where to find a cut that sounds like the song you brought—and that it might have taken you hours to find if you hadn't brought an idea-starter. (See Chapter 8, "Television," for more on music.)

If your approach is a song or jingle, then your musical needs go beyond just needle-drop music. You're going to have to contract with a jingle house to create and perform an original composition. For about $500, the jingle house will create a demo tape, which will sound quite finished: Instruments and voices will be mixed to sound as much like the anticipated result as possible. You'll make suggestions, and the house will produce the final product at a cost of $2,000 and up. You will be the complete owner of that piece of music, copyright and all.

A Note about Working with Music

Sound can be lush or stark, melodic or dramatic. Let's take a look at how these effects are achieved.

First, listen for the low notes. Here's where rhythm is established. You might hear a bass drum and a bass guitar setting up the fundamental rhythm of the piece.

In the midrange you'll hear first the melody and then, as you listen more closely, the harmony. This is where the voice of the lead singer will be pitched, and maybe some instruments or back-up voices to round out the sound. A little reverb, or echo, can add a lot of mood here; swelling strings convey excitement and a big, expensive sound. It's elements like these that create the "texture" of a song.

Your lyrics have to come through clearly, so be careful not to clutter the midrange. Your rule of thumb: If you can't hum the song after hearing it once or twice, it's not simple enough. Pare down the midrange, and let the melody come through.

At the high end come the "garnishes" to the sound. Extra percussion can give it "snap." High strings contribute a romantic sound. Special sound effects might add a memorable touch. Experiment and have some fun with "extra" sounds.

Sound Effects (SFX)

Radio is all about sound. Be sure to sweeten your production with any little extra sounds that might help paint a picture for your listener. Crickets chirping can turn a banjo tune into a summer evening on the back porch. A howling wind in the background can turn a coat sale pitch into a powerful sense memory. Sound effects evoke sensations and bring the imagination into play. Use this technique to boost your commercial's entertainment value. You'll be rewarded with memorable advertising.

Don't use sound effects that don't make sense. It's such an obvious trick! You don't want to promise something and not deliver on it. You build credibility with the sounds as well as the words in your commercial.

As with needle-drop music, an amazing array of sound effects is available from prerecorded sources. Producers typically don't even charge for using them (although you are paying by the hour, so the time you spend looking for one is a factor).

If you and your producer resort to creating your own sounds, be sure you do it right. Badly produced sounds are as destructive as illogical ones. If you want your voice to sound like you're talking on the telephone, your studio should suggest a special audio filter, not hand you a paper towel tube to speak through.

Summary

We've talked about why you should use radio, how to negotiate your buy, and how to produce your ad. Radio is the simplest medium to experiment with: The production and air time are inexpensive, and with the use of co-op programs and some sharp negotiating, you can get your costs down to just about zero. For many advertisers, that's reason enough to try radio.

Radio's key advantage is that it delivers a highly targeted audience. Whether radio is right for you depends entirely on whether that audience is your *market*. If it's not, who cares how cheap it is? It's money you don't need to spend. If it is a good fit, start humming. You're about to be on the radio.

Case Study: Heartland Litho

Heartland Litho is a commercial printing business that began fifteen years ago. The business started in a different location and under a different name. Along the way it acquired another business. This began to be a problem, as the business outgrew its name. Owners Ralph McCall and Mike Couey felt that their growing business deserved an updated image. They held a contest among their customers, chose a new name, and with that decision chose a course of action that would require a well-planned marketing campaign.

Ralph took on the search for a marketing solution. Mike stood by to manage the press room. When I met with Ralph and his advertising consultant, Scott Rippe, this is the story I heard.

Since Heartland Litho was a printer, the first ideas that came to mind were for direct mail pieces. But a thorough marketing review convinced Ralph to give radio a try.

Scott coached Ralph through a process of setting goals and defining strategies, much as this book will do for you. Ralph found that his goals centered around "stretching the peaks, raising the valleys." He wanted to extend his busy season and bring in more sales during slow seasons. Printing is a highly competitive market, and radio was attractive to Ralph partly because other printers weren't advertising on it. So Ralph and Scott developed a marketing strategy with a one-year media plan concentrated on radio.

Where to advertise? Radio, but which station? Heartland Litho surveyed its top fifty customers. It learned that the buyers were predominantly women, between twenty-five and forty-four, working in offices in secretarial, managerial, or marketing positions. To find them, Ralph and Scott compared the available stations' rankings for various day-parts. They found the women listening to adult contemporary stations and a little rock 'n' roll.

Heartland Litho contracted for a schedule that included three different stations, each beginning with a six-week heavy-up sequence followed by a continuous maintenance stream (Example 7-10).

Example 7-10: media calendar

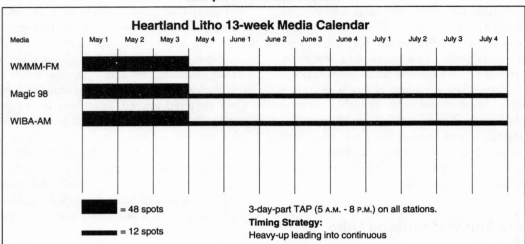

Heartland Litho 13-week Media Calendar

Media	May 1	May 2	May 3	May 4	June 1	June 2	June 3	June 4	July 1	July 2	July 3	July 4

WMMM-FM

Magic 98

WIBA-AM

■ = 48 spots

▬ = 12 spots

3-day-part TAP (5 A.M. - 8 P.M.) on all stations.
Timing Strategy:
Heavy-up leading into continuous

The schedule began in May, jumping in just prior to the summer slow time. For three weeks Heartland Litho ran forty-eight commercials a week in three day-part TAP plans that kept them on the air, all over the dial, from 6 A.M. to 7 P.M. That's aggressive, a big commitment. Ralph was ready.

The blitz rolled out—and the shop experienced its worst month in years! Ralph had the sense not to pull the plug, and in the next two months the program started to show its effect.

Ralph didn't track results mathematically, but he swears that the prospects who call are better qualified, the cold calls are warmer, and the sales he closes are the right kinds of jobs for his shop.

He's letting the maintenance schedule flow on through the end of the year, when he'll evaluate whether to use radio again. I think Ralph will decide that it has a permanent place in his plan.

Example 7-11: Heartland Litho Script
Used by permission of Heartland Litho.

Commercial Copy: Heartland Litho
Subject: Phase Three: Environmental
Copy Date: 6-30-94

ANNCR:	There's a lot more to being an environmentally friendly printer than you might think. Heartland Litho President Ralph McCall explains. . .
RALPH:	Using recycled papers, and soy or other vegetable based inks are just the beginning (edit). That's the raw materials coming in. What we are concerned with at Heartland Litho is the byproducts of the printing process, and what goes out of the plant (edit). We recycle all of our waste papers, trim stock, run-in stock, waste sheets (edit). We recycle all of our plates, our negatives (edit). We contract with (edit) EPA-licensed haulers and disposal companies to deal with our waste inks, our waste darkroom chemistries, our waste solvents. . . to make sure none of those get into the waste stream of our company and prove harmful to the environment (edit). They're all picked up and dealt with in an environmentally responsible way.
ANNCR:	Environmentally responsible—*more*than just recycled papers and soy-based inks. Does *your* printer care that much?
RALPH:	I don't know the procedures and policies of most other printing compa-nies. I know that Heartland Litho lives up to environmental standards that haven't even been written yet.
ANNCR:	Heartland Litho. . . Atwood Avenue across from the Barrymore Theatre.

Injecting Warmth into a Cold, Technical Business

Heartland's creative approach is evident in the tone of the commercials. You have to imagine Ralph, in his gravelly baritone, speaking from his heart. Here's how the script in Example 7-11 evolved.

Scott counseled Ralph to spend the first five months on positioning, spreading his message of warmth in a cold, technical business. The creative hook is the voice, and the informal conversational style of the production is the audio equivalent of the hand-held camera we've all seen in TV advertising. The voice you hear becomes a personality to you. Ralph's style of delivery is untrained, but relaxed and conversational. You liked Ralph after you heard a few of his commercials.

This is an image campaign, designed to create a bond with prospects before meeting them. It's soft-sell; note that there's no phone number mentioned—just the location. The goal was simply to differentiate Heartland Litho from the competition, to elevate its image to that of a bigger business, with more capabilities and higher quality, than people had expected from the shop under its old name, Newsletter Press.

Scott and Ralph chose several topics for commercials based on the key benefits defined in their positioning. Then they created commercials on those topics. The way they went about it was unorthodox.

Scott has a background in radio, and knows how to do studio production. The two went into a production facility at one of the radio stations and sat down with the microphones on. With no prepared script, Scott interviewed Ralph about the quality of his work, the excellence of his customer service staff, the stringent environmental standards he sets. The casual format captured Ralph at his most persuasive. His sincerity shone through as he talked about his dedication to his business and his customers' satisfaction.

The material recorded that day gave Scott all he needed to produce six commercials. He wrote introductions, transitions, and closings for each spot, and edited Ralph's comments into a capsule version of their conversation. The evidence in the printed transcript is the many places marked (edit).

Scott and Ralph are very pleased with the results this campaign is generating. Their advice to you: "Decide how much you're going to put into radio, because *it is going to work*. You decide how much success you want."

Chapter 8

Television: Who Needs It? Maybe You

We are listening to the opening strains of the Blue Danube Waltz. Before us, a man is standing alone, looking downcast. His white suit is spattered with paint. His look of concern changes to one of delight as the stains start to fly from his clothes. In seconds the stains are gone. His expression is now relief and gratitude as he looks at the logo appearing in front of him. "Klinke Cleaners" (Example 8-1).

Example 8-1: Storyboard from Blue Danube
Used by permission of Klinke Cleaners.

TITLE: _KLINKE CLEANER – "DRY CLEANING"_

LENGTH: _:30_

NOTES: _FLASHING TITLES. "BLUE DANUBE WALTZ" UNDER THROUGHOUT._
ANNOUNCER HAS BRITISH ACCENT.

FLASHING
TITLE → _AMAZING DRYCLEANING DRAMATIZATION_

(STAINS BEGIN LIFTING OFF & FLYING AWAY)

(MUSIC)

(MAN DRESSED IN WHITE SUIT
COVERED IN STAINS, STANDS
BEFORE A DROOPY BACKDROP.)

ANNCR: THIS CLEANING DEMONSTRATION IS BROUGHT
        TO YOU BY KLINKE CLEANERS.

CAMERA: CLOSE UP BEGINS PULLING SLOWLY BACK.

FLASHING
TITLE → _DON'T TRY THIS AT HOME_

FLASHING
TITLE → _TRUST KLINKE CLEANERS_

ANNCR: WHILE WE CAN'T PROMISE EVERYTHING
       WILL COME CLEAN THIS EASILY...

..., WITH OVER A DOZEN STATE-OF-THE-ART
LOCATIONS AND SAME-DAY SERVICE....

TITLE: → _Klinke_
        Cleaners

ANNCR: ..., YOU CAN TRUST KLINKE CLEANERS TO
       MAKE ALL OF YOUR CLEANING CONCERNS VANISH.

That's just one example of a successful TV ad. It's entertaining, and it's simple. It relies on the unique visual power of television to get its point across. Not only that, it was simple to film on a budget. Entertaining, effective, and cheap—that adds up to a commercial that works from every perspective. We'll look more closely at this commercial and a companion spot when we get to the case study at the end of the chapter. So stay tuned for more of this exciting story. In the meantime...

Television is an emotional medium. It combines sound and sight to involve us at our deepest levels. TV advertising can create great longing for the products it depicts; it can deliver life-altering messages. The visual imagery it uses to communicate becomes part of our culture. The "slice of life" commercials we see are the stories we tell ourselves about who we are and what we can be. Using visual images, verbal persuasion, and music, TV advertising delivers information while it entertains. Although we often don't like to admit it, it's one of our favorite—and most universal— forms of pop culture.

TV gives an experience. It demonstrates what it's like to own and use whatever's being sold. The advantages come through loud and clear when you use sight and sound. Audiovisual demonstrations are one of the best teaching methods known.

For you as a marketer, television advertising is the next best thing to delivering your sales message in person. Don't get me wrong; TV can't sell a product to someone who doesn't want it or can't afford it. But it can do a good job of getting someone to stop and think about what you're saying. TV conveys prestige. Your ad on TV translates into credibility for your company and your product. It can give your sales force a boost.

Don't be intimidated by television. Too many businesspeople believe that it's too expensive and complicated to consider, but that's simply not true. You can produce a spot and buy a decent schedule of air time for as little as $3,000 ($1,000 for production and $2,000 for a few dozen spots in one of the cheaper day-parts). In this chapter you'll learn how—and why, and who. We'll talk about television advertising from three angles:

1. Strategy: Who uses TV, and for what purposes

2. Buying TV: What it costs and how it's sold

3. Creating TV advertising

When you have finished this chapter, you'll be able to create a plan for a TV commercial or a complete campaign. Your plan will include a timing strategy, a creative approach, and a production plan, including schedules and budgets.

Who Should Use Television?

Retail stores. Restaurants. Car dealers and repair services. Service firms whose clients are consumers—anyone from a drycleaner to a law firm specializing in personal injury. The answer to "who" is this simple: Whoever is trying to reach a broad general audience, or whose selective market is matched by the demographics of certain television programs. If you fall into that group, read this chapter!

Television is going through a revolution as I write this. Cable television is expanding like crazy. Already in large markets you can buy time on programs reaching cable subscribers on almost a block-by-block basis. Think about it—now you can focus the amazing emotional power of television on precisely the people most likely to buy your product, with little waste of circulation.

Whether you should use television— broadcast or cable—depends on who your customers are and whether they are found in the audience television offers. Television is a mass-market medium. That means that a broad spectrum of people are sitting on the other side of that screen. Whole families watch TV together—people of different ages and genders, in different income brackets, and with different interests. Obviously the advertisers who succeed on television are those whose products or services have broad appeal.

Over 60 percent of America's households have more than one TV set. People spend on average five or six hours, or even more, watching television each day. That's much more time than they spend with radio or print. These are persuasive reasons to use television to spread your message.

What are the wrong reasons to advertise on television? Your commercial on TV can make you seem larger and more prosperous, because viewers don't consciously draw distinctions between local and national advertisers. But you shouldn't choose to advertise on TV simply because you have a high opinion of your importance, and you'd like to share it. Make sure your plan for advertising on TV is part of a complete and well-thought-out marketing plan.

You might be tempted to advertise on TV because you'd like to play Steven Spielberg. It's true that producing a television ad is exciting. But it can also be expensive, and costs can go up quickly. The possibility of messing up is great. Cheap production looks bad and hurts your image. Don't get into TV advertising without the resources to do it right. If you're going to produce a commercial, choose an appropriate production facility (we'll talk more about production later in this chapter) and plan to run your commercial for a long time to maximize your investment. In other words, think of TV advertising as an investment in your business. Approach it in the same way you would other business investments.

Television: The Big Picture

Until the mid-1980s, all television signals traveled out from local broadcasting towers in an expanding circle. This is still true today for local stations, but cable companies offer the alternative of receiving your signal through a wire. These cable TV companies offer viewers additional "free" channels and pay-per-view movie services. In my county, 63 percent of the homes are hooked up to cable. Statistics for your community might be even higher. The proliferation of special-interest material on cable segments the viewing audience in ways that weren't possible when nearly everyone sat around one TV in the living room and watched one of the three network-affiliated broadcast stations available in their area.

Network affiliate stations still bring you the "Big Three" channels you've known since the 1950s: ABC, CBS, and NBC. And now the Fox network is making that the "Big Four." These broadcast stations deliver the broadest audience demographics. Cable stations offer access to more specialized audiences. Just as different radio stations appeal to different types of listeners, so do cable channels appeal to different types of viewers.

Today, cable companies offer a choice of channels:

- MTV, for the youth and music culture
- Lifetime, which appeals to women
- BET, aimed at African-Americans
- A&E, for those interested in culturally oriented programs
- ESPN, for sports fans
- CNN, for news junkies

and many others. Each of these allots time to local cable operators for local advertising.

You can see how cable stations succeed by appealing to specific segments of the mass market. The demographics of cable users are very attractive to advertisers, partly because they are self-selecting for a narrow and more loyal audience, and partly because the presence of cable in the home skews the demographics toward people with a level of disposable income that permits spending $20 to $50 a month on entertainment. Even if their income is toward the low end, these people are demonstrably willing to buy consumer goods and services.

Should you consider advertising on a cable station? Advertising on local cable is very popular with retailers. You'll see a full spectrum of your local merchants on cable, from dry cleaners to department stores. Why? Cable time can be inexpensive in comparison with broadcast time, and, as we have already noted, the audience is narrowly defined by demographics. If you have a limited budget, cable is a good way to target a specific audience. But viewer levels are usually much lower than for broadcast stations, meaning that your cost per viewer is higher. Therefore, cable advertising might not be as inexpensive as it seems.

However, as an advertiser, you can have a degree of control over the audience you buy that once only direct mail could approach, and you're getting it at a cost competitive with radio. The cable television company in your area will have information on its customers that gives you a good demographic snapshot of the people you're able to reach.

When is broadcast television a smart choice? Look into broadcast television if you're trying to reach a market that's broad demographically, but narrow geographically—no bigger than the area covered by your local stations' broadcast signal (usually a four- or five-county region). Here's an example: Suppose you sell cars. Who buys them? And who decides which brand to buy? Typically a husband and wife are both involved in the decision, and each has different priorities for the vehicle they buy. She may be interested in safety features and seating arrangements; he may care more about sporty lines and performance claims. So your car advertising has to reach and persuade both, in separate ways. Decisions about major appliances are also joint decisions, and that's why you'll see local appliance retailers on broadcast TV.

Seasonality brings some advertisers to broadcast television who would never advertise on TV at other times of year. A Christmas tree farm advertises on a local broadcast station every year. It buys a flight of commercials that starts two weeks before Thanksgiving and runs until two weeks after. Who decides when and where to get the Christmas tree? The whole family. That's why broadcast works for Christmas tree farms, even though it's more expensive, especially in that season. The spot is low-budget—just some on-site footage of the farm and the happy families selecting their trees. It never changes from year to year, but the campaign works each time.

During the holiday season you'll see a lot of local retailers using broadcast TV because the mass market it delivers meets their needs. Everyone young and old needs new ideas for holiday shopping.

In short, if you sell a product or service whose market is spread across demo-graphics—age, income, gender—then broadcast TV makes sense for you.

On the other hand, suppose you run a neighborhood grocery store. No matter who you reach out to, your primary market is going to be residents of the surrounding streets. You'd be better off buying a mailing list for your Zip code and dropping some loyalty-building coupons. Your market is too narrow geographically for broadcast television. Even cable television might be too broad.

Or suppose you're a brokerage firm specializing in investment planning for CEOs. You're not going to reach them efficiently on television. The demographics of your market are too narrow.

What size is the marketplace you're doing business in? If you're in a smaller or midsize market—population of 100,000 to 400,000—TV may or may not be cost-effective. You'll need to look closely at audience figures and costs. Study your local broadcast and cable TV marketplace carefully. (We'll show you how later in this chapter.) Some towns are very retail-oriented in TV advertising, with lots of sale events and prices-slashed commercials.

Other markets might feature more image advertising from hospitals, manufacturers, and service firms. Watch the ads in your area, and see where you fit in.

That's a taste of what lies ahead—planning a campaign, figuring out the best stations to advertise on, creating a budget, and producing the commercials. In the next sections of this chapter, we'll look at each of these topics in more detail.

Planning the TV Campaign: Choosing What You Will Accomplish

Marketing Objectives: Two Approaches to TV Advertising

As an advertiser you will choose from two possibilities in your approach, depending on your marketing objectives.

The news/entertainment approach. Most advertisers, especially those in retail, use their TV commercials to relay news. This might be a discounted price, or the dates of a sale, or a time-sensitive event like a grand opening. These commercials are planned to be disposable, running for a few days or weeks. They can be very inexpensive to produce. Sometimes they're as simple as a voice-over accompanying slides of the product. These are perfect examples of an ad that it is appropriate for a TV studio to produce—but more about that later. There is often an entertainment component to these ads, to sweeten the delivery of the news. There is always a call to action, a concept you should be familiar with if you've looked at the chapters on print advertising, radio, and direct mail. Most of the information elsewhere in this book referring to direct response advertising will apply to the news/entertainment approach to television advertising.

Image advertising. The other type of advertising we see simply builds awareness of a company or product. This is done very effectively by national advertisers, but may not be practical or wise for the local business, whose pockets aren't so deep. For regional consumer companies, it may be appropriate.

Image advertising builds awareness of a service or product, whereas news advertising is geared to sell more of it. Either approach can be used to position yourself against a competitor. Television is marvelous for that, because it leaves an instant impression. It can work quickly to shift opinions—which is one of the main goals of advertising.

Image advertising by its very nature requires a serious production budget. Partly to offset that cost, but also for strategic reasons, the ads generally stay on the air longer than news ads do. That makes the amortized cost of the spots comparable to that for the simpler news approach. If image advertising is a key part of your overall advertising strategy, take a close look at TV. It is more effective than radio or print at building image, because of its emotional impact. The problem is, it's expensive.

To choose your approach, think about your goals. If you were to use television advertising, what do you think it should do for you? What effect would you expect it to have? What result do you want? Look back to your work in the early chapters of this book, where we talked about marketing objectives, positioning and promotional strategies, and choosing a creative approach. What does that information reveal that should be reflected in your choice of news or image advertising here? Obviously, if you are a retailer planning a special sales event, your TV advertising will probably run to news ads announcing the time and place of the event and a persuasive reason for attending, such as a door prize or a deep discount.

For most people reading this book, especially those trying television for the first time, the news approach to advertising is a better choice. Your up-front production costs will be lower, and your results will be easier to measure. Later, when you have more experience with television, you can use what you've learned to create convincing image advertising if that seems appropriate for your business.

So you think TV might be right for you? Start educating yourself. Finish reading this chapter. Then talk to sales reps; contact the local stations and ask to tour their facilities. Ask questions of production studios and ad agencies, too. Get each one to define the difference between its services and those of the others: What makes it appropriate for you? Study the commercials you see on TV. Which would you like your ads to resemble, and where were they produced? Call the TV station or the advertiser and ask questions. You might learn a lot from talking to someone who has already been through the experience you're anticipating.

How TV Sells Advertising Time

Day-Parts: The Ratings Game

Like radio, TV is sold on the basis of day-parts, each of which commands a different price range.

Morning, 6 A.M. to 9 A.M., will have programming that is heavily slanted toward news, weather, and talk. The audience is typically people getting ready for work.

Midday, 9 A.M. to 4 P.M., is filled with soap operas, game shows, Donohue-type talk shows, and movies. The audience used to be stereotyped as homemakers, but we now recognize that there are many shift workers, work-at-home professionals, and other people with nontraditional lifestyles in the audience.

Early fringe, 4 P.M. to 7 P.M., segues from talk and game shows into after-school kids' programming, syndicated reruns of old shows, and local and national news programs. The audience varies greatly depending on the programming, but it is more likely to feature families watching together than the earlier day-parts.

Prime time, 7 P.M. to 11 P.M., features the networks' lineup of comedies, dramas, spe-cials, and movies. This time slot delivers the broadest general audience and is the most expensive day-part available.

Late fringe, 11 P.M. to 1 A.M., brings another round of news, syndicated reruns, and talk shows. Infomercials (usually half-hour programs) blur the boundaries between advertising and other programming. During this time slot, teens begin to outnumber adults as the hour gets late.

Late night, 1 A.M. until sign-off or 6 A.M., carries mostly movies and old sitcoms in syndication. The viewing audience will be teens and adults. Advertisers have found that since the videotape player has become so ubiquitous, the late night day-part delivers a bonus. Many people record movies for later viewing. Despite their intention to "zap" commercials, people find themselves playing back prerecorded programs as if they were real time.

Cable channels, like ESPN or MTV, muddy the distinction between day-parts, since their programming is likely to be more homogeneous throughout the day. Look carefully at their audience figures to see who the different day-parts are reaching.

Cable time is sold a little differently. There is a larger time inventory available—cable stations allow more advertising per hour than broadcast stations do. (Broadcast is more closely regulated by the FCC.) Because more spots are available to be sold, cable advertising rates are more negotiable than broadcast rates. In short, cable is sold more like radio than like broadcast TV.

Audience Ratings

Each day-part has a different rate structure, but the complexity doesn't end there. Each individual program in a day-part will have a *rating*, which indicates the percentage of TV-owning households that have their sets tuned to that program. These ratings are measured by Nielsen Media Research. It uses surveys and other techniques, such as people meters and diaries, to collect statistical information on how many households are watching any specific program. These measurements are taken regularly (the frequency depends on how large the market is), and ratings change rapidly. A program can be hot one month and cold the next. This is one reason media buying is a full-time job for large advertisers. A schedule planned far in advance must be constantly adjusted to accommodate changes like these.

Your local TV stations will sell time based on a Nielsen book (Example 8-2) for your metro area and your DMA, or designated market area. This is a geographic area defined by how far your local broadcast signals reach.

A rating is the percentage of all households in the DMA who are viewing a specific station or program. Ratings are always expressed as a percentage of the television universe. Ratings will also be broken down by demographic groups—total women or men of different age brackets, teens, and children.

A lot of media buyers look at *share of audience* rather than ratings. Here's the difference: A show's rating will measure how many (for example) women between twenty-five and forty-nine are watching, as a percentage of the total number of women twenty-five to forty-nine *living in that DMA*. That show's share measures how many women between twenty-five and forty-nine are watching, as a percentage of the total number of women twenty-five to forty-nine *watching TV at that time*. You would be more interested in the share, because the women not watching TV are completely irrelevant to your TV advertising strategy. Buying a different program or station still wouldn't reach them. Your goal is to buy the program that reaches the most TV-watching members of your target demographic group.

Ratings and share are important, but they are not the only factors to consider when you choose your advertising schedule. Often a show that garners low rating points—a "Sewing with Nancy" or "Yankee Carpenter," for example—delivers such a narrowly targeted audience that it can be an excellent buy for your business if the audience matches your product.

TV Sales Reps

All this may sound complicated, but don't let it keep you from exploring TV advertising. It is the job of the TV stations' sales reps to understand the ratings game and present the information to you in a way you can understand.

TV stations don't typically have as many sales reps as radio stations do, and so you won't find the TV reps calling on you quite as hungrily. You might have to take the lead by calling the stations in your area. Your first meeting should focus on conveying your goals about the audience you want to reach and the amount you want to spend. Let the rep come back to you with recommendations about the shows that deliver that audience. Don't fall into the trap of buying time on the shows you personally like to watch! Let the reps discuss the ratings and shares for their recommended schedules. Together you'll arrive at a plan that delivers your message to your potential customers. Three or four meetings might be necessary to arrive at a schedule that meets your needs.

Buying Reach and Frequency

As with radio advertising, a proposed schedule of TV ads has to balance reach and frequency. Reach is the number of different households or persons that watch a particular schedule of TV shows. A 30 percent reach means that in 30 percent of households in your DMA, the TV sets are on and tuned to the particular show in your schedule.

TV viewing isn't like radio, where people tend to be very loyal to their favorite stations. With TV, people don't watch stations, they watch programs. If you buy a little time on many different stations, you'll reach a lot of *different* people—that's a schedule planned to achieve reach. Another way to achieve reach is to buy a spot during a very popular show, where you'll find a large, demographically broad audience tuning in.

Frequency is the average number of times a household or person sees a schedule of ads. If your goal is reach, you might buy a short flight of commercials on a number of stations in your area. If your goal is frequency, you would buy a longer flight of commercials, but concentrate them on just one or two stations. The benchmark is this: Your schedule must deliver enough frequency for typical viewers to see your commercial at least three times. Your potential customers must be exposed to your message often enough for it to sink in. If you buy more spots on one show or one type of show—news or sports—you're apt to get the same viewer more times. For $1,000 you could buy a decent flight of commercials on a cable station, reaching a very specific audience. For another discussion of reach and frequency, see Chapter 7, "All About Radio Advertising." The concepts are the same for any medium.

Retailers promoting a specific sale will use short flights. For example, a women's clothing store with a big sale scheduled for Saturday might run a lot of spots on a lot of different shows in all day-parts, but in a very compressed time period—just Wednesday through Friday.

If you have a small budget, don't look at prime time first. Your budget will limit you to a very small schedule, and you won't get the frequency you need. Look at buying daytime instead, especially if your audience includes women. You could sample a lot of shows, getting better reach and frequency, and stretch your ad dollar farther.

Seasonality and Inventory

Seasonality affects the cost of each specific commercial slot. This is because the demand fluctuates throughout the year. As a general rule, January, February, and March are the slowest months. If you plan it right, this may be your best season to try TV. A lot of people are stuck at home watching, and the rates are low because of slow post-holiday demand.

In April, May, and June, the demand increases. Why? Locally, seasonal events from Mother's Day through the Fourth of July give retailers occasions for sales and promotions. That fuels a surge in demand for television advertising. Consequently, the rates increase.

In July, August, and September, things slow down again—in fact, radio can outpull television in the summer months, because so many people are outside and active, and take their radios along for company! As September closes, the new fall season starts, and rates go up again. In college towns you'll find that the third quarter won't slow down as much—back-to-school advertising from national advertisers keeps the rates higher because of supply and demand.

In October, November, and December, demand outreaches the supply of commercial spots available, because of the impact of retail's holiday season. Unless you plan early, cable may be your only option if you want to advertise in the fourth quarter.

If you're trying TV for the first time, look at the first quarter! Your dollars will buy you more frequency. If your business is not of a seasonal nature, you'll be getting a bargain without making any trade-offs.

How Long Should a Commercial Be?

TV commercials run from ten-second spots (:10s) to half-hour infomercials on cable TV. The most popular length for a TV commercial is thirty seconds (:30s); however, :15s are becoming more widespread, for their cost savings. You will find, though, that price is not a straight arithmetic progression. A :30 might cost almost as much as a :60.

How do you decide what length is feasible for you? Focus your message. To do this, start by defining and then prioritizing the key benefits your company offers customers (see Chapter 2 for more about this). Then, choose a creative approach that dramatizes your number one key benefit. (See Chapter 5 for more about the creative approach.) Then, work with your production facility or ad agency to answer the question at the core of this inquiry: What is the least time increment in which you can effectively communicate that message? If the answer isn't immediately obvious, try storyboarding a script. It will quickly become clear how long your commercial will need to be—or how your creative strategy will have to change. You will be juggling budget against marketing impact as you explore your options.

TV is more expensive than other advertising in two ways: the cost to produce a commercial and the cost to put it on the air. Production is expensive because it takes a team of specialists to get an idea from script to final film.

As with radio, but more so, air time is expensive because the inventory is limited and it is often in high demand. Behind this generalization lies a spectrum of price and availability. Late-night cable TV, for example, can be purchased for as little as $10 for a thirty-second spot. This is comparable to what that time slot would cost on a local radio station. Prime time on a broadcast station during the fourth quarter might cost $400 for a :30 in a midsize market.

Timing Strategies and the Price of Air Time: Finding a Happy Medium

Cable stations will typically offer you packages that combine a certain number of spots in certain time periods, with the exact time of airing left open for the station to decide. Shorter increments—the :10s and :15s—can get "shoehorned" into an attractive time slot easily, making short commercials on cable stations a good strategy for some.

Broadcast stations rely less on packages; they sell spots during specific commercial breaks in the scheduled programming. Because of the wide variety of programming aired, you need to look at more than just dayparts to decide your advertising schedule. The sales reps from each station will be happy to explain their offerings to you. See Chapter 4, "Writing a Media Plan," for more background on planning your media strategy.

For maximum efficiency, advertise at predictable times of day for at least two or three weeks. Don't make the mistake of putting all your budget into "creative" production and neglecting to reserve money to cover sufficient frequency. How frequent? Three to five commercials in a week is the absolute minimum. Where and when to run? Let your customers help you decide. Remember, the goal is to find more customers just like them.

Ask the leading stations for proposals based on the budget you plan to spend. Take a look at the schedules of ads they propose. Do these schedules meet your objectives regarding reach and frequency? Use a media calendar like the example in Template 8-1A to compare the different proposals. A budget summary (Template 8-2A) will also be helpful in evaluating the different scenarios. Set up blank templates like these on your computer (Templates 8-1B and 8-2B). Plug in the numbers and schedules your sales reps propose. Do you like the way the budget and timing shape up?

Template 8-1A: Example Media Calendar

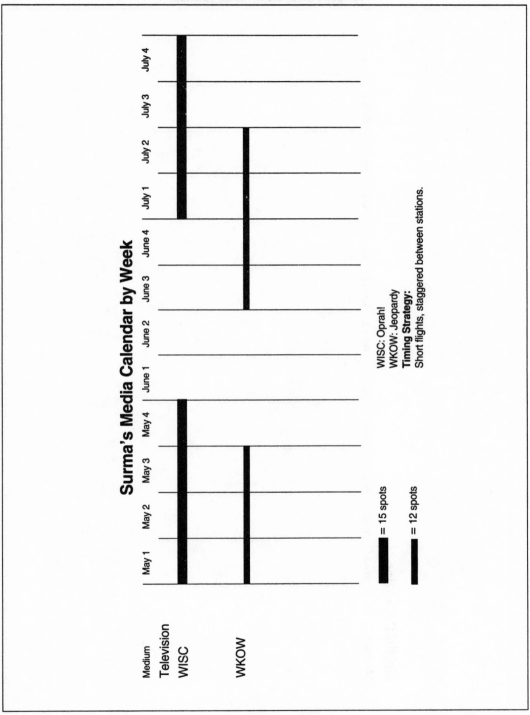

Template 8-1B: Blank Media Calendar

Media Calendar

Medium	Week 1	Week 2	Week 3	Week 4	Week 1	Week 2	Week 3	Week 4	Week 1	Week 2	Week 3	Week 4

Template 8-2A: Example Budget by Week

Media Budget
Spending by Station and Week

Date: 11-22-94
Title: Surma's Restaurant
Assumptions: See Media Calendar
Costs based on rate cards 10/26/94
WISC 30 second spots, Mon-Fri, Oprah! $50/spot, 15 wks
WKOW 30 second spots, Mon-Fri, Jeopardy, $65/spot, 12 wks
Prepared by: SW

Medium	December				January				February				Total ($)	Total (%)
	Week1	Week 2	Week 3	Week 4	Week1	Week 2	Week 3	Week 4	Week1	Week 2	Week 3	Week 4		
Television														
WISC	750	750	750	750					750	750	750	750	$6,000	52%
WKOW		780	780				780	780	780	780	780		$5,460	48%
Total by Week	$750	$1,530	$1,530	$750	$0	$0	$780	$780	$1,530	$1,530	$1,530	$750	$11,460	100%
Percent of Total	7%	13%	13%	7%	0%	0%	7%	7%	13%	13%	13%	7%	100%	

Template 8-2B: Blank Budget

Media Budget
Spending by Station and Week

Date:
Title:
Assumptions:

Prepared by:

Medium	Week1	Week 2	Week 3	Week 4	Week1	Week 2	Week 3	Week 4	Week1	Week 2	Week 3	Week 4	Total ($)	Total (%)
Television														

Total by Week

Percent of Total

As with the other media, you will want to compare CPM, or cost per thousand. In Chapter 4 you will find a complete explanation of CPM calculations, including how to set up your spreadsheet and how to keep your comparisons "apples to apples." The subject is treated in detail in Chapter 6, "How to Create Print Ads that Sell," as well. The same principles hold true for radio and TV. As with any comparison, make sure you are comparing audience figures for the same period—Arbitron for November 1994, for example.

Television media buyers analyze cost efficiencies by evaluating CPP (cost per point), which is similar to CPM. For example, if a show's rating is 8 points and the cost for that commercial is $400, its CPP (cost per point) is $50.

Buyers use a ranking system that involves share, ratings, and CPM and CPP calculations. This is complex statistical stuff, kids; don't try this at home! Have your sales reps prepare CPP and CPM reports for you. Ask them to print out CPP calculations for every show in the proposed schedule of commercials.

And remember, TV alone does not a media strategy make. Review your overall strategy, and the nature of your plans for radio, print, and direct mail, before you finalize your TV plans.

Negotiating the Deal

Everything is negotiable in television advertising, as in most areas of business. There are no hard and fast rules. Rates can be very negotiable, or not very. It depends on:

- *Your loyalty.* The more you advertise with a station, the more negotiating power you'll have.

- *The time of year.* Rates for the first and third quarters are usually more negotiable than those for the second and fourth quarters, when demand for inventory is higher.

- *Supply and demand.* Rates for a show in high demand will not be very negotiable at any time during the year.

- *Your flexibility.* Some broadcast stations will allow advertisers to negotiate a "bump rate." You buy your schedule at a lower rate, but without a guarantee that the ads will run as scheduled. That way, if an advertiser who is willing to pay a higher rate comes along, your commercial is "bumped," and you're offered a make-good spot at some future time. This can be a good deal because it can get you an attractive time slot later on, but you're taking a risk. Don't try for a bump rate if timing is critical. Suppose you're looking at advertising on Wednesday and Thursday for your Friday night event. If your commercials get bumped, the station's make-good offer will be too late to be of use.

Television is changing rapidly, with developments in cable, satellite technology, and more. Program ratings swing up and down; other advertisers change their schedules; the perfect television buy is clearly a moving target. It takes time to stay on top.

As an advertiser, you can purchase TV time by working directly with the TV stations or by going through a media broker or advertising agency. If you're buying direct, you will be paying the full rate without receiving the 15 percent commission given to agencies. You'll also be coordinating the proposals from different stations for yourself, evaluating them, and making decisions without the assistance of a neutral adviser. All this is time-consuming, which may suggest that you need the help of an outsider who specializes in placing ads on TV.

Help in Planning and Placing Ads

There are alternatives to working with advertising agencies, if you're not interested in placing your account in the hands of a full-service firm. You can look for a media broker. This is a specialist who performs the same function as an agency media buyer, but does it from outside the agency structure. Often these individuals have worked as either TV sales reps or agency media buyers before going out on their own. TV stations can recommend media brokers, if your professional network doesn't turn up a recommendation.

Whoever you talk to, negotiate the rate: Offer to split the 15 percent commission, and see what the response is. Depending on the size of your budget, media brokers will often agree to a discount.

If your budget is significant—over $250,000—you should probably have a professional media buyer working with you. A buyer's knowledge and access to timely information will earn their keep.

If you can't get the rates you expect for the spots you want to run, look at your schedule from a new angle. You might discover a creative solution, like advertising on a quirky late-night syndicated show that delivers a good audience for your product. Look at the popularity of the Star Trek spin-off series, "Star Trek: The Next Generation," and "Deep Space Nine." A narrowly defined audience watches these programs—solid gold, if you sell something they want. Remember the importance of frequency over reach. It's more effective for you to reach a small audience with a sufficient number of repetitions of your commercial than to spread your commercial around and risk spreading it too thin.

Budgeting? Don't Forget Co-Op!

It is worth mentioning here, as I have in other chapters, that co-op support programs from manufacturers can be a critical component in making television advertising affordable for you. If you are in a retail or distribution business, you may be familiar with these programs. Almost every product for sale has co-op dollars behind it. Ask your sales reps to help you discover co-op opportunities—it's part of their job.

There are restrictions that apply when you work with co-op. The manufacturer will issue guidelines regarding the wording, visuals, and timing. It's up to you to decide whether this "interference" is worth the money you'll save. Do the math to compare different manufacturers' offers; you could find the support you need to upgrade your goals for television.

To qualify for a co-op program, you will have to submit your script and storyboards in advance, get approval, and then file the necessary paperwork to prove when and where the ads ran. The filing procedures can be complicated, but don't let that hold you back. Too many advertisers let the complexity of co-op keep them from collecting much-needed dollars.

Summary: Buying TV Time

To summarize your approach to buying TV: First establish your primary target audience. Study their viewing habits (via your current customers) to create a short list of potential stations that will reach them. Ask the stations' sales reps to prepare a list of available spots and packages. Make sure their proposals include audience size and ratings information, and check that they draw on comparable sources. Calculate your CPM and project the frequency of your advertising to arrive at your total air-time budget and the schedule that that budget will buy.

And don't forget the magic words: Ask your sales rep, "Can you do better than this?" Let the reps know they're competing for your business, and you'll see some very sharp pencils flying. That leaves you more money to budget for production—our next topic.

Crafting the TV Ad

The structure of a television commercial follows a proven sequence. While the style varies, all commercials essentially unfold the same story: the AIDA formula that we've talked about in other chapters. All advertising, whether print, broadcast, or direct mail, has to do these things: get attention, arouse interest, create desire, and motivate action. Commercials all begin with an introduction, move into a center sell, and end with a closing call to action.

If you're planning to create a message for television, now is a good time to review your positioning statement from Chapter 2 and your creative approach from Chapter 5. In working through those exercises, you laid the foundation for the work you're about to do.

What you want your ad to say, and how you want to say it, will drive every facet of television production. Your decisions will determine how much you'll spend, how much you'll do for yourself, and who helps you with the rest. Of all the media, television requires the most specialized skill from the most people. It's a lot easier to take a do-it-yourself approach with print or radio advertising. Creating a complicated direct mail program is fairly straightforward, too. But to produce a television commercial, you are going to need help. That's why I'm going to start my discussion of television production with a survey of the production sources available to you.

Your production partner might be

- A TV station
- A video production studio
- An advertising agency

Each competing facility tailors its skills and equipment to serve a certain type of client. You will need to interview several to find the firm that is best suited to help you.

TV Stations

A local TV station won't put much emphasis on creative services, but it will have the ability to produce simple spots cost-effectively. For $1,000 to $3,000 you can produce a workable thirty-second commercial. Since you will be responsible for creating your own script, you'll want to know what kind of setup you're writing for. Tour the station's facilities

and view its demonstration tape. How is the lighting in the scenes? Is the sound quality clear, and is the acting good? These are indications of professional skill. You need to get an idea of what it's practical to do in your commercial, without stretching the station's capabilities. Take note of whether the camera goes on location, how complex the in-studio sets seem, and whether the station produces special effects. If you choose this option, write to fit the skills the station demonstrates.

Video Production Studios

These companies are specialists at making thirty- to sixty-second movies. A thirty-second spot working with a studio might cost $5,000 and up, but you're paying for proven creative talent and high-quality production values. If your idea for a commercial is more complex than an off-camera announcer or a shot of you in your store talking to the camera, budget for the services of a production studio. The higher production value your money buys will be a good investment.

Ad Agencies

Ad agencies develop around different businesses in a community. In some towns, each ad agency will have the account of a competing auto dealership, and everybody will develop experience in retail advertising. In another city, agencies might focus on manufacturers or the home office of a major insurance company. These agencies might excel in very different media. Whether there are ad agencies in your community who should be doing your commercial production depends on how well you fit the local mold.

Few agencies have production facilities in-house; most will be hiring production studios to execute their creative work, and often they work closely with the same professionals over many projects. This experience results in a like-mindedness that can be a big advantage in getting an idea safely over the hurdles of execution. Production requires coordinating the efforts of many people, from location scouts to postproduction technicians. When they work together regularly, they often develop a common vocabulary and common standards for various tasks. The work that results is cost-efficient and productive.

If you're not confident of your creative talents—brainstorming, writing, and visualizing your advertising—this may be another reason to work with an agency. (We'll talk more about this in Chapter 12.) An agency-produced commercial might cost from $8,000 to $15,000. This is worth the cost if it saves you time and delivers an effective commercial with the message you want to send. But if you're not interested in having someone create your commercial for you—the concept, script, and storyboard of a commercial—don't hire an agency. You're not matching the tool to the task. Instead, just work with the TV station or a local production company based on your own development of concept, script, and storyboard.

The Production Learning Curve

The first time you advertise on TV, you might produce a simple spot at the TV station. That experience will give you ideas that might lead you to a production studio for your next effort. Later, when you know more, you can work effectively as part of the client/agency team, producing more ambitious concepts to dramatize your product or service.

When you've decided which type of business to work with, then you must choose the specific vendor. As with any professional service, start by contacting your network for referrals. Then ask to see samples, and ask detailed questions about money and technique. Ask, "What did it take to get that shot?" The "war stories" you hear will be an education. Notice the lighting, and the degree of clarity in the shots you see. These reveal the skill of the technicians you're about to hire.

As you tour facilities, note the technology you see. State-of-the-art production equip-

ment changes fast, and it's a Catch-22 situation. The latest equipment, like off-line editing computers, adds great flexibility to production but also adds overhead, and so the rate you pay goes up. Your goal is to buy the highest level of quality *you* will need, not the highest level available.

Your Creative Approach Affects the Cost of Your Commercial

These factors contribute to cost.

What Style of Production Will You Choose? A commercial can be slide-and-voice-over, video on location, or video in studio. The slide-and-voice-over is the least expensive. You can add background music, and it's easy to change the ad just by replacing slides or adding a "crawler" (moving words) across the bottom of the screen.

Where Will You Shoot? On location or in studio? Going on location gives more variety to the advertising, but there are a host of negatives as well. It's the difference between preparing meals at home and cooking over a campfire. The degree of improvisation required in the wilds of location shooting naturally makes each task take longer, and the crew is costing you every minute. Somebody blows a fuse while testing the lighting, and the whole production comes to a halt while somebody finds out where the circuit breaker is. Watching money burn like this can be painful. On the other hand, it is a necessary cost of shooting on location, so be prepared for it.

Permission must be arranged for most locations, and there are often rental fees involved. Going to your place of business offers no great cost savings. While you don't pay rental fees, you do incur downtime among your staff from the disruption of business as usual. You are still paying all the hourly fees for the travel and setup time required. Going on location costs money.

Working in a studio offers the producer a much more controllable environment. The sound quality will be better. The lighting is quicker to arrange. With the home court advantage, your production team works faster and better. The difference in the end result—and the final invoice—is noticeable.

How Will You Be Using Talent? Talent is the people in your ads. The least expensive use of talent is to design your ad around an off-camera announcer. You first record the announcer reading the script, then shoot your visuals, and edit the pictures to fit the sound.

If your announcer will appear on camera, more takes will be needed to get the scene right so your costs will go up. If you hire actors, your talent fees can go up exponentially.

In larger markets, labor unions are an issue. Ask your potential vendors about union and nonunion talent.

What Type of Music Will You Use? You might be tempted to use a recording you like or imitate it with your own lyrics. Explain these ideas and listen when your producer tells you about needle-drop music (see Chapter 7, "All About Radio Advertising," for more on this). The issue here is copyright law. Music publishers license the rights to popular songs. To use a Motown hit, for example, your producer would negotiate with an agent from ASCAP or BMI to arrive at a use fee based on how many times you will run the commercial and how big a geographic area it will reach. This could add a lot of expense to your commercial.

You can produce your own music through a producer who hires composers and performers, and you could try for a sound-alike performance that stays just shy of copyright infringement. Some advertisers do this, but you'll want to seek the advice of your producer—and your lawyer—before you commit to the idea.

Needle-drop music is the answer for most advertisers on a budget. And it works very well. Needle-drop is the "clip art" of sound. It's high-quality music in a wide variety of styles. You pay once for a license to use it; usually the charge is under $75.

You get professional sound quality, flexibility in usage, and speed—it's already recorded, you just have to choose the cut you want. Almost all locally produced advertising is accompanied by needle-drop music.

Control Your Production Costs

To establish a production budget, talk to TV stations, production studios, and ad agencies. You viewed their demo tapes before, when you were thinking about creative approaches; now view them again, and ask specific questions about the dollars spent for what you see. Try to match what you like creatively to what you can afford.

There are four stages to producing a commercial, and each will call for a budget line item:

- Preproduction—Creating the script and storyboard, and planning the shoot

- Production—Filming or videotaping the scenes, and recording the sound track

- Postproduction—In-studio editing to mix visuals and sound track into the final commercial

- Duplication—Copying the final commercial and distributing it to each TV station in fulfillment of your media buys

Template 8-3A shows the budget for creating commercials for Klinke Cleaners, a company we've talked about in other chapters. Template 8-3B is a blank version of this form that you can use.

Template 8-3A: Example Budget for Klinke Spots

Client: Klinke Cleaners
Contact: Jeff Berry
Date: 11-30-94
Project Description:

Two :30 spots, same cast/set
Actor in studio; music + flashing titles + voice over

Description	Quantity	Unit Cost	Total
Preproduction			
Script, cast, & props	20	$50.00	$1,000.00
Production			
Shoot 2 spots	6	300.00	1800.00
Postproduction			
Create title slides	6	75.00	450.00
Music from library	1	55.00	55.00
Audio production	4	150.00	600.00
Video sweetening	1	150.00	150.00
Duplication			
3 sets 3/4"	3	26.00	78.00
1 VHS	1	15.00	15.00
Other			
Purchase 2 used suits	2	50.00	100.00
	Subtotal		$4,248.00
	Tax		233.64
	Total		$4,481.64

Template 8-3B: Blank Production Cost Estimate

Client:
Contact:
Date:
Project Description:

Description	Quantity	Unit Cost	Total
Preproduction			
Production			
Postproduction			
Duplication			
Other			
		Subtotal	
		Tax	
		Total	

An estimate will typically show the unit cost for each category, and then the total projected for that job. An invoice will show similar information with the final costs. The cost line items you can expect to see basically match the stages of development:

- *Preproduction.* This will be an hourly fee from your production studio, writer, or ad agency.

- *Production.* Whether in studio or on location, production time is based on an hourly rate; the price in studio will range from $100 to $200 an hour in a mid-size market to $500 and up in a big city. Going on location might double that charge. The rate reflects a combination of factors: the technological sophistication of the facilities you use, the creative skill of the producer, the demands of a location shoot. Your production company might be negotiable on this line item; if it seems high, ask for a justification.

- *Postproduction.* Editing suites are billed at an hourly rate that covers your use of the equipment and personnel for however long it takes to mix your production visuals and sounds into the final spot. Again, if this figure seems high, ask for an explanation. See the tips coming up for ways to keep these costs in line. On the estimate should be a description of how the time estimate is allotted. The description might include mixing, special effects, generating title graphics, etc.

- *Duplication.* Most commercials are produced on film, $3/4$-in videotape, or Beta format. Once the commercial is produced, you will need duplicates, or dubs, to send to other stations. These will be on $3/4$-in videotape or Beta cassettes as well. You will also want to have a standard videocassette copy made for your own files. There should be a line item on your budget with an explanation of how many duplicates will be made, and in what format.

- *Other costs.* Commercial production might include costs for actors, stylists, art and lighting directors, and other technicians who assist in the production. There will also be fees for props, location rental fees, and perhaps fees for animation or other special effects. As we discuss the production process in the following pages, you'll gain an understanding of these costs, and how you can control them.

Costs always go up. To fight that natural tendency, you can adopt these resolutions:

1. Nobody gets to be the star. You, the producer, the talent—you're all working together to create a successful production. You didn't hire these people to be yes-men. Ask their opinions, and then shut up and listen. But don't let one of them become a prima donna either.

2. Don't accept solutions that call for "tricks." Special effects often hide a lack of ideas behind technical flash. Flash is expensive. Calling for unusual effects is asking for unexpected cost increases. Keep the focus on your message.

3. Get comfortable with making irreversible decisions. On location is no time to waffle. If you second-guess your producer with requests of, "Let's shoot it both ways and decide later," you're asking for a cost overrun. Don't make revisions to the script after approving it for production.

Now, let's go through the process of producing a TV commercial.

Example 8-2: Klinke's Dry Cleaning Script

Used by permission of Klinke Cleaners.

KLINKE CLEANERS

Thirty-Second Television Commercial #1

"Dry Cleaning"

Music: Blue Danube waltz under throughout.

(Open on man dressed in a white suit covered with dirt and stains.)

Flashing title: Amazing Cleaning Dramatization.

(Cut to close-up and begin slowly pulling back.

Man looks at his suit as dirt and stains begin lifting off and flying
        away.)

Announcer: This cleaning dramatization is brought to you by
        Klinke Cleaners.

(Stains continue lifting off of clothes and flying away.)

Flashing title: Don't try this at home.

Announcer: While we can't promise everything will come clean
        this easily...

(Stains continue lifting off of clothes and flying away.)

Announcer: ... with over a dozen state-of-the-art locations and
        same day service ...

Flashing title: Trust Klinke Cleaners.

(Camera stops pulling back when man is full frame. Final stains lift
        off of clothes and fly away.)

Announcer: ... you can trust Klinke Cleaners to make all of your
        cleaning concerns vanish.

(Man looks down at clothes, up at camera, and smiles.)

Title: (Dissolve over video)
        Klinke Cleaners.

Step One: Decide the Contents of Your Spot

Example 8-2 is the script that goes with the storyboard in Example 8-1. Notice how the announcer delivers the sales pitch.

The first seconds of a commercial should be entertainment. In this example, the music and the visual gimmick of the paint flying out of the clothes set the tone of sophisticated wit. Your commercial will need a "hook" like this to get your viewers' attention and set them up for your sales pitch.

The rest of the spot should be *sell*. You have to answer, "What's in it for me?" with entertainment and news of your key benefit. In this example, the visual makes the main pitch. You can't watch paint disappear from a man's suit without getting the point.

Just as the visual delivers the benefit message, the script uses puns to drive home the point with humor. The phrases "come clean" and "your cleaning concerns vanish" help you remember what is being sold.

Closing with a compelling offer or call to action is just as important as crafting a good beginning and middle. The announcer tells us that Klinke's has over a dozen locations and same-day service. The phrase "Trust Klinke Cleaners" closes the thirty-second script, flashing on screen at the same time the announcer speaks the words. That's a humorous, soft-sell approach.

Start watching commercials and paying attention to how they sell. Watch for the AIDA formula in action. Notice how two commercials can share a very similar outline but seem quite different, simply because of their difference in style.

Example 8-3 gives the script for a commercial for a restaurant with two locations in south suburban Chicago. In Chapter 3 we mentioned how this commercial became part of a special promotional campaign. Now let's look at how it sells:

Example 8-3: Surma's Script

SURMA'S CARRY-OUT
Thirty-Second Television Commercial
"Delicious Meals to Go" (2 versions: change final address tag)

(Open: camera pans L-R across exterior sign.)
Announcer: "Stop in at Surma's Carry-Out for delicious meals to go."
(Cut to chickens turning on rotisserie.)
Announcer: "Rotisserie chicken is our newest item, but it's not all we're
               famous for. Surma's Carry-Out offers complete home-cooked
               dinners..."
(Cut to chicken parts spilling from fryer basket into steam table pan.)
               "...Fried chicken! Barbecue ribs!..."
(Pan L-R across steam table—show at least a dozen items.)
               "Dozens of hot and cold side dishes..."
(Cut to table top with carry-out boxes behind array of decorated cakes.)
               "Daily specials! Fresh-baked desserts and decorated cakes."
(Interior of carry-out area; pan R-L down glass display case. Two women walk to
               register. Clerk hands them a bag.)
               "If you're looking for great food fast, not just fast food, stop in at
               Surma's today."
(Pull back across table covered with entrees, side dishes, and dessert.)
               "And don't forget, Surma's can cater any size party."
(Logo superimposes over woodwork in dining area.)
               "Surma's Carry-out. 9189 West 151st Street in Orland Park. Or
               call 403-7797."
(Address and phone number join logo on screen.)

[For second version, change address and phone.]

Here's the script without all the directions:

Stop in at Surma's Carry Out for delicious meals to go. Rotisserie chicken is our newest item, but it's not all we're famous for. Surma's Carry Out offers complete home-cooked dinners. Fried chicken! Barbecue ribs! Dozens of hot and cold side dishes. Daily specials! Fresh-baked desserts and decorated cakes.

If you're looking for great food fast, not just fast food, stop in at Surma's today. And don't forget. Surma's can cater any size party.

Surma's Carry Out. Ninety-one Eighty-nine West Hundred Fifty First Street in Orland Park. Or call (phone number).

This commercial opens with a headline that could be a tagline for this business. "Delicious meals to go" lets you know right up front who we're talking to: hungry, busy people.

Remember, the first seconds of a commercial are entertainment. This commercial gets its entertainment value from a tight-cut fast-action camera style that highlights the superb food and matches the choppy writing style nicely. Short phrases work well on TV; don't feel you have to write English that would please your grammar teacher when you write a script.

The rest of the spot is sell. Watch how this script rolls through the benefit points. Entrees, side dishes, and desserts each get their turn, as does Surma's catering service. The visuals alone deliver the benefit message—this food really does look good. The production value of this commercial is great, and it has to be. Bad food photography would be the worst kind of advertising. The script supports the visual appeal as a narrator lists tempting dishes.

How many times is the restaurant's name mentioned? That's the build-up to the call to action. The end of the commercial delivers the

final hook. Again the writer uses a phrase that could be a great tagline—"great food fast, not just fast food." Then we get a final selling point, an address and a phone number, and it's over and out.

This commercial has several memorable hooks. The great food shots, with their tumbling action and dramatic pans, make you look forward to seeing the commercial again. And the copy, while not of the dramatic, rule-bending kind, gets the job done fast and hot.

This commercial involved going on location, and some intricate planning was needed to have the right foods ready for the shoot. Other than that, it is an example of a very simple production, really. There is little about it that would be difficult or expensive to do. The people who appear on camera are real customers, not actors. The shots of food are all so tightly cropped that no extraneous detail distracts from the main message. This technique keeps the shooting area limited, meaning less disturbance of business-as-usual in the restaurant. Postproduction was the most complex aspect of this commercial: The fast cuts mean lots of editing. This commercial contains eight scenes, which is rather a lot for thirty seconds. Most commercials use five or six scenes.

These examples should illustrate how a TV script is the result of many decisions about content and style.

Here are some tips to help you decide the content of your ad.

Be sure you balance the impression of your announcer with the impression of your product. Show the product prominently—at least three times. Repetition is important. For advertisers of service businesses, a tagline or service description can take the place of a product image on camera. A demonstration shot—showing the lawyer in conference with the client, for example—can show the "product" in action. The Klinke spot uses a parody of a demonstration to make its point. Look for ways like this to make your service tangible.

Keep it simple. Focus on one key benefit, and don't try to make too many points. (You might want to review Chapter 2, "Positioning," to help you simplify your message.)

Don't pay too much attention to national advertisers. National brands often lack meaningful comparative differences. Whether the advertisers are selling beer, home appliances, or athletic shoes, they're using entertainment to try to create a sense of difference. Their tools include everything from expensive special effects to celebrity spokespeople. You're playing a different game, and the rules are different in local television. Focus your ideas on a simple, newsworthy concept, and explore that until you find a creative way to dramatize it.

To get the most mileage out of your money, produce a series of commercials in "donut" style. Follow this structure:

- Introduction (common to all)
- Center sell (multiple version for different spots)
- Close (common to all)

Use the introduction to get attention and to establish context and tone. Film several different messages for the center sell. You might feature different product/price specials, or you might pitch a different benefit in each message. Use the close to make your call to action. Show your logo, address, and tagline or theme. Now you have parts that can be combined to give your advertising variety and longevity, at the lowest possible cost.

Step Two: Decide the Style of the Production and Start Writing

Your commercial is either a slide and voice-over, a location shoot, or an in-studio production. What you write will vary depending on which style you've decided to use.

To plan a slide and voice-over commercial, plan on about four seconds per slide at most. For a feel of fast action, speed up to one second per slide. Think about what reproduces well on TV. You've probably noticed that striped clothing goes wild on TV—it's broken into flickering patterns by the rasterized screen. Any busy patterns—backgrounds, clothing, whatever,—will be a disaster on-screen. Avoid busy or dark shots. Mix close-ups and long shots to give an illusion of action. Close with your logo and call to action, and leave that on the screen for at least four seconds.

For any commercial, start with visual ideas. What will move? In what color? What dramatic situation might demonstrate your key benefit? On television, words only support images. Most beginners try to say too much. Let actions speak louder than words.

Ask yourself, "What do I want the viewer to *feel* about my company?" Remember, TV is an emotional medium. You will be more effective if you recognize that and convey feelings rather than specifics. Music is one of the most immediate ways to convey feeling, and it works even when all eyes aren't on the screen. Memorable characters are often chosen to convey certain emotions. And sometimes it's just a sense of place that gets you there.

Decide the tone you want to establish. Will you be screaming price price price, or delivering a quietly professional image ad? Pick your tone, then be consistent. Watch the commercials in your community and pay attention to which type of advertiser chooses which tone or style.

How are you going to unfold your story? Most of the copy approaches we discussed in Chapter 6, "How to Create Print Ads that Sell," are applicable to TV. You might use a demonstration, or humor, or story telling. Testimonials work especially well on TV. Only the "seven reasons why" approach is inappropriate. This detailed approach, which is so persuasive in print, is too much, too fast on television.

Look for an approach that speaks person-to-person, to exploit the powerful emotional appeal inherent in television. You might depict a slice of life, or use humor to establish a common bond with your audience.

How do you make your commercial break through the clutter of other advertisers? The human brain always tries to place things in patterns. You can get attention by challenging that trait. That's just what the Klinke commercial does.

Rule breaking stimulates viewers to participate on an intellectual level. Here's another example: An advertiser is selling paint. The commercial shows streams of the stuff pouring and splashing about, while an off-camera voice describes it as creamy, thick, smooth, and so on. The pattern-making mind wants it to be food, but something doesn't quite fit. When the payoff comes, fifteen seconds into the commercial, the viewer has a good laugh at this desire for rich, creamy white paint. That creates a good impression—it ties a product attribute to a key benefit in a memorable way. That's good advertising.

The Storyboard Format

Whether you can draw or not, it helps to work out your ideas in storyboard format. Like panels in a comic book, the storyboard shows frames that unfold the story. The sequence of images adds visual representation to the audio and video instructions you write.

Don't sit down at your computer to write a TV commercial, start doodling on a pad. You can buy blank storyboard paper with frames drawn at the proper aspect ratio for the TV tube at most local art supply stores. Or photocopy Template 8-4 as many times as you need. Start drawing action in the panels, and describe underneath what is happening. Even crude line drawings are very helpful in telling a producer what you want done.

Template 8-4: Blank Storyboard

TITLE:_____

LENGTH:_____

NOTES:_____

The storyboard you create will be the focal point of your discussions as you and your producer plan the shoot.

Tips for Crafting Good TV Ads

Keep focused on what you're trying to accomplish. Picture the customer transaction you're trying to make happen, then work back from there.

Make good use of your viewers' time. They decide whether to give their attention to your ad based on the entertainment or news value you offer them.

Writing a TV script is entirely different from writing a print ad. It's not a medium for details. In print, you might say, "Offices in Green Bay, Madison, Minneapolis, and Milwaukee." On TV, you'd settle for "Offices in four cities, including yours."

You have both the video and the audio mode to work with. You can make the two work together, or you can challenge the viewer by creating unlikely combinations. Do you remember seeing a bleach ad that featured a man in formal dress silently demonstrating the washing process, accompanied by classical music? This is a good example of challenging the pattern-making mind, and it was amusing because of its incongruity. Good entertainment invokes good feelings toward your company.

Good entertainment is important, but be wary of delivering it via humor. Writing "funny" can be dangerous for the novice writer. It's tough to get the timing right, and it fails if you fall short. When it works, it only works once—after that, it's a joke you've already heard. There are exceptions, but be careful unless you've always been a funny person, and humor is appropriate to your company's style. Radio is a better medium if you want to explore humor.

No writer expects a first script to be accepted without changes. Have someone critique your work. Or see your work only as preliminary guidance for the writer/director you hire, who will refine it into a final script.

When your script and storyboard are final, you will hold a preproduction meeting, or "prepro session," as it's usually called. Here the production is broken into minute steps and every foreseeable eventuality is considered. Responsibility for each task is assigned to different members of the production team.

There are two technical judgment calls that you must make at this juncture.

Decide whether to shoot on film or videotape. Most ads are shot on $^3/_4$-in videotape for two reasons: It is much less expensive, and it allows you instant playback, so that you can check whether you're getting what you want as you go along. However, videotape is of poorer quality than film. It has a "gritty" look that is appropriate for a newsy event, but it lacks the finished quality that film delivers. And we're not talking about your VHS recordings here. Your VHS camera produces images that are much too low in resolution for television playback. Resist the urge to shoot your commercial with your home equipment!

Film has an aesthetic depth that is psychologically powerful. It seems more timeless, and that's appropriate for image advertising. If you are selling intangibles—as is done by service providers like doctors and lawyers—using film may be wiser. You cannot afford to look low budget in your advertising.

Decide whether to record sound on location or not. Does your script call for a lot of dialogue? Then you'll be filming *and* recording the actors as they work. Avoid this if possible. It is easier, and less expensive, to capture your sound track in the studio. Design your commercial to fit your budget.

At the preproduction stage, listen to your producer's advice, and be ready to commit. You'll work together better if you make decisions once, and make them early.

Step Three: Production

Who's at the shoot? A minimum crew might be just one person, but that's not typical. You will hire a producer, who might also wear the hats of writer and director. There will be a camera operator, and there will be actors. If there are more bodies around, they are assisting these three in doing their jobs. Let's look at the role of each. (A note about pronouns: I use "he" for simplicity, but the people who perform these roles might be of either gender.)

The producer is the boss of the production. He knows the client's vision and the technical processes that must be manipulated to achieve it. He is your advocate on the set, keeping control of the production so that it does not outrun your budget or depart from your script. He communicates your wishes and comments to the rest of his crew.

The producer is often the writer of the script, or if you wrote it, he has helped you flesh out the details.

On all but very large productions, the producer is also the director. In TV advertising, the term *producer* means the one who coordinates everything, and the term *director* refers to the person who directs *people* on the set. The director gives the actors and the camera operator their instructions, but doesn't get involved in directing the rest of the activity around him—that's the producer's job. Your job, as the client on the set, is to work through the producer to get what you came for.

It's important to follow protocol on the set. The director handles the actors. If you see the actors moving or talking in a way that you don't like, you are *not* to talk to them about it. As a client, you must work through the producer/director to communicate with the talent. This may seem ridiculous to you: What's wrong with communicating directly with the people involved?

Acting is a skill that requires intense focus. Instructions coming from too many angles, especially if the instructions are contradictory, can unhinge the actors. Your production will get worse, not better, if you do not follow the protocol.

The director holds the completed commercial in his head and is responsible for continuity from one take to the next. The order in which the scenes are filmed will probably not be the order in which they appear in the final cut. Suppose that your commercial begins with you in your china shop, and you react in horror when a bull walks in. You will film the bull at a different time from the reaction shot, because of the rearrangement of camera and lighting positions between the two shots—not to mention the rearrangement of the breakables for the animal sequence! If your reaction is to look up and to the left, then the bull must appear to enter from the left. The shooting order is determined by the logistics of moving lighting setups, episodes of shooting on location and in-studio, and so on. Therefore someone—the director—has to imagine the final edit and keep the individual scenes working as part of the whole.

That's the basic crew: a producer, a director, a camera operator, and one or more actors. For a complex production, additional specialists will join the crew. If the commercial is to look very "high style," there might be an art director and a lighting designer. If you're recording critical sound on location, there will be an audio track producer. If there are several actors in the cast, and especially if fashion is involved, there will be stylists for hair, make-up, and wardrobe. The producer will have production assistants to help in advance of the shoot with permits, clearances, logistics, and props. Once the production begins, the assistants will be helping everyone in the crew to work together smoothly, right down to the caterers. (Since working fast is critical to working on a budget, most producers will arrange for a buffet, so as not to stop production over a lunch hour.)

Does commercial production sound complicated and expensive? It can be—if you let yourself think big. If you need to keep a tight rein on the budget, your insurance is to work closely with the producer in advance of the production so that your desires are clear to all. You should attend the shoot—you'll learn a lot—but don't second-guess the crew. Make your decisions once and stick to them. If you try to micromanage this process, you will certainly create cost overruns.

Large productions are affordable only by larger retailers and others with fairly large advertising budgets. If you are going to spend this much on producing a commercial, you'd better be buying a lot of air time to give it some exposure.

Smaller businesses use television too, obviously—with every feature of production scaled back quite a bit. One specialist might fill every role from producer to camera operator to off-camera announcer. Your local cable station will show lots of these lower-budget productions, since the air time on cable is less expensive too. If you will be producing a commercial on a slim budget, study the commercials you see on cable.

Step Four: Postproduction

The producer/director will review all the raw material, sound and video, and edit it into the final mix. Do you need to be present for this process? That depends on the equipment being used and your decision process.

The technology, as I mentioned before, is changing rapidly. Until recently, all postproduction involved on-line editing. Using this technique, you began at the beginning, chose each element of sound or video, and copied it onto the master tape in sequence. If you changed your mind about something later, you'd have to redo all your work from the changed portion on. This virtually required the presence of the client, because finality of decisions was the only way to keep the costs in line. Postproduction facilities charge by the hour.

Everybody hates being asked to approve something with a gun to his or her head. "Like this or spend money" was about the size of it. But offline editing equipment is changing that picture. Offline editing uses computers to cut

and paste sound and images, like moving paragraphs around in a word-processing program. This means that you can change anything in the commercial without having to redo the work that comes after it. All the sequences are held in computer memory until the final downloading to videotape or film. This makes the editing process much more flexible. Here comes the Catch-22: That flexibility means that you can explore more options, which can take longer and cost you more money!

What can you do? If off-line equipment is available at the studio you've hired, don't be afraid to use it. But know your ability to make decisions, and don't let yourself fall into exploring too many alternatives. Too many cooks not only spoil the broth, they take longer making it. Let the experts you've hired do their jobs.

Step Five: Duplication and Distribution

At last the hard part is over! You've got your commercial "in the can." Don't let bad duplication bring down your hard work. The production studio will have the ability to make duplicates; the quantity you need will determine whether it should do the work or you should work with a firm specializing in video duplication. Your producer can recommend suppliers.

Volume is the big issue. How many duplicates do you need? Maybe just three to five, for the different stations where you've contracted for time, and a VHS version for your personal collection. If you're running spots on more than a dozen stations, look for an outside duplication house. Your film or videotape master will be "dubbed down" to videocassettes. Be sure to find out each station's desired format; it might be $^3/_4$-in tape or Beta cassettes. You want to make sure you get the best quality possible on the air.

The services provided by a duplication house will include

- Setup
- Duplication

- Labeling (on the tape and on the container)
- Containers
- Shipping per instructions

Get several cost estimates. Quality is important, but difficult to judge. Ask your producer for recommendations and use them to guide your decision.

Who does the shipping, and who makes sure each station gets the right instructions? If you've worked with a media buyer to place your advertising, that person will coordinate with the duplication people. If not, the job's up to you, but it's not hard. In a local market, the TV stations will be making daily runs to the various production houses. Simply contact your station's sales reps and let them know where to pick up the tape.

Summary

TV advertising is the most complex and expensive way to get a message in front of your market. It's also the most exciting, and the closest to show biz you're likely to get. If you plan to use TV, make a solid commitment to give the process the support it needs in both dollars and energy. Then you can view this as an investment that will pay off for your business in increased sales. If you don't learn how to do it right, though, it can be an expensive waste of time.

Case Study: Competition Makes Retailer Flex His Creative Muscle

Anybody can succeed in a retail business if he or she can throw unlimited dollars at the advertising budget. But have you ever met anyone who fits that description? Even the largest retailers in your community want to make every penny count. Here's the story of one such retailer.

Joe Golde started The Bedroom Store two years ago. You got it—he sells bedroom furniture. As you would suspect, he finds competition everywhere he turns. Department stores, mass merchants, other furniture stores—they're all competing for the same consumers, and they're all using television to advertise.

Joe's smart. He tracks his advertising by asking every customer whether they saw his ads on TV, on the radio, or in the newspaper. Let's look at Joe's overall advertising strategy before we zero in on the TV commercials he's produced.

Joe has found that the newspaper brings in his best prospects (remember, print is the medium for communicating detailed information), and so 60 percent of his ad budget goes there. He buys a half-page color ad next to the weather forecast every Saturday. That's high visibility! Those ads are straightforward "catalog" ads, with products and prices featured, and he gets plenty of co-op support from the manufacturers to help pay for them.

But Joe needs to be on TV as well—because his competitors are there, because his store is relatively new, because TV is a good way to reach a wide variety of people. So most of the other 40 percent of his ad budget goes to TV.

Joe worked with salespeople from the local NBC, CBS, and Fox affiliates to design a media strategy that was a "shotgun" approach, not a "rifle shot." He chose to stay away from the cable stations. He liked the solid numbers the broadcast stations presented. He kept careful track of the ratings of the shows in his schedule to make sure he was getting enough reach and frequency with his desired audience—those aged twenty-five to fifty-four. (See "Timing Strategies and the Price of Air Time" for more on this.) Once Joe had his buy figured out (Example 8-4), he set about creating commercials to fill the schedule.

Example 8-4: Media Calendar for Year

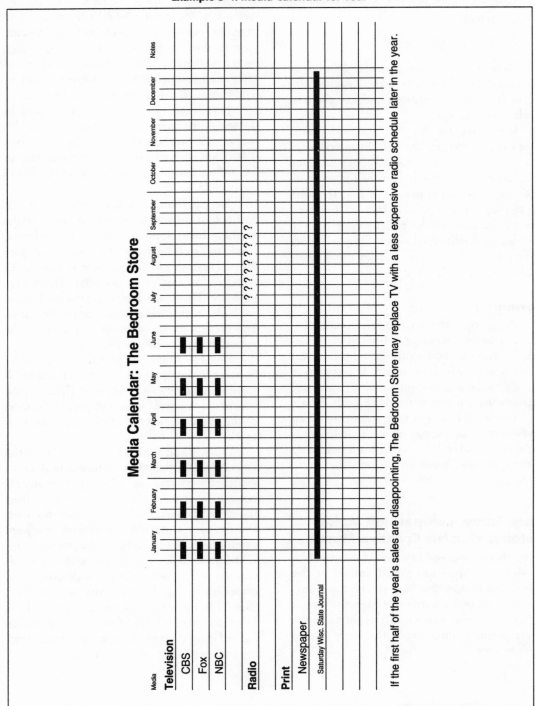

Media Calendar: The Bedroom Store

Media	January	February	March	April	May	June	July	August	September	October	November	December	Notes
Television													
CBS	█ █ █	█ █ █	█ █ █	█ █ █	█ █ █	█ █ █							
Fox													
NBC													
Radio							? ? ? ? ? ? ? ?						
Print													
Newspaper													
Saturday Wisc. State Journal													

If the first half of the year's sales are disappointing, The Bedroom Store may replace TV with a less expensive radio schedule later in the year.

Joe studied other businesses' advertising, using them as mentors. Then he began to work on his own spots, collaborating with an independent video producer, David Braga. They started from Joe's positioning strategy, which he sums up as "low prices and a pleasurable place to shop."

Joe committed to a promotional strategy that was quite aggressive. The Bedroom Store has a sale going every week of the year. "People expect sales in retail," he says. "The department stores, with their one-day and two-day sales, have conditioned the consumer to shop that way. You have to play the game."

So Joe knew that his TV commercials, while partly there to build the general image of his store, would have to announce sales as well. Joe and David settled down to work. The creative process went something like this: The two brainstormed together, David came back with a script, they discussed it, David revised it. After about three rounds like this, they went into production. Joe gave David free rein, letting him choose the actors for the spots, and making the showroom floor available for shooting. "It really tore up the store—he was everywhere with his lights—but that's neces-

sary." David's in-store footage got the point across that this store had a great selection displayed in a pleasing way. The script emphasized product selection and price.

In postproduction, jazzy introductory titles were added to punch up the sale message. Fast cutting brought the story line together. Each commercial has a little plot in it. In a category where most commercials are "flying boxes" with products and prices and an announcer yelling "sale, sale, sale," these commercials come across as high-style, whimsical, and yet hard-hitting on product value.

Joe and David produced only one commercial at first, and it pulled well. A second commercial was less successful, and the two returned to elements that had worked well in the first for their third production. Each time they shot lots of in-store footage, and so as the year goes on, Joe will have an increasing library of images to use. He'll be able to take this quick-cut visual style a long way on his initial investment. It gives his advertising a unique personality. Plus, it packs a lot of message into his 30-second movies (Examples 8-5 and 8-6).

Example 8-5

The Bedroom Store
Thirty-Second Television Commercial #1
"January Sale"
Music: humorous fast-tempo classical strings, a king of "Hungarian" sound.

Open on blank screen; type sails in from all sides.

Titles: Sale Sale Sale
                 We're practically giving them away!
                 Our buyer bought wrong, now you can too
                 $1 over invoice

Announcer: It seems that everyone has a clearance sale this time of year, with
                 Christmas season leftovers and what-not.

(Fade to scene of man with nose pressed against glass. He goes inside.)

Announcer: So what's so special about a January Clearance Sale at The
                 Bedroom Store?

(Quick pans across furniture in showroom.)

(Title: Save 60%, Bedroom Store logo)

Announcer: The new year brings new models, and there's simply nowhere to
                 put them.

(Camera cuts between man trying out lots of beds and pans over furniture. Very
fast style, 7 cuts.)

Announcer: So everything is on sale! Stylish, versatile futons. Sealy
                 mattresses. Solid cherry and oak bedroom sets.

(Title: Guaranteed Lowest Prices. Rule fades in under "guaranteed.")

Announcer: Futons and beds for every budget at guaranteed low prices.

(Cut to shot of store exterior, dramatic sunset shot.)

(Title: The Bedroom Store (logo). January Clearance Sale.)

Announcer: The Bedroom Store. Odana Road. Where January means it's
                 always good sleeping weather.

(Cut to closing shot: man hands coat to clerk and curls up in bed with his
stuffed animal.)

Example 8-6

The Bedroom Store
Thirty-Second Television Commercial #3
"March Sale"
Music: Jazzy riff with snare drums and a blues-y walking bass.

Open on blank screen, type sails in from all sides.

Title: Are you Sick & Tired of painful shopping experiences?
Announcer: Are you sick and tired of painful shopping experiences?
(Cut to salesman with customer in showroom. Quick cut: 3 scenes.)
(Flash Title: The Bedroom Store logo)
Announcer: We think you'll like our bedside manner.
(Quick cuts of man in pajamas tossing and turning on bed. Sports equipment is on the bed too. 7 cuts total as he changes position, very fast.)
Announcer: Are you not on the ball because you're just not sleeping well?
(Camera cuts to pan across beds. Announcer is quiet.)
(Title: The Bedroom Store logo)
(Music up: jazzy walking bass.)
(Camera cuts to feet on bed; sneakers, pajamas, and basketball visible. One foot "kicks" at the logo, which flies off-screen top.)
Announcer: Come be part of our dream team. You snooze, you win!
(SFX: basketball gym sounds.)
(Cut to pan across mattresses.)
Announcer: The Bedroom Store. We must move to a new warehouse!
(Cut to pan across furniture.)
(Title: Save up to 60%)
(Title: 6 Months Free Financing)
Announcer: Save us the moving charges and you'll save big bucks at our
                gigantic in-store warehouse sale.
(Cut to shot of store exterior, dramatic sunset shot.)
(Title: The Bedroom Store logo)
(Title: Warehouse Sale)
Announcer: Guaranteed lowest prices. The Bedroom Store.

Joe gave this advice for anyone considering using television to advertise:

"If you're going to go on TV, it's important to have good production value. If your production doesn't make it, the value of your message us diminished exponentially." He reflected for a moment on his experience with television, both in his two years with this store and in the previous decade, which he had spent in a related business. "It takes guts to go in, fortitude to stay with it, and intelligence to fine-tune the message so you're always improving." That's true of all areas of business—television advertising included.

Case Study: Two Commercials for Klinke Cleaners

Example 8-7

KLINKE CLEANERS

Thirty-Second Television Commercial #1

"Dry Cleaning"

Music: Blue Danube waltz under throughout.

(Open on man dressed in a white suit covered with dirt and stains.)

Flashing title: Amazing Cleaning Dramatization.

(Cut to close-up and begin slowly pulling back.

Man looks at his suit as dirt and stains begin lifting off and flying away.)

Announcer: This cleaning dramatization is brought to you by Klinke Cleaners.

(Stains continue lifting off of clothes and flying away.)

Flashing title: Don't try this at home.

Announcer: While we can't promise everything will come clean this easily...

(Stains continue lifting off of clothes and flying away.)

Announcer: ... with over a dozen state-of-the-art locations and same day service ...

Flashing title: Trust Klinke Cleaners.

(Camera stops pulling back when man is full frame. Final stains lift off of clothes and fly away.)

Announcer: ... you can trust Klinke Cleaners to make all of your cleaning concerns vanish.

(Man looks down at clothes, up at camera, and smiles.)

Title: (Dissolve over video)

           Klinke Cleaners.

Example 8-8

KLINKE CLEANERS
Thirty-Second Television Commercial #2
"Shirts"

Music: Blue Danube waltz under throughout.
(Open on man in dress slacks and an undershirt ironing his shirt in fast motion.)
Flashing title: Don't Try This At Home.
Announcer: We'd like to remind you there's an irony in laundering your own shirts.
(Man continues frantically ironing.)
Announcer: Even if you worked fast, you'd be pressed to match the same day service and wrinkle-free quality waiting for you at over a dozen Klinke locations.
Flashing title: Trust Klinke Cleaners.
(Man sets down iron, pulls necktie from pocket, puts it on, and walks off stage.)
Announcer: We say, why even try?
Title: (Dissolve over video)
              Klinke Cleaners.

A man in an undershirt is ironing a white shirt. He moves in fast motion, like an old Laurel and Hardy movie. He works very hard, but is obviously dissatisfied. Finally he tosses the shirt aside, pulls a necktie out of his pocket, puts it on, and walks offstage. The Klinke Cleaners logo appears in his place (Examples 8-7 and 8-8).

Two Klinke commercials were filmed at the same time, making maximum use of a small production budget. We described the "Dry Cleaning" spot at the opening of this chapter, and we analyzed its script in Example 8-2. The second commercial is clearly part of the family. Repeating elements of visual style, script, and music tie the two together.

With only one actor and a few props, these spots keep costs to a minimum, relying on sight gags and witty writing to get the message across with humor.

In the first example, "Dry Cleaning," the commercial was filmed and then the tape played backward to create the illusion of paint flying out of the suit. Actually, off-screen assistants were firing paint at the actor using super-soaker squirt guns. The actor rehearsed his facial expressions to act the scene in reverse, making the transition from sad to happy in the final result. The announcer's voice, the classical music, and the flashing subtitles were added in postproduction.

In the second example, the tape is played in fast motion to create the humorous visual effect, which underscores the point of the commercial: Let the dry cleaner do it!

For continuity, both commercials use the same piece of classical music, the same style of flashing titles, and the same announcer voice. He uses a British accent, which adds to the classy but humorous tone of the spots.

Example 8-9

TITLE: KLINKE CLEANERS: "SHIRTS"

LENGTH: 130

NOTES: FLASHING TITLES, "BLUE DANUBE WALTZ" UNDER THROUGHOUT. SEE SCRIPT.

FLASHING TITLE: → DON'T TRY THIS AT HOME

(MUSIC STARTS. MAN IRONS
SHIRT IN FAST MOTION)

(MAN IS IRONING FRANTICALLY)
ANNCR: WE'D LIKE TO REMIND YOU, THERE'S
AN IRONY IN LAUNDERING YOUR OWN SHIRTS.

FLASHING TITLE: → TRUST KLINKE CLEANERS.

, ANNCR: EVEN IF YOU WORKED FAST, YOU'D BE PRESSED
TO MATCH THE SAME-DAY SERVICE AND
WRINKLE-FREE QUALITY WAITING FOR
YOU AT OVER A DOZEN KLINKE LOCATIONS.

(MAN SETS DOWN IRON, PULLS NECKTIE
OUT OF POCKET, PUTS IT ON AND WALKS
OFF STAGE.)

(ANNOUNCER IS SILENT. MUSIC CONTINUES.)

ANNCR: WE SAY, WHY EVEN TRY?

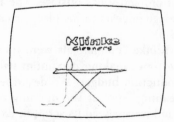

These spots were scripted by an ad agency, but produced at a TV station rather than a production studio. Both commercials make good use of TV's unique qualities of sight and sound. The "gimmick" of playing the tape in unusual ways—fast or backward—could work only on TV. Each is inexpensive to produce, and as a pair they are a real bargain. Template 8-3A shows the budget for these.

These commercials are not just creative. They're sound from a marketing standpoint too. They communicate a key benefit of convenience and quality, through parody of the usual product-demonstration technique. They're cheap, hot, and on-target—just what you'd like your TV advertising to be.

Chapter 9

Direct Mail Advertising: Generating Leads, Winning Responses

Analyze, strategize, create. You've heard me use this formula before. It's my tried-and-true way to get a handle on big subjects. These three words organize the challenge ahead of you:

● Analyze the purposes and characteristics of direct mail.

● Decide whether those attributes fit the strategies you've chosen.

● Then create a mail piece that accomplishes your goals.

Whole books have been written about the topic. *The Perfect Sales Piece* by Robert Bly is a good one for analyzing and strategizing; *Getting It Printed* by Beach, Shepro, and Russon is thorough on the creative end. You say you have no time to read books on the subject? Then browse this chapter. Take what seems to fit your situation, and dive into direct mail.

Analyzing the Direct Mail Program

Why would you want to use the mail to deliver a message? Because direct mail is *the* medium for control freaks. Better than with any other

medium, you can select who gets your message, when, and where. You control the offer. You control the list. You control the costs. You measure the results. With direct mail, you can test and alter your mail piece until it's a finely honed machine.

Direct mail can be designed to fit any budget. At the low end, it can be much more cost-effective than print or broadcast advertising. At the high end, it can cost more than an entire ad campaign—and be effective enough to justify the cost. The two ends of the price spectrum reach different objectives; somewhere between the extremes might be a good promotional program for you.

We'll talk about budgeting in detail when we get to strategy. First I should define what I mean when I use the term *direct mail*. Let me explain how I think it fits into your sales cycle.

Defining Terms

Direct mail is not a scientific term. People use it in different ways. It might cover any type of communication that passes through the post office. To simplify what I mean when I use the term, let me start backwards. Here is what I *don't* mean by direct mail.

Direct mail is not *direct marketing*. That term stands for a category of business that is neither retail (i.e., sold in a store) nor whole-sale (sold to people with a store). Direct marketers sell their products directly into people's homes via catalogs. Lands' End is a direct marketer. So is L.L. Bean. You may or may not fit into this category; whether or not you do will certainly affect how you use direct mail. But don't confuse the two terms. Direct marketers use direct mail as their primary way of reaching their customers and selling to them.

There's also a difference between using direct mail and mailing out brochures. As I see it, your brochure is part of your corporate identity. It behaves like a salesperson for your firm, telling your story as you would present it if you were there in person. It will probably be just as "hard sell" or "soft sell" as you would be. Even if you often send brochures to customers in response to a request for information, I don't consider this "using direct mail." This is a device to facilitate personal communication. That can be a very effective tool for customer communication, and you should certainly have a brochure to respond to such requests. That's why we'll talk about the company brochure and corporate identity in Chapter 11. But don't confuse that brochure with a direct mail advertising program.

Direct mail, as I use the term, means printed literature that goes out to a chosen audience, asks for a lead or an order, and results in a response that fits into your sales cycle in a way you have planned. In other words, it is specifically designed to help you sell something.

This printed literature goes by many names. *Lead generators* and *order request* pieces are the most popular. They are relatively quick in their results, and cost-effective. *Catalogs* and *price lists* are another form used by businesses every day. They are complex to manage, but are a necessary tool in many industries.

Product *sell sheets* and *tech-spec (technical specification) sheets* are a staple of business-to-business marketing. *Invoice stuffers* or *bill inserts* are popular in the consumer marketplace. A *sales letter* is typically a package of the type subscription and other single-product marketers use, where a personalized letter and several other pieces arrive in an envelope. *Dimensional mail* identifies pop-ups and bulky enclosures of all sorts. *Flyers* (or fliers—you'll see both spellings) is a catch-all term to cover the rest of the universe of printed pieces.

These different formats for the printed page all have one thing in common: Each is intended to encourage a specific action. I group them into three categories, each serving a different purpose in the sales cycle. I'll talk about each of these in turn:

- Lead generators
- Inquiry fulfillment pieces
- Order request (often called direct response) pieces

I like to visualize the sales cycle as a big funnel. Outside the lip are people you've never heard of, and who have never heard of you. But you know that some of them would like to hear about what you sell. You will find yourself using the broadest forms of advertising—print and broadcast—to bring those people to the edge of the funnel. You can't reach them any other way, because you don't know exactly who they are. You can also use a form of direct mail called lead generators to do this. All of these forms of advertising are designed to motivate potential customers to give you a call or send in a coupon. The appeal of your advertising tips those outsiders over the edge into your funnel. They give you an invitation to make your pitch. We have already covered print and broadcast. So now let's discuss lead generators.

Lead Generators

A lead-generating direct mail piece works like print or broadcast advertising; it reaches out into the marketplace and gets customers interested in your offerings. Lead-generating direct mail can be the most efficient way to reach people who buy what you sell. Your success in this, though, depends a lot on the mailing lists you choose. That's where you get your control over direct mail. The more precisely you tailor your message to a list, the stronger your results can be.

If you haven't built your own list of leads, you will probably use a mailing list broker. These brokers create sophisticated custom mailing lists from their databases. You describe your typical prospect by demographics, lifestyle, purchasing habits, and other factors they've surveyed. Your list broker should then be able to come up with hundreds or thousands of names and addresses that match your description.

Renting a targeted list is an attractive alternative to advertising in print or broadcast media. There is less wasted circulation. You have a greater ability to track who receives your message and who responds. You measure your results, and you get your information quickly. It's a great way to drum up business in a down cycle.

Even if you are certain that print or broadcast advertising is the way to reach new prospects, you should give lead-generating direct mail some thought as well. Compare the numbers; CPM calculations will help you see your best option. (We'll talk more about list brokers and calculating direct mail costs when we get to the section on strategy.)

A lead generator will include a specific call to action, and sometimes a reward, like a premium or a discount price. *Order request* pieces use offers too, but the purpose of the lead generation offer is different. It is not intended to generate the *sale*—just the lead. Why not ask for the sale? Some products, like computer hardware or industrial equipment, are simply too complex to sell to cold prospects through the mail. You wouldn't buy that way, and you don't expect your customers to.

A lead generator works at the beginning of the sales cycle. It creates initial interest. That interest will result in high-quality sales leads if the list and the piece are properly coordinated to communicate your ability to fill a need or solve a specific problem that the people on the selected list have (see Example 9-1).

Example 9-1A: Lead Generator (Jefferson Home Health Care)
Used by permission of Jefferson Home Health Care.

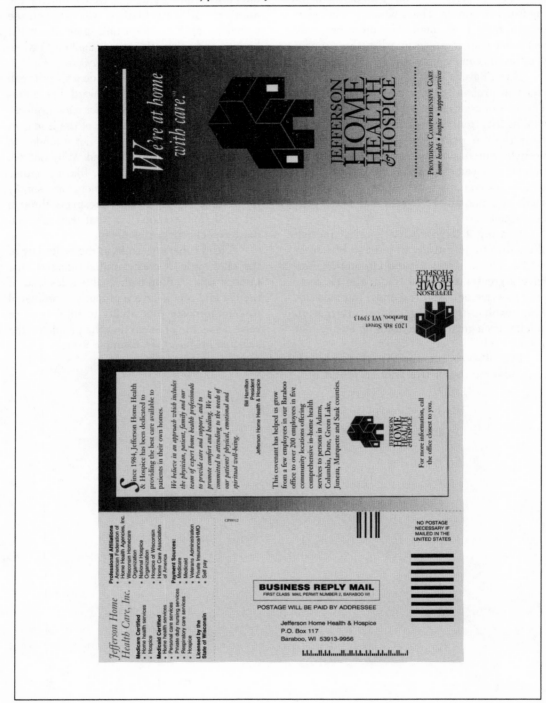

Example 9-1B: Lead Generator (Jefferson Home Health Care)
Used by permission of Jefferson Home Health Care.

Skilled Home Health Services

Jefferson Home Health Care, Inc. provides in-home nursing care, therapy and other skilled services to individuals of all ages. These services may be in lieu of hospitalization or may follow a stay in the hospital to continue the treatment and therapies begun in the hospital. Care is provided under the direction of your personal physician. An assessment for Medicare, Medicaid and private insurance coverage will be done by an R.N. at no charge. We offer:

Skilled nursing visits
Home health aides
Personal care workers
Private duty services
Physical, occupational and speech therapies
Dietary counseling
Medical social services
Patient and family education
Nurses available 24 hours a day, 365 days a year
Consultation on available services at no charge

Jefferson Home Health Care, Inc. provides high-tech care for patients with special needs.

Home Health Support Services

Jefferson Home Nursing Services, Inc. provides supportive home care services such as personal care workers and companion/homemakers to enable clients to remain in their homes. Jefferson also provides supplemental nurse and aide staffing in hospitals, nursing facilities and other health care institutions.

Jefferson Home Nursing Services, Inc. can provide:

Live-in support staff
Companion/homemakers
Respite care
Sick child care
Supplemental staffing through Jefferson Custom Care
Personal care assistance
HHA/PCW training program

Effective caregivers provide affectionate care for all ages, infant through elderly.

Hospice Program

Hospice is specialized multi-disciplinary care available to persons with a life expectancy of six months or less. Hospice makes it possible for patients to stay at home and live as comfortably and fully as possible.

Jefferson provides a caring approach to both patients and their families. The hospice team works directly with the physician, pastor, and family. Services can include:

Pain and symptom management
Psychological, emotional and spiritual support
Nursing care
Respite care
Volunteers
Bereavement counseling
24-hour in-home care during medical crises
Medication, equipment and supplies related to the terminal illness

For more information, call the office direct to you.

JEFFERSON HOME HEALTH HOSPICE

Offices in:

Baraboo
1208 8th Street
Baraboo, WI 53913
608-356-7570

Madison
437 S. Yellowstone Drive
Madison, WI 53719
608-274-8195

Mauston
116 Pine Street
Mauston, WI 53948
608-847-7735

Portage
119 E. Conant Street
Portage, WI 53901
608-742-2555

Montello
35 W. Montello Street
Montello, WI 53949
608-297-7213

It is reassuring to me that we have such outstanding agencies for providing home health care in parts of Wisconsin. I only wish that we had such service everywhere throughout the state...

Dennis G. Maki M.D.
Professor of Medicine
Attending Physician, Head, Section of Infectious Disease
Center for Trauma and Life Support
(UW-Madison Medical School)

Your dedicated program of concern and practical love meets the needs of special situations and permits people to continue to enjoy the security and comfort which their own home means to them.

Congratulations with thanks!
Father Anthony P. Young
St. Thomas congregation
(Poynette)

Do you know someone who needs help to stay at home?

Areas of interest:
Skilled Home Health Services
Home Health Support Services
Hospice Care

NAME
CITY
STATE
ZIP
PHONE

Office nearest you:
Please indicate which office is most convenient for you.
Baraboo
Madison
Mauston
Portage
Montello

Please call to arrange a time for a free consultation in our home. Best time to call:
Please send more information.
I would like to have you speak to our group.
We have a special need.

Let's assume you use a lead generator, and sure enough, it generates a pile of names. Now what's the next step? Direct mail comes into play again.

Inquiry Fulfillment Pieces

If your market is small geographically, chances are that you and your staff will follow up all new leads in person, via phone calls and visits. But if your market is more far-flung, that's not an option. You'll want to plan instead for printed pieces to continue your sales cycle.

We're back to the metaphor of the funnel. Your prospects are now swirling around somewhere near the lip, looking for reasons to climb back out or welcome the trip in. They need information. They need to build confidence in you; they need a good sales pitch. Inquiry fulfillment pieces are designed to deliver all that. Besides conveying the neces-

sary information, printed literature establishes credibility. It sets a professional tone; it demonstrates your stability and follow-through.

Product *sell sheets* and *tech-spec (technical specification) sheets* (see Example 9-2) are used by business-to-business marketers of everything from food ingredients to stucco. Typically they're formatted to a standard $8^1/_2$ x 11 page size, sometimes with holes drilled in the left margin so that they go easily in a ring binder. These pieces are designed with a purchasing manager in mind, right down to the convenient uniformity of size. Sell sheets show performance data, exploded views, test results, process photos—whatever it takes to explain the product concisely. They provide the information necessary to do comparison shopping. They help close the sale, but they're not expected to do the work alone.

Example 9-2: Sell Sheet (Great Wall)

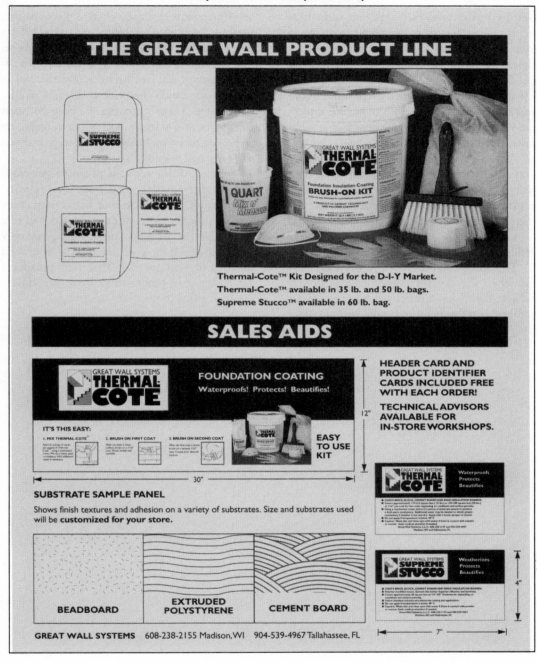

One kind of inquiry response piece often used by business-to-business and industrial supply companies is a catalog with an attached price list. This catalog differs from the consumer marketing type piece that comes from L.L. Bean, for example. Its main purpose is to deliver information about the products covered by this type of company, with the understanding that the actual sale may come from contact with a salesperson.

As you plan your inquiry fulfillment literature, calculate your costs and potential payback. Then you can decide how much information to send how early. More about this when we get to budgeting.

Order Request Mail Pieces

The sales cycle moves toward a conclusion when the prospect becomes a customer and actually makes a purchase. You can trigger that final trip through the funnel with an *order request* mail piece. You might make it an announcement of a special price discount or a limited term of availability, or it might be a description of featured products that are in high demand. The point is, it closes with an order form or toll-free number, and the call to action says "buy." The price and terms will be right there. There's nothing standing between prospects and parting with their money: no "send for more information," no "call and our sales rep will stop by."

For an order request piece to generate successful results, you have to lay your groundwork. Make sure your list is reasonably well qualified and the offer you make is of real value. Is the product something genuinely desirable? Have you created a sense of urgency in your tone, so that your prospects act rather than procrastinate? Are you timing the mail effort to your best advantage?

Example 9-3A: Order Request piece (Bi-Folkal Scoops Piece)
Used by permission of BiFolkal Productions.

Example 9-3B: Order Request piece (Bi-Folkal Scoops Piece)
Used by permission of Bi-Folkal Productions.

Here's the scoop!

We don't like to raise our prices; we have to. Before we put our old prices on **ice**, we have a special offer for you—the **cream** of our customer and mail list contacts.

We don't want to be **jerks**, so we are offering you the opportunity to purchase any of our complete program kits at the 1989 price of $210 for slide versions and $220 for video versions.

We know you don't have much **fat** in your budget, and that's why we make you this **really cool** offer. If you can **dip** into your budget now, send, fax or call in your order. We are usually here 9–5 weekdays (not on Saturdays or **Sundaes**).

Remember—we guarantee you will like Bi-Folkal Productions. Return any kit within 30 days for complete refund or credit—we'll never do anything to **shake** your faith in us.

Here's the **topping**—order now and pay only $5 per kit for shipping.

Why not buy all 16 flavors?

Act quickly—this offer will **melt** on April 1, 1993.

REMEMBERING	Slide kit will be $235		Video kit will be $240		Slides & video will be $270	
PETS	PT101	$210	PT103	$220	PT108	$245
MUSIC	MU101	$210	MU103	$220	MU108	$245
THE FASHION	FS101	$210	FS103	$220	FS108	$245
WORK LIFE	WL101	$210	WL103	$220	WL108	$245
HOME FRONT	HF101	$210	HF103	$220	HF108	$245
SUMMERTIME	ST101	$210	ST103	$220	ST108	$245
BIRTHDAYS	BD101	$210	BD103	$220	BD108	$245
AUTOMOBILES	AU101	$210	AU103	$220	AU108	$245
FALL	FA101	$210	FA103	$220	FA108	$245
FARM DAYS	FD101	$210	FD103	$220	FD108	$245
THE DEPRESSION	DP101	$210	DP103	$220	DP108	$245
SCHOOL DAYS	SD101	$210	SD103	$220	SD108	$245
1924	TF101	$210	TF103	$220	TF108	$245
TRAIN RIDES	TR101	$210	TR103	$220	TR108	$245
COUNTY FAIRS	CF101	$210	CF103	$220	CF108	$245

CIRCLE YOUR CHOICES

SEND TO:
BI-FOLKAL PRODUCTIONS, INC.
809 Williamson Street
Madison, WI 53703

Subtotal _____
Shipping (add $5 per kit) _____
(HI, AK and foreign orders will have shipping added.)

Total order _____

DEADLINE APRIL 1, 1993.

PURCHASE ORDER # _____
PHONE NUMBER _____

SHIP TO:

Name (and title if applicable) _____

(Institution) _____

Street _____

City _____ State _____ Zip Code _____

BILL TO: (Complete if different from *Ship to*)

Name (Title) _____

(Institution) _____

Street _____

City _____ State _____ Zip Code _____

Phone or fax your order for quick response:
Phone: 608/251-2818 or fax: 608/251-2874

Cardholder's name _____
Signature _____
Card Number _____
Expiration date __ __ __ __ ❑ MasterCard ❑ Visa

Example 9-3 is from a company that is selling activity kits used by people who work with older adults. Later in this chapter we'll look at this piece more closely, in a case study of its budget, mailing list, timing, and results. This order request piece offers a price discount if you purchase within a three-month window. In creating your offer for an order request piece, you need to answer such questions as, Will you offer a discount or a coupon in your order request mail? Can you make an offer that is substantial enough to be attractive? Look at Chapter 3, "Promotions," for more ideas on developing the successful offer.

Here's a tip: Order request mailings work very well with repeat customers. Your in-house mailing list is a gold mine if your customers frequently need what you sell. Refills and other often-used products are easy to buy, in bulk, by mail. Your customers know this. If you sell personal-care products, or fashions, or office supplies, or industrial materials like paint or cleansers, you should look into order request direct mail. Figure out your customers' timing, mail to them at appropriate times, and you'll see loyalty building along with your sales.

Cross-selling is important, too. Treat people who have purchased one of your products as prospects for others. The same goes for services! We all tend to assume that our customers are either loyal or gone, that they buy either everything they need or nothing from us. The truth is, almost everyone who shops with you could be buying more from you if you took the trouble to ask for their additional business.

A *sales letter* is a variation on the order request direct mail piece. As I said at the start of this chapter, this consists of an envelope containing a personalized letter, a flyer, a reply card or order form, and probably several other pieces as well. See Example 9-14 near the end of this chapter for a closer look at the sales letter. You will find a sidebar there with a detailed review of the complete sales letter.

Who Uses Direct Mail?

You are likely to benefit from using direct mail if you:

- *Get requests for information*. No matter how you generate those leads, you need inquiry fulfillment literature for answering their requests.

- *Sell to businesses with multiple decision makers*. Comparison shopping is common, and you need sell sheets and other informational pieces to present your case when you can't be there in person. Chances are you will never meet everyone who has input into whether your product will be purchased.

- *Have the ability to manage a list in-house*. Too many businesses I know neglect the power of their in-house customer lists. Who's the most likely person on the planet to buy from you? Somebody who just did, and had a good experience. Figure out how soon that person will need more, and direct mail to them. It works for your dentist, doesn't it?

- *Can procure a mailing list that offers focused distribution of your message*. This is less desirable than a well-managed in-house list, but it's a useful way to explore potential markets. Magazines, newspapers, or other media may serve your market, but they will always be less focused than a well-defined mailing list.

- *Are interested in fast growth*. Direct mail can build credibility, inform, educate. If your business is new, a mailer can go a long way toward educating prospects about who you are and what you do. If you have moved to a new location, you will want to establish your credibility with your new potential customers. Perhaps you have recently added products or services. Your current customers need to be told about your new offerings. Does your business need a jump-start? Look over

Chapter 3 for ideas on promotions, then plan a direct mail strategy that makes an irresistible offer.

- *Sell through agents or salespeople.* Reps, distributors, and other agents who carry your products expect you to support them with printed literature. These salespeople are in the best position to know what they need to help them make the sale. Maybe they want a sell sheet they can customize with their own logo and address. Maybe they want a confidence-building piece with pictures of your manufacturing plant, order center, and delivery fleet. Let those in the field choose their tools. Then get their input as you create your mail piece.

Do any of these situations fit your business? If so, then direct mail advertising could help you.

Advantages of Direct Mail

Direct mail delivers a very high degree of control. It allows you to choose exactly who receives your promotion. You can measure results precisely by recording the number of responses your mailing brings in.

Direct mail delivers a captive audience. Unlike radio, which is on in the background while people are doing other things, your mail piece holds center stage, once it has gotten someone's attention. That's why direct mail sells products and services that take detail to explain. Long-copy advertisements can do that too, but seldom as efficiently as direct mail.

Disadvantages of Direct Mail

There is the "junk mail" factor to consider. A growing number of recipients simply throw such pieces away without even looking at them, much less reading them. However, if you have chosen your list well, it is likely that your recipients will at least briefly check what you have to say. They read direct mail pieces for the same reason you do. So think about why you read such ads and what kind you

read, and that probably will help you understand why others may or may not read what you send.

More people today are also concerned about environmental issues. To address this concern, make sure you aren't sending duplicate pieces to one person. Use recycled papers and earth-friendly soy inks whenever possible—and state that fact somewhere on your piece. You can avoid a guilty conscience by making your offer valuable and your piece attractive and environmentally friendly. If you mail it to reasonably good prospects, you are doing them a service.

Another disadvantage of direct mail can be cost. Producing and mailing the piece can strain your budget. Be careful to match your objectives with your budget. Prepare detailed estimates before you proceed, to keep your production costs under control. If your target is not well defined, you may be wasting a high percentage of your mailings—a costly problem. The list you choose has to be the *right* list before direct mail can do its job for you.

Some Facts of Life About Using Direct Mail

1. You need measurable goals. Clearly define your projected results. Be as specific as possible. Make quantifiable goal statements, such as "Bring in ten new customers each day" or "Sell twenty-five upgrade features." At the end of the mail program, you must be able to tell precisely how close you came to reaching your goal—or by how much you exceeded it. Then you can adjust your projections when you plan your next mail piece.

2. Direct mail is not a general advertising medium. Give it a specific job to do. Target a specific audience. Then develop copy and a layout that fits.

3. Make it easy to take action. Always think ahead to precisely what you want the recipients to do. Then remove any barriers

that might prevent them from taking that step. If you want them to send back a reply card, make it postage-paid. If you want them to call you, get a toll-free number. If you want them to place an order, provide the payment terms, the shipping charges, and all the other pertinent information. Test-drive your response vehicle! Have someone use the order form before you finalize your layout.

4. Use coupons and redemption offers. Give an interested prospect a reason to act soon. Coupons have expiration dates for a reason: to give urgency to the offer. You can get more out of your mail pieces by using promotional techniques. (See more about this in Chapter 3.)

5. Test and refine both the mail piece and the plan. Don't give up after giving it just one shot. So many factors affect the response your piece draws! You could have wonderful design and copy and a great offer, but if you mail it at the wrong time, you can shoot down your chance for a successful result. It works the other way, too. Good timing can't save a bad mail piece. In the end, you have to test until you see what works for your situation.

6. Develop your skills. If you find that direct mail holds promise for you, learn as much about it as you can. You probably get as many mailings about how-to seminars as I do. Attend workshops, look for books and articles on the subject. Educate yourself.

7. Work closely with the post office. Why make expensive and unnecessary mistakes? The main post office in your town will have a bulk mail acceptance unit and an automated mail-handling specialist. Each has a responsibility to provide you with the information you need to bring

mail the way the post office wants it prepared. Simply call them up or visit and ask.

In my graphic design business, I fax the post office a copy of every mail piece I design. I want to make sure I'm not costing my client money or delaying the delivery of our mail pieces by the way I've laid them out. Nonstandard sizes or ink colors, certain placement of type, and other graphic "whims" can have a bad effect on the speed and cost of bulk mail processing. Business reply cards have their own set of rules. Familiarize yourself with the whole postal-compliance aspect of direct mail before you complete your layouts.

Tracking Your Sales Leads

There's one final step to the sales cycle: You have to keep track of your results. You need to set up a system, whether on paper or on computer, that records responses and organizes the information you collect about each. You will want to know:

● The source of the lead (what mailing list was used, when it was sent, etc.)

● The date of response

● Contact name, business name, and address

● Relevant facts, such as computer applications used or other demographic/lifestyle. information that give you a profile of your prospect

You will also want to maintain a log of follow-up activity. Record what literature was sent and when. Also keep notes on personal contacts, whether in person, by phone, or by mail (see Template 9-1).

Template 9-1: Sales Contact Tracking Form

Sales Contact Tracking Form

Date of contact_____From what mailing list_____

When was mailing sent? _____

Method of response: ☐ Phone ☐ Response Card ☐ Visit

Name_____Title_____

Company _____Phone_____

Address _____

City _____State_____Zip _____

Brief description of business (what market served, what product or service offered, etc.)

_____

_____

What (service/product) sparked this response? _____

What additional (services/products) might this firm need? _____

_____

Describe this firm's purchasing habits:_____

_____

Status:

Response sent on (date) _____

Enclosures: _____

Next Step:

Likely to purchase? (Circle one.)   VERY HOT   WARM   LUKEWARM   COOL   COLD

Contact Record:

Date:	Summary of Conversation	Phone/Fax/Mail?
_____	_____	☐ ☐ ☐
_____	_____	☐ ☐ ☐
_____	_____	☐ ☐ ☐
_____	_____	☐ ☐ ☐
_____	_____	☐ ☐ ☐

Do you need to use a computer to do this record keeping? Maybe not. If your projected number of responses is in the dozens, a three-ring notebook or a set of index cards might be all you need. But if you deal with more than a hundred prospects, you're missing the point if you don't use a computerized database. You want to be able to print mailing labels; you want to be able to find out who has responded to certain mailings and target them for similar offers in the future. Using database programs to track sales activity is an important concept.

For the small-market business, like a professional practice or local retail shop, the system you use to track sales leads can be minimal. But it must do two important things. It has to give you mailing labels, so that you can reach respondents repeatedly. And it has to give you a way to report how many responded to a specific mailing in a specific time period. A simple tally sheet, with rows for the weeks or months and hash marks for the number of responses, will tell you what you need to know when it comes time to calculate the return on investment for the mail program. A separate list in a word-processing program or typed on label masters will give you the mailing labels you need. But if you're tracking your direct mail program with tools like these, you're missing the power of databases. The information on your sales tracking form becomes invaluable to you when you can search for patterns and learn from your successes. If you plan to make direct mail an ongoing component of your promotional plans, you'll want to find out more about database marketing.

Organizing Your Follow-Through

There is an administrative side to a direct mail program that requires a little planning. You will have to stock, mail, and reorder the printed literature. You will need to organize a supply cabinet or mailing center for filling requests for additional information. Recognize that managing the direct mail program—both mailing the piece and following up on the

responses—is a distinct function that must be taken care of in a timely way. Make it someone's specific duty. Don't let it get back-burnered—you'll hurt your credibility, or worse.

Many businesses use codes printed on their mail pieces to help manage the system. Look over the reply card on the next flyer you get in the mail. See if you can find a code that conveys the date, quantity, and perhaps a short description of the piece you've received. For example, it might be "CA5M593." To the administrator, that means "Connecticut Area, 5,000 pieces printed, May 1993." This helps in making key decisions—whether to rent the Connecticut area mailing list again, for instance, may depend on how many responses with this code were tallied.

A code is an easy way to track print quantities used over time. That's a big help when it's time to reorder.

Testing Response to Direct Mail

Everyone will tell you how important testing is to the success of your program. Ideally, you will test variations in the offer, the headline, and the layout until you find the combination that pulls best. However, testing each component is hardly affordable on a small-business budget. When your total quantity is under 10,000 pieces, how can you afford to print 1,000 with one offer and 1,000 with another, just to see which gets more response? The answer is, you probably can't. But you can keep track of responses to each mailing, and alter your mail program each time you implement it based on how many responses each approach generates. Track each change in layout, mailing list, or timing against the responses received. The administrative codes will help you compare results from one direct mail program to the next. Over time, you will arrive at the most effective direct mail piece possible for you. The case study on Bi-Folkal Productions at the end of this chapter shows a simple method of tracking results over time.

Response Rates: Hopes and Fears

The truth is, it's hard to generalize about response rates. Business-to-business marketing is different from consumer marketing, so what applies in one area may or may not apply in the other. One fact is true across the board: In either market, the quality of the initial mailing list has the most profound effect on the probability of response.

Contact the Direct Marketing Association (mentioned later in this chapter), or your industry's trade association to get specific response statistics for making your projections. I can give you these ballpark estimates:

Your in-house list, created as people have responded to your previous marketing efforts, should garner a response of 3 to 5 percent. Even 7 percent is possible if the leads are fresh and the mail program is persuasive.

If you're renting a highly specific list and delivering a desirable offer, you might expect a 1 to 2 percent response.

At the other extreme is renting a very large, nonspecific mailing list. Suppose you sell needlepoint craft kits. You want to reach a national consumer audience with your catalog of holiday gifts. You purchase a list covering a four-state region of women over forty-five who have made credit card purchases at hobby stores. While that sounds targeted, it really isn't very narrow. We don't know whether those women have any interest in needle-work—maybe they were buying furniture refinishing supplies or oil paints.

Even if your offering is good, you will probably have to settle for no better than 0.5 percent response. Why? The difference is the liveliness of the names on the list—a purchased list is likely to be less current than your own. And the very breadth of the list means that your offering will be less tailored to the individual. The unavoidable waste of circulation brings down your response percentages and drives up your cost.

In a local market, you can increase your response rate if you use other media to tie in with the program. Announce your upcoming mailing in your radio commercial. You could say, "Look in your mailbox for the exciting offer coming your way." You get the idea. Try it for Grand Openings or Anniversary Sales. Look at Chapter 3 for more ideas on special promotions and tie-ins.

Summary So Far...

We've been analyzing how a direct mail program can be used to generate leads, fulfill inquiries, and make requests for orders. We've covered in general terms who uses direct mail, and what goals it can accomplish. I've tried to give you some facts of life about direct mail and its advantages and disadvantages.

Because so many businesses use sales letters effectively, I recommend that you study the components of these packages. To learn more about how the envelope, the letter, the flyer, and the reply card work together to speed a prospect toward the order, study the sidebar on page 357.

I hope this introduction gives you some ideas as to how direct mail might fit into your marketing plan. I've tried to convince you of the importance of tracking your activity from initial contact on. And I've also touched on testing the direct mail piece, and how to maximize its results.

By this point in the chapter, you should have an idea about whether direct mail makes sense for your business. Next we'll discuss strategy—how to design the direct mail program that fits your objectives—and then we'll get to the creative task.

Strategize! Putting Direct Mail to Work for You

So you think a direct mail program has potential for your business. It's time for you to develop a strategy—a plan that explains how you will put direct mail to use. As in any planning process, I recommend that you develop several alternative scenarios, then decide which strategy serves you best.

You'll be weighing options and making decisions about the list you'll use, the offer you'll make, and the physical format of the piece you'll mail. You'll decide how to produce it—whether through an ad agency or graphic designer, or as a do-it-yourself project. Of course you'll calculate a budget, and project a return on investment, before you proceed. And when you've examined all your choices and made all your decisions, you'll need to develop a schedule for the program's execution.

Add it all up and you've got a comprehensive plan for a direct mail program. Skip the planning, and your thinking will remain fuzzy. Your direct mail programs will be less successful than they should be.

Let's take a look at each of the dimensions of your direct mail strategy.

- The mailing list
- Postal compliance, coming and going
- Response goals and sales goals
- The physical format of the piece
- The production path

The Mailing List: Deciding Who, Then What

A good plan for direct mail starts with a question: Who receives the mail piece? From your answer tumble all the rest of your decisions, from what your offer will be to what your piece will look like and say, to what your printing will cost. So it's the logical place to begin developing your strategy.

Choose a list based on the goal you want your direct mail program to accomplish. Do you want to be writing to your friends, or to strangers?

Writing to your friends—in other words, using an in-house list you've created from your customer contacts—is a powerful tool to increase your sales. I'd like to see you keep a prospect/customer list that tracks leads from initial inquiry right through that "sales funnel" to the purchase. Are you in retail? Capture the names of people who write checks or use charge cards in your store. Every week or every month, routinely add these to your database. You'll build a list of people who have had good experiences with your product or service in the past. That list should respond very well to direct mail order requests, coupons, and other special promotions.

The other potential use of direct mail is to connect with strangers. If you don't have an in-house list, or if your goal is to find new names to add to it, you will be renting a mailing list. Your entire strategy concerning timing, the offer, and the call to action will be entirely different with a rented list.

Think about the sales funnel. A rented mailing list brings you people who are outside the lip of the funnel. Using a rented list is the direct mail equivalent of cold calling. Your goal is to take those strangers and make them friends. All you really need them to do is to contact you with an open mind, so that you can provide persuasive follow-up. Your mail piece in this case will be a lead generator.

When you use your in-house list, you are speaking to people who are already in your funnel. They are known to you as current or prospective customers. You will use direct mail in the inquiry fulfillment and order request categories to encourage their repeat business, or to motivate them to a higher number of average transactions.

Be aware that renting means that you get one-time use! Anyone who provides a mailing list to you in label form will include "ringers"—make-believe names that bounce back to the provider's address. If you copy that list and remail to it, you'll be hearing from the provider—or its lawyers. Purchasing permanent use of a list, as you'd expect, is more expensive. Your better choice is to build your own permanent list from the responders to your rental-list mailings.

There are many sources for mailing lists. We'll talk about each in turn:

- Mailing list brokers
- Subscriber lists
- Professional association membership rosters
- Trade show attendees

List brokers are listed in your Yellow Pages under "Mailing houses" or "Mailing list consultants" or "Advertising, direct mail." They will prepare a list by sorting for your specific criteria, like "women between forty-five and sixty who have a driver's license and a college degree." You can expect to pay a setup fee, and then a cost per thousand based on the complexity of your sort. The price you pay might range from $30 per thousand to upwards of $200 per thousand.

As you negotiate for your list, the broker will run a count using your search criteria, so that you have an anticipated total number of mail recipients to plug into your projections. This number is the circulation for your mail piece, and fits into the CPM equation just like the circulation of a magazine goes into its cost-per-thousand equation. Use a CPM analysis spreadsheet to compare different mailing list scenarios. Template 9-2A shows an example of such a comparison; Template 9-2B is a blank form for your use.

Template 9-2A: CPM Analysis, Mailing List Comparisons

Date: 10-24-94
Title: Mailing List Comparisons
Assumptions: (Describe the mailing lists and how the rate was established.)
This spreadsheet compares a countywide business market reached through either magazine subscribers or zip-code-sorted lists from two potential vendors.

The rate and circulation figures are from the respective companies' proposals.

Mailing List	Rate	Circulation in 1,000s	CPM ($)	Index
In Business subscribers/SIC	$425	2.9	$146.55	100%
Accurate Business zip sort	$125	3.2	$39.06	29%
Total Mail Solutions zip sort	$188	3.1	$60.52	44%

For a full explanation of CPM calculations, see Chapter 6.

Template 9-2B: Blank

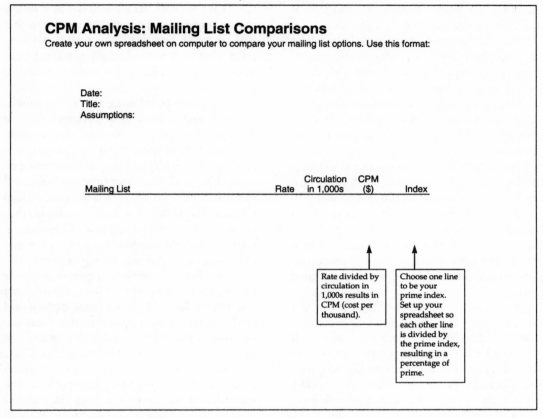

CPM Analysis: Mailing List Comparisons

Create your own spreadsheet on computer to compare your mailing list options. Use this format:

Date:
Title:
Assumptions:

Mailing List	Rate	Circulation in 1,000s	CPM ($)	Index

Rate divided by circulation in 1,000s results in CPM (cost per thousand).

Choose one line to be your prime index. Set up your spreadsheet so each other line is divided by the prime index, resulting in a percentage of prime.

The most common selection criterion for mailing lists is the Zip code sort. You can target certain parts of town—the blocks surrounding your grocery store, for example. List brokers will typically be able to give you breakdowns by demographic data, lifestyle factors, and purchase history, too, although you'll pay more as you add criteria to the sort description. List brokers may offer you packages: the first three criteria at a base price, for example, and three more criteria for a set additional fee.

Meet in person with your list broker; the brainstorming that results is likely to be more fruitful than a phone conversation. There are probably several mailing houses in your town that rent lists and provide the accompanying services—affixing the labels, sorting and bagging the pieces according to postal regulations, and delivering the final product to the post office. Tour their facilities if you think you might use their services. You want to get an impression of their thoroughness and attention to detail, and their quality control. Quality varies in this business, and you don't want your bottom line to suffer because of sloppy handling of your mail.

If you want to do a larger mailing, beyond your county or region's geographic boundaries, you may want to rent a mailing list from a national broker. Consult the SRDS (Standard Rate and Data Service) book of mailing lists. Ask for it at your library's reference desk.

Most magazines rent their subscriber lists, often at a cost that's lower than a list broker's fees. If you sell business-to-business, your industry's trade journal subscribers may be the best targeted prospect list that you can buy. Study the publication's media kit and look at the demographic information it provides.

Another source of mailing lists is the membership rosters of professional associations. I have seen insurance agents and investment counselors turn membership rosters into prospect lists with great success. However, some associations do not make their lists available, so you'll have to check on this in your planning.

The attendees of trade shows are recorded by the shows' management, and these are another prime source of prospects, whether you are looking for consumers or business-to-business buyers. Big-ticket consumer shows, like home remodeling product fairs or boat shows, can deliver highly targeted prospects. Look into attendee lists if you sense a good match.

Subscriber lists, membership rosters, and event attendee lists are likely to be more current than brokered mailing lists, although every vendor tries to keep its information up to date. Keep this in mind when figuring your response rates. There are other ways to build a mailing list—using a business card fish bowl by your cash register, for example. Look around you, and use your ingenuity.

So what exactly happens when you rent a mailing list? If you are using a mailing house, you will simply have your printer deliver the literature to the mailer, and wait for confirmation that the order has gone to the post office. (Make sure one piece is mailed to you, so that you find out how long the postal delivery takes.) You will never actually see the labels, since everything takes place under the mailing house's roof.

If you are purchasing the actual labels, you will need to know in what format they are available. Smaller lists, like association memberships, will typically come on pressure-sensitive labels, on $8^{1}/_{2}$ x 11 pages. These must be applied by hand. For larger lists, the labels will probably be available in a format called Chessire labels. You may have seen these; they are in columns of four and rows of twelve, on continuous-feed computer paper. These can be processed by machines at high speed.

Let the service that is preparing your mailing for the post office tell you what format it wants the list in. Even for hand application I find Chessire labels easier to use than the pressure-sensitive kind, which can be difficult to persuade to come loose from their backing!

You see why you should start planning your strategy by researching mailing lists. The nature and number of names on the list affects everything from your printing and postage budget to your creative approach. So start here: Do your list research before you take your plans further. Use Template 9-3 to collect and compare your cost information.

Template 9-3: Mailing List Cost Estimate Worksheet

Date:
Vendor:
Describe
Sort Criteria:

1. List Rental

$_____ Setup cost
Chessire labels?
$_____ Surcharge for pressure-sensitive, if needed?
$_____ List cost (cost per thousand multiplied by number of names matching sort criteria)
$_____ List Rental Subtotal

2. Mail Prep Costs
   a. Tabbing
$_____ Setup
$_____ Tabbing cost (cost per thousand multiplied by number of names)
   b. Labeling
$_____ Setup
$_____ Labeling cost (cost per thousand multiplied by number of names)
   c. Bundle and deliver to post office
$_____ Setup
$_____ Bundling cost (cost per thousand multiplied by number of names)
$_____ Mail Prep Subtotal

3. Postal Charges (Check with post office for details)
$_____ Bulk permit ($75/year; must be at least 200 pieces, properly sorted)
$_____ Postage (letter or flat rate? Any automation or presort discounts?)

$_____ Business reply permit ($75/year*)
Reply postage (service charge)
*40 cents each if less than 500 responses
9 cents each if more than 500 responses
You must pay $185 accounting fee if over 500 responses
$_____ Figure your anticipated response rate, then calculate reply costs.
$_____ Postal Charges Subtotal

$_____ Grand Total: Mailing Costs

New Technology Offers Alternatives

In the last few years, several alternatives to direct mail have surfaced. You have probably received "junk faxes"—flyers arriving through your fax machine. I look down on this, since you are inconveniencing your prospective customers by using up their fax machine's paper and tying up their equipment. The exception is this: If you are communicating with current customers about a special offer, such as a discount on products they've been known to buy, you are doing them a service that's likely to be welcomed.

E-mail represents another potential avenue for distribution of advertising messages, but the etiquette—and legality—of advertising through on-line computer services is still evolving. You wouldn't want advertisements popping up in the middle of your library books or personal conversations—and that's what advertising on-line is likely to resemble.

Technology is letting us deliver more interesting messages through the traditional mailbox as well. Video mail pieces have a high success rate, and can be an excellent way to demonstrate your product, process, or service. Interactive computer disks are used to sell all kinds of software products. Consider these options before you assume that a traditional direct mail program is the answer for you.

Working with the Post Office

I promised I would go into more detail about working with the post office. Here it comes. This can of worms is called *postal compliance*.

Let's take a lead-generating mailing as an example. You intend to send out a flyer, a three-panel self-mailer with a reply card (sometimes called a "bounce-back card," because you want it to bounce back). You will need to get both the outgoing mail surface and the reply card approved by the post office. Template 9-4 shows what the post office is looking for.

Template 9-4: Outgoing Mail Panel

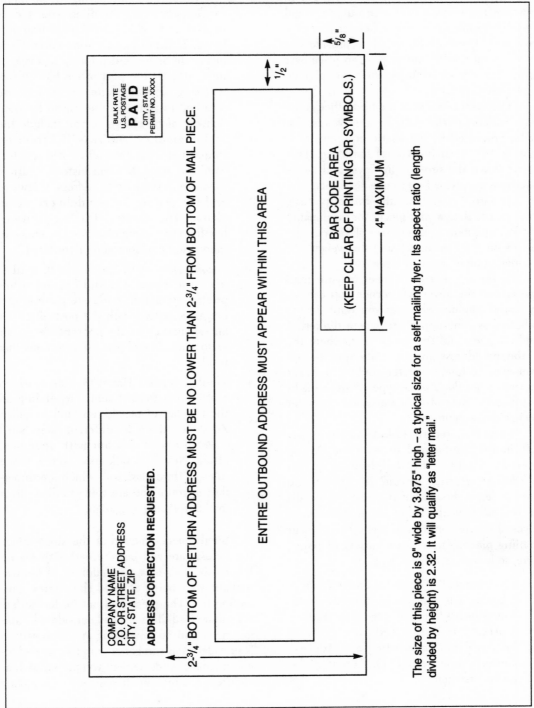

COMPANY NAME
P.O. OR STREET ADDRESS
CITY, STATE, ZIP
ADDRESS CORRECTION REQUESTED.

BULK RATE
U.S. POSTAGE
PAID
CITY, STATE
PERMIT NO. XXXX

$2\text{-}3/4$" BOTTOM OF RETURN ADDRESS MUST BE NO LOWER THAN $2\text{-}3/4$" FROM BOTTOM OF MAIL PIECE.

ENTIRE OUTBOUND ADDRESS MUST APPEAR WITHIN THIS AREA

$1/2$"

$5/8$"

BAR CODE AREA
(KEEP CLEAR OF PRINTING OR SYMBOLS.)

4" MAXIMUM

The size of this piece is 9" wide by 3.875" high – a typical size for a self-mailing flyer. Its aspect ratio (length divided by height) is 2.32. It will qualify as "letter mail."

Follow the diagram in Template 9-4 to position the elements on your outgoing mail panel, or contact your post office for your own template. It should be happy to provide you with a clear plastic overlay you can place over your mail pieces to judge their compliance with postal regulations.

The main concern of the post office is the *machinability* of the mail. In other words, can it be processed by automatic equipment? If not, it will need individual handling. This slows down the process by days, and keeps you from qualifying for postage discounts.

To earn discounts on the cost of postage, you want to design your pieces for machinability. Pay attention to where you place your elements on the mail panel, and the weight and configuration of the mail piece itself.

In the upper right corner of your mail piece, and the lower left corner, you can lay type and graphics wherever you want. In the other areas—the upper left, where the return address goes, and the lower right, where the outbound address and bar code appear—you will need to follow stricter guidelines. What you must *not* do is place type where it might confuse the post office's automatic character recognition equipment.

Keep your return address in the upper left, in a straightforward arrangement. Do you want incorrectly addressed pieces to be forwarded or returned to you? If so, then you have to learn about what the post office calls *mailer endorsements*. These are additional messages of instruction for the post office on your mailing piece. There are a variety of issues here, so let's review them.

- *First-class mail.* The endorsement for first-class mail is the phrase directly under your return address. It might say "Address Correction Requested" or "Do Not Forward" or "Forwarding and Address Correction Requested." Or there might be no endorsement.

Because you are paying the premium for first-class mail handling, your pieces receive comprehensive forwarding services. If there is no endorsement, the piece will be forwarded for up to a year at no charge. If the post office has no forwarding address, the piece will be returned to you with the reason for non-delivery, at no charge. If you include the endorsement "Address Correction Requested," the post office will not forward the piece, but will instead return it to you with the correct address, if known, and the reason for nondelivery, at no charge. The wording "Do Not Forward" has the exact same effect as the endorsement "Address Correction Requested."

- *Second-class mail.* This class of mail is used for magazines and certain other printed literature. If you are publishing a magazine, check with the post office for an explanation of the appropriate mailer endorsements and post office actions that result.

- *Third-class mail.* This is the rate at which most direct mail is sent. Depending on the number of pieces sent and to which Zip codes, there are different rates. You'll have to check this out with your post office. Now let's talk about some of the rules of third-class use, which are important to you if you are going to do a direct mail advertising campaign.

Single pieces mailed at the single-piece third-class rate will be returned with reason for nondelivery or a new address, if known, without your being charged the address-correction fee. The piece will not be forwarded. All other third-class mail is considered *bulk-rate* mail, and no forwarding or return service is provided. You can get around this by including the mailer endorsement you prefer, such as "Address Correction Requested," and paying an additional service charge. Here's how it works.

If your bulk-rate piece has no endorsement, undeliverable mail will go in the trash. It will not be forwarded or returned to you. The same is true if your piece has the phrase "Do Not Forward."

If your bulk-mail piece has the mailer endorsement "Address Correction Requested" under the return address, the piece will be returned with a new address or reason for non-delivery. If the piece weighs one ounce or less, the entire piece will be returned, you will be charged the first-class single-piece postage rate (just as if it were returned with a first-class stamp), and there will be no address correction fee. If the piece weighs over one ounce, you will pay an address correction fee of 50 cents, and you will not get the piece back—just the correct address, if available, and the reason for nondelivery.

If your bulk-mail piece has the endorsement "Forwarding and Return Postage Guaranteed," the piece will be forwarded at no charge (but you won't get a clue that your database address is wrong). If the piece is not forwardable, the entire piece will be returned to you with the reason for nondelivery, and you will be charged the appropriate fee. If your piece carries the endorsement "Forwarding and Return Postage Guaranteed, Address Correction Requested," it will be forwarded, you will receive a notice of the correct address, and you will be billed the 50-cent address correction fee.

Your final option for bulk-mail pieces is the mail endorsement "Do Not Forward, Address Correction Requested, Return Postage Guaranteed." This piece will be returned with a correct address or reason for nondelivery, and you will pay a single-piece third-class rate for its return trip, but not the 35-cent address correction fee.

These last three options might make sense if you are mailing catalogs with timely merchandise, and you don't want to incur the expense of wasting printed pieces or the delay in delivery. In any other bulk-mail situation, I'd recommend using the mailer endorsement "Address Correction Requested." You'll keep your database up to date, and you, not the post office, will be in charge of seeing to it that the right piece is mailed to the right address. If you are working with your own in-house list, always request address corrections. It's well worth the cost to keep your list current. If you are renting a list, however, you will want to negotiate this with your broker.

Confusing? I've tried to make it simple, but working with the post office successfully requires meeting its sometimes complex rules and regulations. Call your post office and ask questions. Then take your completed layout for review before you order any printing. This is how I work, and I've never had a problem with the post office that couldn't be resolved.

Example 9-4 shows a sale flyer that got approval from the post office.

Example 9-4: Stardust Sale Flyer
Used by permission of Stardust Corporation.

P.O. Box 930189
Verona, WI 53593

Address Correction Requested

Use Your Charge Card
When You Buy from the
Price and Inventory Leader!

VISA
MasterCard

Jerzees Fleece Mega-Sale!

SET-IN SWEATSHIRT	FASHION SWEATSHIRT	SUPER SWEATS	COTTON SWEATSHIRT
Style #562M	Style #5663MS	Style #4662M	Style #7662M
S-XXXL	S-XXL	S-XXL	S-XXL
All Colors and Sizes	Birch and White Stripes	All Colors and Sizes	All Colors and Sizes
50/50 cotton/poly 7 oz	50/50 cotton/poly 8 oz	50/50 cotton/poly 9 oz	80/20 cotton/poly 10.5 oz

$2.⁰⁰/dozen off!

GET THE SHIRTS YOU NEED FROM THE PRICE AND INVENTORY LEADER.
Call 1-800-747-4444 and mention "Jerzees Mega-Sale" to get these great savings.

Sale good through November 30, 1993.

1-800-747-4444

ATTENTION: BUYER

BULK RATE
U.S. POSTAGE
P A I D
MADISON, WI
PERMIT NO. 2116

Most pieces you mail will fit the postal category of "letter mail." To keep your postage costs down, keep within the definition of letter mail. Avoid unusual sizes. Letter mail that is nearly square incurs postage surcharges because it is not machinable; good mail pieces will have an aspect ratio (length divided by height) of between 1.3 and 2.5. To calculate the aspect ratio of your piece, take the length and divide it by the height. The resulting number should lie between these two limits to qualify as letter mail.

There are maximum and minimum dimensions that you must take into consideration as well. The height must be at least $3\frac{1}{2}$ inches and not more than 5 inches. The length must be at least $6\frac{1}{8}$ inches and not more than $11\frac{1}{2}$ inches. Larger pieces, like catalogs or envelopes, will be considered "flats"; they follow a different set of rules, and you will pay a higher postal rate.

The weight and color of the paper your mail piece is printed on affects its machinability too. Paper colors that are too vivid or too dark can confuse the automatic sorting equipment. Paper that is too flimsy or too stiff can be a problem, too.

Self-mailers must fold along the bottom edge in orientation to the name on the mailing label. Using tabs or "wafers" (round sticky dots) to seal the open edges of your piece will increase the speed and accuracy of your mail's delivery. If you plan to apply for postal discounts, such as Zip+4 or barcoding discounts, your pieces may have to be tabbed or sealed to qualify.

Before you finalize your design, the post office would like to see a complete folding mock-up of your piece, on the weight and color of paper you intend to use. With this tool, it can help you plan for both cost savings and prompt delivery of your mail pieces. All these are issues for your local post office's automated mail-handling specialists. Consult these experts early on in the process of designing your mail piece.

The other postal people you must communicate with are those in the business mail entry office. Here's where you get your mailing permit, or indicia.

The indicia is the information in the upper right of the mail panel that states the post office of origin, the rate (and class of handling) for the piece, and the permit number against which the cost of mailing that piece is billed. It works like this.

You apply to your post office for a permit number, which opens an account for you. You pay a deposit into that account when you buy your permit. Each time you bring a mailing to the bulk-mail acceptance unit, it must be properly sorted, labeled, and tallied. If you don't know how to do this, and you intend to prepare your mailing yourself, bring your questions to the post office before you bring in your mail. The personnel there will provide you with the supplies you need: sticky labels for the different classes of sorting, rubber bands for bundling, mail bags if your mailing is large, and the proper forms to fill out. The acceptance officer will help you figure your postage rate, based on the amount of presorting you'll do, the size and weight of your piece, and the class of service you want to buy (first, second, or third class). Multiply that rate by your number of pieces, and you have the cost of your mailing. You will pay that amount into your account at the time you present the pieces to the post office. The bulk-mail acceptance form (Example 9-5) should be presented at that time.

Example 9-5A: Post Office Bulk Mail Acceptance Form

UNITED STATES POSTAL SERVICE

Statement of Mailing with Permit Imprints
First-Class Mail (For Priority Mail Use Form 3605-R)

MAILER: Complete all items by typewriter, pen, or indelible pencil. Prepare in duplicate if you need a receipt.

Mailer's Information

Post Office of Mailing		Date	Processing Category	USPS Authorized Mailing ID Code(s)
Permit No.	Federal Agency Cost Code	Mailing Statement Seq. No.	☐ Letters (DMM 128.2) ☐ Flats (DMM 128.31) ☐ Automation-Compatible Flats (DMM 128.32)	
Permit Holder's Name & Address (Include ZIP Code)	Telephone Number	Receipt No.	☐ Irregular Parcels (DMM 128.5)	

No. Sacks	No. Trays	No. Pallets	No. Other

Weight of a Single Piece ___ . ___ ___ ___ pounds

Total Pieces in Mailing	Total Weight of Mailing

Name & Address of Individual or Organization for Which Mailing is Prepared (If other than the permit holder)	Name and Address of Mailing Agent (If other than the permit holder)	Check All That Apply
		☐ Centralized Postage Payment ☐ Plant Loaded to ☐ BMAU Entry at ☐ Orig. ☐ Dest. A/O ZIP _____ ☐ Orig. ☐ Dest. SCF 3D ZIP _____ ☐ Orig. ☐ Dest. ADC _____

Postage Computation

- For mailings of automation-compatible letter-size pieces (DMM 521), other than cards, go to Part A on the reverse of this form.
- For mailings of non-automation-compatible letter-size pieces (DMM 128.2), other than cards, weighing .6875 pound (11 ounces) or less, go to Part B on the reverse of this form.
- For mailings of non letter-size pieces (DMM 128.2) other than cards, or of automation-compatible flats (DMM 522), weighing .6875 pound (11 ounces) or less, go to Part C on the reverse of this form.
- For mailings of postal cards and postcards (DMM 311, 322), go to Part D on the reverse of this form.

Postage (From Reverse Side) ►

Part A	$
Part B	$
Part C	$
Part D	$

Additional Postage Payment (State reasons for Additional Postage)	No. Pieces	Rate/Piece $. ___ = $

Total Postage ──────► $

Certification

The signature of a mailer or its agent certifies that it will be liable for and agrees to pay, subject to appeals prescribed by postal laws and regulations, any revenue deficiencies assessed on this mailing. If this form is signed by an agent, the agent certifies that it is authorized to sign this statement, that the certification binds the agent and the mailer and both the mailer and the agent will be liable for and agree to pay any deficiencies.)

The submission of a false, fictitious or fraudulent statement may result in imprisonment of up to 5 years and a fine of up to $10,000 (18 USC 1001). In addition, a civil penalty of up to $5,000 and an additional assessment of twice the amount falsely claimed may be imposed (31 USC 3802).

I hereby certify that all information furnished on this form is accurate and truthful, and that this material presented qualifies for the rates of postage claimed.

Signature of Permit Holder or Agent (Both principal and agent are liable for any postage deficiency incurred)	Telephone Number

USPS Use Only

Single Piece Weight ___ . ___ ___ ___ ___ pounds	Are the figures at left adjusted from mailer's entries? ☐ Yes ☐ No If "Yes" Reason

Total Pieces	Total Weight	
Total Postage		

Check One ☐ Verif. Not Scheduled	Presort Verification Performed as Scheduled ☐	Date Mailer Notified	Contact	By (Initials)

I CERTIFY that this mailing has been inspected concerning: 1) eligibility for the rate of postage claimed; 2) proper preparation (and presort where required); 3) proper completion of the statement of mailing; and 4) payment of the required annual fee.

Round Stamp (Required)

Signature of Weigher	Time	AM PM

PS Form **3600-R**, June 1992   Financial Document – Forward to Finance Office

Example 9-5B: Post Office Bulk Mail Acceptance Form

Form 3600-R — First-Class Other than Priority Mail — Permit Imprint

Postage Computation

Presort/ Automation Discounts	Net Rate	Count (Pcs)	Charge	Presort/ Automation Discounts	Net Rate	Count (Pcs)	Charge
Automation-Compatible Letter (DMM 521)				**Non-Automation-Compatible Letter – .6875 lb. (11 oz.) or Less**			
ZIP + 4 Barcoded (5-Digit)	_____ ×	_____ pcs. = $ _____		Carrier Route	_____ ×	_____ pcs. = $ _____	
ZIP + 4 Barcoded (3-Digit)	_____ ×	_____ pcs. = $ _____		Presorted First-Class	_____ ×	_____ pcs. = $ _____	
ZIP + 4 Presort	_____ ×	_____ pcs. = $ _____		Single-Piece Rate	_____ ×	_____ pcs. = $ _____	
ZIP + 4 (Nonpresorted)	_____ ×	_____ pcs. × $ _____		Nonstandard Surcharge (If Applicable) Presorted First-Class and Carrier Route	.05 ×	_____ pcs. = $ _____	
Carrier Route	_____ ×	_____ pcs. = $ _____		Single-Piece Rate	.10 ×	_____ pcs. = $ _____	
Presorted First-Class	_____ ×	_____ pcs. = $ _____					
Single-Piece Rate	_____ ×	_____ pcs. = $ _____					
Total – Part A (Carry to front of form)		$ _____		**Total – Part B (Carry to front of form)**		$ _____	

Check one: Automation-Compatible Flat (DMM 522) ☐ Other Nonletter ☐ – .6875 lb. (11 oz.) or Less				**Postal Cards and Post Cards**			
ZIP + 4 Barcoded* (3/5-Digit)	_____ ×	_____ pcs. = $ _____		ZIP + 4 Barcoded* (5-Digit)	.155 ×	_____ pcs. = $ _____	
ZIP + 4 Barcoded* (Nonpresorted)	_____ ×	_____ pcs. = $ _____		ZIP + 4 Barcoded* (3-Digit)	.161 ×	_____ pcs. = $ _____	
Carrier Route	_____ ×	_____ pcs. = $ _____		ZIP + 4 Barcoded* (Nonpresorted)	.177 ×	_____ pcs. = $ _____	
Presorted First-Class	_____ ×	_____ pcs. = $ _____		ZIP + 4 Presort*	.164 ×	_____ pcs. = $ _____	
Single-Piece Rate	_____ ×	_____ pcs. = $ _____		ZIP + 4* (Nonpresorted)	.180 ×	_____ pcs. = $ _____	
Nonstandard Surcharge (If Applicable) 3/5-Digit ZIP + 4 Barcoded, Presorted First-Class, and Carrier Route	.05 ×	_____ pcs. = $ _____		Carrier Route	.152 ×	_____ pcs. = $ _____	
Nonpresorted ZIP + 4 Barcoded and Single-Piece Rate	.10 ×	_____ pcs. = $ _____		Presorted First-Class	.170 ×	_____ pcs. = $ _____	
				Single-Piece Rate	.190 ×	_____ pcs. = $ _____	
*Available only for Automation-Compatible Flats (DMM 522)				*Available only for Automation-Compatible Cards (DMM 521)			
Total – Part C (Carry to front of form)		$ _____		**Total – Part D (Carry to front of form)**		$ _____	

PS Form **3600-R**, June 1992 *(Reverse)*

*U.S. GPO: 1992-318-489

You can use the same permit number to mail any class of mail. What changes is the wording you print on the indicia. Be very careful what words you choose! Make sure you discuss it with the post office before you print anything. First-class mail receives the same handling individual letters do. Second class is reserved for magazines and certain other printed literature. Bulk rate is the correct term for third-class mail, which is the least expensive but also the slowest. Working to the specifications of automatic handling equipment can speed your bulk-mail delivery time by over a week. It can also save you several cents in postage on each piece, so this is well worth the time it takes to research it with your local post office.

Business Reply Mail

Remember we were talking about a flyer with a reply card? Getting that reply card through the post office and back to you brings a whole separate set of regulations into play. Again, there are height and width ratios to work within (see Template 9-5).

Template 9-5: Business Reply Mail Example

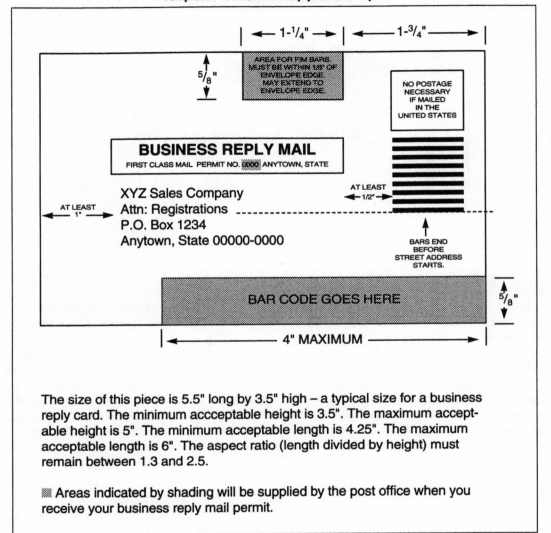

The size of this piece is 5.5" long by 3.5" high – a typical size for a business reply card. The minimum accceptable height is 3.5". The maximum acceptable height is 5". The minimum acceptable length is 4.25". The maximum acceptable length is 6". The aspect ratio (length divided by height) must remain between 1.3 and 2.5.

▨ Areas indicated by shading will be supplied by the post office when you receive your business reply mail permit.

The weight of the paper the card is printed on must be at least 55# Offset to meet postal standards, which means that your whole flyer will have to be on heavier paper than you might otherwise pick.

From the post office, you will purchase a business reply mail permit. Along with a permit number, the post office will give you two sets of marks for your reply card. One is the FIM (facing identification marks), which are the bars at the top and left of the indicia. The post office will also give you a bar code that conveys your own mailing address to a scanner, and gets positioned below and to the right of the return address. These two bits of art (see Example 9-6) will come to you along with your paperwork and instructions, and you must provide them to your printer or graphic artist.

Example 9-6: FIM and bar code

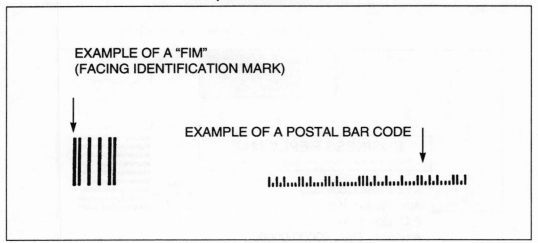

EXAMPLE OF A "FIM"
(FACING IDENTIFICATION MARK)

EXAMPLE OF A POSTAL BAR CODE

The post office is very ready to work with you on all aspects of your business mail. Just call or stop by and start asking questions. You're likely to learn more than you ever wanted to know—and everything you *need* to know.

What Goals, What Format?

Now it's time to talk specifically about the format of your direct mail piece. Once you define that, you can get cost estimates and prepare return-on-investment comparisons.

And that's the final step in choosing your direct mail strategy.

Example 9-7 shows some different formats for direct mail pieces. These standard sizes have developed from the printing industry, where dimensions of paper and presses have been standardized for efficiency. To break away from the common sizes and shapes is a strategic decision. You might gain in impact, through breakthrough originality, but you stand to lose substantially in cost efficiencies.

Example 9-7: Formats for Mail Pieces

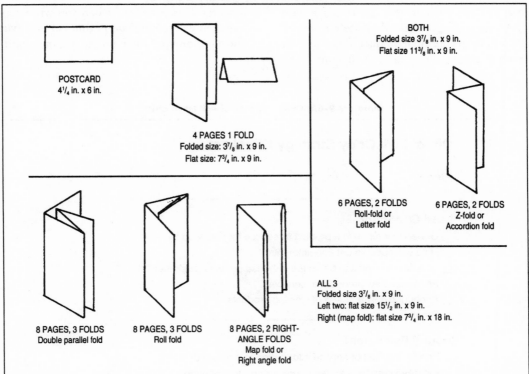

POSTCARD
4¼ in. x 6 in.

4 PAGES 1 FOLD
Folded size: 3⅞ in. x 9 in.
Flat size: 7¾ in. x 9 in.

BOTH
Folded size 3⅞ in. x 9 in.
Flat size 11⅜ in. x 9 in.

6 PAGES, 2 FOLDS
Roll-fold or
Letter fold

6 PAGES, 2 FOLDS
Z-fold or
Accordion fold

8 PAGES, 3 FOLDS
Double parallel fold

8 PAGES, 3 FOLDS
Roll fold

8 PAGES, 2 RIGHT-
ANGLE FOLDS
Map fold or
Right angle fold

ALL 3
Folded size 3⅞ in. x 9 in.
Left two: flat size 15½ in. x 9 in.
Right (map fold): flat size 7¾ in. x 18 in.

What format you develop depends on how much information you have to convey. So let's get specific about that. You will need to estimate the following:

- *Copy outline.* Make an outline of each point you want to discuss, and estimate how many words it should take to cover each point.

- *Visual survey.* You might need photographs, diagrams, charts, cartoons, creative illustrations—the possibilities are many. They can add excitement, convey information, or support the copy in other ways. What accomplishes your goals?

- *Print specifications.* Define the size, shape, paper, and ink colors for the mail piece. A low-budget direct mail piece might have one or two ink colors on a col-

ored paper stock. A larger budget can buy a full-color (also called four-color process) printed piece. As you decide the size and shape of your piece, cut and fold a blank sheet of paper to make a life-size mock-up. It's important for you to get a tangible sense of the piece you are creating.

Describe each piece you plan by describing its copy, its visuals, and its printing techniques. Consider each component of your direct mail program. If you are doing a sales letter, your must prepare a copy outline, a visual survey, and print specifications for each piece: the envelope, the letter, the response card, the flyer, and any other enclosures.

Template 9-6A is a worksheet to help you decide what belongs on your copy outline. Template 9-6B gives an example of how this worksheet is used. Later, when you write the copy, you can refer to this list to make sure each important point is adequately covered. This will keep your final product aimed at your strategic target. For example, if you check "Qualify a prospect to be on the in-house potential customer list," when you write copy, this item will remind you to think of qualifying questions and put them on the response card.

Template 9-6A: Copy Strategy Checklist (Blank)

Direct Mail Copy Strategy Checklist

Piece:

_____

Lead Generator
__ Generate interest in a product or service for follow-up by mail
__ Help salespeople get appointments
__ Qualify a prospect to be on the in-house potential customer list
__ Announce new products or services
__ Announce new features of existing products
__ Other _____

Inquiry Fulfillment
__ Provide product or service information to educate prospect
__ Establish credibility for your company or your offering
__ Support distributors and sales representatives
__ Add value to the product
__ Serve as reference material for sales representatives and customers
__ Create desire for the offering
__ Other _____

Order Request
__ Produce orders for the product
__ Help distributors and sales representatives close sales
__ Offer an incentive to buy through a promotional offer
__ The promotional offer is: (see Chapter 3)
__ Other _____

Date prepared _____ By _____

Template 9-6B: Jefferson Home Health Care Example

Direct Mail Copy Strategy Checklist

Piece:

Jefferson Home Health Care Flyer

Lead Generator

✓ Generate interest in a product or service for follow-up by mail

✓ Help salespeople get appointments

✓ Qualify a prospect to be on the in-house potential customer list

__ Announce new products or services

__ Announce new features of existing products

✓ Other _Let us see which office should follow up._

Inquiry Fulfillment

__ Provide product or service information to educate prospect

__ Establish credibility for your company or your offering

__ Support distributors and sales representatives

__ Add value to the product

__ Serve as reference material for sales representatives and customers

__ Create desire for the offering

__ Other _____

Order Request

__ Produce orders for the product

__ Help distributors and sales representatives close sales

__ Offer an incentive to buy through a promotional offer

__ The promotional offer is: (see Chapter 3)

__ Other _____

Date prepared _9-14-93_ By _Sarah White_

This checklist describes Example 9-1 at the beginning of this chapter. Note that the reply card has a section titled "office nearest you." This was included to let Jefferson Home Health Care print one version of the reply card, then distribute those leads for follow-up by the office nearest the prospect.

Template 9-7 is a worksheet to help you define the graphics needed for your direct mail piece.

Template 9-7A: Visual Survey Checklist (Blank)

Direct Mail Visual Survey Checklist
Piece:

_____

__ Tables (columns and rows of information; an example might be a table of items available and their prices)

__ Graphs (visual representation of statistical data)

__ Diagrams (exploded views, renderings, assembly instructions, etc.)

__ Icons (informative symbols)

__ Product photos

__ Conceptual artwork (illustrations or photos that convey concepts rather than facts about the product or service)

__ Other graphic treatments; background motifs, etc.

_____

_____

__ Logos:

__ for the company

__ the product

__ logos of manufacturers, trade associations, etc.

__ Are you applying for co-op credit?

Date prepared _____ By _____

Template 9-7B: Jefferson Home Health Care Example

Direct Mail Visual Survey Checklist
Piece:
  Jefferson Home Health Care Flyer

__ Tables (columns and rows of information)
__ Graphs (visual representation of statistical data)
__ Diagrams (exploded views, renderings, assembly instructions, etc.)
__ Icons (informative symbols)
✓ Product photos
__ Conceptual artwork (illustrations or photos that convey concepts
  rather than facts about the product or service)
✓ Other graphic treatments: background motifs, etc.
  Graduated blend in logo color
  Dots as a graphic motif
✓ Logos:
  ✓ for the company
  __ the product
  __ logos of manufacturers, trade associations, etc.
__ Are you applying for co-op credit?

Date prepared _9-14-93_ By _____ Sarah White _____

This checklist describes Example 9-1 at the beginning of this chapter.

Even though we are selling services here, I consider these "product photos" because they demonstrate our caregivers at work.

Use Template 9-8 to describe the piece you are planning in a way that allows a printer to estimate its cost. You can also use this template when developing your piece to make sure you have included everything you thought appropriate.

Template 9-8A: Print Specifications Worksheet (blank)

Direct Mail Print Specifications Checklist
Piece:

Dimensions: flat size	_____
Final (trimmed) size	_____
Number and location of bleeds	_____
Number of pages in the finished piece	_____
Number of ink colors	_____
What ink colors?	_____
Paper stock	_____
Proofs required	_____
Bindery operations	_____
Delivery arrangements	_____
Quantity	_____
Price	_____

Date prepared _____ By _____

Bleeds: Ink extending to the edge of the sheet, which requires that the piece be printed on oversized pieces of paper and then trimmed down.

Bindery: Scoring, folding, collating, stapling, trimming, diecutting, embossing, etc.

Quantity: Often phrased "base quantity" and "plus cost for additional 1,000s" to a maximum range, e.g., base 5,000 pieces and plus cost for additional 1,000s to 10,000 pieces. Since you may be comparing projections using different mailing lists, and therefore different total numbers of pieces for circulation, you want to avoid wearing out your welcome with your printer by repeatedly asking for slight variations in your quote. Phrasing quantities this way will give you all the numbers you need to plug into your different cost calculations.

Template 9-8B: Jefferson Home Health Care Example

Direct Mail Print Specifications Checklist
Piece:

Jefferson Home Health Care Flyer

Dimensions: flat size	15.5" x 8.75"
Final (trimmed) size	3.875" x 8.75"
Number and location of bleeds	Bleeds 4 sides
Number of pages in the finished piece	8 panels
Number of ink colors	2
What ink colors?	Black + PMS 328
Paper stock	65# Matte Cover
Proofs required	Dylux + Press Check
Bindery operations	Score, perforate reply card, roll fold
Delivery arrangements	To customer in Madison
Quantity	5,000 10,000
Price	add'l 1,000s to 50,000

Date prepared 9-14-93 By Sarah White

The easiest way to get apples-to-apples print quotes is to find a sample piece that resembles what you'd like to do and ask for quotes on that specific piece. In fact, finding a sample you like is very helpful in guiding your copy outline and visual survey, too.

Of course, you're not committed forever to any decision you make at this stage. Print specifications often change dramatically between the planning stage and the final execution! We will talk in more detail about print production planning when we get to the third section of this chapter, "Creating the Perfect Direct Mail Piece."

Remember, you really should fill out each of these worksheets—copy outline,

visual survey, and print specifications—for each printed piece that is part of your direct mail program. This is the best way to really think through the whole proposed strategy and gather the information you need to prepare budgets—the next step.

At this stage you may find it very helpful to meet with the vendors you are considering as the creators and producers of the actual printed piece. Some creative services offer strategy consulting as well as technical expertise in execution. If you'd like a second opinion on the strategy you've developed, now's the time to look for it.

Deciding How You'll Produce Your Direct Mail—And Who Will Help

Desktop-publishing equipment has put much more power in the hands of do-it-yourselfers in the last five years. You may have all the tools and skills you need to produce your direct mail piece. Should you do it yourself? Ask yourself these two questions.

1. *What are the demands of the piece as planned?* Are there photos that must show small details of the product? Is the marketplace so dog-eat-dog that you'll need the competitive edge a creative specialist gives your piece? The most important consideration is that you must avoid looking poor and amateurish. If you have the right talents and the time to devote to the project, go ahead and proceed on your own. You might do everything yourself right up to delivering a disk to your printer, or you might take a component approach to producing your piece. Often it makes sense to buy elements from individual freelancers. You might hire a copywriter, a graphic artist, or a photographer. But you will provide the coordination between their activities, do much of the work yourself, and communicate directly with printers to get the final product. Before you commit to this approach, ask yourself the next question.

2. *Is this the best use of your time?* Most of us aren't artists, writers, or photographers. Few of us have the technical knowledge to prepare complex materials for printing. Learning to do each step may be an interesting challenge that excites you, but is it what you should be doing? Most of us have our hands full with our jobs' other demands. Making time for a direct mail project may cause other tasks to go undone, or disrupt the intended timeline for the mail program.

Time, Budget, and Quality

Whether you do everything yourself, hire and manage a team of independent specialists, or go the advertising agency route, you first need to get your priorities straight. You've probably heard of the time/budget/quality equation. It goes like this: On any given project, you can reasonably expect to have two of these factors meet your expectations. But it's unrealistic to think that all three will be completely to your satisfaction. Think about these scenarios. To achieve the quality you want at the price you want to pay, you may have to let timeliness suffer. To save money, you might take advantage of your printer's post-holiday slow time, for instance—but now your printer is controlling your timing, not you. Or to use another example, to get a timely delivery, you may have to pay rush charges for some services. Now you've achieved timeliness without sacrificing quality, but your budget is paying the price. And to get something fast and cheap, you may not be able to use the quality of vendors you would prefer.

Let me give you a glimpse of the process from the agency side. When I meet with prospects to discuss a potential project, I am always asking questions that help me place their priorities on the time/budget/quality scale. I also ask about what their decision-making process is going to be. The reason? So that I can quote a price that accurately reflects a process and end product that meets their criteria. To be blunt, I charge more for working with multiple decision makers. It's fair because it takes longer to please a committee.

It is reasonably realistic for me to promise that I can deliver quality, on time, and on a low budget when I am working with one decision maker. Make that two decision makers, and it gets harder. I have more wishes to accommodate as I develop creative solutions—and that means more time, and of course more time means more money. There will need to be an adjustment in either the timing or the budget expectations to allow us to work together well. When the number of decision makers goes beyond three, it becomes much harder to deliver timeliness and quality without spending more money to do so. This is not a problem if the client has resources. If not, I try to gracefully pass on the project. Give me realistic expectations of a budget, timeline, and definition of quality in the final product, and no job is too large or too small.

Template 9-9: Time, Budget and Quality

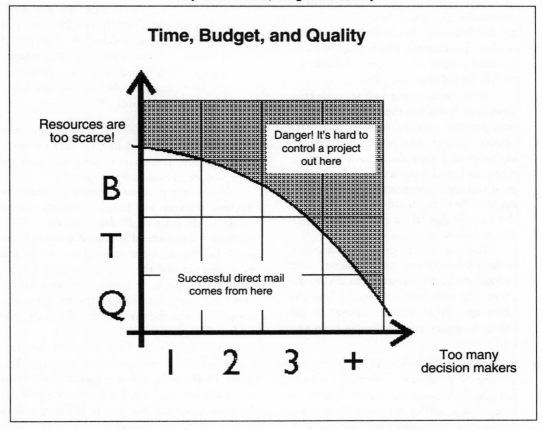

Think honestly about where you belong on Template 9-9. (Do you have a committee of five inside your head?) Be clear in what you communicate about your priorities when you meet with potential vendors.

Who can help? There are all sorts of organizations and individuals you might call on at different points in the process. In Chapter 12 I discuss the subject, from ad agencies and design studios to the many individuals who make up the freelance and consulting scene.

Look over that chapter to get an idea of the possibilities.

Your budget, as well as your time and expertise, will tell you which option to choose.

Budgeting for Profitable Direct Mail

Your costs for a direct mail program will fall into the general categories of producing the piece, delivering the piece, and fulfilling its response. Let's take a look at each category. Refer to Template 9-11A on page 356 and you will see how these items appear on the budget spreadsheet. You'll find each category described in more detail in that section. For now, let's get the overview:

- *Production expenses.* Your costs for production will be very similar to those for print advertising; you might want to review the discussion under "The Budget for the Print Ad" in Chapter 6. Template 6-12 in that chapter, which gives costs for a complex print ad, is very similar to the budget for a direct mail piece.

    If you are working with separate freelancers to bring together the elements of your program, you will need to keep track of costs for a creative approach, copywriting, graphic design, illustration or photography, and producing art ready for a printer. If you are working with an agency, your estimate from it should include details of the costs budgeted for each of these production expenses.

    The last area of production expense is the printing of your piece. You will want to look at various quantities to decide the most cost-efficient approach. Use the print specifications worksheet to get apples-to-apples cost estimates from several printers.

- *Delivering your piece.* Work with your mailing list vendors to determine the costs not just for renting the names, but for all aspects of preparing the piece for mailing. In the case of a sales letter, for example, this estimate would include the charges for collating the cover letter, flyer, and response card into the outgoing envelope.

    There might also be charges for sorting the pieces by Zip code, to qualify for bulk rate postage, and other charges related to getting the mail pieces accepted by the post office and into the mail stream. Your final charge will be the bill for postage.

Do you need to purchase a bulk-mail permit? Will you need a reply-mail permit for a response card? If the answer is yes, contact the post office for current rates, and include this in your budget.

- *Fulfilling the response.* What offer does your mail piece make? You must include in your estimate the cost of any discounts or freebies you've offered. Project your response rate, and calculate the cost of fulfilling that response. You will probably want to do a worst-case, most-probable, and best-case projection to find the range of possible responses.

See the topic "Direct Mail Budget and Schedule" at the end of this section for a checklist and flowchart to help you prepare your budget and manage your project.

When you have an estimate of your production, delivery, and fulfillment costs, you're ready to do your profitability analysis. The method I recommend is *contribution to overhead.* We focus on the sales generated by the mail program and the costs associated with it. Figuring payback, or break-even analysis, is about covering the costs of the program and contributing to the profitability of the company (see Template 9-10).

You identify the fixed costs of the program—creative fees, printing, postage. You make projections about response, and then you estimate your variable costs—the postage for reply cards and the cost of fulfilling orders (called redemption costs), such as the sales forgone by offering a discount.

Even at its highest estimated production and delivery expense and its worst-case projection of response, does your direct mail program break even? If not, you'd better adjust it until the bottom line comes out in a zone you're willing to live with. When do your production costs come due? When do you anticipate that the program will bring in the desired revenue? The answer may affect your ability to execute the program you'd like to propose.

Template 9-10A: Break-Even Analysis Worksheet (blank)

Date:
Description:
List used:
Number of pieces sent:
Time period of offer:
Assumptions:

Description	Worst Case	Most Likely	Best Case
Fixed Costs			
Creative fees	$	$	$
Printing			
Mail handling			
Postage			
Other			
Subtotal: Fixed Costs	$	$	$
Variable Costs			
Response percentage	0.0%	0.0%	0.0%
Number of responses	0	0	0
Cost for response postage	$	$	$
Redemption cost			
Cost of discount on average sale	$0	$0	$0
Total sales forgone:	$	$	$
Other			
Subtotal: Variable Costs	$	$	$
Cost of Promotion	$	$	$
Average Sale:	$	$	$
Sales Generated	$	$	$
Contribution to Overhead:	$	$	$

Template 9-10B: Example of Sales Flyer

Date: 3-31-94
Description: Sale Flyer
List used: Current Customers and Mail List Inquirers
Number of pieces sent: 10,103
Time period of offer: 90 days to order at discounted prices
Assumptions: Letter mail at bulk discount: postage 19.8 cents
                               Response postage 40 cents
                               Cost of discount: 10% of sale

Description	Worst Case		Most Likely		Best Case	
Fixed Costs						
Creative fees		$1,400		$900		$700
Printing		2,550		2,550		2,550
Mail handling		185		185		185
Postage		2,000		2,000		2,000
Other						
Subtotal: Fixed Costs		$6,135		$5,635		$5,435
Variable Costs						
Response percentage	0.3%		0.5%		1%	
Number of responses	30		51		101	
Cost for response postage		$12		$20		$40
Redemption Cost						
Cost of discount on average sale	57		63		95	
Total sales forgone:		1,728		3,182		9,598
Other						
Subtotal: Variable Costs		$1,740		$3,202		$9,638
Cost of Promotion		$3,479		$6,405		$19,277
Average Sale:		$573		$630		$950
Sales Generated		$17,367		$31,824		$95,979
Contribution to Overhead:		$13,888		$25,419		$76,702

Don't Forget Your Co-Op

For any type of advertising you consider, whether it's direct mail or print ads, broadcast or special events, don't forget to look for a little cooperation. I'm talking about co-op programs, the rebates and resources available from manufacturers and some trade associations. These programs, while they have restrictions that may affect your plan, can pay up to 50 percent and sometimes even close to 100 percent of your expenses. It's worth doing a little research to find out if co-op support is available to you. Check with your manufacturers' reps.

Summary: The Direct Mail Strategy

We've been talking about each of the dimensions of the direct mail strategy. Write a paragraph summarizing your projected activities in each of these dimensions—list, post office requirements, format for piece, production, co-op—and you have a good basic written plan stating your direct mail strategy. You'll find it extremely useful in keeping your subsequent activity on track.

- Find your mailing list.
- Work out the logistics of the mail piece with the post office.

- Set goals for the number of responses and volume of sales you'd like to generate.
- Describe the format of your piece. Develop a copy outline, a visual survey, and print specifications for each component.
- Define a production path. Choose vendors, and have them prepare budgets for you.
- Summarize your budget, show your break-even analysis, and describe your funding plans, including payback period (you'll want to see your program's impact on your cash flow) and co-op support.

I suggest you follow the tips in Chapter 12 on finding and working with your suppliers. And now that you're off and running, in the last section of this chapter we'll learn the nuts and bolts of actually creating that printed piece.

Direct Mail Budget and Schedule: Planning for Profitability

As you meet with potential suppliers for each phase of your direct mail project, have them prepare cost estimates for you. You will need detailed cost projections in order to analyze the feasibility of your strategy. Use Template 9-11A to make sure you've covered every angle.

Template 9-11A: Direct Mail Budget

Date:
Title of Piece:
Description:

1. Planning

$_____ List any planning or consulting costs

2. Writing

$_____ Research
$_____ Write
$_____ Review
$_____ Rewrite
$_____ Writing Subtotal

3. Graphic Design

$_____ Initial design plan (and revisions)
$_____ Art direction
$_____ Design Subtotal

4. Production: Gathering the Elements

$_____ Photography
$_____ Illustration
$_____ See Chapter 6 for a full explanation of these costs.

5. Production: Combining Elements into Final Art

$_____ Scanning and color separations
$_____ Typesetting
$_____ Page composition
$_____

6. Print Estimate (See Template 9-8A)

$_____ Prepress (film output, stripping, electronic troubleshooting)
$_____ Press time
Bindery operations
$_____ Delivery/shipping charges
$_____ Print Subtotal

7. Mailing Estimate (see Template 9-3)

$_____ List rental
$_____ Mail prep
Postal charges
$_____ Mailing Subtotal

$_____ Grand Total: Direct Mail Program

I'll describe each of the categories on this worksheet in sequence:

1. *Planning.* You may do all your planning yourself, or you may hire consultants to help you with some components of your plan. You will be ready to proceed when you can complete the statements in this sidebar. If you will be incurring costs as you get to the answers, record them under "planning" on your budget worksheet.

Statement of Direct Mail Strategy

(Name of business) will use (source of mailing list) to promote (benefit) to (audience). This mail program will be a (lead generator) (inquiry fulfillment piece) (order request vehicle). The desired action on the part of the prospect is to (complete this sentence). Results will be measured by (method).

Statement of Mailing List Strategy
Describe each list under consideration.

1. Describe the search criteria (example: women in Chicagoland between twenty-five and forty-five who have used credit cards in the last six months).

2. State the circulation; how many names meet the search criteria?

3. State the cost, including any setup fees, for the list as described. (You'll refer to this number again when you get to Item 7, the mailing estimate. See also Template 9-3.)

Statement of Creative Approach
Describe the positioning strategy and the tone desired for the mail piece. What action should this piece motivate?

As you meet with potential vendors for writing and design, make these planning statements available. Each member of the team will benefit from a clear understanding of your goals, your target audience, and your thoughts on the creative approach.

The total estimate for planning goes in section 1 of Template 9-11A.

2. *Writing.* An estimate from a copywriter should include each of these steps: researching, writing, reviewing the first draft with you, and one (at least) rewrite. You don't need to see costs broken out for the different stages, but you do need to be sure that the writer is including at least the first rewrite in his or her quoted price.

To estimate the job, a writer will need to know what source material is available, approximately how many words will be needed, and whether travel will be necessary.

The estimate for writing, including revisions, goes in section 2 of Template 9-11A.

3. *Graphic design.* An estimate from a graphic designer should include each of these steps: initial layout or design plan, a review meeting with you, revising the layouts, and art direction (coordinating the production of components such as photography or illustration). Again, you don't necessarily need to see costs broken out for the different stages, but you do need to be sure they are covered.

To estimate the job, a designer will need to know the proposed format for the piece, whether the copy will come as an electronic file or will need to be typed, and whether that copy is final or will be revised after layout begins. The designer will want to know the number and type of visuals to plan for (photos, illustrations, charts, etc.). It is useful to know how the piece will be printed, what quality level the printer offers, and also whether the printer wants traditional paste-up boards or a computer file on disk.

The total estimate for graphic design goes in section 3 of Template 9-11A.

4. *Production phase 1: creating the elements.* A photographer will need to know the location and complexity of each proposed shot, the type and quantity of film stock required (transparency film, black and white or color film; how many Polaroids might be used during setup), whether models and stylists will be necessary, and whether any unusual props will need to be located or built.

An illustrator will want to know the type of medium desired—for example, airbrush or oil paint or computer rendering—the size of the finished piece, and how it will be reproduced.

The estimates for photography and illustration go in section 4 of Template 9-11A.

5. *Production phase 2: combining the elements into final art.* Photos and illustrations must be converted from original artwork to computer files suitable for page layout software. This is called *scanning*; in the case of color images, it might be referred to as *color separation*. Technology is changing rapidly in this area, and equipment at the low end of the price spectrum can compete with the highest-priced processes, depending on the type of photo or illustration involved. Ask your potential suppliers for a full explanation of what will be done to turn your image into an electronic file, and get samples of similar images and their results. Talk to service bureaus, prepress houses, or printers, and compare the prices you are quoted. (More about this in Chapter 12, on how to choose your suppliers.)

Typesetting and page composition are the services required to make copy and art into printable artwork, whether that means making mechanical artboards or combining the elements of copy and artwork in page layout software for output as printers' negatives. Typesetting may or may not be broken out on your estimate as a separate charge.

An estimate from a graphic designer might include the entire production process, or might simply cover the designer's work and leave you to approach photographers and illustrators separately. Detail is important in the production budget so that you know that all potential costs have been planned for.

The estimate for combining elements into final art should go in section 5 of Template 9-11A.

6. *Printing.* Use detailed print specifications (see Template 9-8A) to make sure your estimates are apples-to-apples.

Some printers still prefer to work from traditional artboards (also called paste-ups or mechanicals or keylines) to prepare artwork for printing, but these printers are dinosaurs. Everyone in the printing industry is adapting to the technology that's here to stay—page layout software that positions type, photos, and art on electronic pages that can be proofed on laser printers and finalized on high-resolution imagesetters as plate-ready printing film. The process of imaging and positioning this film is called prepress.

Your budget should include some allowance for *troubleshooting* (adjusting trapping, color correction, and dot-gain settings—technical details that vary from press to press, and so are often left by designers for the printer to set to his own specifications), *film output* (the imagesetter creating pages from software), and *stripping* (prepress technicians positioning the pages into printing signatures, adding any remote elements not included in the electronic files).

The actual printing estimate will be the sum of costs for *press time* (is a press check anticipated? If so, the printer will allow an extra hour or two for the job on press), *bindery* (folding, stapling, perforating tear-off reply cards—all the finishing operations required to make the final piece), and *shipping* (where and how the job is delivered).

You will probably not see a print estimate broken out into all these categories, but somewhere behind the scenes the estimator is making a calculated guess about each line item. The prepress tasks might be handled by a service bureau or color separation trade shop instead of by the printer; this industry is changing at lightning speed, and a range of vendors exists to handle jobs of various levels of complexity. Your designer and your printer should be in close communication, to determine the best production path for your job.

The estimates for prepress, press time, bindery, and delivery go in section 6 of Template 9-11A.

7. *Mailing.* Your mailing costs will be a total of your estimates for *list rental, mailing preparation* (sorting, bundling, and delivery to the post office), and *postage.*

Refer back to the earlier sections on the mailing list and on working with the post office. Template 9-3, the mailing list cost estimate, will help you calculate the estimates to go in section 7 of Template 9-11A.

And there you have it: a detailed map of the route from idea to printed piece. Use this as a checklist when you prepare your budget. It's not necessary to have a cost broken out for each subcategory on this template—a total in each area is sufficient. The reason you might want to go into detail is to be absolutely certain that every possible cost is covered.

Looking at this list, you might feel as if you have to just about complete the piece to be able to estimate its cost. It seems that way sometimes. If you are unsure of the answer to any of these questions, finding a sample of a piece you'd like to emulate and discussing it with the vendors involved will help a great deal.

Templates 9-11B and 9-8C show the specifications and budget for a project. The project described is a four-color sale flyer that a major retailer might use to promote a fairly high-ticket item, such as furniture or recreational sports equipment.

Template 9-8C: Print Specifications

Direct Mail Print Specifications Checklist
Piece:

Color Sale Flyer (4 pages, full color, 4 photos)

Dimensions: flat size	17" x 11"
Final (trimmed) size	8.5" x 11"
Number and location of bleeds	Bleeds
Number of pages in the finished piece	4 pages
Number of ink colors	4
What ink colors?	Process color
Paper stock	80# gloss text
Proofs required	Dylux, color proof, press ok
Bindery operations	Collate, staple
Delivery arrangements	To customer in Madison
Quantity	35,000
Price	$3,475

Date prepared __9-14-93__ By __Sarah White__

Template 9-11B: Direct Mail Budget

COST ESTIMATE WORKSHEET

Date: 2-19-93

Title of piece: Sale Flyer

Description: 4 pages, full color, 4 photos

1. Planning

_____ $160 List any planning or consulting costs

2. Writing

_____ $200 Research

_____ 200 Write

_____ 50 Review

_____ 50 Rewrite

_____ $500 Writing Subtotal

3. Graphic Design

_____ $520 Initial design plan (and revisions)

_____ 480 Art direction

_____ $1,000 Design Subtotal

4. Production: Gathering the elements

_____ $2,400 Photography

_____ 0 Illustration

_____ $2,400 See Chapter 6 for a full explanation of these costs.

5. Production: Combining elements into final art

_____ $1,200 Scanning and color separations

_____ 100 Typesetting

_____ 480 Page composition

_____ $1,780 Production Subtotal

6. Print Estimate (See Template 9-8A)

_____ $400 Prepress (film output, stripping, electronic troubleshooting)

_____ 2800 Press time

_____ 260 Bindery operations

_____ 15 Delivery/shipping charges

_____ $3,475 Print Subtotal   35,000 pieces

7. Mailing Estimate (see Template 9-3)

_____ $700 List rental

_____ 1575 Mail prep

_____ 7350 Postal charges

_____ $9,625 Mailing Subtotal

$18,940 Grand Total: Direct Mail Program

Direct Mail Schedule

This checklist is also an important tool in planning your production process. It is arranged in chronological order. However, some of the stages of creating a printed piece can overlap. Flowcharts are very helpful for keeping track of what needs to be done when, so that all the pieces come together in the end. Use Template 9-12 to create a timeline for your proposed project. Fill in dates across the top using a calendar; I tend to pick Wednesdays as milestones, and state the assumption, "This step completed by the end

of day designated." This reduces confusion when the timeline is tight.

Be sure to allow extra time around holidays and vacation seasons. Nothing gets done too quickly in August or December—and where I work, in Wisconsin, it can be nearly impossible to get anything printed during November! Hunting season empties out the press rooms, as everyone with any seniority heads out to their deer camps. You might not want your job handled by the rookies left to mind the shop. By anticipating these scheduling dilemmas, you can achieve better results in your printing.

Template 9-12: Execution Calendar: Steps and Deadlines

Execution Calendar: Steps and Deadlines

Put your target start date in the far left column and your target delivery date in the column at the far right. With a calendar, find a good rhythm for your interim steps. Do not plan on more than two steps a week (Tuesdays and Fridays, for example).

Begin planning
Work out print specs and budget
Plan the creative approach
Plan copy outline and visual survey
Plan the graphic design
Write copy
Shoot photos
Review/revise copy and photos
Approve copy and photos
Create artwork
Review first layout proof
Finalize print specs and budget
Correct or revise
Review second layout proof
Correct or revise
Review final proof
Out for films!
Make negatives
Strip and assemble
Review prepress proof
Correct or revise
To press!
Plate
Print
Bind
Deliver

Creating the Perfect Direct Mail Piece

If you want to create great direct mail, and by that I mean mail that gets results, you've really got to focus. What *exactly* do you think direct mail is going to accomplish for you? You must define your goals. How are you going to get your prospects to sit up and take notice?

Planning the Creative Approach

When everything's an option, it's easy not to choose. So that's where we have to begin: making decisions. In the section on strategy, you got a feel for the options available to you. Narrow your focus now. What is the next step you want your prospect to take? Why?

You need to relate the answers to those questions to the problem of print production. What is the right size, shape, and content for a mail piece that will make that action happen? This isn't like a math equation; there is no one right answer. You have to come up with the answer that's right for you.

Here are three ways to focus your vision. After you've thought about each of these aspects, the perfect mail piece for your situation should start to come into view.

Take a Look at Your Look. Pull out every printed piece your company currently uses. That means your letterhead, business cards, and brochure, and your print advertisements too. How should this new piece resemble the others? Are there colors, logos, or themes you use consistently? Unless your current look is a real mess, it's smart to coordinate your new piece with your current family of printed literature.

Are there themes you have used in the past that should carry through from piece to piece? Maybe you are going to run ads that generate leads. Is there a creative theme established in that ad that should carry through to a follow-up piece?

Get to Know Your Audience. Review everything you know about the people on your mailing list. Successful direct mail speaks person-to-person. You must create for yourself a keen mental picture of that other individual. Try to imagine "a day in the life" of some of the names on your mailing list. When the mail comes, what do they find in their in-boxes?

If you haven't selected a mailing list, get going. You can't create a customer-focused mail piece without knowing who your customer is.

Probe for details about the people who will receive your mailing. If it's a business market, what are their occupations, responsibilities, concerns? Just because it's called business-to-business doesn't mean that you're writing to a desk in a pile of concrete and glass.

Your piece has to open a conversation with the person opening the mail. You do that by knowing as much as you can about that person.

If you're mailing to consumers, this is especially true. Demographic characteristics (geographic location, income bracket, family status) and lifestyle information (hobbies, ownership patterns, etc.) help you draw a mental picture of your prospect.

With those typical individuals in mind, ask yourself what likes and dislikes they might have. What common needs, what style or tone, might stimulate their interest in you?

Look Around. Have you seen your competitors' literature? It's easy enough to call and request information. People do it every day.

You need to know what offers your competitors are making and what creative themes they've chosen. Look at how they are using direct mail: Are they sending out lead generators, or inquiry fulfillment pieces, or order request literature? Or some mix of all three? Look for parallels to the piece you intend to produce.

You may be able to draw conclusions about their target market. The style and tone of the piece, as well as the offer it makes, will provide you with clues.

Your ideas for what you should do—and what you want to avoid—will get much clearer as you critique your competitors' approaches.

In the previous section I gave you worksheets for planning the copy checklist, the visual survey, and the print specifications for your direct mail piece. Review those worksheets now. Apply what we've just discussed.

You know the piece should be consistent with your company's already established look, should be geared to the tastes and concerns of its recipients, and should capitalize on the lessons learned by your competitors in their efforts. Do your worksheets describe a piece that meets these criteria? Make any adjustments now.

Making the Mail Piece Tangible

It's time to make a folding dummy. Cut a piece of paper to the dimensions described in your print specs. Do whatever folding and stapling or taping you need to, until it resembles the finished piece. I like to make these out of clean white paper—it's surprising how staring at that empty white page helps you imagine ways you might fill it. Look back at Example 9-7, "Formats for Mail Pieces," if you need ideas.

That folded piece of paper, your mailing list, your schedule, your budget, your copy outline, and your visual survey make up a complete kit from which you can assemble your direct mail piece. Now that you've developed a strategy and fleshed out the details, the task before you becomes much more straightforward. I use Example 9-8 to explain the production process to my clients.

Example 9-8: The White Space Flow Chart

Have you chosen a creative approach? To fill up these blank white pages, you'll need an advertising strategy and a hook—a Big Idea. Chapter 5 gives you the tools you need to develop a creative approach. Review your worksheets from that chapter now.

How to Write Copy for the Direct Mail Piece

Writing direct mail can be a lot simpler than writing ad copy, or it can be harder. All copywriting is hard work if you're not experienced at it. In Chapter 6 we talked quite a lot about writing copy for print advertising. You may find it useful to review that chapter.

Here's how to get started with your writing. Do you have print ads on the same subject as the direct mail piece you're about to write? Look for blocks of copy you can pick up from there. If you repeat phrases, or even whole sentences and headlines, you will build consistency into your advertising efforts. You want all your advertising to coordinate like a wardrobe. Use your ad copy to get a jump on your direct mail writing.

Make an outline in summary of all the points you want to cover, just as you would if you were writing a print ad. Check it against the AIDA formula (attention, interest, desire, action). Are your copy points arranged in an order that will allow your story to unfold in this way? Juggle the order until the outline fits the formula (see Template 9-13).

Template 9-13: Component Outline for Writing Copy

Component Outline for Writing Copy

Not everything on this list will be relevant to your project, but you don't want to take a chance and leave something out, do you? Review this list for components of your copy outline.

___ Lead-in (get attention)

___ Benefits (in order of priority)

___ Features

___ How it works

___ Types of use

___ Types of users

___ Availability (models, colors, sizes, etc.)

___ Specifications

___ Frequently asked questions

___ Background on the company (demonstrate solidity, back up claims)

___ Product support

___ Call to action

If you are hiring a writer to prepare copy rather than doing it yourself, I would still recommend that you use these worksheets. You are defining the starting point for your writer. You can provide much clearer direction to your hired talent if you work closely together at this stage. Provide these worksheets for background, then ask your writer to respond with suggestions and additions before starting. You will both enjoy having a clearly defined task, as vagueness can be costly.

Long Copy Has Its Place

Does the outline seem long? Don't be afraid of long copy in a direct mail piece. It can work to your advantage by giving the browsing reader more opportunities to see something of interest. Long copy also works to your advantage in this way: Genuinely interested readers will educate themselves, becoming better-qualified prospects. If you sell a relatively unknown product, or one that's technically complex, you will probably find yourself creating a lengthy mail piece.

Long copy is fine, but don't let it be long-winded. If people have to work too hard to get your point, you'll lose too many of them. It's really as simple as this: Use however many words you need and no more. Tell the story and close. Complicated story? Long copy.

Short or long, the operative word is *focus*. *Rewriting will be necessary.* Whittle and shape until every sentence, every phrase, moves the reader along toward one clear goal—the call to action.

How to Keep Your Piece Out of the Wastebasket

Stress the benefits. That's the most important piece of advice I can give you. If your piece delivers some variation on the promise "I'm going to solve your problems," you're on your way to success. You're taking advantage of positioning. In Chapter 2 I dealt with that subject in detail.

Use *lift lines.* The mail panel is the closest contact you're going to have with your reader. When people pick up a piece of mail, they usually check to see if it's addressed to them. To catch their attention, put a selling phrase near the mailing label. In the direct mail business, these are called lift lines (see Example 9-9).

Example 9-9: Sales Letters with Lift Line
Used by permission of Thompson Publishing Group.

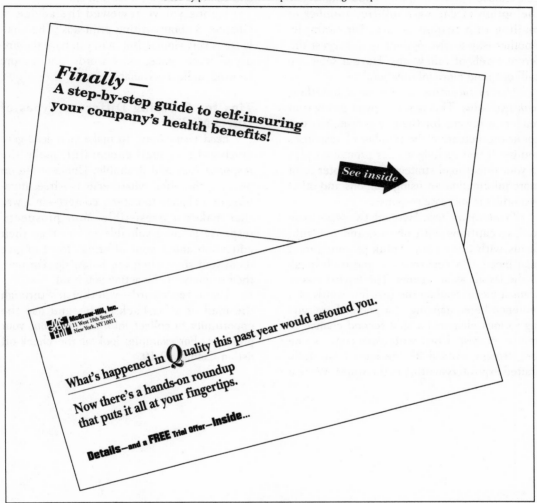

Repeat the offer. You can pretty much assume that nobody will read every word you write—and you can count on the fact that they won't read it in the order you want them to. We're all becoming browsers and skimmers because of the glut of information rushing at us. There is nothing stupid about using a little redundancy to spread your message further.

Repeat the offer in at least three different places in your mail piece. You might want to make a quick pitch on the mailer panel as a lift line, state the offer at the beginning of the copy near your first benefit statement, and state it again at the close where you make the full call to action. You aren't likely to go into all the details of the offer in each place; your goal is to make sure that the maximum number of prospects know what action you'd like them to take. Then give them as much incentive as possible to take that action.

Give several options for response. When your customers have more than one way to respond, they will feel more control, as they can choose between options. You might give the option of calling a toll-free number or mailing in a response card, for example. Another way to give options is to suggest different levels of follow-up: "Have a sales rep call" or "Send more information."

Use an incentive—and make it something with real value. This is your way of giving your readers a reward for their response. You can count on increasing the number of responses you get if you include a sales promotion plan in your direct mail strategy. See Chapter 3 for more information on using coupons and other incentives to increase response.

Break up the text. Here are two ways to do it: Use captions with photos, and use subheads with body copy. Think of your direct mail piece as a conversation, and each break in the layout as an opener. The typical reader scans a piece, reading the first few words of a sentence here, glancing at a photo there, giving various elements a split-second chance to arouse interest. Don't write your copy as one long stream, even if it's the most beautifully crafted expository writing in the world. Write a

main text and a number of side bits, captions and call-outs and lift lines and all.

I hope you've reviewed the advice in Chapter 6 about writing print ads. The challenge is very similar, but here you have the luxury of more space, more words, and a more focused audience available to you.

Tips for Creating Different Types of Direct Mail

Lead Generators. To make your lead-generating direct mail successful, make the response easy and desirable. Concentrate on pitching the offer, whatever it is—free literature, or a chance to enter a contest—in a way that makes it irresistible. Your prospects' response is more valuable to you than their education about your offering. You can give them your story when you follow up. For now, their response is the action you want.

Use a reply card—whether it's through the mail or a fax-back form—and use the opportunity to collect information about your prospect. For example, look at the check-off list on Example 9-10.

Example 9-10: Heartland Litho Mailer
Used by permission of Heartland Litho.

To learn more about Heartland Litho's award-winning customer focus, please fill out this card, detach and mail. *Postage is prepaid.*

NAME_____ TITLE _____

COMPANY _____

ADDRESS _____

CITY _____ STATE_____ ZIP _____

PHONE_____ FAX _____

I am interested in or currently use the following products or services.

☐ Design services ☐ Business forms ☐ Newsletters ☐ Flyers ☐ Business stationery

☐ Mailing services ☐ Brochures ☐ Folders ☐ Desktop publishing

Other_____

If you are laying out a postal reply card, make absolutely certain that you follow post office regulations. Get post office approval in writing before you print *anything*. That suggestion holds true for every mailing surface you design.

Inquiry Fulfillment Literature. Under this general heading falls everything from sell sheets and tech-spec sheets to catalogs and price lists. The key to success with any of these formats is *focus*. You must understand what your customers know about your offering today, and bring them along to the next level of understanding you want them to reach. That's why qualifying questions on the lead-generating response card are important. They help you focus on this customer's needs and desires.

Sell sheets and tech-spec sheets are both ways of describing products to their potential buyers. I find that they are almost always organized along two parallel tracks. There is a narrative describing the product and its benefits. Then there are blocks of data—the performance statistics, the technical descriptions (such as height and weight with a machine, or nutritional make-up with a food ingredient). I like to include suggested uses or applications, and a summary of features and benefits. Your sell sheet is probably speaking to two people: the technical user of the product, and the financial controller who will authorize its purchase. Make sure your piece answers the questions of each. Talk about the financial advantages of your offering as well as the technical benefits.

Catalogs are a subject of such scope that you will probably want to study it in detail, through books or seminars, before you launch into production. The issues that will concern you are:

- What information to include on each product

- How products should be organized

- How the price sheet and order form will function

- Physical format (size and shape, need for color, need for product photographs or illustrations)

Your product information might include physical descriptions, colors, shapes and styles available, explanation of functions, tips on usage, model numbers or product codes, and a lot more besides. Organization of the products should follow a logical system, but there are many to choose from. You might organize by function, or by type of product, or by demand, or by the "hot spots" in the catalog. These are the pages nearest the cover, the center spread, and the order form. You won't necessarily apply your own internal organization structure to the catalog. Listing products by model numbers might be simple for you but confusing to your customers, for example. Successful marketing via catalogs is a high-stakes game. Producing and mailing a good catalog is expensive. Do your homework before you proceed. I recommend you look at Robert Bly's book *The Perfect Sales Piece* for a good overview of the subject, and contact the Direct Marketing Association at (212) 768-7277 to find out about seminars in your area on the subject.

A Mini Case Study on Catalogs

A client came to me with an idea for a direct mail business. A self-proclaimed "soccer mom," she saw a market for products aimed at this special interest group. She developed a line of stationery and gift items, and approached me about developing a catalog to market them.

Example 9-11: Soccer Notes Order Form
Used by permission of Soccer Notes.

Soccer Notes
Products to Express
Your Soccer Excitement

NO MINIMUMS!

ORDER FORM

NAME _____ DATE _____

ADDRESS _____

CITY _____ STATE _____

PHONE _____ ZIP _____

QUANTITY	ITEM NUMBER	ITEM	PRICE PER PACKAGE	TOTAL
	CP901	Coach's Pack	$6.00	
	G901	Goobert	6.00	
	RS90	Rubber Stamp Soccer Ball	6.00	
	SS90	Soccer Stickers: 500 count roll	20.00	
		Holiday Cards in Full Color!		
	HC911	Over The Rooftops	$10.00	
	HC914	Hang Your Stocking	10.00	
	HC912	Keeper Rudolph	10.00	
	HC913	Santa Juggling	10.00	
	PCR	Rudolph Holiday Postcard	$0.60	
	RSG	Goobert Rubber Stamp	0.60	
		"World Cup Stamps" Postcards		
	PCWC	World Cup	$0.60	
	PWIB	Winning The Ball	0.60	
	PCS	The Save	0.60	
		Goobert Postcards		
	PCG	5 Panel Cartoon	$0.60	
	PCGB	4 Panel Cartoon "BLAM!"	0.60	
	S93	Soccer Notes Stationery	10.00	
	SS100	Soccer Ball Stickers: 100 count roll	6.00	
	GM91	Glass Medallion	$12.00	
	TP91	Team Photo Card	8.00	
	F901	The "Flames"	6.00	
	P901	Party Invitations	6.00	
	T926	Thank You Card	6.00	
	CH92	Plexiglass P-O-P Card Holder	6.00	

NEW FROM SOCCER NOTES!

SHIPPING AND HANDLING*	
If Your Order Totals:	Add:
Up to $30.00	$3.95
$30.01 to $60.00	5.95
$60.01 to $125.00	6.95
$125.01 to $200.00	7.95
$200.01 to $300.00	9.95
Above $300.00	12.95

*For shipments outside the continental U.S.
please call for information.

Orders shipped U.S. mail or
UPS. Easy payment: personal
check or money orders
accepted. All orders must be
prepaid. Make checks payable
to Soccer Notes. Phone orders
sent C.O.D. with additional
$4.50 C.O.D. charge.

QUESTIONS?
Call us at 1-800-484-8094.
(Enter security code 4004).

SUBTOTAL	
Wisconsin 5.5% Tax	
Shipping & Handling*	
C.O.D. add $4.50	
TOTAL	

Mail this order form with your
payment to:

**Soccer Notes
529 Charles Lane
Madison WI 53711-1311**

THANK YOU FOR YOUR ORDER!

Example 9-11 shows the order form of the catalog we developed—12 pages picturing families of products, and two price lists—one for a wholesale market, and one with retail prices for selling directly through the mail. She has twenty-three products in all, including a Plexiglas point-of-sale greeting card holder to encourage retailers to carry her products. The catalog is printed in black and white, to keep costs down.

Many entrepreneurs start from similar roots, turning a hobby into a money-making sideline. Have you ever thought about starting a catalog business? Template 9-8D gives an estimate for a simple eight-page black-and-white catalog, using the Print Specifications Checklist. A complete mail program is described using Template 9-11C, the Direct Mail Budget Cost Estimate Worksheet.

Template 9-8D: Print Specifications for 8-Page Catalog

Direct Mail Print Specifications Checklist
Piece:

Product Catalog (8 pages, black & white, 10 photos)

Dimensions: flat size	11" x 8.5"
Final (trimmed) size	5.5" x 8.5"
Number and location of bleeds	No Bleeds
Number of pages in the finished piece	8 pages + order form
Number of ink colors	1
What ink colors?	Black
Paper stock	body: 80# gloss text
	order form: 80# offset
Proofs required	Dylux
Bindery operations	Collate, staple
Delivery arrangements	To customer in Madison
Quantity	4,000
Price	$835

Date prepared 9-14-93 By Sarah White

Template 9-11C: Eight-page Catalog Budget

COST ESTIMATE WORKSHEET

Date: 7-31-92

Title of Piece: Product Catalog

Description: 8 pages, black & white, 10 photos. Mail to rented
list from Soccer America magazine

1. Planning

___$400___ List any planning or consulting costs

2. Writing

    ___$150___ Research

    ___100___ Write

    ___50___ Review

    ___50___ Rewrite

___$350___ Writing Subtotal

3. Graphic Design

    ___$250___ Initial design plan (and revisions)

    ___300___ Art direction

___$550___ Design Subtotal

4. Production: Gathering the elements

    ___$1,100___ Photography

    ___0___ Illustration

___$1,100___ See Chapter 6 for a full explanation of these costs.

5. Production: Combining elements into final art

    ___$350___ Scanning and color separations

    ___200___ Typesetting

    ___170___ Page composition

___$720___ Production Subtotal

6. Print Estimate (See Template 9-8A)

    ___$90___ Prepress (film output, stripping, electronic troubleshooting)

    ___660___ Press time

    ___70___ Bindery operations

    ___15___ Delivery/shipping charges

___$835___ Print Subtotal

7. Mailing Estimate (see Template 9-3)

    ___$155___ List rental

    ___180___ Mail prep

    ___1160___ Postal charges

___$1,495___ Mailing Subtotal

$5,450 Grand Total: Direct Mail Program

Case Stuffers and Bill Inserts. You can use these simple formats to reach your current customers with new offers. This is a marketing technique called cross-selling. Never assume that because a customer buys one product you offer, he or she knows about all your products. The potential for new sales to current customers is amazing. Explore their needs and cross-sell to them. These sales are cost-efficient—you don't have to mine for the prospects; they already have a favorable impression of you and a working relationship with you. With very little investment in the selling process, you can generate substantial sales.

Every contact you have with your current customers is an opportunity to pursue additional sales. When you ship an order, include a case stuffer. You might use a headline like "Special Private Sale for Special Customers." Bill inserts are another common way to promote new sales and to inform about new products or services. Simply reprinting your magazine or newspaper ads can make simple and effective bill inserts.

Order Requests. With order request direct mail, your goal is to convince prospects to become buyers, then give them the vehicle to do so. The key is to make responding as easy as possible.

The secret to getting orders via direct mail is to provide the perfect order form (see Examples 9-12 and 9-13). That means removing any complication or confusion that might create a barrier to placing the order. You've used lots of order forms in your life—you probably remember a few that were really difficult to understand. There's so much information involved in most purchases, from size and color specifications to return policies and guarantees.

One way around the question is to ask the customer to place the order by phone. This is almost the same as filling out an order form, really—it's just that a trained person on the other end of the telephone does the filling out. If you can't afford to have operators standing by to take orders, you will want to make your order form a masterpiece of simplicity and logic. Template 9-14 is a checklist to help you prepare your order form.

Example 9-12: Execution Calendar
Used by permission of BiFolkal Productions.

REMEMBERING	Slide kit will be $235	Video kit will be $240	Slides & video will be $270
PETS	PT101 $210	PT103 $220	PT108 $245
MUSIC	MU101 $210	MU103 $220	MU108 $245
THE FASHION	FS101 $210	FS103 $220	FS108 $245
WORK LIFE	WL101 $210	WL103 $220	WL108 $245
HOME FRONT	HF101 $210	HF103 $220	HF108 $245
SUMMERTIME	ST101 $210	ST103 $220	ST108 $245
BIRTHDAYS	BD101 $210	BD103 $220	BD108 $245
AUTOMOBILES	AU101 $210	AU103 $220	AU108 $245
FALL	FA101 $210	FA103 $220	FA108 $245
FARM DAYS	FD101 $210	FD103 $220	FD108 $245
THE DEPRESSION	DP101 $210	DP103 $220	DP108 $245
SCHOOL DAYS	SD101 $210	SD103 $220	SD108 $245
1924	TF101 $210	TF103 $220	TF108 $245
TRAIN RIDES	TR101 $210	TR103 $220	TR108 $245
COUNTY FAIRS	CF101 $210	CF103 $220	CF108 $245

PURCHASE ORDER #_____

PHONE NUMBER _____

SHIP TO:

_____

Name   (and title if applicable)

(Institution)

Street

City   State   Zip Code

BILL TO: (Complete if different from *Ship to:*)

Name   (Title)

(Institution)

Street

City   State   Zip Code

Phone or fax your order for quick response:
Phone: **608/251-2818** or fax: **608/251-2874**

Cardholder's name _____

Signature _____

Card Number

Expiration date _ _ _ _   ☐ MasterCard ☐ Visa

CIRCLE YOUR CHOICES

SEND TO:

BI-FOLKAL PRODUCTIONS, INC.
809 Williamson Street
Madison, WI 53703

Subtotal_____

Shipping (add $5 per kit) _____
(HI, AK and foreign orders will have shipping added.)

Total order_____

DEADLINE APRIL 1, 1993.

Example 9-13: Component Outline for Writing Copy
Used by permission of ERIC Clearinghouse on Higher Education.

Subscription Reservation Certificate

☐ YES! Please send me the Teaching and Learning Mini-Library (a one-year subscription to the *FORUM* and the five reports listed below) for just $67 – **40% off the combined price of the *FORUM* and the teaching and learning reports.**

☐ I do not wish to order the Mini-Library at this time, but please send me the individual resources I've checked below:

Your 100% guarantee

We stand behind everything we publish. If you're not completely satisfied with the **Teaching and Learning Mini-Library,** you may receive a complete refund of every cent you paid.

Jonathan D. Fife, Director

ERIC Clearinghouse on Higher Education

The George Washington University WASHINGTON, D.C.

Quantity		Amount
_____	One-year subscription to *The National Teaching & Learning FORUM* (six issues) $39	_____

ASHE-ERIC Teaching and Learning Reports

_____	**Learning Styles**	$10	_____
_____	**Critical Thinking**	$15	_____
_____	**Peer Teaching**	$15	_____
_____	**Active Learning**	$17	_____
_____	**Cooperative Learning**	$17	_____
_____	Shipping	$2.50	_____

(No shipping on orders for newsletter only)

Subtotal (ASHE-ERIC Reports) _____

Total Due _____

☐ Check enclosed for $_____ (Please makes check payable to GWU-ERIC.)
☐ Charge my ☐ Visa ☐ MC # _____ Exp. _____
Signature _____
☐ Please bill me/my institution (total order must be over $45)
Purchase order # _____

Name/Title _____

Institution _____

Teaching Discipline _____

Address _____

City _____

State/ZIP _____

Telephone _____

E-Mail _____

Mail to NTLF, ERIC-HE, The George Washington University, One Dupont Circle, Suite 630, Washington, DC 20036-1183.

Look for the similarities and differences in these two order forms.

Template 9-14: Checklist for Order Forms

WHO

____ Space for customer to fill in name, address, phone number. If you are shipping by Federal Express or UPS, the address needs to be a street address, not a post office box.

WHERE

____ Shipping address, which is often different from the billing address. If you're selling business-to-business, a central purchasing office might be ordering products for any of a number of locations in different regions. If you shop by catalog as a consumer, you've probably discovered the practice of having orders shipped to your office while the bill is sent straight to your home.

____ Provide a place to report address changes. There is a good way to handle this, if you can make your order form fall in position where the other side of the printed piece is the outgoing mail panel. Simply include a line saying, "Is the mailing label on the other side of this panel correct? If not, please indicate changes."

WHAT

____ Provide appropriate spaces for your customers to indicate what merchandise they are ordering. You are probably familiar with SKUs, or "Stock Keeping Units." This is a very handy concept which basically means "all the things of one kind." If you had a shoe store, for example, an SKU might be all the red Easy Spirit 3/4" heel stadium pumps in size 7M. A red size 7W would be a different SKU. All the systems of product numbers I've ever come across are basically codes created to differentiate between SKUs.

Your order form should have a blank for every variation available in your offering—and it's easy to see if you've included them all. Simply take yourself on an imaginary shopping trip; make up your wish list, then try to place the order. If you find yourself getting confused, you know your order form needs work.

____ Offer an impulse item near the order form. Statistics show that this is very productive for add-on sales.

HOW

____ What methods of payment do you accept? If you accept credit cards, ask for a signature and an expiration date.

____ How will the order be shipped? Get shipping, packing, and delivery information.

____ Be sure to include a phone number for customers who are confused and would like help.

____ Inform your customer how shipping and handling costs and sales tax are calculated. Sometimes this takes the form of a table.

____ Explain your guarantees and return policies.

CLOSURE

____ Request names and addresses of others who should receive the offer.

____ Include a code number for tracking response to this offer. You will want to test results for each variation in mailing list, timing, and offer you make.

Tips for order forms: Keep them as simple as possible. Number the steps to guide a customer through the process. Leave plenty of room to fill in the requested information. Most important of all, try using the form yourself to make sure it's functional. Fill it out, to test it's "user-friendliness," then try following it through the order-fulfillment process, so that you know that your form is compatible with your in-house way of doing things. If you plan to enter the customer information in a database, for example, you want the sequence of information on the order form to match the sequence of fields in your data-entry screen.

Reply cards, or fax-back forms, are abbreviated versions of an order form. The same logic applies. However you are using order request mail pieces, keep this in mind: You are asking someone to buy something sight unseen. Offer a guarantee!

Sales Letters: There are whole books written on how to do these packages well, and seminars and workshops that might interest you, if you are planning to use this marketing method extensively.

Here are some tips for successful sales letters:

1. Stick to the tried-and-true components: an envelope, a cover letter, a flyer, and a reply card.

2. Personalize the letter on computer, if possible. "Dear John Doe" will provoke more responses than "Dear Boat Owner" (although "Dear Boat Owner" is better than no personalization at all). Make the sales letter look typed, not typeset.

3. Write the cover letter in an informal first-person style. Keep your paragraphs short, and think of the first sentences as heads or subheads—perhaps you'll set them apart with underlines or special spacing. Always include a P.S. at the end.

4. Use a second ink color, like red "notations" or "highlighter" streaks of yellow, to make the piece appear personally handled.

5. Always use teasers or lift lines on the envelope near the mailing label.

The list on pages 384–385 provides a more detailed review of the complete sales letter mail piece.

The Sales Letter

Here's a closer look at an effective sales letter direct mail piece (Example 9-14).

Example 9-14A: Quality Yearbook Sales Letter Components
Used by permission of McGraw-Hill.

McGraw-Hill, Inc.
11 West 19th Street
New York, NY 10011

What's happened in *Quality* this past year would astound you.

Now there's a hands-on roundup that puts it all at your fingertips.

Details—and a FREE Trial Offer—Inside...

3 EASY WAYS TO ORDER:

Return this postpaid card.

Call toll-free **1-800-2-MCGRAW**
(1-800-262-4729) 24 hours a day.

Fax this order card to 1-717-794-5291.

ASK ABOUT 24-HOUR EXPRESS DELIVERY!

The McGraw-Hill Unconditional Guarantee:
You must be satisfied or owe nothing.

FREE-TRIAL ACCEPTANCE CARD

☑ **YES!** I need to keep up with the latest quality ideas, trends, and practices! Please rush me THE QUALITY YEARBOOK, 1994 Edition (024013-2) for just $69.95 plus local tax, postage, and handling. I understand that if after using it for 15 days I'm not convinced it's an indispensable roundup of the best in TQM today, I may return it with my unpaid invoice and owe nothing. If I keep it I'll receive *automatic priority updates* of future annual editions just as soon as they come off press. Each is mine to evaluate on the same no-obligation free-trial basis—and I can cancel my participation whenever I like.

NOTE: For orders over $150 please use a purchase order or call 1-800-2-MCGRAW (1-800-262-4729). Same Free Trial privileges apply. Prices subject to change. Orders subject to approval.

Example 9-14B: Quality Yearbook Sales Letter Components
Used by permission of McGraw-Hill.

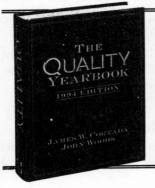

*"The average life expectancy
of an industrial company
is less than half that
of a human being."*

—James W. Lawton and Matthew D. Williams,
"The Learning Trip: Enhancing an Organization's Ability to Learn"

Dear Colleague:

Ever think you might outlive the company -- even the industry -- you work in?

It's a scary thought. And not just because of what could happen to your pension benefits.

I bring up this alarming possibility for the same reasons Hewlett-Packard managers James Lawton and Matthew Williams do in "The Learning Trip"* -- one of the more than 60 probing articles you'll find in McGraw-Hill's bold new QUALITY YEARBOOK.

To make a point about quality ... about competitiveness ... and about perpetually learning to improve both.

Because in a nutshell, that's what THE QUALITY YEARBOOK is all about.

 The brainstorm of quality experts James W. Cortada and John A.
 Woods, this unprecedented annual has only one mission: to help
 you learn (and keep learning) about the latest, most successful
 quality ideas, trends, and practices <u>in the shortest time</u>.

So you can devote more of your energy to building the quality, competitiveness, and total customer satisfaction your business needs to survive -- and thrive -- in the decisive years ahead. To making sure your company outlives you ... NOT THE OTHER WAY AROUND!

Cortada and Woods have "panned for gold" in the torrent of quality literature to update you on breakthrough concepts and results no matter where they're reported -- in magazines as diverse as <u>Quality</u>, <u>Industry Week</u>, <u>Journal of Business Strategy</u>, and <u>Training</u> ... and in pathfinding books ranging from Gregory Watson's <u>Strategic Benchmarking</u> to Michael Hammer and James Champy's <u>Reengineering the Corporation</u>.

The result: a one-stop guide to state-of-the-art TQM strategies in the manufacturing <u>and</u> service industries -- even health care, education, and government.

---

* According to Lawton and Williams, a recent study by Royal Dutch/Shell found
 that <u>one-third</u> of the industrial companies on the 1970 list of Fortune 500
 had gone out of business by 1983.

(Over, please)

Example 9-14B: Quality Yearbook Sales Letter Components (continued)
Used by permission of McGraw-Hill.

THE·YEAR·IN·QUALITY

WHAT's working. WHO's doing it.
HOW they're going about it.
And WHERE they're getting results–in:

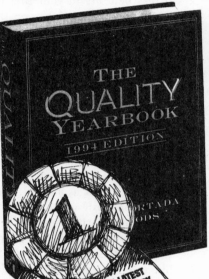

☑ *Benchmarking*
☑ *Reengineering*
☑ *Customer Satisfaction*
☑ *Training*
☑ *Leadership*
☑ *Communication*
☑ *Measurement*
☑ *Standards and Assessments*

TQM WAR STORIES FROM SUCH INDUSTRIES AS
♦ Automobiles
♦ Electronics
♦ Hospitality
♦ Banking
♦ Insurance
♦ Health Care
♦ Education
♦ Government

THE LATEST TQM THEORY AND PRACTICE IN
♦ Sales and Marketing
♦ Purchasing and Supply
♦ Information Technology
♦ Accounting and Finance
♦ Human Resources

Over 60 of the year's top TQM writings from 69 of the nation's leading experts—including all-time classics from Juran, Deming, Feigenbaum, and Ishikawa!

The sales letter is very good at taking a cold prospect through the inquiry fulfillment stage directly to the purchase with one mail shot. It does this by providing lots of information, a persuasive sales pitch, and a response vehicle, all in one package. If you are selling to a fairly broad mass market, and the budget numbers work out to your advantage, this is a technique you need to try. You may do it strictly by the book, or you may borrow something from its format that will lift the results of whatever you create. Let's take a closer look at the sales letter's components.

- *The envelope.* The package starts with an outer envelope. Often it will carry a "lift line" or "teaser" printed near the recipient's name. This is a headline, slogan, or benefit statement, worded to convince someone to look inside. Sometimes businesses will design the envelope to look like a government notice, or a check, or an invitation. These do prove to have a high rate of opening, but I'd be cautious in using these techniques. No one likes to be tricked.

   What sort of postage goes on this envelope? A preprinted bulk mail indicia is the simplest answer, but it clearly labels your piece "junk mail." A standard postage stamp will pull better results than a printed indicia. An unusual commemorative stamp will outdraw a standard stamp. Talk over your options with your post office.

- *The cover letter.* This is your personal contact with the reader. It's the key to the success of your package. If you can have it personalized to the individual from the computerized mailing list, do so! If that is too expensive, write the letter in the most personal style you can. Composing it might be your finest hour as a copywriter. Here are some tips:

1. Use the first person. This is not a letter from your company, but from you, personally, to the reader, alone. Whatever name appears at the bottom, keep the language direct. Make the salutation as personal as possible; if you cannot use the reader's name, look for a phrase like "Dear Boat Owner" or "Dear Information Manager" that describes your reader believably, and shows that you understand his or her point of view.

2. Stress benefits in your first paragraph. Then state your offer, even though you will be enclosing a flyer to promote the offer. Be redundant; repeat the offer several times. You know perfectly well that almost no one will read *every* word of your package. Browsers and skimmers are potential customers too!

3. Make it look personal. Use a typewriter or word processor, or a computer font that looks like one—Courier, Prestige, and Elite are the names of a few such fonts. You want this to look as immediate as possible. Desktop publishing is changing our expectations about what personal communication looks like, but the old standard is still the most reliable. Make your letter look like a letter, and your flyer like graphic design.

   Hold onto the next magazine subscription solicitation that comes in your mail. It's your complete study guide to the sales letter. Look at the cover letter. You'll see that it uses underlines, asterisks, and postscripts to call attention to the main points. Sometimes it will even use a second color, to simulate hand-written notes, or a yellow "highlighter" or Post-it Note. Use these devices to increase your success.

- *The flyer.* "The letter sells, then the flyer tells." This piece answers questions to help make the sale. It should be self-contained. By that, I mean that if it were separated from the rest of the package, it should still deliver all the information your prospect needs to learn about your offering and respond to your call to action. This piece can be as plain or as fancy as the situation—and the budget—call for. The key is that it must be benefits-oriented. It should be well designed—visually interesting, well organized, a quality production.

- *The reply card.* Every sales letter contains a way to respond to the offer. It will usually be a separate reply card, although occasionally it is contained on one panel of the flyer. Either way, this piece will be designed to the post office's specifications, with your name and address and a business reply mail permit printed on one side, accompanied by the necessary bar codes. The other side will have spaces for the prospect's name, address, phone number, and any other information you want to acquire. Sometimes the card will have check-off boxes to indicate level of interest or readiness to purchase. Sometimes it will request information survey-style, like "How many people are in your firm?" or "What type of computer system do you own?"

As with any form you create, be sure to have someone—or several people—try filling it out before you finalize the layout. If you expect people to send money, the reply device should include an envelope, as a matter of courtesy.

There are often more components in the sales letter—a page of testimonials, or a list of area dealers, or a special additional offer. These will follow the same guidelines as the flyer: They should be self-contained, benefits-oriented, and of high-quality production. Make sure all the elements of the sales letter work together in a cohesive way.

You may find it too complex, and costly, to plan and execute a sales letter program. You

might choose instead to use simpler direct mail formats, such as self-mailers or invoice stuffers. There are tradeoffs. Despite the trend toward earth-friendly attitudes, tests prove that in many industries, sales letters pull better results than single-piece mailings. Why? Perhaps it's the perception of value, or the illusion of personal correspondence. I personally would be happy to see all these packages disappear, replaced by simple trifolds and postcards that make their point and don't create a lot of waste. But I can't argue with the statistics. I recommend that you contact the Direct Marketing Association and ask about how you can get statistics for your industry. Then decide what combination makes sense for you.

Direct Marketing Association, Inc.
11 West 42nd Street
New York, NY 10036
(212) 768-7277

How to Design and Produce Your Mail Piece

Once you've gotten this far, the finish line is in sight. You've chosen your creative approach, defined your piece in the tangible form of a dummy, and tackled writing direct mail ad copy. All you've got to do now is to combine the copy and art on pages, print them, and then mail your finished piece.

Check in with your calendar and budget. It's time to start spending money for design services, photography, and printing. Is your project on track? If you're concerned, check back with your chosen vendors and show them how your idea has evolved. Discuss how their estimates might need to change.

You—or the professionals you've hired—can follow the worksheets from this chapter to get organized, and then begin the process of layout and design. I wrote about this process first in Chapter 6, and if you are planning to produce your direct mail piece yourself, I'd recommend that you skim that section now

("Layout and Design"). In that chapter we discussed

- Using grids in layout
- How to use thumbnail sketches
- Bringing the page together (art, copy, and white space)
- Using photographs and illustrations
- Using type
- The design process: steps to completion

Each of those topics is relevant to the task ahead of you now.

As I've said before, direct mail is a medium for control freaks. For that reason, I'm devoting the rest of this chapter to those of you who are going to do it all yourself because you want that level of control.

About Type

Let's start with the words. You will typeset your manuscript in all its complexity—captions and call-outs and diagrams and all. You should use an electronic page layout program to do this; Quark XPress and PageMaker are the leaders. I prefer Quark, but it's really a very individual choice. I've worked in both programs on both Windows and Macintosh hardware, and they all get the job done. For do-it-yourselfers, the power of the desktop-publishing software is amazing.

I have a personal attachment to good typography, and I hate to see standards drop as newcomers take on the job. So I'm going to ramble on about it in more detail.

Typography follows well-established customs, because the way we read is a very habitual thing. Make reading uncomfortable, and our willingness to read drops off dramatically. Wild typography has been trendy, but it communicates style more than substance, in my opinion. You want somebody to get your message? Give them legible type.

You and everybody else who bought a laser printer started out life with about five type families we've all seen enough of. I know font packages sound expensive—anywhere from $50 or $60 to as much as $300, depending on how many fonts (styles and weights) are included and the reputation of the manufacturer. Still, I think one of the smartest things you can do for your corporate identity is to purchase a different font, one that can speak as the unique voice of your company in print.

I covered a lot about typography in Chapter 6, so I'll keep my advice to the minimum. Don't set lines of type that are too long. Use bold or italic for occasional emphasis, but don't get carried away using too many fonts or type styles. Choose serif or sans, whichever seems right to you. Don't set very many words in reverse (light on dark background). Again, check out Chapter 6 on this subject.

Even though page layout software lets you switch easily between tasks like styling type and placing photos, I like to concentrate on first one, then the other. I will apply styles to type—establishing what body copy will look like, and heads and subheads, establishing widths for the columns of type—before I bring any other elements onto the page. In publishing these are called "galley pages." What you have with galley pages is the page layout with type but without the final illustrations in place.

Typesetting is a professional skill, and doing it yourself increases the chances for error. Concentrating on just the type as you make galley pages lets you find and fix problems easily. You might find that your type has neuter quotes (they look like inch marks, rather than the proper open- and close-quote characters) or bad hyphenation. More than two hyphens in a row splitting words at the end of consecutive lines is forbidden, and I personally hate to see split words at all in advertising. Usually a tweak to the layout can solve the problem.

If you use the style-sheet function in your program at this step, you will be taking advantage of its power to keep your typesetting consistent.

Don't be surprised if you find yourself rewriting copy at this step! When you see the words typeset, you see them with a certain freshness. You might spot trouble areas. While I believe in getting the copy polished up before I begin laying it on pages, this is a good time to make any necessary last editorial changes. Each step past this point makes copy changes more of a pain.

Make sure you include proofreading cycles in your calendar. At every step, read the type carefully, and have someone unfamiliar with it read it too. If you are doing the page layout tasks, you will quickly become too familiar with the material to be reliable as a proofreader. Each time you go through the piece, read once for content and then once again for typographic accuracy—just checking for errors of capitalization or punctuation and for typos like transposed or missing letters.

Once the piece is in production, you might think that you only need to review the changed sections, checking the new against the old. Unfortunately, with electronic page layout, it's too easy to accidentally make small, mysterious changes that are hard to find. I call these "mouse droppings"—they're usually the result of an accidental click, deleting or changing some element. You might catch these with random spot checks—but never assume that everything is ready to go to the printer without one last read through everything. That's why it is so important to keep showing the piece to fresh eyes.

About Photos

In Chapter 6 I talk a bit about creating interesting photos. Here I'll talk about getting them into print. As with your copy, you have to get your photographs (and other art) into electronic form. That means scanning, and then separating them into the colors of the printing inks to be used. This might be the four process colors, also called "four-color," "full-color," or "CMYK" (cyan, magenta, yellow, and black). C, M, and Y are self-evident. The K is

for blacK, because if you used a B someone might think you meant Blue. At least, that's how printers always explain it. They've been using K for blacK for almost a century.

So photos are converted into either four-color separations or tritones, duotones, or gray-scale images. Your printer or your imaging service bureau can do the scans for you. If you haven't chosen your printer yet, this might be a good time to finalize that decision. It's really best if the printer does the scanning, if it has the right equipment. That way the printer takes responsibility for seeing that the scans are suitable for the presses. This can make an important difference in quality.

You should be aware that photo scans take up a huge amount of memory on a hard drive. If you have limited memory available, tell the person who does your scans to make you an "FPO" scan—for position only. He or she can sample the image down to a manageable size, and hold the real image in reserve for when you bring your job in. Then the operator replaces the FPO images with the high-resolution ones originally made.

There's a truly amazing amount of magic being done in retouching and augmenting photographic images with today's breakthrough software. If you want to combine images, or change components to correct flaws, or create unusual effects, your options are wide open. An image-setting service bureau is probably your best source for information on what is possible and who is doing it in your community.

Anything good takes time, and for this sort of service, you will pay by the hour. Do not rely on retouching to correct sloppy photography. You are always better off getting things right the first time. But it is nice to know that the new tools exist.

As you place your photos on your pages, you will be sizing and cropping them—reducing or enlarging, and deciding what portion of the image available will be used. For example, you might want just the head and shoulders of a person, even though you have a full-length shot to work from. There's nothing difficult about cropping and sizing images, but you should know the terms. (See the sidebar in Chapter 6 on pages 205–206 that explains other technical terms and concepts for print production.)

Once you have your photos, it's relatively easy to bring together the rest of your layout. Simply combine the images with the stream of text from your galley files. Use the print specifications you've written as a guide when you set up your document's page size. The same goes for the ink colors. At this point, as the words and images are coming together on the electronic page, you have only one step left to go: getting it printed.

What Do You Take to the Printer?

That depends on whether your printer is set up to accept jobs on disk or not. If yes, then you simply finish your layout work, make copies of everything (both the electronic files and the laser-printed output from them), and take everything to your printer. Ask for a copy of its imaging job order form if it has one. Most printers and service bureaus do.

If your printer doesn't have imaging equipment, it should be able to refer you to a service bureau. A service bureau is a company that takes care of certain tasks required before you can have your piece printed. Again, you'll collect your files, both paper and electronic, and provide those to the service bureau. Then a day later (that's standard turnaround most places, unless you want to pay a premium), you pick up negatives and take them to your printer, along with the folding dummy made from your last laser prints. Together you review the negatives against the dummy, and then the job is out of your hair.

Have your service bureau or your printer give you a quote that includes your scanning, high-resolution negative output, and any file "troubleshooting" charges and other fees. Imaging can get expensive in a hurry. Negative output typically costs from $10 to $15 per

page, and if anything isn't prepared properly, you can expect to pay to have the page rerun after corrections. Negatives for a simple three-panel direct mail piece (about 9 by 15 in.) might run $120 or so. Costs go up quickly as you add ink colors or pages. Your films might run $500 to $800 on a more complex job. The cost gets into the thousands for a catalog. So it makes a lot of sense to make sure your proofs are error-free before getting negatives prepared. An ounce of prevention here is definitely worth a pound of cure.

Once negatives are made and stripped or "imposed" into position for printing, you will see one last proof, called a "dylux" or "blueline." Look these over carefully, and make any changes you need—but know that changes at this stage could cost you $80 or $100 in work that has to be redone.

Selecting a Printer

Commercial printing is a multibillion-dollar industry, and it is made up of many niche markets. At one end of the continuum you'll find the copy shops and quick printers who specialize in very short runs (50 to 5,000 pieces) and very simple print jobs, and often combine photocopy and offset printing equipment under one roof. A two- to five-day turnaround time will be their standard.

A notch above them, in both cost and quality, are the local printing firms that carve out niches by specializing in business printing, like letterheads, business cards, newsletters, and brochures. They may have more and better presses and better-trained personnel than the quick printers, and they will give you fast turnaround on short runs.

In your community there may also be large printing firms that do books, magazines, annual reports, and catalogs. Their presses will be more elaborate still, computer-driven, and capable of handling larger sheets of paper, or even paper on continuous rolls (called *web printing*, as opposed to *sheet-fed* printing.)

It's up to you to determine which niche fits your needs. Review your print specifications checklist and make some phone calls. You're about to begin a relationship that might last for years.

I find it comforting that with printing, at least, you do get what you pay for. By that I mean that there does seem to be a direct correlation between price and quality. The printer who gives you the lowest bid very likely can offer that price because it cuts corners in some way the higher bidders do not. You may not be happy with the result.

All printers face the same basic facts of life: They have overhead, both rent to pay for manufacturing space and payments on the presses and other equipment they buy. One way printers keep costs down is to locate out in the suburbs. If you are doing business in a larger metropolitan area, you should definitely look for referrals to printers in outlying areas. You can save hundreds of dollars this way.

If the print job you are planning is fairly straightforward, say a two-color direct mailer on coated stock, with no special binding or die cutting involved, then look for a printer that has suitable equipment, but not a lot more. If you look above the appropriate niche, you will find yourself paying for bells and whistles that are not applied to your job.

Some printers have made the plunge and purchased computer electronic imaging equipment, setting up elaborate in-house prepress departments. Other printers have delayed that investment, and will send you to a service bureau if you want to bring them a job electronically. Working with separate vendors for these two steps can be more cost-efficient, although more hassle. You will have to decide if the inconvenience is worth the tradeoff.

By this rule of thumb, your best bet for quality and low price will be a suburban printer without a lot of electronic prepress equipment in the shop. I say this through personal experience. It holds true if the demands of your print job are simple.

To find the printer that's right for you, ask your business associates where they shop. Contact these printers, describe the piece you're planning, and ask to see samples of similar pieces they've printed. Larger printers may have sales representatives who call on you, although smaller firms may not. Be sure to tell them the quantity you're planning to print. You may find out that a particular printer is above or below the niche you need.

When you have your "short list" of potential vendors, check out each firm carefully. Visit the plants, and learn about each firm's equipment and capabilities. Look around you: Is the shop clean, dust-free, well organized? Ask for names of clients you can contact for references. Make some phone calls. The important questions to ask are:

- Do they deliver when they say they will?
- Is their work clean and consistent from first sheet to last?
- When a problem arises, how is it handled?

The first few times you buy printing, you will want to get three bids. Use the Direct Mail Print Specifications Checklist to make sure the bids you get are apples to apples. Ask to have any confusing charges or terms explained to you. After you've bid two or three jobs around, you'll start to get a handle on who in your community provides the real value in printing. When you find a firm that does right by you, reward it with repeat business.

Most printers are honest, reasonable businesspeople with a strong love of their craft. They all struggle with the fact that each job is custom-produced. There are many chances to get it wrong, from art to ink to paper to bindery, and only one slim chance to get the whole job right. Most printers really want to get it right, and do what it takes—via their systems, equipment, and personnel—to keep their customers happy. Do what you can to make the printer's job easier, like providing reasonable time to produce your orders, and you'll build a true business partner.

Planning the Print Job

The very first step is to establish your quality expectations. The decisions you make about paper and ink, about press types and finishing operations, will all be guided by the impression of quality you want your printed piece to make. When I ask my clients, I often hear the concern, "I want it to look good, but not like we spent a ton of money on it." Look around you until you find samples of paper, and ink colors, that hit that mark for you.

Making printing an environmentally friendly process has become an important concern. Printers now use more recycled paper, and use soybean-based inks that can be cleaned up without solvents and discarded without hazard, unlike the older oil-based printing inks. Recycling of the wasted paper is standard in just about every print shop. Sometimes the environmentally clean processes cost a little more; do the right thing for you.

Use the Print Specifications Checklist (Template 9-8A) or a similar form from your printer to keep track of your print quotes, and to monitor changes as the job evolves. In my experience, the quantity you order, the paper you put it on, and the ink colors you choose are all likely to change once or more during the production process. Using this form will help you stay organized.

There is one trade custom of the printing business that you should be aware of, and in case your printer doesn't remember to tell you, I'll go into it here. It's the rule of "overs and unders." When you specify a quantity in printing, it is understood that the count delivered to you may not be exact. It is just not feasible for the printer to count pieces in every order it prints. And while printers always run extra sheets, or "make-ready," to cover for any lost in finishing operations, there is always the chance they might lose too many getting set up on the folding machine or whatever, and

not have the actual quantity you ordered left at the end of the line. So, the custom of "overs and unders" or "plus or minus 10 percent" has developed. If you ask for 1,500 flyers, for example, you and the printer are really agreeing that you might get 1,350 or you might get 1,650—10 percent less or 10 percent more than you ordered. The price you pay is adjusted down or up by figuring your per-piece cost at the 1,500 quantity, then adjusting the final bill to match the per-piece cost to the actual number delivered. It's a reasonably fair practice. Where it becomes a problem is if you don't know about it in time to accommodate it in your plans.

If you don't want to pay for 10 percent more brochures than you ordered, you'd better talk it over with the printer before you place the order. Otherwise the printer will be within its rights in delivering them to you and expecting to be paid for them. And if you need 1,500 pieces and no less, because you purchased a 1,500-name mailing list, make sure the printer knows that too. You might find yourself placing the order for 1,650 to assure that you get *at minimum* the 1,500 you need.

I could go on for pages about the subtleties of print buying, from specifying papers, to the different print processes, to specialty finishes like embossing, foil stamping, ultraviolet coatings, and so on. But you can learn all this from your print sales reps when you begin to develop working relationships with a few firms over time. Print buying is a challenging, but satisfying, part of the direct mail process.

Summary: Creating Your Direct Mail Piece

In this section we've examined the creative business of direct mail. We've talked about finding the creative approach, writing copy, making a visual survey, and developing print specifications. We've discussed how to design and produce your piece. In the previous section on Strategy, we covered how a mailing service connects your piece to your prospect, through providing first the list and then the service of sorting and labeling the mailing for the post office.

The templates in this chapter should help you feel in control of your next direct mail project. If it all seems a little vague to you still, then review the checklist in Template 9-15.

Template 9-15

Focus Your Vision of Your Successful Mail Piece

Review these topics. Is your thinking fuzzy in any of these areas? Go back and think about it until you have confidence in your decisions. You can't create a focused direct mail piece with fuzzy vision. Once you start, the process will suffer if you second-guess yourself!

__ Objective of the piece

__ Format

    __ Copy outline

    __ Visual survey

    __ Print specs

__ Creative approach (see Chapter 5)

__ Supporting information available for writing copy

__ Source to find data, testimonials, or other new material to write

__ Audience demographics and lifestyle

__ Positioning statement (see Chapter 2)

    __ Key benefit

    __ Supporting rationale, features

__ Competitive environment

    __ Name of closest competitors

    __ Description of their style or tone

    __ Their positioning strategy

__ Your sales cycle:

    __ What step precedes use of this piece?

    __ What step follows its use?

__ Budget (see section on budget, then fill out Template 9-10A)

___ Schedule (fill out Template 9-12)

Case Study: How Bi-Folkal Productions Uses Direct Mail

Small businesses tend to fall into two categories: those that serve a local retail market, and those that serve a national but narrow market. Both have the problems inherent in smallness—a shortage of resources to apply to marketing and advertising, for example. For businesses in the latter category, direct mail is the way to go. Here's how an unusual niche business uses solid direct mail techniques to build sales. Its approach can serve as a useful model for any small business.

Bi-Folkal Productions is a nonprofit corporation that creates resources to encourage older adults to remember and share their stories. Libraries, nursing homes, adult day centers, schools, and other settings use the resources it sells to enhance their programs and activities. Some of the resources are kits with many components; others are simply books, tapes, and sets of slides or activities. All have subject matter that stimulates memories and encourages intergenerational sharing. Prices range from $6 to $25 for the single items to $270 for multicomponent kits.

One popular kit is called "Remembering Automobiles" (see Example 9-15). If you were to order this kit, you would receive a large duffle bag, packed with a tray of slides, a cassette tape with songs and stories, a skit, and some paraphernalia to encourage reminiscing. The "Remembering Automobiles" kit contains, among other items, a scrap of old auto upholstery, an interstate map, and a hubcap for a Model A Ford. Kits also include posters, a program manual, and booklets to help the librarian or program director plan activities using the kit.

Here's an example of another kit:

Example 9-15: Bi-Folkal Catalog Cover and PGTS Page
Used by permission of BiFolkal Productions.

REMEMBERING
PETS

Library of Congress

Encourage people to remember the animals they have known and loved, and to share those memories. Perhaps you will prompt the purchase of a guppy or two. This is a kit to interest groups in your community who may be new to Bi-Folkal—the Humane Society, 4-H groups and Scout troops, churches, and civic organizations. *Pets* is a great choice for intergenerational programming!

"The kits are so complete that they can be effectively used by a person who has had no experience in audiovisual presentations and no background in the subject matter."
The Gerontologist

KIT CONTENTS:

SLIDE/TAPE AND/OR VIDEOTAPE
The Family Pet offers a look at the animals who have found a place in our homes and hearts. 80 images with a warm and fuzzy 14-min. narration.

CASSETTE TAPE #2
Side 1 is a set of six sing-along songs about dogs. Side 2 offers *Cat Tales* (a poem, an essay, and a story) for discussion.

MANUAL
How to use the kit pieces, ideas for pet projects and an extensive list of resources.

25 BOOKLETS
Reigning Cats and Dogs. Six sing-along songs (Tape #2), plus a choral reading, some poems, and quotable quotes for discussion and fun. Everything in large, easy-to-read type.

PICTURE SET
Paws for Pictures. Twelve historical photos in black-and-white to look at and discuss. Questions in large type accompany each picture. *See page 30 to order the picture set separately.*

2 SKITS
"Cat Chat" and "Fighting Like Cats and Dogs". Three large-print scripts for each. Includes one cat mask and one dog mask to use with the skits.

PARAPHERNALIA
Things to touch include a squeaky toy *(The Doggie News)*, a curry comb, imitation Dalmatian and lamb fur, and a bit of catnip.

KIT AVAILABLE IN 3 VERSIONS
Kit with slides PT101 **$235**
Kit with VHS video PT103 **$240**
Kit with slides and video PT108 **$270**

The beginning

It was 1975 at the Library School at the University of Wisconsin at Madison. The assignment was to design a library service for one group in the community.

Two students decided to take a library program out of the library to a nursing home and a senior center. Those students were Kathryn Leide and Lynne Martin Erickson.

Our goal was to encourage the sharing of memories and stories on the topics of fall and Halloween. We couldn't find the program materials we wanted at the library, so we made our own. We took fall slides and poetry, adapted a ghost story, borrowed some old rubber masks, and made some fresh applesauce.

We heard some great stories about fall activities and ambitious Halloween pranks both at the nursing home and the senior center. A famous time was had by all. Word spread and we got lots of requests to bring the program other places.

UW WISCONSIN

2 KITS

The company markets seventeen of these resource kits, and other related products, through a forty-page catalog. It publishes a quarterly newsletter that is mailed to all purchasers and active leads. And it does special mailings to promote new products and to reintroduce existing ones.

The thing that impresses me about Bi-Folkal Productions is the way it tracks the results of its direct mail program. It developed the spreadsheet shown in Template 9-16 to report the effectiveness of different mail pieces. (I have altered the numbers to protect confidentiality.)

Template 9-16: Bi-Folkal Direct Mail Sales Tracking Spreadsheet

Ave. Sale	Sales	Total Cost	Cost Piece	List Rent	Mail	Postage	Ave.
116.65	2,799.50	1,384.86	0.811	0	261	355.26	0.208
696.34	29,246.25	1,802.97	0.178	0	237	1,121.43	0.111
	32,045.75	3,187.83					
138.49	10,248.00	2,216.03	0.184	0	280	1,334.78	0.111
183.45	64,206.42	32,360.91	X	X	X	X	X
41.06	2,546.00	2,449.95	0.192	0	517	1,220.18	0.096
X	X	942.07	0.469	0	63	222.78	0.111
64.68	7,955.95	2,609.16	0.193	0	594	1286.7	0.095
442.28	1,326.85	209.29	1.011	0	35	48.02	0.232
	9,282.80	2,818,45					
45.6	228	3,042.33	0.214	0	600	1,390.64	0.098
	118,556.97	47,268.83					

Example 9-3, early in this chapter, was a flyer Bi-Folkal mailed just before it planned to increase prices. It appears on this spreadsheet on the second line in 1993. Look back at the printed piece. You'll notice that it contained very little product information—just a lot of sales pitch worded in a humorous style.

Note in Template 9-16 how this flyer performed compared to others. The response rate was 0.42 percent, near the lower end of the responses Bi-Folkal has learned to expect. But the size of the average sale was phenomenal. The reason: The offer had real value, and it was made to the right people. The piece offered a discount off today's price for purchasing before a deadline. The incentive to buy now comes from the fact that prices will

not just return to the undiscounted price, but will go up after the deadline.

The potential customers—the librarians, teachers, and activity directors—have many things in common, including that they all work with limited financial resources. They look for bargains and shop at sales like anyone on a budget. This offer clearly was such a good value that it brought customers out of the woodwork.

I'll explain the columns on the spreadsheet from left to right.

Date: Date the piece was mailed
Order Code: A tracking number assigned to
            some mail shots.

List: Key phrase describing different mailing lists. Cust & Mail is the in-house list that Bi-Folkal carefully maintains.

Pieces: What was mailed. (Code names stand for different promotional mailings.)

Total Piece: Cost per piece for printing.

Sent: Number of pieces mailed.

Order: How many orders could be attributed to the mailing.

% Return: Number of orders generated divided by number of pieces sent.

Ave. Sale: The total sales divided by the number of orders.

Sales: Total dollars in sales attributed to the mailing.

Total Cost: Production and delivery expense for the piece(s). This would ordinarily be a higher number, but Bi-Folkal Productions has staff with the talent to write and produce mail pieces in-house. These numbers reflect only printing, list rental, and postage costs.

Cost/Piece: Total cost divided by number of pieces.

List Rent: Mailing list rental. (No charge here when in-house list is used.)

Mail: Mail prep, including labeling and sorting for the post office.

Postage: Actual postage costs.

Ave.: Postage cost divided by number of pieces sent, for average postal rate per piece. (This organization has nonprofit status, and so can mail at special rates.)

Bi-Folkal Productions is benefiting from using this kind of analysis as its direct mail programs evolve. Here's an example: It mailed a flyer pitching program kits. The hook was a panicked cartoon character saying, "Oh No, My Program Didn't Show!" The benefit stated was that Bi-Folkal kits are a convenient backup when scheduled programs fall through. Response to this piece was so good that it mailed the same piece to the same list again, but this time raised the price two dollars. The piece pulled just as well a second time.

There's one more form the folks at Bi-Folkal use, and that's a spreadsheet that lets them track the growth of the mailing list on a monthly basis (Template 9-17). With this information, they can see how many people migrate from "active lead" status to "current customer."

Template 9-17: Mail List Status Report

Date	Mail List #	# Added	Customers from Mail List	New Customers	
7/1/94	12728	124	27	34	
8/1/94	13490	762	41	52	
9/1/94	14212	722	52	74	
10/1/94	12795	232	24	29	Note: Mail list went down due
11/1/94	14817	2022	85	104	to cleaning out old names.
12/1/94	15237	420	34	42	

I'll explain the columns from left to right:

Date of Report (Month)

Mail List #   Total names on "active leads" status and also current customers.

Added   How many names have been added this month.

Customer from

Mail List: How many names from the "active leads" list made their first purchase this month.

New

Customers: How many new customers (total) were gained this month, both those who converted from "active lead" status and those who came from no attributable source.

You can and should develop a sheet like this to track your own direct mail advertising efforts. By doing that, you will be able to correctly assess the costs versus the benefits of direct mail advertising.

It's care and feeding of a mail program with analysis like this that makes a company a direct mail dynamo.

Chapter 10

Publicity: The Almost-Free Alternative

If you've read Chapter 7, "Radio Advertising," you're familiar with the story behind the news release in Example 10-1. In 1992, when this release was created, failing savings and loans were hurting the credibility of banks. Independent community banks not only were experiencing the fallout from that, but also were seeing competition from large financial institutions that were expanding into their home towns. To fight back, the Independent Bankers Association of Wisconsin produced a marketing kit for its members. Among its other components, the kit contained several news releases, including this one. By sending the news releases in the kit to local media, the community banks were able to gain press coverage that built confidence in their stability. Bankers don't tend to know much about advertising or publicity—and that's why they needed a marketing kit.

If you've ever sent out an announcement about your promotion or an award you've won, you've participated in the publicity game. How successful were you? Could you do better when your next big news comes along? The goal of this chapter is to see that you do.

In this chapter I will attempt to define publicity activity, show you how it works, and provide the templates and tools you need to get started doing publicity for your business. Through case studies, I'll show you two styles of publicity activity—one centered on using word of mouth to promote business-to-business, and one focused on using traditional press relations techniques to heighten awareness of a nonprofit foundation's work.

The nebulous world that some people call publicity and some call public relations does not have to be overwhelming. In this chapter I hope to make you aware of its potential, and give you a handle on how to use its power to your advantage.

As I see it, there are two aspects to publicity; one is working with the news media, and the other is "other." This could be networking, or doing good works in your community, or hosting a special event—anything you personally can do to keep people saying good things about you and your business. When it comes to working with the news media, there are standard methods and procedures that public relations people have developed over the years. I've collaborated with an expert in that field to bring you the tips and pitfalls in this chapter.

Example 10-1: Press Release from IBAW Kit
Used by permission of Independent Bankers Association of Wisconsin.

Independent Bankers Association of Wisconsin
Independently Healthy™ Promotion

News Release

For more information contact:
Robert Gorsuch, President
David Glomp, Executive Director
Independent Bankers Association of Wisconsin (IBAW)
7818 Big Sky Drive
Madison, WI 53719
(608) 833-4229

For immediate release:

Wisconsin Independent Bankers Fear Proposed Banking Reforms Could Hurt State

Proposed changes in the banking system have sparked national controversy but nowhere is the discussion hotter than with the over 400 independent community banks of Wisconsin. "If the current broad banking reform package were to pass as proposed it could have a major negative effect on Wisconsin's economy," says Robert Gorsuch, president of the Independent Bankers Association of Wisconsin (IBAW), the trade group for Wisconsin's locally owned and operated banks.

Current treasury proposals being considered include limiting deposit insurance coverage, toughening regulations, allowing banks to branch nationwide, affiliation with securities firms, and enabling industrial companies to own banks.

Gorsuch, who is also president of Madison's Park Bank, was among a group of Wisconsin bankers that took their concerns to Washington, D.C. recently for a meeting with the staffs of all nine Wisconsin Congressmen and two U.S. Senators. They presented their "Summary of Wisconsin Banking Industry Posters On Deposit Insurance Reform and Related Federal Financial Legislative Issues."

The bankers say they acknowledge that the nation's deposit insurance is in need of reform, but they want changes to be undertaken carefully and with a full understanding of the implications of the various proposals on the nation's banks, economy and financial delivery system. They presented their suggestions for what they believe would be more responsible changes.

"Deposit insurance is fundamental to our proposals which are designed to make the system safer and more equitable while avoiding problems for the economy," Gorsuch says. "We're urging Congress to enact comprehensive legislation this year that strengthens the financial marketplace, banking and the overall financial system. Addressing FDIC insur-

Example 10-1: Press Release from IBAW Kit (continued)
Used by permission of Independent Bankers Association of Wisconsin.

ance fund and the related deposit insurance reform issues must be dealt with to insure continued overall consumer confidence in the system. It is also recognized that some of the financial reform issues may require more time and study."

One of the major concerns of the IBAW is that current proposals will take the control of deposits and lending away from Wisconsin community banks and put it in the hands of large institutions elsewhere. David Glomp, the organization's executive director, met recently with Governor Thompson's office and State Banking Commissioner, Toby Sherry to present the banker's views at the state level. "We need to raise awareness with the business community and public on what these changes will mean in Wisconsin," Glomp says. "The potential negative effects of these dollars leaving our state should be of major concern."

Glomp echoed the sentiments of Toby Sherry when he spoke in favor of keeping Wisconsin dollars close to home. "Our deposits are best managed by local people who know their customers and invest back into the communities they serve. Our banks help entrepreneurial start-ups and aid greatly in Wisconsin's overall growth and prosperity. If these dollars end up in the control of large national banks with only branches here, a lot of money is going to go elsewhere."

Add to these concerns the fact that larger, nationally operated financial institutions are more likely than Wisconsin banks to have problems. According to the Federal Deposit Insurance Corporation, while the number of troubled banks is actually falling, more assets are in danger because more large banks are having problems. And George Gregorash, an executive in the Federal Reserve Bank of Chicago's supervision and regulation office confirms that cautious tactics have kept banks in the Great Lakes region operating as the pillars of strength while some banks in other regions struggle.

The Wisconsin Independent Bankers believe that Wisconsin shouldn't be penalized for the mistakes of financial institutions in other areas of the country. "The safety and security of our banks is a shining example of our conservative midwestern banking practices," Glomp says.

Even though proposed changes haven't yet been enacted, a Wall Street Journal report confirms that at least some of the Wisconsin banker's fears are justified. According to their report, banking reform proposals are already rattling the system and making the credit crunch worse. Large depositors concerned about limits on deposit insurance are reducing the amount of deposits beyond the current $100 per account ceiling. The loss of these large depositors makes it difficult for small banks to make loans which hinders economic recovery.

"Our banks are already losing some of their biggest depositors because of the proposals being considered in Washington to limit the scope of deposit insurance," Glomp says. "We're not against reform, but policy makers need to consider the impact of what they are proposing," he says.

The IBAW is currently conducting a letter writing campaign from their banks to government leaders and plans further lobbying efforts at the state Capitol and in Washington. Efforts to rally the support of financial, business and consumer groups in Wisconsin who will be impacted by the proposed changes are also planned.

What Publicity Is—And Isn't

Publicity is an often misunderstood component of communication programs—misunderstood even by professionals in the related fields of advertising and marketing. It is often easier to define publicity by saying what it is not.

Let's separate publicity from the other communications functions:

1. Publicity is not public relations; it is only a part of that larger concept. While public relations often includes a major publicity component, it embraces overarching strategy, tactics, public opinion research, internal management decisions, relationships with multiple audiences, and more. Describing the entire public relations function is beyond the scope of this book. We are going to focus on only one of its tools, publicity.

2. Publicity is not paid advertising. If you pay for advertising time or space to distribute the message, that message is advertising. If you pay to create the message, but offer it to news media and other sources of distribution as potential editorial material, that is publicity.

   It is not free advertising, either, because it does generate business costs and should be budgeted for like any other expense. It is often thought of as free advertising because any space or exposure it generates is not billed for.

   Publicity generates coverage in the news sections of newspapers, magazines, and broadcasts. It should never be referred to as free advertising. *News organizations do not do free advertising.* They will be offended if you even suggest that you think of it that way. They provide their readers, listeners, and viewers with the information they think is newsworthy. If that information concerns your business or organization, that's great for you—but it isn't free advertising. It's publicity.

3. Publicity is not marketing. Publicity can be an important supporting component of marketing, providing name recognition for businesses and products, but marketing is a broad category of activity of which publicity is only one component.

Here is a working definition of publicity: Publicity is the result of any action, by any means, taken by any person or business, to let at least one other person (but often hundreds or thousands more) know something about that person or business.

Publicity is a very powerful communications tool. Like any other tool, it can be very effective in advancing the fortunes of those who use it. However, if its power is ignored or if it is handled in anything less than a systematic and well-thought-out way, it can lead to widespread and long-lasting damage. Later in this chapter we'll talk about bad publicity—what to do when bad news makes the media come looking for you.

Tip: Remember, it is impossible to retrieve the sound of a rung bell. If you are going to use the publicity tools in this chapter, use them wisely.

The Big Picture: Publicity's Place in the Advertising Process

Publicity often enjoys an intimate, integrated relationship with other advertising methods. A well-managed publicity program is a partner with your paid advertising campaign or direct mail program. It puts additional power behind those thrusts.

For example, news about the launch of a new advertising campaign is an awareness builder, prompting audiences to look for the paid campaign when it appears. If it is innovative, the publicity campaign can generate additional mentions and coverage, boosting the impact of the paid advertising when it runs.

Here's an instance of this in my community in Wisconsin—Mosquito Country in the summer. A company that installs screen rooms and porches bought a billboard at the busiest intersection in town during the hottest part of the year. It went up (just by coincidence) during a warm, wet spell that had record mosquito hatches popping out. The graphic was a picture of a giant mosquito with a stinger extending 18 feet out from the board—and the owner of the business had the sense to know a "photo opportunity" when he had one. His publicity efforts got a local TV news crew out in front of the billboard doing their weather forecast. The advertiser got more exposure than if he'd paid for a sixty-second commercial in that time slot.

The same principle applies to marketing efforts. Publicity can be an amplifier of product expansions and introductions. Are you introducing new products, changing your pricing structure, expanding a line of goods, or making other strategy innovations in your marketing? Publicize it! The trade press is particularly interested in this type of news. The marketing publications, like *Adweek*, *Business Marketing*, and *Advertising Age*, and the trade publications for your industry will be likely to use this type of story.

Perhaps the most notorious example of a marketing decision generating tremendous amounts of worldwide publicity was the introduction of New Coca-Cola in the 1980s. When this product was introduced as a replacement for traditional Coca-Cola, the company garnered much more publicity than it had intended. It seems that in all the Coca-Cola Company's communications about the new product, it had never fully explained that the new brand would replace the traditional favorite product. This was to be a product substitution, not a line extension. When the public realized that the old favorite was disappearing, the publicity generated went global to millions. As a result of the outcry, the traditional product was re-introduced and named Classic Coke.

Some media insiders speculated that this was all calculated to generate such publicity.

According to one Coca-Cola advertising executive, however, "We are neither that stupid nor that clever."

This example reminds us that not all publicity originates within a business. Quite often internal decisions create powerful outside publicity forces. Sometimes that publicity is favorable—and sometimes not.

Some publicity is geared to stand alone. Other publicity programs are integrated with the other components of your advertising and marketing. How are these two approaches different? If you send out a news release on your election to office in a service club, that's *stand-alone* publicity, carried out to keep your name high-profile in your community. If you are opening a new store, and you invite the press to attend a public grand-opening event, timed to coincide with a paid advertising campaign, that's *integrated* publicity. The other components might be radio, print ads, or direct mail (sending out invitations) to publicize the event, and of course the event itself is a planned promotional activity.

Obviously, in order to participate in a publicity program, you are going to have to get organized. The next section of this chapter deals with how you will plan your activity and how you will manage your follow-through.

Organizing Your Publicity Activities: A Place and a Plan

Every aspect of your business deserves a plan. Your publicity efforts are no different. We've introduced the practice of publicity. We've talked about how it relates to the other aspects of your advertising and promotional activities—where publicity overlaps, and where it stands alone.

You'll need to learn a lot more about publicity before you're ready to finalize your plan—and that's what this chapter is about. Let's take a look at where it's all going. The publicity plan will be a document you write, composed of an assortment of calendars, budgets, and templates for letters and news releases. I recommend a ring binder for keeping this plan organized and up to date. In addition, you'll have a collection of files and collateral materials—your press kits, brochures, photos, stationery for correspondence, files on your contacts, and more.

There's an administrative aspect to a publicity program that requires some organization. Since you'll be stocking and mailing materials, you'll need a mailing center. Design a system for yourself that includes a way to keep files current and storage space for the printed pieces. You'll need at least twenty-five file folders and labels to get your system started. If you're comfortably computerized, then most of this can be a hierarchy on your hard drive. Even so, you will have physical elements as well—newspaper clippings, letters received, copies of enclosures, and other "hard copy." If you don't want to scan all this into your computer, you'd better set up your physical files.

Your contact files are a very important component of your publicity activity. Your contacts might be reporters and editors at the newspapers or radio or TV stations, or they might be industry leaders, political pace-setters, or others who influence public opinion that affects you. Set up a file for each person. Then each time you send a person something, note what it was in his or her individual file or include a copy.

As you might imagine, the same kind of follow-through in contact maintenance that gets some salespeople to the top is what you need to make your publicity efforts hit new heights. Create a system that lets you build information about each contact. It's critical that you keep track of who got what. You will be filing

- Letters (both received and sent)
- Copies or notes of everything you've enclosed with letters
- Notes on phone conversations and personal contacts

- Clippings and notes that might help you tailor your future correspondence more closely to this person

In addition to contact files, you will have general files where you will put

- Media lists (names and phone numbers, and photocopy label master sets)
- Glossy photos for sending to media
- Industry news clippings
- Quotes (testimonials, or anything newsworthy)
- Rough ideas and brainstorms

A calendar is one of the most important tools of your publicity plan. There will be a copy of the calendar in your notebook, but it won't work for you unless it's integrated with (1) your daily appointment calendar and (2) the calendar you use for setting overall business goals and timelines. Take some time to think this through. Where will you post a master calendar for the year? How will you follow through on your commitment to use it, updating it as plans change? Remember, you don't want it where the public might see it—your competitors would love to know what's coming up. Also, don't post it where it will drive you crazy wondering how you'll get it all done. That rules out directly over your desk.

On the wall near your mailing center, or wherever you store often-used supplies, a wall calendar showing the full year will help you keep your "big picture" business plan connected with each component of its success, including publicity activity. The calendars available from Re-Markable Products are good because they allow you to wipe off old notes and replace them as plans change. Many printers give away printed year-at-a-glance calendars as a planning tool for their customers. It shouldn't be hard to find the tool you need.

To use your time efficiently, keep all your marketing-related materials and activities together. You should have a place for files in or near your desk where you can keep your marketing and advertising plans, your media planning notes and rate kits, your direct mail program materials, and your publicity plans and contact files.

Let's take a closer look at the publicity planner—your ring binder. The notebook you keep will have sections for

- *Goals*. Summarize the objectives you expect to accomplish.

- *Strategy*. Explain your action plan and the rationale supporting it.

- *Distribution channels*. This is the place to summarize your contact lists and intended media outlets. Reference where the supporting information is filed—where the actual photocopy label masters are kept, and that sort of thing.

- *Audience*. Describe the audience you are expecting to reach through your publicity channels. Who is the end consumer of the information you are disseminating?

- *Calendar*. Keep a current copy of your year's schedule here. Update it as plans change.

- *Budget*. Summarize the estimated costs for each area of activity, from the supplies necessary to set up your filing system to the cost of each mailing. For example, let's assume you want to create a press kit. It will consist of a printed folder housing a news release, a glossy photo, several pages of background material, a copy of your corporate brochure, and of course a business card. (Later in this chapter we'll describe each of these components in more detail.) You will need to estimate the cost of printing the folder and the cost for printing or copying the news release and background information. You might have a detailed budget elsewhere for the brochure. Look up that total, and figure the per-piece cost. Then calculate how many pieces will be set aside for use in

the press kits, and carry that cost here. We'll talk about budgeting in more detail later in this chapter.

- *Templates for standard letters, news releases, etc*. In this chapter you'll find templates for all kinds of publicity correspondence. Adapt these for your own use—you will find your own customized templates very useful. Set these up in your word processing program.

Your publicity notebook is a master plan. It guides you in the execution of your publicity activities throughout the year. It stands ready to help you answer questions when the media call—in response to your mailings, or out of the blue. The rest of this chapter will deal with the specifics of each area. When you are finished with this chapter, you will have the necessary tools to create and implement your own plan.

Choosing a Publicity Strategy

Developing Your Message

The rock on which any publicity effort depends is message development. Simply put, what is it you want to say about your business?

Believe it or not, this step is often overlooked by many businesses. Without a clear message, clearly communicated, it is impossible to "stay on message," as the political consultants say. Without this foundation, it is impossible to prevent fuzzy focus, not to mention confusion about what it is you want to say.

Developing a clear, concise message about your business is a useful exercise. The review of your business activity stimulates a fresh look at what you are doing. It can foster creative approaches to old problems and help you discover new areas of opportunity for publicity. See Chapter 2, "Positioning," for worksheets to help you do this. Template 10-1 will help you organize your publicity strategy. Template 10-1A gives the strategy for the independent community banks. Template 10-1B is a blank form that you can use.

The fundamental message that you develop can be simple or complex, but it must be simply stated here. Otherwise, you might seriously overload the attention span of your audience by giving them too much information.

Tip: The sound bite in modern American politics has its origin in the demands of television. In that medium, thirty seconds is an average story, and three minutes is a long one. If your message won't fit, it might not be used at all—or worse, it might be distorted by cutting.

Message development depends on a series of basic questions and answers: Who are you? What is it that you do? Where do you do it? Why do you do it? What benefits are generated by your doing it? Why would this be of interest to anyone else? What proof do you offer for your claims and statements?

You can't talk about message development in a vacuum. You must know your target audience. Who do you want to know what?

The answer to the audience question (and there often are multiple audiences) will suggest the publicity methods you should use.

For example, suppose you are a manufacturer of bread-making equipment and you are bringing out a new line of ovens. If that is your message, the baking trade press is your medium of choice, and the message should be tailored to that audience. If your new line of ovens requires a 50,000-square-foot addition to your manufacturing facility and the addition of 150 new skilled trade jobs, that is a story of great interest to the media that cover your community. Now you have added a different message, and it should be tailored accordingly.

The first message will require a press release to the trade magazines this company subscribes to, or advertises in. It also goes to the local business reporters.

A second news release will not go to the trade press, but will be of great interest to local city beat and business reporters.

This company could even come up with a feature story angle, perhaps some recipes designed for the new oven, and send that news release to the food editor.

Example 10-2 shows how a news release to the trade press would read.

Example 10-2: News Release

NEWS RELEASE
contact information
For Release: April 2, 1995
Headline:

HABBERT HOT-SIDER STANDS OUT BY STANDING BACK

Oven technology takes on a new dimension with the arrival of the Hot-Sider from Habbert. It stands only 36" out from its wall mounting, but through unique engineering manages to produce more baked goods per hour than other ovens even twice its size.

Company President Delbert Habbert, Jr. stated, "This is a breakthrough for our industry. We were the first to develop this technology."

For more information, contact the Habbert dealer in your area or dial 1-800-HOTSIDE.

-30-

Photo enclosed

Example 10-3 demonstrates the difference when the story is pitched to the local
business press.

Example 10-3: News Release

NEWS RELEASE
contact information
For Release: April 2, 1995
headline:

HABBERT MANUFACTURING TO ADD 150 JOBS TO LOCAL ECONOMY

COLUMBUS — The Habbert Manufacturing Company, local manufacturers of bakery equipment and supplies, has announced today plans to hire more than 150 workers in a variety of positions to bring on-line its new production facility located outside of Columbus.

Company President Delbert Habbert, Jr. has stated that the success of his company's new Hot-Sider oven, an innovation in baking equipment, has met with such strong success that the new production facility will be brought on line as soon as possible. "This is a breakthrough for our industry, and since we were the first to develop this technology, our facility is the only one that can meet what we feel will be strong demand for years to come," he said.

While the new facility is being built, production of the ovens will continue at the Habbert Lane facility downtown with a second shift added.

Construction bids for the new building have yet to be let. Meanwhile, the company is seeking applications from skilled workers from welders to electricians to staff the new facility. All interested workers are requested to contact the Habbert personnel office starting on Monday. Written applications are suggested, but for those with questions, call 1-800-555-OVENS.

NEW OVEN FACILITY FOR HABBERT — ADD 1

In a related development, Mr. Habbert released a letter from the Mayor of Columbus and Rye County executive Ed Wheat stating that this development is most welcome for the employment picture in the city and county. "This will again show that the people of Rye County and Columbus have the skills required to meet the needs of this modern plant," said Mayor Bunn.

The plant, when fully staffed, is expected to be able to make 250 of the ovens per day. Mike Yeast, representative of the local labor union, also praised the move. "We knew our workers were the best in the business, and this is yet another opportunity for them to show what they can do. We look forward to this new facility."

Mr. Habbert said that further information, including that on the awarding of major construction contracts, will be released at the appropriate time.

-30-

Message development is different for each of these audiences. The trade journal is interested in the performance of the oven. The hometown press is interested in the performance of the company. And the food editor is interested in the performance of the recipes. With each pursuing its own interest, the net result is good publicity exposure for the Habbert company. For each audience, you would fill out Template 10-1B differently.

To prepare your publicity message, you will want to review your answers to the business review exercise in Chapter 1, as well as the positioning exercises in Chapter 2. The theme you developed in Chapter 5, "The Creative Approach," will be relevant here as well. While those chapters are talking about crafting an advertising message, there are many overlaps with the publicity activity. Everybody's trying to sell something to somebody—and only a fraction of the time are we using paid advertising to do it.

Template 10-1A: Statement of Publicity Strategy

Statement of Publicity Strategy

Publicity will convince _____ business decision makers _____
(audience(s))

that _____ an independent community bank _____
(your product or service)

is or will _____ provide stable, conservative service _____.
(message)

This will be attributed to _____ local ownership, independent decision making _____.
(feature/rationale)

This is newsworthy because _____ failing savings and loans are _____
(describe benefit to audience of knowing this information)

_____ hurting the credibility of banks in general _____.

Distribution of the message will be via _____ local newspapers and radio stations.
(describe media channels)

_____.

Template 10-1B: Statement of Publicity Strategy

Statement of Publicity Strategy

Publicity will convince _____
(audience(s))

that _____
(your product or service)

is or will _____.
(message)

This will be attributed to _____.
(feature/rationale)

This is newsworthy because _____
(describe benefit to audience of knowing this information)

_____.

Distribution of the message will be via _____
(describe media channels)

_____.

Finding Opportunities for Publicity

Before you can put your publicity campaign into action, you've got to choose the mix of methods you'll use to distribute the message. There are four basic ways to spread publicity.

Word of Mouth. This is perhaps one of the most effective publicity methods known. It is very slow to work in many instances, especially where new products are concerned, but it is very quick when bad news is involved. For example, a survey taken in the past by a major automobile manufacturer revealed that if a car owner had a good experience with his or her dealer, he or she was likely to tell three people. If the experience was a bad one, the car owner was likely to let more than ten people know of it.

Sponsorships and collaborations with other businesses are an excellent way to stimulate word-of-mouth publicity. If you sponsor a local sports team or support a fund-raising event, make sure your business name is prominently featured in that activity.

The first case study at the end of this chapter shows one individual's creative use of word of mouth to market his real estate consulting to other businesses.

Employee Communications. You might think this applies only to larger organizations. Not so! No matter what the size of your business, your employees are very effective communicators about it because, among other things, they are insiders. They must know your message and communicate it to their friends, families, colleagues, and others. They are a prime source of personal information about your business in your community. This points out the importance of effective message development. Do your employees have the right message on the tips of their tongues? Don't leave this up to chance. I know of one company that used a little game during a staff meeting to develop employee publicity skills. Employees were asked, "If you had five minutes on David Letterman's show to talk about this business, what would you say?" The resulting conversation (which was hilarious) gave the employer an opportunity to brief the staff on the right message to communicate.

It's possible that you or your employees will be asked to speak at service organizations, knife and fork clubs, and similar gatherings. Don't let this opportunity go to waste! Before you or one of your employees speaks in public, review the message. Is it current and correct?

Pitfall: It is a great mistake for anyone to talk about a business without knowing all the facts. Make sure your designated spokespeople have accurate information.

Creating a speakers' bureau is an excellent idea. If members of your staff have expertise in different areas, find out who would be comfortable speaking on what topic, and make local organizations aware of what you have to offer.

Special Events. These planned events can be a great source of publicity, when carefully thought out and executed. The event itself can generate news coverage and often expand the audience for your message. Get involved in your community, and get your community involved with your business. You can do this through events, open houses, plant tours, and hosting visits for the media. In Chapter 3, "Promotions," we talk more about this technique.

Traditional Publicity Methods. When we talk about publicity, most people think of working with the news media, via releases tailored for print media or broadcasters, pictures and graphics, press kits, and news conferences. And indeed, this is a primary activity in generating publicity for your company. So let's talk in more detail about how you go about generating publicity in the local media. We'll talk about how to choose a story angle, and how to work with the news media to increase the chance that your story will be used. We'll address the problem that arises when negative publicity comes looking for you. The templates provided will help you write the pieces you'll need to execute a publicity campaign.

Story Angles

Publicity has this advantage over advertising: It has credibility. When people read an advertising message, they often respond cautiously, on guard against a sales pitch. On the other hand, publicity presents straightforward information in the same familiar form in which other news reaches them. Your audience will often accept your message more willingly in the news media.

However, your news has to compete with other news stories for space and time. The key to getting your story placed successfully lies, therefore, in the newsworthiness of the material.

Your message is going to be scrutinized by hawkeye news editors long before the public sees it. They are the gatekeepers, holding the keys to your access to the media. Their chief question about your materials will be: Is this of interest or service to my readers, viewers, and listeners? If the answer is no, the editors won't use it. If it is yes, and the story is strongly and clearly presented, they probably will use it. Unlike paid ads, publicity comes without guarantees of any kind.

Pitfall: Be aware that when you call attention to yourself with a publicity effort, the news media won't limit themselves to reporting only good news. That's not their job. Informing their readers, viewers, and listeners is. If you have some news that you would rather the fewest number of people know about, think twice about publicity. If you have adverse news of some kind, develop a strategy to deal with it, and then go ahead.

When you present your story to the media, you can choose one of two approaches. You might send a news release informing them about an event or issue that they can write a story about. Or you might actually send a story, written by you, that they can choose to use as is or rewrite to suit their needs. The approach you choose will depend on your skill as a writer. If you can write the story well, do so. All journalists are overworked, and your help with the legwork will be appreciated. (But remember, your story should not be overtly promotional of your own interests. You're not writing advertising copy.)

Whether you are doing a news release or writing the full story, you will need to think about the story angle you will present.

Here are some categories into which your stories might fall:

- *Straight news.* This includes announcements of information or events that are of potential interest to the general public or specific groups. You can manufacture newsworthy events by sponsoring a workshop, hosting a celebrity appearance, etc. Your introduction of new products or services may also qualify as straight news. On a slow news day, even a story like the one in Example 10-4 can get in the paper.

Example 10-4: White Space Moves

State Journal photos/JOSEPH W. JACKSON III

Graphic design office on the move

Sara White, owner of White Space, a graphic design business with two employees, spends part of her first day in her new, mostly white office getting organized Monday. White, who moved out of an office at 121 S. Pinkney St. because of a lack of parking, is the latest of a series of new tenants in the old Gardner Baking Co. building (left photo) at East Wash- ington Avenue and Paterson Street. A spokesman for Hyperion Studios, another tenant, says the building's 32,000 square feet on the first and second floors are now more than 80 percent leased. Roberts Construction Associates, which has been renovating the building, occupies a middle portion of the building, including a penthouse office.

This is a minor example of the "photo op," or opportunity. Many straight news stories include announcements of photo opportunities. The 10,000th visitor to your miniature golf course or the first class of graduates from your flight training school or the first pot out of your new kiln can qualify. It's easy to imagine what might make a good photo op for your business. Study the business coverage in your local media and you'll quickly get an idea of the types of photos or footage they like to use.

- *Feature stories.* Features explore subjects of interest to the public that are not related to a current or future event. Ask yourself, "What do I know well that the general public should know, or would find interesting?" In your answer lies your potential feature story. How-to stories are particularly good. The benefit to you comes from the way a feature story establishes your credibility. See the first case study at the end of this chapter: Derrick used a feature story approach when he placed his story on lease vs. buy decisions.

  Feature stories are usually of greater length than straight news stories. Many features are written so that they could run at any time; these are called "evergreen" stories.

- *Concepts.* A concept article describes the basic concept of your area of business, and why people should take advantage of what you and your competitors offer. For instance, a graphic designer might write an article on why a business considering a brochure should hire a design firm specializing in print rather than a full-service ad agency. Note that the article will be general, not specific in recommending the author's firm. The reader will not miss the unstated message that the people who wrote the article, or are quoted in it, are experts in the field.

- *Opinions.* Where controversy exists, so do opinions. You can reinforce your leadership image by taking a stand and publicizing it. You could write a letter to the editor, or detail your point of view in an article and submit it to the appropriate news contacts. Over time, the media may come to rely on you as a source of input for issues relevant to your field. Don't be afraid to have an opinion! To those who agree with you, it confirms your reputation as an expert in your field. To those who disagree, you are still perceived as one who is willing to speak your mind.

- *Public service announcements (PSAs).* The media run PSAs free, when time and space are available. Because of the law of supply and demand, broadcast media are more willing to run PSAs than print media will be. The broadcast media have a set number of minutes to fill, and if the time is not purchased, your PSA is a good candidate to fill the unused time. Are you involved in good works in your community? Put together a PSA script for radio or TV and get the good word out.

  Pitfall: It is unfair, and damaging to good media relations, to request that one medium run public service announcements for no fee when you are paying for advertising time or space in another medium.

  Example: For more than 100 years, the State Historical Society of Wisconsin had used publicity to promote its activities. In recent times, the Historical Society began an extensive PSA operation to promote visits to historic tourist sites. It sent both written and recorded public service announcements to radio stations, to be aired free of charge. When the Historical Society finally began a small paid advertising program, the nature of the message (maps, coupons, dates, hours) dictated that the medium be print newspaper ads.

But what about the public service announcements in the hands of radio stations? The society solved the dilemma through a firm commitment to good media relations. It sent a letter to radio stations outlining the strategy on the paid print campaign, including a request that the PSAs continue to be used, and also explaining that if it was not given air time, the organization would fully understand in light of the paid campaign. Many stations dropped the PSAs in favor of those of other organizations they wished to support that had no advertising budget. However, many other stations continued to use the spots because they believed in the goals of the Historical Society. The launch of the paid campaign even received some publicity.

Result: The paid campaign was launched without ruffling the feathers of long-time supporters from the media, and the society got good marks for being a square shooter in media relations.

When you work closely with your media contacts, feeding them newsworthy stories on a regular basis, you gain an additional publicity advantage. Business editors need local contacts that they can turn to for commentary or background, to make a national news story more relevant on a local level. By demonstrating your knowledge, you position yourself as a local authority in your area of expertise. Being quoted as an expert is excellent publicity for you.

When Do You Meet The Press?

Most publicity work is done by phone, fax, and mail—you send out news releases and press kits; you find story angles and pitch them to your contacts. You mail things, and you follow up. Once in a great while you meet the press face to face, when they select you for an interview or your photo opportunity brings them out. Sometimes you call a news conference, if your announcement is so sensi-

tive that advance information can't be released. A news conference is an essential tool for releasing news to the widest possible audience at the same time. But be sparing in your use of the news conference. Stick to traditional announcements via news releases. You're more likely to see your story covered the way you like.

A politician called a news conference on the steps of the state capitol. He did reasonably well at promoting its importance, and he was joined by a dozen reporters from the local media. Unfortunately for him, the city jail was just a block away. An inmate chose that moment for a breakout attempt. Word came over the cellular phones to the reporters, and off they dashed in pursuit of a hotter story. The politician had no control over a situation that left him without the coverage he expected. While in this case the story was eventually picked up and used, you get the point. Outside events dictate the nature of the coverage. If you have a ribbon cutting scheduled for a new facility, and an hour before, the oil refinery on the other side of town blows up, don't expect much coverage. News releases may not be as gratifying to the ego as a news conference, but the written release is more reliable.

Working with the News Media

Good media relations are a basic cornerstone for the success of any publicity program. Guidelines for establishing good media relations are simple to state, but they often prove difficult to carry out. Your commitment to follow-through is so important that it bears repeating.

The force of public opinion is powerful. Perhaps the most important underlying fundamental of good publicity is that you should act ethically. Your performance as a corporate citizen is always being judged. Good media relations enhances the story of your good performance. It can minimize the damage done by negative events, but it can't change the stripes on the cat.

The following guidelines are suggestions and pointers gained through years of experience and study of media relations. It's up to you to adapt them to your particular message, audience, and situation.

When you are writing news for publicity, you are wearing the hat of a reporter covering your business. For the moment, you're working for the press. The editors who decide to cover your story are the bosses you've got to please. You will have a list of media contacts, including business writers, general news reporters, feature writers, and others, working in both print and broadcast media. If you familiarize yourself with each specific contact's needs, you can prepare your news to fit each audience. By supplying your contacts with accurate, timely information, you will earn their help in presenting your message.

Media Relations Guidelines

Once you start sending out publicity material, you will hopefully start hearing from the media. Be prepared for that phone call! They may simply want to verify information, or they may want to get additional details. Better still, they may have decided to use your material, and want to contact you for a quote, or to arrange an in-depth interview. News people are always under deadlines—drop whatever you're doing and give your full attention to that call. Have your publicity planner up to date and close to hand, so that you can answer questions on the spot.

If someone from the broadcast media contacts you, the tone of your response is especially important. You are being "auditioned" for a possible on-air interview. Be enthusiastic, speak clearly, and don't oversell.

If you should be asked to give an interview, do your homework. Be prepared to answer questions accurately and briefly. The hardest part of being interviewed is to avoid making statements that might be misunderstood if taken out of context. Make sure you understand all questions before you answer.

Ask the reporter to clarify if you find the question ambiguous. How do you keep this presence of mind when the microphones are pointed your way? Practicing in advance can help.

It is often helpful to play what might be called "Twenty Questions" as a way to prepare yourself. Ask yourself every possible question about your story and your operation. Prepare short answers. This exercise will help prevent you from being surprised by questions. It is also an exercise that can be profitably done with your staff and employees. Edited, it becomes your "Sample Interview Questions" to include in your press kit. (More about that in the next section.) Role-play the situation with someone you know, if you tend to be nervous in public-speaking situations.

Here are some pointers to help you succeed with the media.

1. *Give good service.* Provide your media contacts with all the help you are able to. This will enhance your credibility, and in time the media will begin to rely on you for the timely, factual information that they need about you, your business, or your line of work. Give direct answers to direct questions. If you don't know the facts involved, say so and offer to help find out what is requested. Always follow up.

2. *Be quotable.* Your goal is to give the media your message in a package they can easily use. One technique that works well is to restate the question as part of your answer.

   Example: Question: "Why did you decide to open a bookkeeping service?" Bad answer: "To help clients and make money." Good answer: "I decided to open my bookkeeping service because, after working part-time for a number of small businesses, I saw an opportunity to serve clients better while being my own boss."

3. *Use comparisons to add color to your comments.* Rather than describe your product by its size or weight, say, "It's about the

size of a toaster" or "It's lighter than a gallon of milk." People find comparisons more entertaining—and memorable—than straight statistics.

4. *Don't be overpromotional in your statements.* An interview is not meant to be free advertising. When you allow the interviewer to mention your product or service, you gain further credibility.

5. *Get to know the reporters who cover your activities.* They can be a good source of information that you might not otherwise obtain. When you have an opportunity to do a kind deed for a reporter, do it!

6. *Don't complain about the coverage your operation receives if it is negative, but be aggressive in correcting errors of fact.* The news media pride themselves on accuracy, and will appreciate your efforts to help them achieve it.

7. *Be available to the media whenever required—at all times if that is necessary.* You know the demands placed on the media when they are doing their job. Be especially aware of the constraints of deadlines on news people.

8. *Always assume that what you say is on the record.* If you do not want to be quoted, do not speak. There is no such thing, or at least to any reliable degree, as "off the record." Do not hesitate to say "off the record" when dealing with the news media on sensitive points. Often your wishes will be respected. But *don't count on it.*

9. *Speak in sound bites.* When you are in a news conference situation, especially with the electronic media, start with the most important item you want to express. Keep the point as simple as possible, and do not hesitate to repeat it as often as necessary.

10. *When answering questions on television, make eye contact with the questioner, not the camera.* The camera will do its work.

You concentrate on being accurate, sincere, and credible.

11. *Think positively.* Avoid comments that sound critical of others, or are generally negative in tone. Negativity reflects unflatteringly on you, even if your facts are correct.

12. *If you tell a reporter that a story is exclusive, honor that promise.* "Exclusive" means that you've released information to only one particular media outlet. This can be a useful but dangerous approach. You run the risk of offending other newspapers and stations if they did not have a chance at the story. Exclusives are to be distinguished from "enterprise journalism," when a reporter or editor initiates coverage of your operation. If a medium has "enterprised" the story and asks for an exclusive, it is generally best to honor the request. If other media complain, explain that the story was "enterprised" by someone else. Have another story ready for those who did not get the exclusive. And never play one medium or outlet off against another in any way. If you do, you will soon find yourself alone on the playground.

Before you put your foot into this heavy media traffic, note that the street goes both directions.

What if Publicity Suddenly Starts Chasing You?

Don't panic. Pull out your publicity plan and review it. Do a new set of "Twenty Questions," if needed. If publicity is now chasing you, you have either a very big hit or a world of trouble on your hands. Either way, your publicity plan will help get you through.

When the Beatles landed in New York for the first time, they thought the crowd was for someone else. And the owners of the White Star Line never planned for the fact that their unsinkable *Titanic* wouldn't reach that same city on its first voyage.

What are you prepared to say when the big lights hit you? Is your background statement in order and up to date? Are your people informed about company policy? Are they ready to spread the right message on a moment's notice?

Have you ascertained the facts of the item that has caused all this attention? What can you say with certainty? Remember, you may have to live with the things you say now for a very long time.

Many events over which you have no control can bring the media to your door. Natural disaster can strike. Product recalls and lawsuits may be possibilities. A lean financial year can result in layoffs and cutbacks that have the press at your door looking for explanations.

Here is our advice on how to handle any publicity, but especially the negative kind:

1. Honesty is the best policy. This may be painful at certain times, but you *must* be honest with the media. It is better to say nothing (and that is quite appropriate under certain circumstances) than to give out falsehoods. This does not mean that you need to tell all you know. It means that what you say should be truthful to the best of your knowledge. In the long run, honesty is always the best path.

2. When answering a question, do not repeat a reporter's incorrect statements. The repeated inaccurate information might be the only part of your words that are quoted. You don't want to be quoted in the paper as saying, "Who cares if he says I'm a crook?" It doesn't cast you in a very good light.

    Tell only what you know and want to state publicly. Remember the impossibility of retrieving the sound of a rung bell.

3. When you have given your complete answer to a question, and a silence ensues, *leave* it silent. Provide additional information or details only if it will help clarify information.

4. Don't try to kill a story. You may know that the media already have a story that you would like to see suppressed. Resist your urge to use your influence to bury it. Work with the media on unfavorable news and you will be rewarded with less damage than you might have otherwise sustained.

    Attempts at censorship or suppression will backfire every time, and are likely to have two immediate undesirable consequences: (1) increased interest in the matter and (2) unfavorable coverage of your attempt to suppress information.

    Note: This point is negotiable. There may be very valid reasons for information not to be reported. It may not be proper or safe for you to tell all you know. Trouble comes with situations involving death, theft, or fraud. If there is a police investigation, details may have to be withheld for purposes of identifying suspects. Explain the circumstances. News reporters will often respect your wish not to release information about sensitive matters. Remember, information evolves in troublesome situations. Once you know the facts, release them.

In all your dealings with the media, keep in mind that you can control what you say during any interview or other contact. It is your responsibility as a communicator to be in control. It is your job to present a fair, complete, and accurate picture of the story you are involved with. Protect your credibility at all times. You will need it in the future.

Implementing a Publicity Plan

How do you deliver your publicity message? Early in this chapter we talked about four methods: word of mouth, employee relations, special events, and communication with the traditional news media. The first three are fairly easy to implement once you've decided to take action. You simply lay the groundwork, plan the event, hold the meeting, make the speech—whatever your plan calls for.

Dealing with the news media takes more formal implementation.

Let's assume that you want to generate favorable publicity in your local newspaper, and on radio and television stations. What is your next step? Make a list of publicity materials that you will need. This includes the following:

- *News release letterhead.* This can be a variation on your business stationery. If your letterhead is appropriate, just add the word NEWS at the top of the sheet. Some companies print special news release stationery in attention-getting colors.

- *Press kits.* If you have multiple materials—fact sheets, photos, etc.—you will need a way to package them. A simple file folder will do. Most newsrooms are jammed with paper, and a fancy cover won't make much difference if it lands in the round file. However, a file folder might just end up in a vertical file or desk cubbyhole, to your advantage. We'll talk more about creating special-subject press kits in the next section.

- *Envelopes.* Your standard business envelopes may not be large enough for the publicity materials you mail. Get printed mailing labels, or have large envelopes (9" x 12") printed with your address. If you're mailing an announcement of a specific event, promote that on the envelope. If your press kit includes audio tapes or videotapes, buy appropriate mailers.

- *Audio tapes.* These can be used to send recordings of interviews with key personnel or short public service announcements about your business or event. They should be clearly labeled.

- *Videotapes.* There is some debate about the value of this rather expensive item in the publicity mix. If you can easily afford a few

nonreturnable tapes, fine. Make sure the video is of high quality, shot by a professional. Before you proceed, find out what format tape the stations in your area can most easily use.

Tip: Stock footage of your operation might be of value to television stations, particularly if parts of your operation are difficult for a TV news crew to capture. When the press has videotapes available, it is easier for them to cover ongoing stories about your specific business or your field in general. Provide them with a tape including shots of your operation, production processes, or service staff in action, your building, and key personnel. Again, clearly label what segments are on the tape and their running time in minutes and seconds. Remember to send the media updated material every year or so if you expect to be dealing with them on a regular basis.

The video press release is a special animal. If you feel this medium is appropriate to you, consult a public relations professional before you proceed on your own.

The Press Kit: Beyond the News Release

For a simple announcement like a staff promotion or hiring a new employee, a straight news release and perhaps a photo is all you will need to prepare. In most situations, however, you will want to have additional materials ready to go, and that means building your press kit. A press kit can be generic, simply describing your company and its offerings, but press kits usually have a specific subject. A press kit is very useful in the introduction of a new product or announcing a special event. The press kit will have one or more of these components:

- *How to contact you.* Enclose a business card or a Rolodex card with your name, address, and phone number.

- *News release.* Write the story the way you'd like to see it told. Create a headline that tells succinctly what the story is about, who should be interested, and why. Write a lead paragraph that contains the elements a journalist looks for: who, what, where, when, why. Choose your story angle, and write as much or as little as necessary. If you're unfamiliar with writing news, study the subject. Read the paper and pay attention to how each story is structured. Most news stories follow the pyramid structure: All the most important facts are in the first paragraph, then the supporting information unfolds in a hierarchy leading down to the least important fact. This way the story can be edited quickly by simply lopping off the last paragraphs if there is no room for the complete article as written. You'll find more tips on writing the news release in the templates at the end of this section.

- *Photos.* Take, or have taken, high-quality photographs of what you want to illustrate. Even though we all own cameras, very few of us should take our own publicity photos. Proper lenses, lighting, composition, and exposure are critical to creating a good photograph. And the press won't use a bad one. There is no point in incurring the expense of multiple sets of duplicate photos if your original photos are bad. Always include a caption (often called a cut line) firmly attached to each photo, including the date taken.

  Tip: Good photography can serve multiple purposes in your promotional efforts. Photos can be used in brochures, advertisements, company manuals, and other applications. Plan your photo shoot accordingly. Prepare a schedule of shots for your photographer. A day of shooting can provide a bank of material for use well into the future. If you are planning a special event, don't forget to arrange for a photographer (video or stills) to be there!

- *Fact sheet.* State the bare-bones information about your business. This can include number of employees, date of founding, principal officers, lists of products and services, dollar volume of business, locations of operations, and other such information. It should not be more than one or two pages. Type it on your business stationery with the words "FACT SHEET" at the top of the page. Its purpose is to provide the media with instant information on the background and significance of the subject of the kit.

- *Background information sheet.* This can include information on your particular business and its relationship to its community, its past achievements, how it fits into its related industry, trends in the business, outlooks for the future. In short, it summarizes anything that might be useful for news people to know when they write about you or your business.

- *Personnel sketches.* This can include brief one- or two-paragraph statements about the people who are involved in the story you want to get across. This helps news people set up interviews and know who the players are. This is not a full resume, but a summary of the facts that best illustrate each person's relevant credentials. You might include education, awards received, professional experience, and other achievements.

- *Other components.* A press kit can include many more pieces, depending on the subject for which it is organized. For example, a simple black-and-white line-drawn *map* can be a key element if the location of your business, event, or activity is crucial to coverage of your story. This can also be a useful part of general information material and can be used in brochures, ads, etc. A map can be vital to news people who want to come and cover your story. (Be sure to include times of operation and when gates and doors are open for visitors.)

Copies of *news articles*, or quotes from them, are helpful in conveying the newsworthiness of your subject. Preparing *sample interview questions* can help harried reporters fit you into their schedules by reducing the time they need to spend preparing. Base these questions on the main points you'd like to get across.

Your *brochure* or *catalog* belongs in the kit if it's relevant to the subject. Your *financial information* may be pertinent. Copies of *testimonials* and *complimentary letters* may be included as well.

Once you've assembled your press kit, put a complete copy and a description of how you've used it in your publicity plan notebook. Also note who received it, and when.

Table of Contents for a Press Kit

Must have:
File folder or pocket folder to hold everything
Business card or Rolodex card
News release
Photos
Fact sheet
Personnel sketches

Maybe:
Map
Press clippings or quotes from them
Sample interview questions
Brochure
Catalog
Financial information
Copies of testimonials and complimentary letters

Timing Your Publicity Efforts

Timing of your publicity activity can be a crucial element in its success. Is the publicity operation keyed to a date-specific event, such as a special event or the release of a new product? Ask yourself the key question, "When do I want people to know about this?"

Getting your materials into the right hands on the right date is a *big* factor in getting your story into the press. There is such a thing as being too efficient! Don't mail materials to the press too early. A general rule is that the news people in the daily media should have your materials in hand between ten and five working days before your announcement or event, or when you would like to see coverage. For magazines, lead time is much longer. Send materials eight or nine weeks prior to the issue you'd like to be in. If you send them earlier than this, the materials can get lost. If you send them later, they may get passed over in the rush of other stories, leading to less coverage or no coverage at all for your story.

Pitfall: If at all possible, avoid last-minute distribution of news materials by fax machine. Such machines are overused, and often overjammed with material pouring into newsrooms across the country. Don't fool yourself by thinking that faxing will convince your contact that the news you've sent is urgent. The fax can be helpful in announcing press conferences if it is sent in time for the media's "budget session," when each reporter's schedule is determined. A fax is useful in accommodating last-minute changes. But don't overuse the fax; this is a pet peeve with many journalists.

Follow this timing checklist as you develop your publicity campaign:

1. Develop your message.

2. Prepare and review and double-check all materials for clear writing and accurate facts. Have someone else read your writing. Be prepared for criticism. Correct any typographical errors. Allow time in your schedule for revisions.

3. Assemble and mail or deliver materials.

4. Allow for delivery time, then make one phone call to each of the people you have sent them to, to gauge their reaction. Ask

if they have any additional questions.

Pitfall: Don't be a pest. Newsrooms are full of people who are on short deadlines. Know when those deadlines are, and do not call at busy times. The busiest time for afternoon papers is in the morning, and conversely, the busiest time for morning papers is in the afternoon and evening. Don't call television stations just before their evening news programs. The morning is better, when they are planning their coverage needs.

5. Prepare for coverage by making sure that you and others in your firm are available, well briefed to talk about your story, and aware of all the facts you are publicizing. Review your message and prepare for the phone calls that will come.

6. Keep records of all coverage. Maintain a master log or diary describing coverage, including a list of broadcast coverage. You want to get copies of the coverage whenever possible. Don't ask your news contacts to clip stories for you. Do that yourself, or work with the newspapers' public service desk for back issues. Don't ask televisions stations for copies of broadcast coverage. You or your employees can monitor broadcasts and make recordings at home, with a different station assigned to each person. File copies of the press clipping and tapes in your contact files.

7. Follow up. If you have received favorable coverage, a short thank-you note to the news people involved is always welcome. Resist the urge to call—it's just an interruption. Thanks in writing is permanent; a phone call isn't. If there have been inaccuracies in the coverage, then call and point them out so that they can be corrected. But make sure you didn't supply the inaccuracy! If you did, own up to it, and correct it as soon as possible.

8. Analyze. Look back on your effort to determine: Did you receive the kind of coverage that was helpful? What could you have done better? What worked and what didn't? Did you receive any feedback from the news media on your effort? Did the news people seem to approve or disapprove of any particular aspect of your effort or materials? Determine if any new publicity opportunities were revealed that you can use in future campaigns.

News Release Templates

Follow this outline for writing a news release. In Example 10-5, the sections have been keyed to show you how the structure works in practice.

Example 10-5: Crane Foundation Press Release
Used by permission of International Crane Foundation.

International Crane Foundation

(A) # News Release

1

(B) FOR IMMEDIATE RELEASE

(C) FOR FURTHER INFORMATION CONTACT:
David Thompson, International Crane Foundation
(608) 356-9462 (w)
(608) 233-9589 (h)

(A) **SECOND FRONT IN BATTLE TO SAVE WHOOPING CRANES
OPENS AT WISCONSIN'S INTERNATIONAL CRANE FOUNDATION**

(B) An important turning point in the battle to prevent the extinction of North America's rarest crane will be realized this November in Baraboo, Wisconsin, with the arrival fo 22 whooping cranes. The birds are being shipped to the International Crane Foundation (ICF) from the only captive flock of these birds, located at Patuxent Wildlife Research Center in Laurel, Maryland.

2

(C) Dr. George Archibald, co-founder and Director of the International Crane Foundation, commented on the transfer: "The slow but remarkable recovery of the whooping crane is a consequence of the species' tenacity for survival and of the cooperation between Canada and the United States. ICF is honored to join in this team effort. The whooping crane's success provides encouragement to conservation efforts for endangered species worldwide."

(D) (more)

Example 10-5: Crane Foundation Press Release (continued)
Used by permission of International Crane Foundation.

(E) Whooping Crane Transfer -- Add 1

The single captive flock is being divided for two reasons.
Establishing a second captive flock will protect the population from
potential epidemics or other disasters. In addition, the creation of
a second flock is intended to capitalize on the Foundation's record
of success in breeding cranes. Since its start in 1973, the
Foundation has successfully bred 13 of the 15 crane species, fledging
nearly 200 chicks. The Foundation was the first in North America to
breed Brolga cranes, native to Australia, and it was the first center
in the world to breed the rare Siberian and hooded cranes from Asia.

ICF ganed worldwide attention in 1982 for its breakthrough in captive
breeding, when a whooping crane named "Tex" was induced to lay eggs
after joining in mating dances with Archibald. Tex would not produce
eggs because she had become imprinted on humans, and could not
establish her natural cycle of courting and egg laying. Onceshe was
ready to produce eggs, Tex was artificially inseminated with semen
flown to ICF from the Patuxent Wildlife Research Center. Tex produced
a son named "Gee Whiz", who is now on display at the Foundation.

The plans for establishing a wild flock are dependent on producing
surplus whooping crane chicks at ICF and at Patuxent. If past ICF
success in breeding is any guide, then the future looks bright for
the endangered whooping crane.

(A) -30-

(B) Photos available: see Archibald and Gee Whiz photo enclosed in press
kit. More photos available from ICF.

(C) For further information, contact:
David Thompson, International Crane Foundation
(608) 356-9462 (w)
(608) 233-9589 (h)

George Cutlip, ICF Public Information Consultant
(608) 356-9462 (ICF)
(608) 233-3507 (h)

1. Header section
   A. This may be on your company letterhead or a specially designed news release letterhead. Either way, it should have the word "NEWS" prominently displayed at the top.
   B. Release date: "FOR IMMEDIATE RELEASE" or date. Your story will be held until this date, unless some intervening event makes it hot.
   C. Contact information. "For additional information, contact: Your name, title, company, phone, and fax."
2. Body
   A. Headline. This demonstrates your story angle and sells its key newsworthy element. You have the luxury of space in your writing, since your headline doesn't have to fit a specific hole in the page layout—yet. Use all the words you need to single out the target audience and present your news hook. Rewrite it until it's short, sweet, and sharp.
   B. Lead paragraph. This must tell the story so that if nothing else is published, your reader can still get your main point. Readers pay most attention to the first paragraph, whether they are aware of this or not. Picture an individual in your chosen audience as you write. Get his or her attention—and then explain why. Writing a good lead is very difficult. Try many before you decide on the one you'll use.
   C. Body copy. Everything after the lead paragraph is an expansion on what you've introduced. To make the copy readable, move from the abstract to the personal as quickly as possible. Quotes are an excellent tool for making your copy personal. Unfold the story as follows: Use a subhead to introduce a point; state it in the next sentence; then use a quote to illustrate it, add commentary, or describe a point of view. Continue until you've conveyed each point in the message you've developed.
   D. If your release goes on for several pages, write "more" at the bottom of each page, centered.
   E. At the top of each additional page, write a slug line—a two- or three-word name for your story. Follow that with "add 1," "add 2," etc. Note that the second page is not "page 2" but "add 1."
3. Closing
   A. Sometimes you will see the notation -30- used. Copy editors are trained to signal the conclusion of the story with this mark. Words following this are information to the editor or notes to the typesetter, not text to be printed. You may include this to indicate a break between the end of your story and subsequent information.
   B. Enclosures and available materials. List photos, audio tapes, and videotapes available or enclosed with the release. (Don't forget to caption any photos you enclose.)
   C. Contact information. Repeat the contact information from the header of the release.

Example 10-6: George Archibald Photo, Crane Foundation
Used by permission of International Crane Foundation.

International Crane Foundation

News Release

International Crane Foundation Director Dr. George Archibald works with "Gee Whiz," a seven-year-old male whooping crane hatched at the Foundation, located near Baraboo Wisconsin. Dr. Archibald helps the crane to "feel better" by allowing it to dominate him with aggressive postures and calls.

Gee Whiz will soon be joined by 22 other whooping cranes, shipped to the Foundation in November and December to establish the second captive breeding flock of the endangered species.It is hoped that Gee Whiz will find a mate among the newly arrived birds.

Credit: David H. Thompson

September, 1989

E-11376 Shady Lane Rd., Baraboo, Wisconsin 53913, USA   608-356-9462

Example 10-6 shows a typical format for submitting photos. Make yourself a template like this to label and caption your photos.

Example 10-7A: Speakers at Press Briefing Upon Arrival of Whooping Cranes
Used by permission of International Crane Foundation.

International Crane Foundation

News Release

FOR IMMEDIATE RELEASE
FOR FURTHER INFORMATION: David Thompson (608) 356-9462 (o)
                                          (608) 233-9589 (h)

SPEAKERS AT PRESS BRIEFING UPON ARRIVAL OF WHOOPING CRANES

George Archibald – International Crane Foundation (ICF)
Director and Cofounder of ICF. Dr. Archibald was recently placed on the Recovery Team for the Whooping Crane. Dr. Archibald will introduce other participants, and speak about the significance of the transfer of Whooping Cranes from the Patuxent Wildlife Research Center to ICF.

Charles Collins – National Fish & Wildlife Foundation.
As Executive Director of the National Fish & Wildlife Foundation, Mr. Collins will represent the foundation, and speak on the Foundation's role with the Whooping Crane. Whitney Tilt, who has coordinated the Foundation's work with the bird, will also be present.
The National Fish and Wildlife Foundation is a private foundation authorized by Congress in 1984. It plays a behind-the-scenes role as an instigator and catalyst in wildlife conservation projects. By providing help with funds, logistics, and administration, the Foundation brings life to many projects, and speeds others that otherwise would be delayed. For example, the Foundation provided as grant of $200,000 to ICF for construction of pens for Whooping Cranes, and helped to arrange today's flight, in cooperation with the Department of Navy and the US Marine Corps.

Maurice LeFranc – National Wildlife Federation
As Director of the Federation's Institute for Wildlife Research, LeFranc will present a $25,000 check to the National Fish and Wildlife Foundation, to help reimburse the Foundation for funds they gave ICF.
This donation is part of the Federation's continuing involvement with endangered species. The Federation has been involved with Whooping Cranes since they and the State of Nebraska filed an injunction against the Grayrocks Dam in Wyoming. This action forced the dambuilders to establish a $7,500,000 fund for mitigation of the dam's effects on the Platte River. The Platte River is critical habitat for Whooping Cranes and many other species of birds during migration. The Federation is now one of the three parties in the Platte River Whooping Crane Habitat Maintenance Trust, Inc.

more

Example 10-7B: Speakers at Press Briefing Upon Arrival of Whooping Cranes
Used by permission of International Crane Foundation.

Speakers Upon Arrival of Whooping Cranes -- Add 1

Jim Lewis - U.S. Fish & Wildlife Service, Region 2.
   Dr. Lewis is Head of the US Whooping Crane Recovery Team,
and National Coordinator for the Whooping Crane program of the
USFWS. In cooperation with the Canadian Wildlife Service, the
USFWS is responsible for the management of both the wild and
captive flocks of Whooping Cranes. Dr. Lewis will speak on how
the young Whooping Cranes produced at ICF will be used, three or
four years in the future, to help establish a new wild flock in
Florida.

Gerry Luther - Luther Builders, Inc.
   Luther Builders of Rock Springs served as general contractor
for 12 "Crane Condominiums," built this fall with funds from the
National Fish & Wildlife Foundation. The involvement of six
Wisconsin contractors shows that conservation means jobs for the
local economy.
   Mr. Luther said: "The most interesting thing was watching
the cranes. Everyone got a big charge out of them. You don't
see that kind of thing everyday on the job. I found out how much
work it means to keep that species going. It's a lot more work
than chickens. It changes your whole attitude about
conservation."

Glenn Olsen - U.S. Fish & Wildlife Service, Region 8.
   As the Center Veterinarian at Patuxent Wildlife Research
Center, Glenn Olsen (DVM and Ph.D.) is in charge of medical
quarantine for the birds before the flight, and care of the birds
during the flight. He will be accompanied by Animal Caretaker
Renata Tramontana.
   Dr. Olsen has just returned from a week in Puerto Rico,
where he has been studying disease problems of the endangered
Plain Pigeon.

Mary Wickhem - International Crane Foundation
   As ICF Board of Trustees President, Wickhem has been a long
and steadfast supporter of ICF. She provides a long-term
perspective on what has been achieved since ICF was founded in
1973.

-30-

The example of a personnel sketch in Example 10-7 describes the speakers who will be at a news conference. Note how each speaker is "sold" as having a particular expertise or significance that contributes to the news value of the event.

If your press kit is designed simply to describe your company and its offerings, you will want to put together a personnel sketch of your key officers and spokespeople. Include education, professional accomplishments, credentials—whatever gives each person credibility as a voice for your business. Avoid padding with irrelevant details or ancient history. Give in to the urge to include colorful background, like interesting hobbies or unusual experiences.

Example 10-8: Crane Foundation cover letter
Used by permission of International Crane Foundation.

INTERNATIONAL CRANE FOUNDATION

WORLD CENTER FOR THE STUDY AND PRESERVATION OF CRANES

E-11376 SHADY LANE ROAD   BARABOO, WI 53913-9778, USA
TEL. 608-356-9462   TELEX 297778 ICF UR

Dear Newspeople,   October 25, 1989

Enclosed are materials about the up-coming transfer of half the captive flock of Whooping Cranes from the Patuxent Wildlife Research Center near Laurel, Maryland, to the International Crane Foundation (ICF) near Baraboo, Wisconsin.

This is an exciting and important development in the 50-year struggle to prevent extinction of this magnificent crane. The good news is that the species is coming back! The enclosed materials will give you the details.

The birds will be flown to Wisconsin by VMGR 452, a Marine Corps Reserve KC-130 Unit from Stewart International Airport, Newburgh, New York. <u>Media are welcome on the flight</u>. <u>Return flights from Wisconsin are the responsibility of the media</u>.

The flight will depart from Andrews Air Force Base, Navy Ramp, Washington, D.C. Loading will start at 9:30 a.m. EST, on Wednesday, November 8, 1989. Media covering and/or going on the flight should arrive at the main gate, Andrews AFB, no later than 9:00 a.m. The flight will arrive at the Baraboo, WI airport at 12:30 p.m. CST, plus or minus 30 minutes. Media personnel wishing to travel on the flight to Wisconsin <u>must</u> contact <u>both</u> the ICF and Marine Corps Public Affairs Office.

Marine Corps contacts are: Staff Sergeant Barbara Vaughan, or Captain Elizabeth Kerstens at (202) 694-1494, or 694-1495, Marine Corps Headquarters, Washington, D.C. The ICF contacts are: David Thompson, (608) 356-9462 (ofc.), (608) 233-9589 (h.); or George Cutlip, ICF Public Relations Consultant, (608) 233-3507.

You must also arrive at Andrews Air Force Base on your own. The names and Social Security numbers of all people planning to make the flight must be submitted in advance to the Marine Corps Public Affairs Office.

This will be a memorable event in the world of conservation. We welcome your participation. Let us know how we can help you.

Sincerely,

David H. Thompson   *George C. Cutlip*

David Thompson   George Cutlip
Education Director, ICF   Public Relations
                                       Consultant, ICF

Some press kits include a fact sheet. Example 10-8 shows a cover letter serving this purpose. If your press kit is not about a special event, but is more generic to your company, your fact sheet might have a rundown on your company similar to that in a stock prospectus.

Checklist: The News Release

Review your writing. Put what you have written to this test and you will avoid glaring errors.

1. Will readers have the complete message if they never get beyond the first paragraph?

2. Of each statement, ask, can it be read in only one way?

3. Does the story include at least one quote attributed to a credible source who is known to my anticipated audience?

Have someone else read your story. Does it leave them with questions? Revise your work. Go away and come back. Does the draft read well to you now? Then you can proceed with disseminating your news. Follow these instructions in preparing your release for distribution.

1. Use white paper.

2. Double-space all copy. (The headline may be single-spaced if it runs to two lines.) Word processing or desktop publishing software makes it easy to produce a clean final document for printing.

3. Use only one side of each sheet. Write *"more"* at the bottom of each page.

4. Number all pages and include a slug line (short title) at the top.

5. Invest in high-quality duplication. Use a laser printer if you need only a few copies. You can use high-quality photocopying for larger quantities.

6. Staple all elements of two or more pages in the publicity materials.

7. Weigh the whole publicity packet and apply sufficient postage.

8. Mail the release. When time gets short, it is helpful to have a list of post boxes with late pick-up times. You can also deliver by hand and maybe meet your media contacts, if they aren't too busy.

Examples 10-9 to 10-12 will help you write news releases for your business. Follow the outline in Example 10-5 to structure your news release in the appropriate format.

Example 10-9: News Release Announcing Staff Promotion, Sent to Local Business Press

NEWS

contact information
For Immediate Release
(Note: usually no headline is included with a staff announcement.)
    Dennis Johnson, formerly a partner with McCoskey & Johnson, has joined the Madison law firm of Borders, Stein, Hastings, and McDowell, practicing in the area of family law.

-30-

Example 10-10: News Release Announcing New Products, Sent to Industry Trade Journal

NEWS

contact information
FOR RELEASE: April 1, 1996
headline: AMERICAN SPORTSMAN LAUNCHES PREPRINT LINES
    The American Sportsman has two new preprint lines. One is an upscale nine-shirt collection featuring high-quality reproductions of action photographs by sports photographers. The other is the Big Ten merchandise, incorporating slogans and symbols for Big Ten sports teams under licensing agreements with the schools. Some of the proceeds from sales of the T-shirts, coffee mugs, caps, and other items will go to sports scholarships for talented youth. For more information, contact American Sportsman at (phone number).

-30-

Example 10-11: News Release Announcing Product News, Sent to Regional Business Magazine

NEWS

contact information
FOR IMMEDIATE RELEASE
Headline: PERSOFT PROGRAM "MEETS ALL" FOR MOTOROLA
    Madison-based Persoft Inc. recently received certification from Motorola that its software product, SmarTerm for Windows, meets all criteria and expectations for Windows-based terminal emulation products.
    SmarTerm is a connectivity program that allows PCs running Microsoft Windows to access UNIX and VMS host machines by making the PC behave as though it were just another network terminal. Motorola reported very good user productivity and better than normal terminal emulation.

-30-

Example 10-12: News Release Announcing Seminar, Sent to Local and Regional Business Press

NEWS

contact information
FOR IMMEDIATE RELEASE
Headline: VOICE, DATA, AND VIDEO CONFERENCE

   The Governor's Conference on Voice, Data, and Video Communication—Wisconsin's Industrial Competitive Challenge will take place in Madison on December 14. The one-day conference features case studies of tools that companies are currently using to improve customer service, build customer relations, train staff, communicate R&D, and access worldwide networks such as the Internet. There will be demonstrations and presentations on the latest technology.

   For more information, contact John Klus in UW-Madison's Department of Engineering Professional Development at (phone) or (fax).

-30-

Pay attention to the tone of this writing. It is straightforward and clear, never overpromotional. Adapt these examples for your purposes.

Conclusion: Forming Your Publicity Plan

We've covered the components of your publicity activities, talking about your strategy, developing your message, finding opportunities for publicity, choosing story angles, and working with the media. As your knowledge base about publicity has grown, I assume you have been forming ideas for your business. It's time to get them in writing.

   Your publicity plan is a document, as I described at the start of this chapter. Now it's time to make some decisions so that you can summarize your activities into a written plan.

- *Goals and strategies.* The purpose of advertising is to shift public opinion, and that is also the reason for performing publicity activities. What is your publicity goal? What change in perception would you like to effect? Each goal implies a strategy for achieving it. Use Template 10-1B to summarize your publicity strategy.

- *The action plan.* Implementing that strategy will demand resources—time and money. Make your estimate now about the staff time required to accomplish the tasks you envision. Decide who will do what, where, and when (this becomes your publicity calendar). Summarize those decisions as an action plan (see Template 10-2).

Template 10-2: Action Plan

Publicity Action Plan

Who	Action	Target Date	Date Completed

● *Distribution channels.* You will need to keep track of the distribution channels you've chosen—your media contacts and/or your business associates. This requires building a database, or at least a filing system and a set of photocopy label masters for a mailing list. Develop this list now, so that you know how many people you will be keeping in touch with. This will be important as we get to budget setting. Then make a commitment to keep this list current. Responsibilities change frequently in the newsroom.

Tip: If your media list is large, it is often more efficient to address the news release to a responsibility in a newsroom, not a specific person—for example, Business Editor or Business Desk, City Desk, State Desk, Features Editor, Food Editor; for television and radio, News Director, Sports Director, Public Service Director, etc.

● *Audience.* Your publicity contacts are the linchpin of your publicity activity, but they are not the only audience you are speaking to. Remember that your contacts are the communicators, not the end consumers, of your information. Now is the time to define your audience—those end consumers. Are you sure that the media contacts you've listed are the best, most efficient way to reach your audience? Check back with your advertising media plan. How do your plans for paid media match up with your publicity contacts? Are you advertising in the same publications you anticipate will give you editorial coverage? Then you are creating a synergistic effect in the audience for that medium. Good work.

Pitfall: Don't ever get caught in the trap of confusing the advertising side of the news business with the editorial side of the news business. Threats to pull your paid ads will fall on very hostile ears in the newsroom. Keep your paid advertising and your publicity efforts in separate worlds. They don't mix.

- *Calendar.* Review your action plans. Do you see a year's activity taking shape? Do you have a promotable event scheduled for at least every quarter? An event every month is even better, but only if each is newsworthy. I don't mean a major special event necessarily—all sorts of occasions are suitable for publicity. The anniversary of your business is one. The accomplishments of your employees may be newsworthy. Are you active in a community group or service club? If you will be elected an officer, that is an occasion for publicity. If you attend a seminar or receive professional certification or recognition, these events deserve news releases as well.

Activities Worthy of News Releases:

Anniversaries
Personnel changes (promotions or
    new hires)
Club/civic special events
Club/civic service (election to office,
    etc.)
Hosting a seminar
Holding an open house
Attending a seminar
Running a contest
Receiving professional certification or
    recognition
Achieving a sales goal
Release of a new product
Development of a new process
Purchase of new equipment
Opening a new office
Moving to a new location
Releasing a new advertising campaign
Local angles on national trends,
    where your expertise is valuable
Unusual personal anecdotes about
    you or other people in your firm
Did a mother duck build a nest in
    your parking lot?

Make sure your calendar includes one or two high-profile events like an open house or grand opening. Decide which of your efforts will be small, and which will require more time to develop. Prepare a timeline of activities for each. Does it look realistic? Make sure the proper resources will be available at the critical times. Cash flow or work flow can have an effect on your schedule. Don't plan an open house at the peak of your busiest season.

Budget

Now that you know what you're doing and when, you can draw up a budget (see Template 10-3A). The first category will be the setup cost of your activity. This will include the physical tools you need—the wall calendar, the filing system, the folders and labels you'll use. It will also include the production costs for the printed supplies you'll use—stationery, business cards, etc. If you are creating a company brochure and plan to use it in publicity, a proportionate part of its cost should be accounted for here.

Each mailing you plan to do will require a cover letter on stationery and probably several enclosures, requiring copying or printing charges.

There may be photography fees as well if you plan to include a special photo—costs for studio time to shoot it, and costs for materials as you reproduce the necessary number of 8 x 10 glossies. Duplicate photos can be produced by photo finishing houses. Get price estimates and ask to see samples. Prices, delivery times, and quality can vary widely. Multiple hundreds of duplicates, should you need them, can be obtained from specialty duplication services in larger cities by mail. Allow enough time for your order to be processed—three weeks at least.

If your mailing includes a press kit, that will have its own set of costs. Develop a special budget for it. Your press kit will include a cover and other printed pages, which might include a cover letter, a fact sheet, biographies, press clippings, and more. There may be brochures included. Some people print up a customized Rolodex card. There may be "freebies"—promotional giveaway items like pens, mugs, or whatever. You will need cost line items for each.

Postage is the final category you must estimate for. Using your media list and your calendar, you can make a reasonable estimate of how much you will spend on postage during the year. Make a sample of a press kit so that you can determine exactly what mailing it will cost.

Template 10-3 will help you summarize your publicity budget. You will find templates throughout this book that will help you with estimating costs. The templates in Chapter 7, "All About Radio Advertising," and Chapter 8, "Television," are relevant to estimating the cost of producing audio or video news releases. The templates in Chapter 9, "Direct Mail Advertising," will help you estimate design and printing for the other components of your press kit.

Set up a template like Template 10-3A as a computer spreadsheet.

Template 10-3A: Publicity Cost Estimate Worksheet

Date:
Title of Campaign:
Description:

1. Planning

$_____ List any planning or consulting costs

2. Setup

$_____ Calendar
$_____ File system
$_____ Printing (special news release letterhead)
$_____ Other
$_____ Setup Subtotal

3. Press Kit

$_____ File folders/covers
$_____ Photography (time and materials to take photo)
$_____ Photo duplication
$_____ Envelopes/special mailers
$_____ Audio tape production/duplication (see templates in Chapter 7)
$_____ Video tape production/duplication (see templates in Chapter 8)
$_____ Other
$_____

4. Special Event Costs

$_____ Celebrity spokesperson fees
$_____ Travel costs
$_____ Lodging
$_____ Meals
$_____ Equipment rental (tents, tables, audiovisual, etc.)
$_____ Other
$_____ Special Events Subtotal (see Chapter 3 for more on special events)

5. Postage

$_____ Cost per piece to mail news release X number to be mailed
$_____ Cost per piece to mail press kit X number to be mailed
$_____ Special delivery charges
$_____ Postage Subtotal

6. Other

$_____ Special giveaway items
$_____ Other
$_____ Other Subtotal

$_____ Grand Total: Publicity Program

I like to express budgets in quarterly terms so that my clients can plan the necessary cash flow. Template 10-4A shows both the total budget and the quarterly cash requirements.

Template 10-4A: Publicity Budget by Quarter

Spending by Activity and Quarter

Date:
Title:
Assumptions:
Prepared by:

Medium	First Quarter	Second Quarter	Third Quarter	Fourth Quarter	Total ($)	Total (%)
Planning						
Setup						
Press kit						
Special events						
Event 1						
Event 2						
Event 3						
Event 4						
Postage						
Other						
Total by Quarter:						
Percent of Total:						

A case study at the end of this chapter describes the launch of a product, Boccone Chocolate Morsels. Templates 10-3B and 10-4B show how these templates might appear for that publicity campaign.

Template 10-3B: Cost Worksheet

Date: 12-15-92
Title of Campaign: Boccone Chocolate Morsels Product Launch
Description: First Year's Activity; 2 food shows, 50 media contact names

1. Planning

_____$0_ List any planning or consulting costs

2. Setup

_____$15_ Calendar
_____40_ File system
_____170_ Printing (special news release letterhead)
_____25_ Other
_____$250_ Setup Subtotal

3. Press Kit

_____$80_ File folders/covers
_____450_ Photography (time and materials to take photo)
_____140_ Photo duplication
_____80_ Envelopes/special mailers
_____0_ Audio tape production/duplication (see templates in Chapter 7)
_____0_ Video tape production/duplication (see templates in Chapter 8)
_____450_ Other: Product Samples (retail value)
_____$1,200_ Press Kit Subtotal: 50 Pieces Produced

4. Special Event Costs

_____$500_ Celebrity spokesperson fees: chefs' honoraria for food fair
_____700_ Travel costs
_____240_ Lodging
_____90_ Meals
_____400_ Equipment rental (tents, tables, audiovisual, etc.)
_____2,000_ Other: Product samples for giveaway (retail value)
_____$3,930_ Special Events Subtotal (see Chapter 3 for more on special events)

5. Postage

_____$65_ Cost per piece to mail news release X number to be mailed
_____140_ Cost per piece to mail press kit X number to be mailed
_____25_ Special delivery charges
_____$230_ Postage Subtotal

6. Other

_____$350_ Special giveaway items: Custom logo napkins for food fair
_____0_ Other
_____$350_ Other Subtotal

$5,960_ Grand Total: Publicity Program

Template 10-4B: Budget by Quarter

Date: 12-15-92
Title: Boccone Chocolate Morsels Product Launch
Assumptions: First year's activity: Food show in 1st 2 quarters.
Mail press releases 4x/year
Prepared by: Bill Davis

Medium	First Quarter	Second Quarter	Third Quarter	Fourth Quarter	Total ($)	Total (%)
Planning	0	0	0	0	$0	0%
Setup	$250				$250	4%
Press kit	$1,200				$1,200	20%
Special events						
Event 1	$1,965 Chicago Food Fair				$3,930	66%
Event 2		$1,965 Philadelphia Food Show				
Postage	$182	$16	$16	$16	$230	4%
Other	$350				$350	6%
Total by Quarter:	$3,947	$1,981	$16	$16	$5,960	100%
Percent of Total:						

Hiring Publicity Services

You may feel ready to begin your publicity activities now—or ready to turn this responsibility over to the pros. Two factors affect the decision to use outside sources. First, do you have the time to follow through on your publicity plans without fail? Is this the best use of your time? Second, do you have the writing skill to do your own publicity effectively? We each have our own comfort level with the written word. Publicity is very much a craft of writing. If you are not a competent writer, don't waste your time trying to do your own publicity. Hire someone who can be effective on your behalf.

You will find a spectrum of firms offering publicity and public relations services, from specialty shops to full-service advertising and marketing agencies. Publicity is a specialty, and you will need to peek behind the promises to find out if the agencies you talk to have real expertise in this area. The best way to find this out is to check references. Ask specifically for the names of clients for whom they perform publicity services, then speak to those people and ask for anecdotes about the work the agency has performed for them. You could even call a reporter or editor or two! In Chapter 12, you will find my recommendations on how to select an agency, and also how to get the best results after the decision has been made.

Case Study 1: Selling a Consulting Practice via Publicity

Derrick Van Mell is a management consultant. He specializes in real estate issues. He is not a broker—and that fact constitutes both his unique niche and his biggest publicity challenge. His prospects simply don't understand what he can do for them.

Derrick helps business decision makers with real estate issues. The question he is asked most often is, "Should I lease or buy?" but his help goes beyond lease vs. buy decisions. He helps clients build strategies for use

or adaptation of their current buildings. He manages the bidding on and construction of new facilities. He is a soloist—a guy with an office in his home—yet he is selling to the top brass in the largest organizations in his area. His entire prospect pool is no larger than fifty or seventy-five people.

Derrick must appear conservative, knowledgeable, and professional. High-profile advertising methods have little relevance for him. No radio commercials. No billboards. Even advertising in the local business press makes no sense, given the size of his target market.

Instead, Derrick has made skillful use of creative publicity techniques to keep his business image high-profile. Here's how.

He developed three principles that help him keep his publicity efforts on target. They will work for you as well. If you are in a service business, selling to other businesses, and work for yourself, this case study is for you.

Principle 1: Your Network Is Your Sales Force

The way to sell a service business is through referrals. If you're a specialist, selling an abstract and intangible range of business services, paid advertising is of very little use to you. Instead, you must build your network, and train it as you would a sales force.

Derrick met with a public relations consulting firm early on, and developed an ongoing working relationship. He doesn't pay the firm a retainer, but he occasionally uses its services—paying an hourly fee—when he needs someone to brainstorm with, or someone to check his work.

As a result of working with the PR firm, Derrick learned to take his network seriously. He set goals for frequency of contact with his network, and he explored the style of publicity that would project the right attitude or image for him. He was reminded, as I'll remind you, to think about this question: Who belongs in your network? Remember that publicity doesn't necessarily have to do with influencing your prospects—it has at least as much to do with swaying the network of people who influence their decisions.

For some people the answer to "who" will be professional media people—the editors and reporters who control what information appears in the press, and who we've talked about in detail in this chapter. For others, like Derrick, the "who" will focus more on those who are influential with business decision makers. This is a surprisingly broad group. For Derrick it included builders, bankers, lawyers, other management consultants—all those who are in close and trusting business relationships with the top CEOs in town. Derrick took this concept and did his research until he had a name-identified list of influencers. He then set about recruiting and training them to be part of his network.

Networking is not just "grip and grin," Derrick would like to remind you. He has spent considerable effort making sure his associates know what he does. He sees himself as a sales manager, and his network as his staff. How do you keep your "sales staff" enthusiastic and motivated? As with actual salespeople, you remember what's in it for them.

- Making a good referral is a favor people remember. Derrick makes sure that his network knows that he appreciates their referrals.

- Explore possibilities for joint projects. Can you think of people who stand to benefit from your prosperity? Make sure they know how and why they should refer prospects to you.

- Your network is an information link to your prospects. You don't want to appear overeager in calling on a prospect—and risk antagonizing him or her—but you don't want to be out of the prospect's information loop either. Exchanging information with others who call on the same firm can keep you in the know without always being in their face.

You can see how training your business associates as a sales force can work to your advantage. But here's an issue you should consider: Once you've "hired" these people, how do you "fire" the nonperformers? Derrick makes the extra effort to maintain a database on the people in his network. Over time he evaluates their utility—are they active, making referrals, providing information, proposing joint projects? If not, he retires them from his active list. In his view, a good contact is always in training, always in need of a better understanding of what he does, always capable of performing at a higher level with the right encouragement. When contacts do well, he rewards them—Derrick is a source of referrals as well.

Here's another key concept about your network. Your clients are potential members. Have the self-confidence to press them into service. Each client firm knows what you did for it, but it may not know what other firms you work for, or what other types of projects you do. Include your clients in your network, and (presuming you've done your usual brilliant job for them) you will find them the best source of referrals of all.

Principle 2: Triangulation Helps Clients Find You

Credibility is the absolutely most important attribute of your public image. Derrick learned the principle of triangulation from sailing. "It takes two sitings before you know where you are and where you're headed," he says. "In the same way, it takes two sitings before people can find their way to you. They need to hear recommendations from several sources. They have to get their bearings." Those professionals with a long track record don't have to worry about this—their credibility has built naturally over time. But as a newcomer in the community, just establishing his practice, Derrick had to take control of his publicity to get the necessary triangulation effect. He had to build it with his own sweat and blood.

Derrick chose two activities to raise his profile: He developed several seminars (the most popular was "Lease vs. Buy?"), and he wrote articles on general-interest real estate topics, which he submitted to the business press. To these activities he applied the same AIDA formula we've talked about elsewhere in this book in relation to writing advertising copy. Remember, "AIDA" stands for "get attention, arouse interest, create desire, stimulate action." Both in his articles and in his seminars, he used this sequence to sell the concepts he wanted to get across.

The public relations firm he worked with helped a great deal, Derrick feels. It got him introductions to and contacts with the local business press. Then it helped him craft articles that would be easy to market to his new contacts.

In a midsize or smaller market, the business press will be hungry for your material if you can give them something of substance. Your name in print is an excellent credibility builder with both your network and your prospects. Derrick was able to get four articles placed within the course of a year—almost too many.

While he was writing and placing articles—and serving his clients—Derrick also pursued seminars as a way to get his name in front of the public. First he spoke as a panelist at other business seminars, then he developed his own. "It's the best form of publicity," says Derrick. "People see you and hear you—a live demonstration. And the setting is under your control." He recommends that you pick an issue that's fairly broad, and provide solid but general information. Bring in other experts to develop a panel approach—a team will have more credibility and a broader network to draw on. And there's a synergy effect. "It works like a comedy team," says Derrick. "Each thanks the last presenter, and pumps up the next. You all look good." In short, if you can learn to talk about yourself without being vain and if you can be comfortable and "on"

before an audience, this is a direct path to new business.

The two parts of Derrick's approach, the articles and seminars, were equally successful. The result? A steady stream of prospects, most resulting in contracts—the triangulation effect at work.

Principle 3: Look through Your Prospects' Eyes

As we mine for prospects, it doesn't hurt to look at our current clients. When we back up from the individuals we do business with, we are able to generalize a description that will help us find more like them.

Derrick hired his PR firm to do a modest survey. It developed a questionnaire, then conducted phone interviews with eight current clients that Derrick thought were most typical of the type of business he would like to attract in the future. He discovered how they viewed what he did for them—which was quite different from what he thought he did. In fact, the results helped him decide to call his activities "management consulting" rather than "real estate consulting," since he saw how his expertise reached across categories in his clients' operations.

Derrick developed new action plans for his publicity based on what he learned, and continued his emphasis on publishing and networking.

Summary: Case Study 1

What has Derrick's experience taught him that's relevant for you? Certainly we all could benefit from managing our professional networks the way Derrick grooms his.

Derrick's theories about triangulation are useful for those of us who are just starting out and need to make ourselves known to our community in a hurry. My experience bears out his belief that multiple referrals from unrelated sources are very influential in bringing in new business. You can't *make* this happen, but by pursuing the kind of activities

Derrick describes, you can increase its likelihood.

And Derrick's last point—that we should learn from our prospects and clients—is certainly relevant. Survey techniques don't need to be complicated or expensive to be effective. Simply asking your associates how they see what you do will teach you a lot about how to present yourself. Is this publicity, strictly speaking? Of course not. Is it good advice? You bet.

Case Study 2: Send In the Marines to Save the Cranes! A Good-News Story Angle Nets Good Press

The press kit examples in this chapter (see Examples 10-5, 10-6, 10-7, and 10-8) tell the story of a very special event. A conservation organization received the cooperation of the Marines in arranging an airlift of endangered birds from another breeding center half a continent away. This event had two potential news angles: its interest to conservationists, and the participation of the Marine Corps in this activity. Read the two press releases and note the two story angles. One focuses on the significance of "splitting the flock" in preventing extinction of the species. The other focuses on the arrival and transportation of the birds, giving a clear picture of the military involvement (the birds were allowed to "tag along" on a regularly scheduled training flight). This release made clear where and when the photo opportunities were along the way.

The first press release, "Second Front in Battle to Save Whooping Cranes," Example 10-5, appears on page 419–420, where we dissected it for the elements of a news release. This example presents the story of the International Crane Foundation and the arrival of some exciting new tenants.

This second press release, Example 10-13, plays up the Marine Corps angle.

Example 10-13A: US Marine Corps Reserves Flight
Used by permission of International Crane Foundation.

International Crane Foundation

News Release

FOR RELEASE: Immediately
FOR FURTHER INFORMATION:
David Thompson, ICF: (608) 356-9462
                     (608) 233-9589
George Cutlip, Public Information
  Consultant, ICF: (608) 233-3507
Capt. Elizabeth Kerstens,
  Marine Corps Public Affairs;
                     (202) 694-1494
                     (202) 694-1495

US MARINE CORPS RESERVE FLIGHT TO ESTABLISH BEACHHEAD IN BATTLE TO SAVE WHOOPING CRANES

BARABOO, WI -- The United States Marine Corps will give approximately eight rare whooping cranes a flight assist on November 8, 1989, when the birds are flown from Andrews AFB, Washington, D.C. to Baraboo, Wisconsin, home of the International Crane Foundation (ICF). The aircraft will be flown by Marine Corps KC-130 Reserve Squadron VMGR 452, based at Stewart International Airport, Newburgh, NY, as part of a regularly scheduled training and proficiency flight. The cranes are now at the Patuxent Wildlife Research Center, near Laurel, Maryland.

The Baraboo/Dells Airport, S 3440 A Highway 12, is located three miles north of Baraboo, Wisconsin. The Marine Corps KC-130 is one of the largest aircraft to land at the Baraboo airport.

When the plane lands, a short news conference will be held by officials involved in the program. Expected to speak are George Archibald, Director of ICF; Jim Lewis, Whooping Crane Coordinator for the U.S. Fish and Wildlife Service; Jim Range, Chairman of the Board of the National Fish and Wildlife Foundation, and ICF staff.

The arrival of the Whooping Cranes in Wisconsin represents the opening of a new front in the battle to bring back the cranes from the brink of extinction. Forty-five years ago, just 21 of the birds survived in the wild.

Approximately eight birds will be shipped on November 8, the first of three air shipments of approximately half the captive Whooping Crane flock. The birds are being sent to ICF to guard the flock from a possible outbreak of disease or other accident, and to establish a second breeding flock. ICF will maximize the production of Whooping Cranes in captivity. Eventually, with a larger breeding flock, ICF will be able to contribute birds for release into the wild. ICF is known world-wide for its success in breeding rare cranes.

(more)

Rt. 1, Box 230C   Baraboo, Wisconsin 53913, USA   608-356-9462

Example 10-13B: US Marine Corps Reserves Flight
Used by permission of International Crane Foundation.

WHOOPING CRANES TO TAKE MARINE CORPS FLIGHT -- ADD 1

The program to establish a second breeding flock accelerated this summer with the construction of new pens at ICF, funded by a $200,000 grant from the National Fish and Wildlife Foundation. The Foundation is a non-profit private organization established by Congress to raise funds for wildlife conservation projects in the United States and abroad.

During their flight, the birds will be attended by a veterinarian and an animal caretaker. Two additional shipments of birds are tentatively scheduled for late November and early December.

Upon unloading from the aircraft, the Whooping Cranes will remain in their shipping crates for their protection. (Media representatives are invited to accompany the arriving birds to ICF headquarters, two miles north of the airport, on Shady Lane Road. Media may be able to photograph the new arrivals in their houses through an open door, after they have been released and have settled down. Media will be allowed to photograph "Gee Whiz," ICF's famous seven-year-old male Whooping Crane. It is hoped that Gee Whiz will receive a mate in the shipment.)

The birds have undergone a quarantine at the Patuxent Wildlife Research Center to ensure that they won't bring disease to the cranes already at ICF. They have also been given thorough checks for their overall health by Patuxent staff.

Only one self-sustaining wild flock of whooping cranes now exists. The 144 to 150 birds in this flock migrate twice each year between Wood Buffalo National Park in Canada and Aransas National Wildlife Refuge on the Gulf Coast of Texas.

The shipment of these magnificent birds to ICF is an a cooperative effort by the National Fish and Wildlife Foundation, the U.S. Fish and Wildlife Service, and the International Crane Foundation. The birds in the captive flock are owned jointly by the governments of the United States and Canada.

Since its establishment in 1973 by Director George Archibald and the late Ron Sauey, ICF has provided worldwide leadership in the preservation of cranes. ICF serves as a breeding facility and international clearinghouse for information, in cooperation with more than 800 conservationists from 59 countries.

-30-

The arrival of the crane plane was greeted with a press conference (an example of a good occasion for one), combining photo opportunities with availability to the press of a number of speakers. The personnel sketches describing the speakers (Example 10-7) helped the media plan how to cover the event.

One of the more visible aspects of the Crane Foundation's work is the spectacle of staff members dancing with cranes. George Archibald, the director, is pictured performing this dance in the photo in Example 10-6. The caption gives this "evergreen" photo timeliness by explaining, "It is hoped that Gee Whiz will find a mate among the newly arrived birds."

If you study the components of this press kit, you will find a red-carpet treatment prepared for the media. A cover letter tells them succinctly when and where the action takes place. Two news releases cover the story from two angles. A personnel sketch describes speakers at a press conference, giving editors background to help them prepare for the conference. A photo gives them material to use if they choose not to attend, but also suggests the oddball picture possibilities at the on-location photo opportunity described.

This is media relations as done by the pros. Make or find the news, send out the word, follow up with phone calls, coordinate the event so that it all comes off without a hitch. Treat the media like guests. Anticipate their needs, and help them do their jobs with speed and accuracy.

Case Study 3: Boccone Chocolates—A Sweet New Product Launch

A man saw a market and designed a product to fill it. The market was upscale chocolate; the product he created was a premium chocolate chunk packaged in a resealable bag, delicious either for snacking or as an ingredient in baking. The product turned out to have a cross-category appeal that gave it real "sizzle."

Since he had a very low budget for advertising, our man knew that publicity would have to be the key component of his marketing. He was the president of an advertising and public relations firm, and he applied what he knew to the project. Here is his story.

Bill Davis started with a savvy observation about grocery retailing. Specialty grocery shops were enjoying a boom. Cooking was growing as a hobby. Some baby boomers were happy to nestle in with their Nestlé chocolate chips, but some longed for something better, something more luxurious. That's where Bill's product came in.

Bill set out to sell the best chocolate he could find, broken into sweet fragments that dwarfed traditional chocolate chips in both flavor and size. He named the product "Boccone Chocolate Morsels"—*boccone* means "mouthful" in Italian. He packaged the chocolate in a resealable bag, making snacking as convenient as baking with his product. His goal: to create a small but reliable niche market—a cult following, as he put it.

The next step was to find distribution for the product. To do that, he had to create demand. Bill mapped out a publicity campaign designed to reach consumers. If he could get them clamoring for the product, distributors could be convinced to carry it.

Breaking into grocery distribution is a tough challenge, and if you know anyone who's tried it, you've heard it's getting tougher. It's a commodities game in which volume and efficiency make all the difference. When a distributor takes the risk of carrying a new product from an untried company, the demand for it had better be there. Bill set about making sure it would be.

In short, Bill's publicity goal was to give consumers the idea that premium chocolate chunks should be on their shopping lists, and often.

Bill designed a publicity strategy for Boccone Chocolate Morsels that concentrated on the nation's gourmet magazines, the vehicles that reach consumers who appreciate fine food. He used news releases, product samples, and demonstrations to spread the word to the writers and editors. He gave each contact he made plenty of personal follow-up. In a few months his product launch was well under way.

Template 10-1C shows Bill's statement of publicity strategy.

Template 10-1C: Boccone Chocolate Morsels Publicity Strategy (filled in)

Statement of Publicity Strategy

Publicity will convince ___chocolate-loving upscale consumers___
(audience(s))

that ___Boccone Chocolate Morsels___
(your product or service)

is or will ___be a delightful versatile any-time treat___.
(message)

This will be attributed to ___delicious premium flavor, resealable bag___.
(feature/rationale)

This is newsworthy because ___it breaks the rules, bringing "eating chocolate"___
(describe benefit to audience of knowing this information)

___and "baking chocolate" together in one bag.___

Distribution of the message will be via ___food consumer press___
(describe media channels)

___.

Bill Cooks Up a Press Kit

Bill targeted about a dozen magazines for his launch. He chose two cities for his initial distribution, and the local city magazines headed his media contact list. Right behind them was the national food press: *Gourmet, Food and Wine, Chocolatier,* and other magazines like them. Related "lifestyle" magazines made the list too: *House Beautiful* and the like. The common element: an audience with an appreciation for life's gastronomic pleasures.

As soon as a package for Boccone Chocolate Morsels had been designed, Bill arranged a photo shoot. "Don't skimp," he advises, "especially with food. It's got to look delicious. Make sure you get both black-and-white prints and color transparencies; you might need either, and you want to be ready." He also recommends that you plan advertising and publicity shots at the same time, for efficiency in the shooting.

Bill designed a news release format for Boccone and drafted a press release, tailoring it slightly for the different magazines. "Ask yourself what the benefit is for that market," he says. To each magazine he sent a free package of the chocolate, along with his press release and photo. He followed up the next week with phone calls, asking how each recipient enjoyed the chocolate. The response was tremendous. Within three months positive mentions had appeared in five magazines.

Story Angles and the Consumer Press

Bill's press releases varied from story submissions to fact sheets and teasers. He found that the trade journals liked him to submit news in story form, since all they had to do to use it was edit it for space. "If you're a thorough, concise writer, they'll be grateful for your help," he told me. He found that the consumer press was more interested in information that would help their staff writers prepare their own stories. Bill accommodated his approach to each magazine's tastes.

Bill's first press releases were simple new product announcements. The message was basically, "try it, you'll love it." And that proved to be true. But to "keep the sizzle on the steak," Bill had to keep finding new story angles.

He took the chocolate around to restaurants and asked chefs to develop recipes with it. He then printed the recipes on cards and distributed those in new press releases.

He went to food trade shows and made appearances at events, always giving baking demonstrations and lots of free samples. "Events are crucial," he says. "With food, people have to sample the wares." Each appearance gave him a new angle for publicity. As the food press got to know Boccone Chocolate Morsels, the word began to get around.

Examples 10-14 to 10-16 show some of the press releases Bill sent out. Notice how the material is tailored for different audiences.

Example 10-14: News Release Announcing New Product, Sent to Industry Trade Journals

---

(contact information)
(release date)

Headline:

Chocolate Delight

    BD Chocolates introduces Boccone Chocolate Morsels, chocolate chips so big they're really chocolate chunks, made with fine bittersweet, not semisweet chocolate. Gourmet cookie shops have long known the value of using eating-quality chocolate in chocolate-chunk cookies. Now consumers can make cookies just as good, thanks to these delicious pre-formed chocolate chunks. A resealable bag makes them convenient for snacking as well as baking. Boccone Chocolate Morsels can be found in gourmet shops and the specialty section of groceries. For information on distribution opportunities contact BD Chocolates at (phone number).

**Example 10-15: Press Release Announcing New Product, Sent to Local City Magazines
(This release was targeted for a regular section featuring local products and innovations)**

(contact information)
(release date)
Headline:

Chocolate Chunks So Good You'll Eat Them
Before You Can Cook With Them

    Be careful—my kids finished mine before I could add them to my recipe. Luckily I had a second bag stashed away! What are these mystery chocolate chunks? They're called "Boccone Chocolate Morsels." They're marketed by BD Chocolates, a local company started by Bill Davis, owner of Davis Advertising and Promotions. Actually small chunks of fine bittersweet chocolate, the chips make cookies even gooier and more delicious. But if you're the type who never gets around to baking, the chocolate chunks also taste great right out of the resealable bag.

    These gourmet chips are currently for sale at (list of local gourmet shops). The average price is $9 per pound.

Example 10-16: News Release to Food Consumer Press Announcing Line Extension Event

(contact information)
(release date)
Headline:

Delicious Taste-Off

Attendees at next month's Chicago Food Fair will find a battle in progress. But it won't be Al Capone versus Elliot Ness. No, BD Chocolates is hosting a contest to select Chicago's Favorite Flavor from their newly expanded line of gourmet chocolate chunk products.

Five chefs have offered to create special treats, each selecting one product from the Boccone Chocolate Morsels line-up, which includes the new Macadamia Nut, Pecan, Raisin, and Mixed Fruit flavors, as well as the Boccone original flavor, Bittersweet Chocolate Chunk. Baked goods ranging from brownies to truffle cake will be available for sampling all day during each day of the show. In addition, the product line in its trademark resealable bag will be offered throughout the event.

Sweet tooths beware! You can vote as often as you like in this unscientific popularity contest. For more information, call (phone number) or stop by Booth #447 at the Chicago Food Fair.

Bill limited his paid advertising to only one magazine, *Chocolatier*, the most narrowly targeted magazine available, with an aim pointed directly at his best customers. Bill's ads brought in 200 to 300 responses a month, with an average order size of three to five one-pound bags. Each responder went on the mailing list. Publicity brought inquiries too—not as easy to tally, but just as valuable.

Now Bill could move into his next phase: building distribution for his product. From the start he developed and wooed a prospect list. Each time a new piece of favorable publicity appeared in the press, he made a nice presentation of it and mailed it to each potential distributor. For instance, he would make reprints showing the magazine cover with the article clipping displayed on top.

As distributors picked up the product, Bill listened to their needs. They asked for a broader product line—not uncommon, given the efficiencies of bulk distribution. Bill added nut- and fruit-filled mixes to his line. He looked to Europe and beyond in search of new products, allowing his distributors to guide the growth of his business. Bill's sales enjoyed steady growth at a reasonable pace. Sales in

the first year topped $300,000. At about $9 a bag, that's over 33,000 units, not bad for a start.

I asked Bill what surprised him most about his publicity campaign. "Nothing surprised me," he said at first. "We got the response we expected, in about the time we anticipated. It worked just the way we hoped." Then he thought a bit more.

"The direct mail was unbelievably great," he added. "The ads brought in names, we followed up, and the people ordered. We sent them more mailings, and they ordered more. We sent them a little catalog, and they ordered even more. I could have just worked with that and built an entirely different business."

When I asked Bill about the budget for his publicity, he hedged. Remember, he owns an advertising and public relations firm, so his PR budget would look a little different from yours. "Some of our press kits probably cost $50 a pop," he mused. "The packaging, the product sample, all that. The ads cost about $500 a month, but of course that's not PR." In short, what Bill spent isn't relevant. It's how he spent it that matters.

Using his professional expertise and his entrepreneurial savvy, Bill took a bag of chocolate from $0 to $300,000 in one year. That's something to be proud of.

Why isn't there a bag of Boccone Chocolate Morsels in your cupboard right now? Not every story has a happy ending. The clue was hidden a few paragraphs back. Bill's inexperience in overseas trade had some unfortunate side effects, and a good company ran aground on that shoal. At this time he is choosing not to pursue his interest in chocolate—except recreationally.

For most of us, Derrick's style of publicity is more familiar than Boccone Chocolate's or the Crane Foundation's. But either may be appropriate. You be the judge: pick your methods, develop your tools, follow through on your plans. Use this chapter to organize your activity and prepare for the attention that results.

Chapter 11

Your Corporate Image: Keeping that "Together" Look

By now you've figured out that the image your company projects through its advertising is important. In this chapter we're going to talk about the facet of your image called *Corporate I.D.*

Remember that image is earned, not made. You can produce and disseminate an array of materials designed to spread your identity, but in the end your image will be created by your community, as it responds to your advertising, public relations, and identity program. Do people remember you? Do they think well of you when they do? Then you've arrived at a good image.

One important part of that image is your corporate identity program. A corporate identity is the look you give the pieces called "print collateral," meaning items that support or work alongside your advertising.

In this chapter we'll talk about

- Logos
- Business stationery
- Company brochures
- Catalogs
- Newsletters
- Displays (retail and trade)
- Signage

From your storefront to your mailing label, how your business looks is under your control. Why overlook this opportunity to maximize your success?

Your corporate identity is the way you communicate your personality when people can't see your face. It helps to humanize your company. It evokes an emotional response from its viewers. It might give an appearance of power, or of elegance; it might communicate your sense of experience, confidence, or tradition. Developing an image is a slow process. You will arrive at a sound corporate image after years of carefully managing your corporate identity.

An identity is more permanent than an ad campaign. When you arrive at a strong graphic look for your firm, you won't change it—except to reflect major changes in your company or to update outmoded elements of style.

Your Logo and Stationery: The Building Blocks of Style

What is a logo exactly, and why is it so important? *Logo* refers to a collection of elements that identify a company. The logo consists of the business name in a distinctive typeface, often accompanied by a distinctive graphic element. Sometimes there is a tagline or positioning statement at the feet of the type. How these elements are placed with relation to one another is what we mean by a logo. You need one. Example 11-1 shows some different logos.

Example 11-1: Six Logos

Your Logo

The graphic symbol that represents you is a visual trigger that leads to simple associations about your service or product. You need a logo that makes the right associations for you. An outdated or unprofessional logo may be making the wrong associations. Pull out your business card and take a critical look at your current identity.

Your logo will fall into one of three categories: typographic symbols, abstract symbols, and descriptive (see Template 11-1).

Template 11-1: Test to Categorize the Logos Mentioned Above

Can you categorize the logos in Example 11-1? Decide which are abstract, typographic, or descriptive — before you look at the answers to the right.

	Abstract	Typographic	Descriptive
Columbia County	☐	☐	☐
Domus Equity	☐	☐	☐
Wisconsin Whey	☐	☐	☐
Space-metrics	☐	☐	☐
J.Kinney, Florist	☐	☐	☐
Klinke Cleaners	☐	☐	☐

Answers:

Columbia County
Descriptive symbol. The symbol describes the location of the county within the state of Wisconsin.

Domus Equity
Abstract symbol. The houselike shapes don't tell you anything about what Domus does.

Wisconsin Whey
Abstract symbol. Five spheres are abstracted from the molecular structure of whey.

Space-metrics
Typographic symbol, with border and rule under the type. These graphic elements add uniqueness but do not describe the company in any symbolic way.

J.Kinney, Florist
Typographic symbol with decorative border. The border could make this qualify as a descriptive logo, since it suggests flowers.

Klinke Cleaners
Typographic symbol. The typeface has been exaggerated to give the logo "attitude."

A typographic symbol might be a distinctive setting of the name in type, or it might be a monogram using the initials of the company. In either case, it's the type style that communicates the personality of the company.

Abstract symbols use a stylized, simplified rendering style to create a graphic icon representing a company. Abstract marks have the advantage of longevity, since they tend to look contemporary even as design trends change. Sometimes the consideration necessary to find the meaning in an abstract mark makes it memorable.

Example 11-2: Wisconsin Whey Protein Molecule and Science Book

A

Abstract symbol for Wisconsin Whey

Page from a scientific text, faxed to me by my client. Describes the molecular structure of whey.

B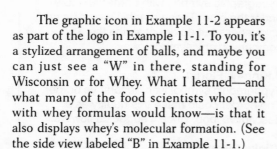

Staggered structures for the octomer of β-lactoglobulin A.

The graphic icon in Example 11-2 appears as part of the logo in Example 11-1. To you, it's a stylized arrangement of balls, and maybe you can just see a "W" in there, standing for Wisconsin or for Whey. What I learned—and what many of the food scientists who work with whey formulas would know—is that it also displays whey's molecular formation. (See the side view labeled "B" in Example 11-1.)

A descriptive mark represents the company by suggesting the character of the company. It might depict its main product or suggest its mission through imagery. It's important to avoid being too descriptive, though. Changing technology could put your logo back in the shop for an upgrade!

Which style of logo is best? There's no formula to predict what will succeed for you. Go with your instincts. If you decide you would like an abstract symbol for your company, I'd recommend that you call in a professional to design it. There is a lot of skill involved in finding the right associations and translating them into simple, compelling visual elements. A logo designed by an amateur will look like a logo designed by an amateur, and

that is not an image you want to project for your company.

Descriptive logos are really best left to strong visual artists as well, because the style of rendering and the scale of the objects described can be so important. Example 11-3 shows an amateur logo and its professional update. Note how it has become more abstract, but retains some of the elements of the wing and the wheel.

Example 11-3: Metro-Ride New and Old
Used by permission of Metro Ride.

If you want to do it yourself, try! But I'd recommend that you stick to typographic solutions in that case. Play with your word processor, page layout program, and/or photocopier until you come up with something you like. Here are some tips for turning type into a logo:

- Start by setting the name of your firm in every font you have available to you. Set it both uppercase and lowercase, try roman (standard type), italic, and bold. Then look the samples over for unusual or interesting features. The shapes of the letters g, a, q, r, and j are often quirky. Look for where they fall in the words. Also look for opportunities for ligatures—places where one letter might flow right into the next. These unusual letterforms could give your name its unique appearance in print. Note the variations in the "Q" in "Domus Equity."

Example 11-4: Domus Equity

BODONI	**DOMUS EQUITY**	**Domus Equity**
CASLON OPEN FACE	DOMUS EQUITY	Domus Equity
TRAJAN	DOMUS EQUITY	**This font has no lower case.**
GOUDY	DOMUS EQUITY	Domus Equity

- Look for attitude! Compress or expand the typeface (play with its horizontal scale) to give it drama. Set words in italic type to imply motion. Use bold type to imply power. Use blocky sans serif faces for punch, classical serif faces for elegance.

  There has been quite a trend in the last five years to mix typefaces in compound words; the best example might be the logo for the TV show "**thirty**something." If your name is a blend of two words, try this graphic trick.

- Try boxing the type with a thin rule, or reversing the words out of a box, so that they appear white on a black square. The Space-metrics logo is an example of a logo developed this way. Words can be asymmetrically placed. Break a rule or two.

- Stack the words, and play with different sizes to emphasize the key words in the name (see Example 11-5).

Example 11-5: Great Wall Systems
Used by permission of Great Wall Systems, L.L.C.

- Try adjusting the size of the first letters, and maybe the last letters as well. Try adjusting the spacing between the letters, making it either abnormally tight or abnormally loose.

As you play with these possibilities, you'll start seeing all the logos around you in a new way. Hang onto examples of anything you react to strongly, either positively or negatively.

Dedicate a part of your wall to your logo project; pin up the examples you've collected, and add your experiments to the wall. See what reactions you get from the visitors, delivery people, etc., who pass by. The reactions of your "focus group" should steer you away from bad ideas.

Before you go too far, try applying your proposed logo to your ads and your business card. If it's not going to hold up in execution, you'll find out now. A logo can look great when seen alone, but turn out to be too long or too tall or too fussy in detail to work in the places you need it.

At this point you may want to go to a professional artist or printer to have the actual final artwork created. By bringing them your initial design, you have saved yourself an investment in time as they try to read your mind. Of course, you have invested a good deal of your own time! Only you can decide, based on your own inclinations and talents, where your time is best spent.

When you hire a graphic designer for a logo process, it will go something like this. You will be interviewed, along much the same lines as the business review in Chapter 1. The designer will be probing for information about your company's strengths and weaknesses, the marketplace you're in, and what your future might bring. From this review comes the raw material of inspiration, and the artist will follow a process similar to that described in Chapter 5, "The Creative Approach." He or she searches for a concise visual depiction of the information gathered. At the end of this exploration phase, you will be presented with a number of designs to respond to. These will be rendered on computer and so will look final, but are really just a first step.

The designer should give you time to react to these "thumbnails," then you and the designer will discuss what directions to explore. In a second presentation the designer will show you two or three ideas that have evolved from this discussion. At this presentation you will probably find your new logo, with perhaps one or two final modifications needed. Then the artist will finalize the artwork, which today means preparing a computer illustration file. You should be able to get copies of this file in any formats you need for your word processing software and for any other document needs you might have, such as CAD drawings.

The designer might also recommend a type family for your firm's corporate identity. Think about the packaging and advertising for Apple's Macintosh products: Not only do you always see the Apple logo, but you see the typeface Garamond Condensed, a classical font with just a touch of whimsy. You see it on everything from the cartons the products come in to the on-air signature at the end of a TV commercial. This kind of consistency builds image. Be open to the idea of purchasing a font for your computer and using it in all your communications.

A logo design might cost from $700 to $3,000, or much more, depending on the degree of complexity in the process and the reputation and billing rate of the design firm you contact. More money will typically buy you an analysis of your business in more depth and more iterations of possible designs as the process unfolds. Some $700 logos knock the socks off some $3,000 ones. But generally in this field, price does have a relationship to the quality and creativity of the final product you'll see.

Your Tagline

In Chapter 2, "Positioning," I talked about the importance of creating a tagline, a phrase describing your key benefit. If you're using one, use it consistently—design it into your logo. Especially if your company is new, or moving into new markets, you need the extra acceleration a tagline gives your logo. You're just another face in the crowd if you don't give your prospects a clue as to what's unique or special about you. Does your name indicate

the area of business you're in? If your name is "Signs Plus," maybe a tagline isn't necessary. But if you're doing business as "Van Mell & Associates," then "Management Consulting" following your name is definitely a good idea. If there's one key thing you want people to remember about your company, find a memorable way to phrase it and lock it into your logo (see Example 11-6).

Example 11-6: Stardust logo

Legalities

A trademark is a word, name, or symbol used to identify a product or company and distinguish it from the competition. For intrastate commerce, you usually apply to your state's secretary of state; to register a name or device for interstate or foreign use, you'll work with the U.S. Patent and Trademark Office. You will be asked to submit a written application, a drawing of the mark, examples of it in use, and a filing fee. While waiting for approval, you may use the letters TM placed near the trademark to indicate that this mark is your property. Once your application is approved, you may use the ®. Lots of people never go through any of these application processes. Their use of their logo in trade alone gives them some basic rights.

I'm no lawyer, and I'm not going to try to tell you how to protect your logo as a trademark. When you've finalized your logo, talk to your lawyer and take the necessary steps to protect it. He or she can perform a search to assure its originality, then help you through the registration process to restrict its use to you. Or contact the U.S. Department of Commerce, Patent and Trademark Office, Washington, D.C., 20231 for more information.

Business Stationery

Whenever my design firm is hired to do a logo for someone, I can bet that we'll soon be doing stationery. About the time we get to that second logo design presentation, somebody starts saying, "I like that one, but how will it look on the letterhead?" So I tend to offer logo-stationery design as a package deal (see Example 11-7).

This book is not the place to go into the many theories about what letterhead should look like, or what makes a stationery design good or bad. However, these two thoughts stand out: Your letterhead should function easily for those who use it, and it should be appropriate to the style of your business. Here is what I mean by functionality: If you write long letters, don't design a letterhead with an address line across the bottom. You'll always be bumping into it as you print out letters, and you'll waste time and materials. Another functional issue: If you use a laser printer, tell your printer that. Some paper stocks work nicely with laser printers. Others don't. The ink cracks or rubs off, or the paper jams repeatedly. Avoid these problems by planning ahead. Test some of the paper stock before you place your order.

With an envelope or mailing label design, make sure you're in compliance with post office regulations. Type placed at angles or up the side of the envelope might appeal to you, but reduce the deliverability of your mail.

Business cards are the Mighty Mouse of stationery. They work the hardest for you, traveling far beyond your range to communicate about you and your business. I feel that the person's name on the business card is of primary importance—not the company name. Some people would disagree with me on this, but here's my rationale. You meet a person. You exchange cards. It depends on the context, of course, but in most situations you're more likely to recall that person by name than by company. Each business card should make it super-easy to find the person's name and telephone number.

Example 11-7: Wisconsin Whey Business Set

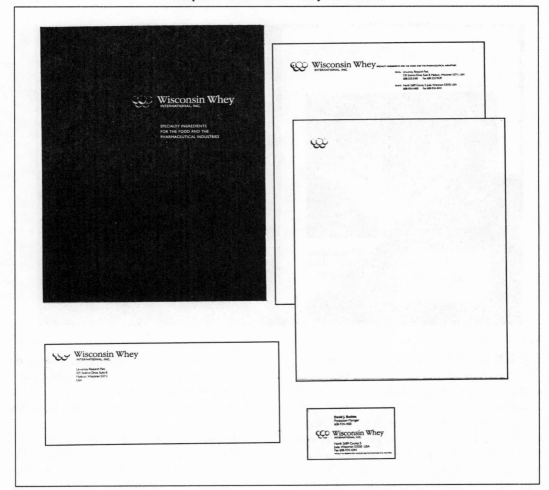

There's a last element of stationery that makes a nice finishing touch: letterhead second-sheet. Some firms just use blank reams of matching paper; others pay to have a second sheet printed. There's a good reason to have a customized second sheet, and it has nothing to do with writing long letters. You'll find additional uses for it—in proposals, staff resumes, product sheets.

Put these sheets together and you'll find that you need some kind of package. Some companies go for the bound-booklet approach, with stiff covers, perhaps a window where a customized title appears, and spiral or comb binding up the side. Other firms opt for folders with inserts. Sometimes these inserts are staggered in height so that the title of each can appear. I've heard this called a "ladderback" style.

Wisconsin Whey is like many companies that purchase folders to package their presentation materials. Information of all sorts goes into the folder—background on the company, nutritional analysis certificates of its different products, sell sheets, and other literature (Example 11-8). And that's a nice segue into the subject of brochures.

Example 11-8: Wisconsin Whey Folder with Inserts

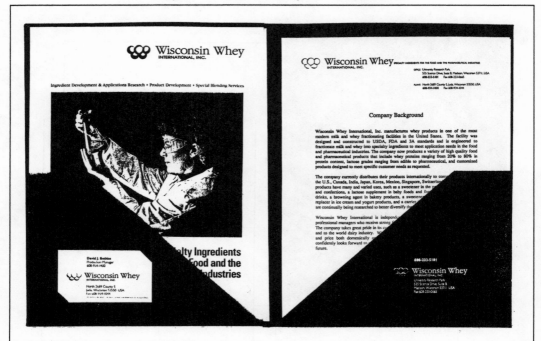

Capabilities and Product Brochures

A brochure speaks for you when you can't be there in person. It should present you as naturally as you would present yourself, projecting your personality through its look, tone, and message. Even though you often send them in the mail, brochures are not direct-mail sales literature. In Chapter 9, "Direct Mail Advertising," I discuss the brochure's close cousin, the *lead generator*. Lead generators are an efficient way to reach people who buy what you sell, and generate interest in buying it from you. Brochures work in a much different way.

A *capabilities brochure* tells your story with a central theme and focus. It unfolds the story purposefully, in a tone of friendly authority. It makes clear what makes you different from your competitors.

It might be printed in four colors on glossy stock, or two colors, or simply consist of sheets of paper in a folder. See Example 9-7 for some diagrams of typical brochure formats.

If you sell products, you might need brochures that introduce each item in the same way a capabilities brochure talks about your company. Sometimes distributors or manufacturers will have product brochures available for you, slick professional products that you can have imprinted with your logo. So look for this kind of co-op support for product brochures.

A brochure may be illustrated with art or photos, or may just tell the story in type. Example 11-9 shows a typical brochure for a small company.

Example 11-9A: Datakeep Outside
Used by permission of Datakeep, Inc.

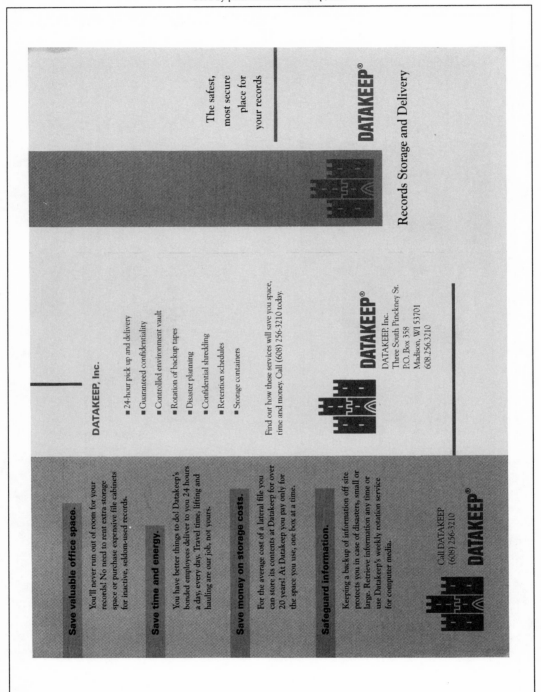

Example 11-9B: Datakeep Inside
Used by permission of Datakeep, Inc.

Karl W. Wellensiek
President

An active member and past officer of the Madison chapter of ARMA (Association of Records Managers and Administrators), Karl Wellensiek is an acknowledged expert in records storage and management.

He has been a leader in recognizing and promoting professionalism in the field of records management. A long-standing member of Madison's business community, Karl has extensive analytical and operational experience in working with both large and small businesses.

Merita Berryman
Records Manager
CUNA & Affiliates

"The security of our information is most important to us. We did a lot of investigating and feel very confident in Datakeep and its controlled environment vault with respect to both humidity-temperature control and intrusion protection. And the cost is reasonable compared to what it would cost to do it ourselves."

David G. Walsh
Partner-in-Charge
Foley & Lardner
Madison Office

"Space is a big factor for us, and using Datakeep frees up valuable office space. Best of all, the Datakeep system both encourages and facilitates our own organization, and in that sense has improved our efficiency."

Bernadette A. Thiemann
Administrative Coordinator
Cellular One

"Datakeep's service is consistently prompt, reliable and has become a valuable tool to us. With Datakeep it's very easy to track archival material, and their rapid retrieval system works very smoothly. I can always depend on Datakeep's professional service."

DATAKEEP® *Our name and logo are derived from the word "keep"—the castle's stronghold, the safest, most secure place.*

In today's world of information and technology, your company's records are one of its most vital assets. Keeping them in the safest, most secure environment possible makes good business sense—and it's our business, our only business.

At Datakeep we combine security and technology to give you the best records storage available—controlled temperature and humidity for micrographic and computer media, industrial strength shelving for documents, computer-controlled inventory systems, maximum security systems.

Karl W. Wellensiek, President

Note the components—the subheads making benefit statements, the testimonials, the credibility-building photo of Karl in the storage vaults, and the humanizing story of the logo. Here's a brochure that covers all the bases.

How do you make a brochure? Start by studying Chapter 9. Keep in mind these tips:

- Start by writing your copy. Write an outline, then write heads, text, and subheads until you've covered all your points. Don't write more than 700 to 1,000 words. Don't omit the housekeeping details: a phone number, address, and of course the logo.

- Think about the art. If your offering calls to mind a dramatic image, you're in luck. But most areas of business are pretty abstract. How will you visually present your company's story? Don't try to get by cheap. Doing without photography is better than using muddy, obscure photos.

- Edit your text. Picture your audience; have you talked about benefits or wasted your words on features? Rewrite. Are you using the passive voice where you could use the active? Rewrite again. Read the copy out loud. Does it have a musical sound? How's the rhythm? Rewrite again. You get the idea.

- Lay out your brochure in a clean, legible way. Establish a uniform format for type and placement of graphics. Make several copies so that you can look at all the panels of your brochure together; they should look like members of the same family.

You'll find lots of help in other chapters of this book. Take a look at Chapter 5, "The Creative Approach"; Chapter 6, "How to Create Print Ads that Sell"; and Chapter 9, "Direct Mail Advertising." You'll find the creative advice in Chapters 5 and 6 helpful, and the production budget and schedule information in Chapter 9 will help you plan your brochure.

What Will You Do with a Brochure?

A brochure is an extension of you, the representative of your firm. It should be used in conjunction with personal contact. If you speak in public, bring your brochure to pass out. If you have lunch with someone you're grooming for business referrals, mail a brochure afterward with a note of thanks. If you're trying to get your foot in the door with a prospect, your phone calls are likely to be met with "send me your brochure." It's important to have literature on hand for the follow-up.

These are all fairly haphazard distribution methods! You will probably want to make an orderly distribution effort when you first print a new brochure. Your mailing list might include all your current clients, your prospect list, and your referral network list. Include a cover letter with a simple statement explaining why you think each one should review your brochure. The letter might be slightly different for each list. Or design a reply card that turns your brochure into a lead generator, like the card from Datakeep in Example 11-10.

Example 11-10: Datakeep Reply Card
Used by permission of Datakeep, Inc.

DATAKEEP®

BUSINESS REPLY MAIL
FIRST CLASS MAIL   PERMIT NO. 1043   MADISON WI

POSTAGE WILL BE PAID BY ADDRESSEE

DATAKEEP, Inc.
PO BOX 358
MADISON WI 53791-8207

NO POSTAGE
NECESSARY IF
MAILED IN THE
UNITED STATES

❑ Yes, I would like to begin saving space, time, and money with Datakeep. Call me!

❑ I am interested in a free cost/benefit analysis of our records storage system. Please call me to set up my free, no obligation consultation.

Please send me more information about
❑ Datakeep
❑ Disaster planning
❑ Offsite storage guidelines

I am interested in
❑ Document storage
❑ Computer and micrographic media storage
❑ Media Protection Service (rotation of backup material)

We are currently storing our records
❑ in file cabinets in our office
❑ in a spare room in our building
❑ in additional rented space offsite
❑ in a mini warehouse
❑ at an employee's home
❑ other

Name: _____

Title: _____

Company: _____

Address: _____

_____

Telephone: _____

Best time to call: ❑ a.m.   ❑ p.m.

Chapter 9 will help you with the logistics of doing this mailing.

When you've just paid for a box of printing, you'll feel much better if you know that it's hurrying out there to work for you. The brochures not distributed in the initial mailing become your supply for filling future needs.

Catalogs

Catalogs are pieces of literature describing all the products a company sells. The product descriptions include information about the physical properties of the product; explanations of functions, features, and benefits; and prices for various quantities. Some have much more detail to help the customer. All catalogs display merchandise and help you find it. If selling through catalogs is part of your business, you're probably already pursuing classes or reading books specific to the topic. Catalog experts can tell you which spots are the hot spots, how the price of an item affects the size of its picture, how to arrange your order form, and more. How well you know the ins and outs has a major effect on your catalog's profitability. We also talked about catalogs in Chapter 9, so see that chapter for more on this subject.

Newsletters

Newsletters come and go in popularity. Some businesses use them successfully to promote, others to inform. They are less formal than a brochure. A good newsletter is an informal, relaxed, person-to-person communication. Its purpose is to remind customers that you're around, remind them of what you do, and provide news in an area in which you both have an interest.

There is a category of newsletter that serves small audiences with special interests. These subscriber-based publications form a limited-circulation subset of the publishing industry. Publishing newsletters is a business that draws many entrepreneurs. But we're not talking about for-subscription newsletters here. We're talking about a free newsletter sent to your mailing list that helps you communicate with clients, prospects, and peers through magazinelike stories about yourself.

A newsletter is a big commitment of time and money. Too often people start off with good intentions, but find they can't maintain the quality or regularity they would like. That's dangerous—faltering publicly is hard on your image.

Why take the chance? Here are some reasons you might want to do a newsletter.

- Instead of making a straight sales pitch, the newsletter delivers a blend of news, ideas, and promotional messages.

- Newsletters build credibility. Repetition builds awareness of your products and services. Your target group of customers and prospects is becoming more familiar with you, even if they never read more than a few lines of it.

- You have the luxury of more words. If your product or service requires a complex sell, a newsletter may be a smooth way to deliver it.

What types of information will you include? News, of course—from your company or from your industry. Answers to questions. Tips and explanations. Case histories. Profiles of employees, customers, community leaders. Reviews and write-ups of conferences. You might reprint articles of interest from trade publications—with permission.

Newsletters can be demanding to publish because doing them right takes time. You have to meet your deadline for each one, coming up with stories and doing all the attendant work of getting it printed and mailed. You may want to contract with a freelance writer to write the newsletter for you. By networking around, you can usually find someone to help you. If your city publishes a business magazine, check with the editor for names of freelance writers.

How should it look? With desktop publishing, there's no excuse for information from any company looking less than professional. Hire a graphic designer to help you with a format design as you start your first issue. Your newsletter will need a masthead—the graphic treatment of its name, which usually goes at the top of the first page. It will need a layout grid, typestyles, and recommendations for the treatment of illustrations or photos.

If you want to produce your newsletter yourself, get a layout template, preferably as a file on disk, in either Quark XPress or Pagemaker, for Windows or Mac, whichever you work in. Newsletter templates on disk are available—look in software catalogs.

Alternatively, you might simply give your designer your stories (on disk) and pay for the layout services. An eight-page newsletter should cost less than $750. Get an estimate and weigh it against the staff time in-house production will cost you.

A newsletter carries too many words to waste your readers' time; make sure the design is legible. Lines of copy should be not more than two alphabets long—about fifty letters to a line on average. Count characters and adhere to this rule. Lines of up to 75 characters can get by if there is plenty of space between the lines vertically (called leading), but this is a style more common in books than in newsletters. You can choose to look like a book, a magazine, or a newspaper page (see Example 11-11).

If you're even thinking about producing a newsletter, start collecting samples that come across your desk. These will help you communicate your likes and dislikes to the designers and others who assist you.

Example 11-11: 35 West Newsletter
Used by permission of 35 West Productions.

How will you know if you're doing a good job? Is the newsletter you're offering of real value? Look at an issue of your newsletter through your customers' eyes. Every now and then, do an informal phone survey. Five or six calls will alert you if your newsletter has grown stale.

Producing a newsletter is a matter of establishing a routine and sticking to it. Template 11-2A gives a typical production schedule for a newsletter.

Template 11-2A: Quarterly Newsletter Production Schedule

Fall Newsletter, 1989

Editor/director meet	June 13
Copy to graphic artist	July 11
Camera-ready art to printer	July 31
Printer delivers to mailing house	August 21
Mailing date	August 28
Hit date	September 6

Winter Newsletter, 1989

Editor/director meet	September 26
Copy to graphic artist	October 20
Camera-ready art to printer	November 3
Printer delivers to mailing house	November 16
Mailing date	November 22
Hit date	December 1

Spring Newsletter, 1990

Editor/director meet	January 8
Copy to graphic artist	January 26
Camera-ready art to printer	February 9
Printer delivers to mailing house	February 23
Mailing date	March 2
Hit date	March 9

Summer Newsletter, 1990

Editor/director meet	April 4
Copy to graphic artist	April 30
Camera-ready art to printer	May 14
Printer delivers to mailing house	May 28
Mailing date	June 4
Hit date	June 13

Use Template 11-2B to schedule your own newsletter.

Template 11-2B: Quarterly Newsletter Production Schedule

Use this blank worksheet to map out your newsletter deadlines.
Use Template 11-2A to get an idea how much time to allow for each
step. For a more detailed production schedule template,
see Chapter 9.

Fall Newsletter   **Cover Date:** _____
Editor/director meet   _____
Copy to graphic artist   _____
Camera-ready art to printer   _____
Printer delivers to mailing house   _____
Mailing date   _____
Hit date

Winter Newsletter   **Cover Date:** _____
Editor/director meet   _____
Copy to graphic artist   _____
Camera-ready art to printer   _____
Printer delivers to mailing house   _____
Mailing date   _____
Hit date   _____

Spring Newsletter   **Cover Date:** _____
Editor/director meet   _____
Copy to graphic artist   _____
Camera-ready art to printer   _____
Printer delivers to mailing house   _____
Mailing date   _____
Hit date   _____

Summer Newsletter   **Cover Date:** _____
Editor/director meet   _____
Copy to graphic artist   _____
Camera-ready art to printer   _____
Printer delivers to mailing house   _____
Mailing date   _____
Hit date   _____

A typical newsletter might be four to eight letter-size pages, and informational or promotional in its content. It is produced on desktop publishing equipment, with graphics from a clip-art library, or photos of products, events, etc.

Template 11-3 is a worksheet to help you calculate a budget for your newsletter.

Template 11-3: Newsletter Budget Cost Estimate Worksheet

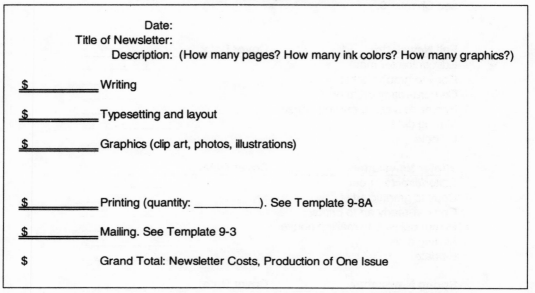

Date:

Title of Newsletter:

Description: (How many pages? How many ink colors? How many graphics?)

$_____ Writing

$_____ Typesetting and layout

$_____ Graphics (clip art, photos, illustrations)

$_____ Printing (quantity: _____). See Template 9-8A

$_____ Mailing. See Template 9-3

$ Grand Total: Newsletter Costs, Production of One Issue

For more detailed information about estimating costs for printed pieces, see Chapter 9.

Trade Show Booths and Retail Space Design

These may sound like two unrelated topics, but they're really very similar. We're talking about merchandising. As your customers interact with your business, you want to control the experience to your advantage. Whether you're at a trade show or in your retail showroom, the space you're in is filled with sights, sounds, and smells. These either encourage or disturb your prospects. You must learn to orchestrate the whole environment. If you're in a retail business, you know how important this is. You may have worked with an architectural specialist in retail design when you planned your store. Maybe you adapted the location of cash registers, fitting rooms, and conference areas to enhance behaviors you observe as customers shop in your store.

If you're in one of the many industries that do business through trade shows, you don't have the luxury of learning from day-to-day experience. Say you go to five or six shows a year. You get a total of at most two dozen days on the floor to accomplish a year's worth of business. You'd better have a trade show booth that's engineered to maximize that opportunity.

You will find specialists in the exhibit industry who will help you analyze your needs and design a booth to suit. Display companies design and construct exhibits, and also coordinate with show personnel so that your booth arrives when and where it should. Many display companies rent displays, sometimes customized to your needs. If your budget requires something more modest, you can purchase off-the-shelf displays, like Skylines (Example 11-12). These collapsible walls are covered with velour panels that allow you to use Velcro to attach posters to them. Racks, lights, and rear-projection screens make them customizable to your needs. The cost of display materials for the posters has come down in recent years. Modular display units like these are available for under $2,000. A set of three or four posters, combining type and photos, might cost between $1,000 and $1,500.

Example 11-12: Skyline Exhibit Diagram
Used by permission of Skyline Displays.

Your exhibit experience is a stage play; your booth is the set. You are the director—and the scriptwriter, too. Think through the action you want to see. Your booth might need a display area for your merchandise and a conference area for deal making. Think through your "props list." Will you be bringing your own furniture, or renting from the show management? There's a whole industry built around the convention/exhibit trade. You can go to seminars on how to make your investment in exhibiting pay off. You'll learn how to greet prospects, manage leads, make sales.

If you are considering exhibiting, talk to the sales agents for several shows and the reps for several types of display systems. You'll get a good feel for the lay of the land in your industry.

How does this tie in to corporate identity? Your booth is certainly an extension of your business personality. It should be strongly identified with the company colors and the logo you use.

Your booth has to function as a billboard—it has to draw people in. Keep the theme and the graphics simple. Keep words short. Make them describe a benefit.

Big pictures draw people in—details of processes, or product photos, or shots of the plant. As long as the quality of the color is gorgeous, these will enhance your display.

A graphic designer or a specialist from the exhibit industry can produce the display pieces for you. Ask to see samples of their work, and look for a good match in materials and budget.

Signage

The last area of corporate identity is the signage that identifies your physical properties. You have a headquarters—perhaps you have additional locations too. Take a look at your building signage. Is it consistent with your company's positioning? Is it in good repair?

Do you have a fleet of vehicles? How are they identified? If you think this is small potatoes, take a look at the statistics on outdoor

advertising. Your vans could be—and should be—hardworking billboards. Especially if delivery is part of your product offering, you should take your vehicle signage very seriously.

The company whose van is shown in Example 11-3 provides archival storage of business files; pick-up and delivery is a key benefit of its service. The company's brochure was featured earlier in this chapter. It has used vehicle identification as a key tool to advertise the business.

Example 11-13: Datakeep Van

Conclusion: How Corporate Identity Supports Advertising

Advertising is about image—creating perception in the minds of the audience. A well-managed corporate identity helps the advertising create that perception. Because the advertising and the corporate identity are parts of an integrated whole, there is synergy—the advertising encourages recall of the corporate identity, and vice versa.

Your logo and your stationery present your face to the world. Your brochure opens your mouth and speaks. Through your trade show booth or retail space, you invite your customers into your home. With your catalogs, newsletters, and advertising, you try to amuse, educate, or inform your guests. The result? Popularity. In the marketplace, that translates into sales.

Look at your business card again. Think for a moment about the times and places you've pulled one out to exchange. Think about the other pieces we've discussed in this chapter—the store floor plans, trade show booths, and signage. Are you putting your best foot forward in every case? And do your socks match?

If you've been following the concepts and exercises in this book, you are definitely planning to grow your business through advertising. New people will be hearing about you for the first time. You are about to make hundreds of first impressions. Get your corporate identity in line with the image you'd like them to see.

Chapter 12

Do You Need Help with Your Advertising? How to Hire and Work with Specialists

It's unreasonable for most of you to think you can—or should—do all of your advertising planning, purchasing, and execution yourself. There are hundreds of specialists in your marketplace who can help you with the various components of your marketing. Deciding how to put together your advertising plan is like planning a meal. You can stop at your grocer's freezer and pop it in your microwave, or you can shop around and put out something you've created from scratch. You'll find an abundance of talents and services in the local market. Here are a few ideas that might help in selecting the best ingredients to suit your tastes.

Before you let your fingers do the walking, though, consider your needs. Think about what you've learned from this book, and where you'd like to begin. Describe what you will need to do to get started. What sort of project might make sense for your business? An ad campaign, a direct mail piece, a coupon promotion? Ask your friends to recommend some of the services that they've had success with. You'll find a spectrum of firms, from individual specialists to full-service agencies, all providing ways to fulfill different needs.

A Survey of Advertising Service Professionals

I'll start by talking about the organizations—ad agencies, design studios, public relations firms, and so on—that produce advertising. Then I'll describe the individuals who make up the freelance and consulting scene.

Advertising Agencies and Other Firms

The main advantage of using an ad agency or another firm with some depth of staff is that it will handle the entire job for you, and the results will be professional. The end product will reflect coordination, from strategy through concept to copy and design to production and printing. This group of people is accustomed to working together and has systems and expertise that show in the final product. The agency (I'm using the term to cover ad agencies, graphic design studios, and other communication firms) will assign an account representative to act as liaison between you and the various departments of the agency. Rather than your meeting with and directing the efforts of a writer, artist, producer, photographer, and printer, the agency will do it all. Your communication with the individual specialists will be through the account representative, who acts as an advocate for your ideas and priorities.

Another advantage of working with an agency is that you get its experience at handling coordinated campaigns. If you're planning a program with many components, an agency's skills may be useful to you. The agency understands marketing and advertising strategy. Agencies act as consultants, helping to improve the plan you've developed, with a resulting increase in return on investment.

The disadvantages of working with agencies are several. One is clearly budget. You will pay to have someone take over the burden of managing a project, and you will pay for the expertise you receive in consultation and technical execution. Also, agencies build their profitability and their reputations on long-term relationships with clients. If yours is a one-shot project and is not likely to result in repeat business with the agency, you may find that the agency is not particularly interested.

The channels of communication at an agency can be a disadvantage as well. I often hear complaints that boil down to miscommunication during a message's journey from client to account rep to artist or writer, and back again. You can avoid this by selecting a smaller agency, where often the account rep also functions as the writer or art director on the project. Now you have more direct communication, and your satisfaction level will be higher.

There is a considerable gray area between the traditional advertising agency at one end of the spectrum and freelance artists at the other. There are small creative agencies and design firms that specialize in project-based rather than retainer-based relationships. These small firms offer a lot of the advantages of freelance talent when it comes to price and flexibility. Sometimes extremely creative people don't fit in well at larger agencies; you will find them working in smaller shops, without the overhead or the creative constraints of the larger firms. Especially if you are not an "idea person" yourself, you may want to look for these firms. The creative edge they give your advertising will be worth it.

Some agencies bill for their services at hourly rates; others work on a retainer basis; most provide some services free in exchange for placing commissioned media buys. When you meet with prospective firms, be sure to ask about their rate structure and billing procedures.

Freelance Talent

Choosing to work with freelance professionals who handle specific tasks gives you access to a wide pool of talented people who will work on a project basis. When you work directly with specialists selected for specific parts of the job, like copywriting, illustration, photography, or graphic design, you gain control. Now you are in charge of the deadline, the budget, and the creative outcome at each step of the way, at the cost of spending more of your time on the campaign.

In every community there are freelance writers and strategists who can help you create your message. Producers, directors, illustrators, photographers, and graphic designers help you get the idea into final form. How do you find these people? The Yellow Pages is one way. Another is through networking with friends in other businesses. Another is to call the advertising office of the local business magazine or newspaper and get some names of people they often work with. From there, you can contact these people and begin to explore with them their abilities to meet your needs.

A new breed of freelance professionals, desktop publishers, have come into being in the last five years. These people prepare artwork for printing, just as graphic designers do, but with a hard-to-define difference of approach. My observation is that those who call themselves desktop publishers have less confidence in their artistic skill than graphic designers. Both will arrange a page for you, often using the same software, and with similar degrees of technical skill. The difference will be one of creativity.

The designer is more likely to propose new or different solutions to you, and more likely to show you several variations of a design and discuss their merits to help you decide which to use. Desktop publishers view themselves more as technicians, prepared to execute the ideas and instructions you bring to the table. You will have to decide for yourself whether creativity is a component that you are willing to pay for. I would argue that it should be.

Most printers have an art staff who, like the desktop publishers, are prepared to take your idea and make printable artwork from it. Their skills are probably comparable, but their equipment may be different (traditional phototypesetting machines instead of desktop computers, for example), and their proximity to the printing process means that they will be responsible for how their work runs on press. They quickly learn what works and what doesn't—an advantage for you.

All of these people work at an hourly billing rate, which may range from $25 to $125 an hour, depending on what you're buying. Any materials or out-of-pocket expenses will be an additional charge. You should be able to get an accurate project cost estimate from these professionals before work begins.

Know Your Copyrights!

When you purchase artistic services, whether through an agency or directly from the creative talent, be sure to ask your vendor who owns the concepts, the original artwork, and the copyright license to that artwork. With illustrators and photographers, it is customary to specify certain use rights when you commission the work. You might request the right to use the work for one-time distribution, for instance, or the right to unlimited circulation for a limited time period, or all rights outright. Ask your vendor's policies before you consider your agreement final. You may want to have a conversation with your own lawyer about the subject.

How to Choose Your Suppliers

How are you going to pick the right person or firm for you? The best way to get started is to develop a project, determine your field of prospective agencies or individual freelancers, and let the project out for bids. Even if you're not 100 percent convinced that the project you describe is what your business should be doing, it will give you something specific to discuss with your possible advertising partners. Their reactions and suggestions will provide you with a fair basis of comparison between potential firms, as close to "apples to apples" as shopping for creative services is likely to get.

How do you decide who makes that short list of candidates? Ask your associates. A good professional referral is absolutely the best source. A firm's track record on similar projects means a great deal when you're shopping for creative services. As you interview these firms or individuals, follow these tips:

- *Look at samples.* Do they match the quality you seek? Even if your project is quite simple, it needs to be clean, sharp, and professional. The portfolio of samples your potential vendor shows you will obviously be the work of which he or she is proudest. If something appears to lack quality, what does that say about the work you *aren't* seeing?

- *Look for experience in your field.* You may not want to hire the agency that is handling advertising for your toughest competitor. But you don't want to spend too much time bringing a supplier up to speed on your industry, either. Firms and freelancers will tend to specialize in different areas and industries, such as business-to-business marketing or fashion or financial services, where they find a good match to their interests and talents. It is to your advantage to find someone who has experience in, and gets excited about, the field in which you operate.

- *Ask to see their client list.* Would you be among your peers if you hired this firm? Or are the firms listed too big, or too bush league, to be appropriate for you? Choose several firms from the client list for which they have done projects similar to the one you're planning. Call for references, just as you would with a potential employee.

- *Does their style please you?* I'm using the word *style* to mean two different things here. First, the style of their work should be appealing to you. You should see in their portfolio work that would be appropriate if it had been done for your business. But also, the style of the people should be comfortable for you. Ask to meet *all* the people who will be working on your account. A business buddy of mine took me aside once and shyly asked me a question. He was working with an ad agency to create a promotional folder. A young copywriter had been assigned to his account. "I don't like his neckties," my friend admitted. "Is that a reason not to work with him?" When you're buying creative services, I told him, yes! Everything about a person—every person who works on your account—goes into the intangible mix of creative services. If you don't like the people, there's too great a possibility that you won't like the work. Maximize your chance for success—choose to work with people you like who do work you like.

Your next step is to interview these firms. You will ask for proposals from each firm; these proposals will generally include a situation analysis, recommendations, cost estimates, and a creative approach. You and each firm should work out a reasonable definition of how in-depth you want this proposal to be. Understand that if a firm can afford to put significant time into speculative business pitches like this, that is reflected in the rates it charges its paying clients. A leaner firm might offer you more casual off-the-cuff observations. Most firms prefer not to prepare creative work "on spec."

As you interview these firms, give them the information from your business review from Chapter 1 (Template 1-1). Make sure you describe your product and identify your market. Include any special suggestions, such as strategies you feel are appropriate. Discuss your anticipated budget range. Set deadlines for the presentations. Make it clear that other firms will be competing for your account; it's a simple courtesy, and ensures that you get the best from those you invite.

Once you've received the responses, set up meetings with the agencies, a few a day, or two or three days in a row. Go to see the agencies, rather than having them come to see you. This gives you a chance to sample the atmosphere and meet the people who might soon be working for you.

Each agency will present its ideas and a justification for the approach. Each knows your budget constraints, so notice whether the proposals stay on target. Consider the balance between the creative and marketing aspects of each proposal, and the process each takes to effect its plan.

Set up some criteria to review the proposals.

You may be tempted to evaluate the proposals under the influence of some pretty persuasive people; don't accept an empty message served up in an attractive wrapper. But don't ignore personalities either. Your working relationship with the chosen agency may be the most important factor of all.

Put together an evaluation of each presentation. Try to make your decision promptly, and call everyone back to tell them the final decision. Don't be afraid to critique any presentation. A thoughtful review of your needs may come back to help you in the future. Template 12-1 provides guidelines you might use for judging presentations.

Template 12-1: Criteria for Reviewing Agencies

Criteria for Reviewing Agencies

Questions to ask yourself about the agencies you interview. You may use this form in the interview situation, or use it to record your comments afterward.

Who will actually work on our account? Do we feel rapport with those people?

_____

Is it evident that they care about details? Are they neat, prompt, etc.?

_____

Do they have clients who market their products or services in the same way we do?

_____

How's the fit? Is our account likely to be profitable enough for them? Will we get their best attention?

_____

Check references; ask how successful the agency's work has been.

_____

Have the staff and clients been around for a while?

_____

Is the agency profitable? Stable?

_____

Regarding the agency's recommendations in response to your project description, ask yourself:
Is the recommendation sound? Consider the rationale behind the media plan, the creative approach, and the suggested executions. Are these recommendations consistent with the suggestions in this book?

_____

_____

_____

What does your gut tell you? Creative relationships thrive on intuition. Are you ready to trust these people with your money? Do you feel you can work together to your mutual satisfaction?

_____

_____

_____

If you are managing a project with several specialists, make certain you have time to attend to the project. You'll be head chef in the kitchen, coordinating the efforts of all. The more attention you can pay to a project, the higher the quality of the work you'll get in return.

How to Get Good Results from Your Team of Specialists

Whether you work with one agency coordinating all the players or you work with many independent freelancers, _you_ have a lot to do with how well the process goes. Here are some tips for getting the best possible results.

- *Give complete information up front.* That doesn't mean giving orders—you are, after all, hiring these people because they have expertise in areas you don't. It means providing the resources that help them to read your mind. When you sit down with someone to initiate a job, bring samples that will help make it clear what you are looking for. Samples of pieces you hate are as useful as samples you admire. Bring anything that helps to communicate what you—and other decision makers on your team—would consider a successful outcome. If you are meeting with a writer, bring everything previously written about the company or product. Your press releases, business plan, and advertisements all give information the writer might need. Literature or advertisements from competitors are helpful, too. You cut down the writer's research time, and you convey what style of language is appropriate and acceptable to you.

  When you are meeting with a graphic designer, bring your company logo, stationery, and other printed pieces, so that your supplier can get a feel for the whole family. If you have strong likes and dislikes in colors or graphic treatments, make that clear.

  Especially when you are working with freelancers, you must take your role as coordinator seriously. That includes coordinating the information exchange.

- *Talk about money, up front and often.* Everyone appreciates it when the money side of a project is handled in a straightforward manner. When you initiate the project, discuss what the process should be as well as the end product. If you want to see several different layouts, so that you have choices to select from, say so. Discuss what the price might be to show you two options, or three. Now you know what you will receive, and the supplier knows how much work you're ready to

pay for.

I find, and it's not unreasonable, that clients always assume that the price we've discussed is firm unless I make a point of opening the subject again. If the project changes course in midstream—which isn't unusual with creative processes—it's important to talk about the cost ramifications. The copywriting budget for a three-panel brochure must be adjusted if we decide to change the direct mail program to a five-component sales letter. In fact, every portion of the budget—creative, production, and printing—will be affected by the change of direction.

Nobody likes surprises when the job is billed. It's always better to talk about costs while there's still time to opt for a cheaper solution if you have to. To keep good relations with your suppliers, keep the money conversation going throughout the project. Not everyone is comfortable talking about money. Many freelance artists have a hard time with the subject, and will avoid it as long as possible. That's why I'm suggesting that you make it your responsibility, and take it seriously.

- *Be available when the project needs you.* It's a terrible feeling to be the one in charge of getting a job to press on time, and to have that last proof in your hands but no client available to check it. Do you punt and send it to the printer without a sign-off? Or do you take responsibility for holding up the job while you track down the elusive client?

  Don't put your suppliers in that position. Discuss schedules as work progresses, so that you can plan to be available when your input is needed. If they submit work for you to review, be timely about approving it or handing it back for revision.

- *Be open to suggestions.* You've hired these people because of their expertise; your project will benefit from letting them do their jobs. Too much direction from you will result in a demoralized crew. We have a word for it in the industry: "hired wrists." Nobody wants to bring his or her skills and expertise to the table, only to be asked to carry out another person's instructions. Let your team of specialists bring you their best shot, and then react. That brings me to my next point.

- *Offer your criticisms in a constructive way.* Don't second-guess your team; don't start rewriting or redesigning the piece. Clearly state your objections to the work as presented, but leave it to the creator to make the necessary adaptations. If facts are wrong, provide the right information or the source to check. If a design layout leaves you cold, try to be specific about why. "I think the type is hard to read" or "My audience is too old to go for those wild colors" will help artists to see where they've missed the mark. This is more helpful than "I just think it needs more pizzazz."

  Managing creative specialists is just like managing your employees. Their egos are involved in the work they present to you, and creative people can be easily upset. Be tactful when you need to, supportive and positive when you can. Keep the lines of communication open and your team will reward you with their best efforts.

- *Establish a decision-making process and stick to it.* Let everyone know from the start who is to be involved in what decisions. Reviewing the copy might involve certain people in your business; technical people should certainly review any descriptions and specifications for accuracy. Reviewing the design layout might involve others on your staff—the sales representatives who will use the piece in the field, and so on. Your lawyer may want to see contest rules or product guarantees—but should not touch the creative approach.

  Too many cooks can quickly spoil this broth. Water it down with committee decisionmaking and the final result may have no flavor at all. Don't change the recipe—or the ingredients—halfway through. You'll find yourself redoing work that you thought was completed, and the budget, timeline, and sense of satisfaction with the final piece will all suffer as a result.

- And finally, *don't waste time!* I have clients who carefully mark up a manuscript with corrections, and then insist on meeting with me for an hour to explain what each mark means. It would cost them half as much if they realized that I can understand written instructions, and simply let me do the work.

  Avoid unnecessary meetings and paperwork. Don't insist that your account representative meet with you in person over each piece of business—phone calls and faxes are often more efficient. Every freelancer and every firm makes money by billing time, and each is in business to make a profit. If working for you is unprofitable for them, they will find ways to cut corners on your job.

Even if others are performing the tasks related to your advertising, you are still the ultimate manager of the job. Using the strategy, calendar, and budget worksheets in this book will help you stay on time, on target, and on budget. Chapter 13 summarizes how those templates work together to deliver your advertising plan.

Your Computer Is Your Advertising Ally

Your computer is an important assistant. The right software can help you in three areas.

Project Management

All projects begin with budgets, and budgets begin with spreadsheets. If you're not familiar with using a spreadsheet, you're missing the power of some of the templates in this book.

Scheduling and tracking software can be very useful too. If you are doing your advertising yourself, or coordinating teams of freelancers, you will want a convenient way to keep on top of tasks and deadlines. There is good software available for both the Windows and the Mac environment. A computer software retailer will be able to make suggestions about products to suit your needs. Quick Schedule + and TimeLine are two possibilities.

Production

Advertising is made out of words and images. The word processing software you already use for your business needs will be adequate for a lot of your work. Writing a positioning statement, scripting a radio spot, writing a press release—these are word processing tasks.

If you're creating your own printed pieces, you may or may not be able to get along with just word processing software—it depends partly on how elaborate your ideas are, but more on how well you know the software in question. The leading word processing programs—I run into WordPerfect and Microsoft Word the most—can do an awful lot of sophisticated design maneuvers.

I and most print production professionals choose desktop-publishing software programs because of their ability to print to more sophisticated Postscript devices, and the flexibility of their layout options. Quark XPress and Pagemaker are the leading programs, and seem to match each other feature for feature; either can accomplish plenty. If you're choosing one, look for recommendations from people who do tasks similar to yours, and then stick with what you pick. Learning more programs all the time shoots a hole in your productivity.

Note: Before you decide which program to purchase, check for compatibility with your hardware. RAM, hard disk size, processing speed, and printers must be selected to work together. While you may have the equipment listed as "minimum system requirements" for a particular piece of software, often much more hard disk space or processing speed is needed to be productive. If you are setting up an in-house desktop-publishing system, *work with a computer consultant who is familiar with this type of work!*

Knowing Your Customers

A good relational database is the power behind your marketing plan. It helps you answer the critical questions about your current customers, to help you find new ones like them. A good database will be open-ended, allowing you to add new fields of information as your understanding broadens. FoxPro and Claris Works are two possibilities; again, I'd suggest you work with a consultant to recommend software and help you get your database up and running.

Chapter 13

Summary:
What You Ought to Do Is...

My mother told me to avoid people who say, "What you ought to do is...." This book contains 3,479 variations (more or less) on that phrase. I'm sorry.

In the sections where I've coached you on advertising copywriting, I've emphasized the need to close with a call to action. Now that I'm finishing this book and you are too, my call to action is this. Stop reading about advertising—go forth and do. Take your templates and your notes and start putting your work to good use.

This book is a tool kit. You are a carpenter. Your ideas, your product, your marketplace—these are some of the materials you build with. This book has shown you how they can be put together to build different sorts of advertising.

In this chapter we'll review your advertising tools by means of a chapter-by-chapter overview, summary of templates, and repetition of key recommendations. At the finish you will be ready to put your knowledge to use.

Even so, you can follow every tip in this book, and you'll still need to start over again every couple of years. Planning is like doing the dishes. Get used to repeating the tasks.

I've used my motto "analyze, strategize, create" more than once in this book. Right now I'd like to emphasize the first two words,

the planning steps. Whether or not you are executing your own advertising, it's a sure bet you're doing your own planning—and you're on the line for its success or failure. If you analyze your situation and strategize your route to your goals, it follows that the advertising you create will succeed.

The Ring Binder

Since planning is so important, it makes sense to organize your planning efforts. In several chapters I've recommended that you use a ring binder for your notes and materials. This system works for students, and it works for me. My reputation for follow-through is a good one, and it's my notebooks that keep me organized. I think a system like this will work for you.

Advertising isn't the most linear subject in the world. For instance, you have to have an idea how much a direct mail piece costs before you can develop a marketing plan that relies on a lot of direct mail. You have to know a little about every area before you can decide which areas are important for you. This book is meant to be browsed, then revisited as your attention turns to different facets of your advertising.

I've introduced some fairly broad subjects in specific chapters, then treated those subjects in less depth when they surface in other chapters. Cost/payback analysis is one such topic. Calculating CPM (cost per thousand) is another. These subjects are relevant to almost every facet of advertising and publicity. In this chapter I'll point out the crossovers, so that you can find the information you may have missed by skimming chapters.

This book is organized in three sections, starting with broad concepts, moving into specific executions, and finishing up with tangential thoughts.

In the first section you were introduced to the underlying structure that gives rise to creative advertising. We laid the groundwork as we talked about setting goals, choosing strategies, exploring positioning, using promotions, planning media usage, and developing the advertising message.

In the next section we looked at the specifics of negotiating the buy and crafting the ad message for print, radio, TV, and direct mail advertising. Templates and examples offered tools for making your own plans and executions.

Then in the third section we looked at other components of marketing that fall outside "pure" advertising: your publicity, your corporate image, and your relationships with ad agencies and other professionals.

Here is an outline of the key concepts in each chapter, with crossover topics noted. I'll describe the templates that help you see the big picture. Some of the templates simply help you clarify your thinking on certain topics. Others are more important to your overall planning. These templates are statements of strategy, calendars, and budgets. Specific chapters generate information about your plans for print, radio, TV, and direct mail. As you complete these templates, you lock in decisions that help you manage your marketing work. Keep these templates up to date in

your notebook and you can refer to them as needed, to keep your marketing work on time, on budget, and on target.

Part 1, Planning the Strategy and Finding the Creative Approach

Chapter 1, Before You Advertise: Determining Your Marketing Objectives

When you are determining your marketing objectives, you are finding a way to connect your personal and business goals with the needs and desires of your marketplace. You do this by analyzing who you are and what you offer today, then choosing objectives based on the strengths, weaknesses, opportunities, and threats that your analysis uncovers. How you move toward those objectives becomes your marketing strategy. Like a map showing you the route from where you are to where you want to go, your strategy helps you plan for and make the trip. In this chapter I recommend a format for the written marketing plan that makes use of a ring-binder notebook.

Chapter 1 Templates

Template 1-1, The Business Review: This is an analysis of your business, challenging to complete but critical to your success.

Template 1-8, Statement of Marketing Objective: This is linked to strategy statements in Templates 2-1, 3-2, 5-1, 5-2, and 10-1. Referring back to Template 1-8 as you develop the others, and as you go about executing your plans, will keep your efforts strategically on target.

Template 1-9B, the Master Calendar, and Template 1-10B, the Master Budget: These templates gather your subplans in one place for quick reference. Keep them in your Marketing Plan notebook. We'll keep referring to these two templates as we talk about timing and budgets for specific media in Part 2.

Chapter 2, Positioning: The Heart of Creative Promotions

Positioning, or finding your unique selling proposition as we sometimes call it, means defining what's unique about your business and presenting it to your potential customers in a way that captures their interest. Positioning is vital for distinguishing your offering from everybody else's. In Chapter 2 you learned to describe your unique position in terms of your key benefits, your target market's needs and wants, and your competition's positions.

Chapter 2 Templates

Template 2-1, Positioning Statement: This identifies your key benefit and the rationale supporting that claim.

Template 2-4, Dimensions of Competition: This reveals your competitive advantage by examining the aspects on which you compete. A key concept, this template is also referred to in Chapter 1, Chapter 5, and elsewhere.

Template 2-5, Positioning Strategies: This uses the information from Template 2-4 to develop a unique selling proposition for your business.

Chapter 3, Promotions: Do They Have a Place in Your Plan?

Promotions work by stimulating sales for reasons other than the product or service's inherent benefits. Discounts, gifts, special events, free samples—there's a world of possibilities to boost your sales that you can discover when you study the subject of promotions. In this chapter we talk about objectives and strategies for promotions. You'll learn how to execute those strategies as you study the specific chapter for each medium in Part 2. I strongly recommend that you include a promotional strategy in your marketing plan. The results of a promotional program are specific and measurable, and come about quickly. This speeds your learning curve when it comes to the ins and outs of advertising.

Chapter 3 Templates

This chapter contains two key concepts that will affect all your marketing activity! Template 3-1, Elements of the Promotional Program: This summarizes your promotional options in terms of incentive, vehicle, timing, and delivery method. It covers all you need to know to design a promotional program.

Template 3-3, Break-Even Analysis Worksheet for Promotional Program: This concept is mentioned in Chapter 1, but it is analyzed in more detail here in Chapter 3. If you decide to use a promotional program as part of your marketing strategy, your estimated cost total here should be carried to Template 1-10B, the Master Budget.

A similar analysis is used in the case study in Chapter 9. If you set up a break-even analysis spreadsheet on your computer, you'll have a tool for calculating cost and payback on any advertising campaign, whether a promotional offer is included or not.

Chapter 4, Writing a Media Plan

The biggest expense in advertising is likely to be your media costs. This chapter teaches you how to manage that investment. Media planning is the process of developing yearly plans for each medium in which advertising will be placed. That plan is then executed by negotiating separate contracts for each media outlet to be used. Using the tool of CPM (cost per thousand) analysis, this chapter leads you to decisions regarding advertising that will guide your work as you choose your creative approach, then craft your advertising message for print or broadcast. This is a chapter you'll want to visit more than once as you develop your advertising plan.

Chapter 4 Templates

Template 4-1, CPM (cost per thousand) Calculations: This is a spreadsheet for ranking advertising vehicles. By stating cost as a percentage of circulation, you can make apples-to-apples comparisons, no matter what advertising vehicle you are comparing. This concept is explained in detail here and again in some detail in Chapter 6. CPM worksheets also appear in Chapter 7 and Chapter 9. The CPM ranking process is relevant to any media decision.

Template 4-5, Media Calendar: This is a useful tool for visualizing the timing strategy you employ. It becomes part of the Master Calendar, Template 1-9B. Other calendar templates appear in Chapters 6, 7, 8, 9, and 10—all should be reflected in the Master Calendar.

Template 4-6, Media Budget: This describes projected spending by medium and by quarter. We'll keep adding to this template as we discuss specific media in Chapters 6 through 9. The total will be carried to Template 1-10B, the Master Budget.

Chapter 5, The Creative Approach: Taking Aim at Great Advertising

There is a process that makes creativity manageable: You analyze, you strategize, and then you create. The creative approach has two components: the advertising strategy and the "Big Idea." Analyzing the audience your media plan delivers tells you who you're talking to. With your ad strategy you define what you want to tell them. With your "Big Idea" you discover how you will capture their interest. This chapter includes a tried-and-true method for finding a creative "hook" for your advertising. In the subsequent chapters you learn how to execute that idea for different media.

Chapter 5 Templates

Template 5-1, Statement of Advertising Strategy: This locks in decisions that you don't

intend to rethink, and so removes your brainstorming from a "try-everything" approach. I suggest that at this point you review Template 1-8, the Statement of Marketing Objective, to ensure that your creative approach takes aim at your marketing objective.

Template 5-2, Summary of Media Plan: This is a reminder to keep your ad ideas appropriate to the medium in which they appear.

Don't-Miss Tips for Part 1

Budgeting. Determine your budget, then stick to it. Don't try to do too much with too few advertising dollars. Match your goals to your budget. Being cheap becomes expensive if you let it pull you off track. When you compare media, you might be tempted by a low cost per thousand (CPM) for a particular vehicle. If you discover that it doesn't deliver the audience you want, it's really no bargain.

Media planning: buy frequency. Frequency is much more important than you'd like to believe. Don't sacrifice frequency to buy bigger ads or longer time slots. All types of advertising gain effect when repeated, but particularly advertising in broadcast media. Since the listener can't play back anything he or she didn't understand the first time, it may take three to five repetitions to get your message across and to generate a response. With broadcast media, expect the response to your ads to improve as time goes by and people are exposed to repeated airings.

Creative approach: Choose the strategy, then the "Big Idea." You need a strategy—it keeps you focused on your key benefit and gives you a way to judge your creative ideas. As you work on the Big Idea, anticipate these stages: preparation, incubation, frustration, illumination, and evaluation.

Go for results. If you're not sure whether to try an image or a response strategy, go with response. It's easier to tell if it's working. In fact, I'd recommend that you design a promotional program (see Chapter 3) to increase the value of the offer in your response ads.

Part 2, Executing Print, Broadcast, and Direct Mail Advertising

Chapter 6, How to Create Print Ads that Sell

Print is an inexpensive, efficient way to reach a broad consumer base (through newspaper advertising, for example) or a targeted vertical market (through trade journals or regional business publications). Unlike the broadcast media, print ads convey information in a way prospects can *study*, making this the best medium for communicating substantive information. This chapter looks closely at the many options, and teaches you how to negotiate, write, and produce print advertising for each of the print media: magazines, newspapers, directories, and outdoor advertising.

Chapter 6 Templates

Template 6-2,: This CPM analysis compares different print media. This chapter goes into more detail on applying this concept to print media than the overview of CPM calculations in Chapter 4. A case study on planning a print advertising campaign explains how to index CPM calculations.

Template 6-5B, the Print Media Calendar: This summarizes your media plan in a format that is consistent with your overall Media Calendar (Template 4-5) and your Master Calendar (Template 1-9B).

Template 6-5, the Print Media Budget: This summarizes your budget and should be reflected in your Media Budget (Template 4-6) and also your Master Budget (Template 1-10B).

Template 6-9 and Template 6-12: These are cost estimates for production of simple or complex print ads. Your estimated cost total here should be carried to Template 1-10, the Master Budget, in the Advertising Production Costs category.

Template 6-10, Thumbnail Sketches for Newspaper Ads and Template 6-13, Thumbnail Sketches for Magazine Ads: These templates are aids to designing your print advertising.

Chapter 7, All About Radio Advertising

This chapter surveys the particular strengths of radio, describes who can benefit from radio advertising, and discusses how to negotiate the buy and craft the radio ad. The key feature of radio as a medium is the narrow audience demographics it delivers. If your target market matches the demographics of one or more local radio stations, this chapter is important to you.

Chapter 7 Templates

Template 7-1. This template shows CPM calculation as it applies to radio advertising. See also the discussion of CPM in Chapter 4.

Template 7-2B, Media Calendar by Week: This provides detail that should be summarized in your Media Calendar (Template 4-5) and your Master Calendar (Template 1-9B).

Template 7-3B, Media Budget: Your estimated cost total should be carried to Template 4-6, the Media Budget, and Template 1-10B, the Master Budget, in the Advertising Media Costs category.

Template 7-6, Radio Production Estimate: Again, carry the total here to Template 1-10, the Master Budget, in the Advertising Production Costs category.

I haven't provided a template for radio scriptwriting, but all scripts look pretty much the same. Follow the format of the examples in this chapter as you type your radio scripts.

Chapter 8, Television: Who Needs It? Maybe You.

Television is powerful entertainment, and that applies to the commercials as well as the programs. This chapter explains television from three angles: who can use TV well, how to negotiate the buy, and how to write and produce TV commercials.

The rapid growth of cable television is making this medium much more accessible for the small advertiser. If you've thought TV too expensive and complicated for you, think again—and read this chapter.

Chapter 8 Templates

Template 8-1B, Media Calendar: This provides detail that should be summarized in your Media Calendar (Template 4-5) and your Master Calendar (Template 1-9B).

Template 8-2B, Media Budget: Your estimated cost total should be carried to Template 4-6, the Media Budget, and Template 1-10B, the Master Budget, in the Advertising Media Costs category.

Template 8-3B, Television Production Estimate: Carry the total here to Template 1-10B, the overall Marketing Budget, in the Advertising Production category.

Template 8-4, Storyboard: Photocopy this template and use it to plot the visual and sound elements of your commercial. The examples will show you how.

Chapter 9, Direct Mail Advertising: Generating Leads, Winning Responses

When you want to control your advertising down to the last detail, direct mail is the medium to choose. You select who gets your message, when, and where. You control the offer, the list, the costs. You measure the results. Direct mail can be a powerhouse, generating leads, conveying information, and producing orders. For many business-to-business advertisers, it's the most cost-effective way to get to your prospective customers. Direct mail is a broad subject, and again I use my "analyze, strategize, create" formula to organize our discussion of the topic.

Chapter 9 Templates

Template 9-2, CPM Analysis, Mailing List Comparisons: This describes CPM analysis as it applies to direct mail. See also the discussion of CPM in Chapter 4.

Template 9-3, Mailing List Cost Estimate Worksheet: This generates a total for mailing costs. Carry this total to Templates 9-10A (Break-even Analysis) and 9-11A (Direct Mail Budget).

Templates 9-6A and 9-7A, Direct Mail Copy Strategy and Visual Survey Checklists: These assist you in creating your direct mail piece, by surveying the elements to be included.

Template 9-8A, Direct Mail Print Specifications Checklist: This is useful in procuring competitive print cost estimates. The cost of printing will be relevant in Templates 9-10A, and 9-11A and in the Master Budget (Template 1-10B).

Template 9-10A, Break-even Analysis Worksheet: Projecting fixed and variable costs related to the direct mail program helps you determine the feasibility of the proposed program.

Template 9-11A, Direct Mail Budget Cost Estimate Worksheet: Subtotals for planning, writing, graphic design, production, printing, and mailing add up to the budget for your direct mail program. Carry these totals to the Break-even Analysis (Template 9-10A) to assess feasibility. If you choose to carry out the program, reflect these totals in Template 4-6, the Media Budget, and in Template 1-10B, the Master Budget, in the Direct Mail category. If you plan to do several direct mail programs in the course of the year, complete this template for each. Show the totals of all direct mail pieces planned (by production, printing, and distribution) in Template 1-10B.

I'm sorry if this seems confusing! Budgets for production, printing, and distribution are interrelated—the mailing list you choose affects how many pieces you print, which affects the style and cost of production you choose, and so on. Planning for direct mail involves balancing many factors, and these templates—no matter what order you prepare them in—will assist you in that process.

Template 9-12, Execution Calendar: This outlines the steps in the production process. It helps you set deadlines for each step and provides detail that should be summarized in your Media Calendar (Template 4-5) and your Master Calendar (Template 1-9B).

Don't-Miss Tips for Part 2

Write "AIDA" ads. No matter what medium you're writing for, good advertising copy follows the AIDA formula. Your copy should get **a**ttention, arouse **i**nterest, evoke **d**esire, and motivate **a**ction. Follow this outline so that your copy establishes context, delivers content, and ends with a conclusion that calls for action.

Print ads: Not too big, not too weird. People associate ad size with company size. Buy the size that describes how your company would like to be perceived. Look at your competitors and buy an ad just a little bigger, if that's appropriate.

What about art versus photos? When in doubt, choose photos. We accept photos as picturing what is real, literally telling the truth without distortion. On the other hand, art—drawings, paintings, animation techniques—communicates a more subjective viewpoint. This is good if your goal is to arouse emotion. If you want to communicate solid information, choose a photo.

Want to try humor? Try radio or outdoor boards. If you have an idea you think is hilarious, see if one or both of these media fit your budget. Billboards and radio are both great for puns, double entendres, and other word play. It's tougher to make humor work on TV or in print.

Part 3, Idea Starters Outside the Realm of Advertising

Chapter 10, Publicity: The Almost-Free Alternative

Publicity, the search for positive mention in the nonpaid media, can be a powerful force for your business. It doesn't have to be difficult or time-consuming, if you are well organized and proactive in your approach. For some professions, such as medical firms or consulting, publicity is more appropriate than the more "hard-sell" techniques of advertising. This chapter explains how to plan and implement your publicity activity and how to work with the news media, and introduces some nonmedia publicity techniques via case studies.

Chapter 10 Templates

Template 10-1B, Statement of Publicity Strategy: This ensures that your publicity efforts are coordinated with your marketing and advertising activity.

Template 10-2, Publicity Action Plan: The target dates you set here will affect Template 10-4A, Publicity Spending by Quarter, and also the timetable you describe in Template 1-9, the Master Calendar.

Template 10-3, Publicity Budget Cost Estimate Worksheet: Subtotals for planning, setup, press kits, special events, postage, and "other" add up to the budget for your publicity program. Reflect the total in Template 1-10B, the Master Budget, in the Publicity category.

Tip: Pamper your publicity contacts like you do your clients. If you want publicity's powerful influence on your side, set up a database and manage your media contacts just as you do your key clients. Keep track of the special-interest areas of each contact so that you can pitch appropriate story angles.

Chapter 11, Your Corporate Image: Keeping that "Together" Look

Logos, stationery, brochures, catalogs, newsletters, displays, and signage are all speaking for you, presenting your face to the world. Each can contribute its support to your overall goal, if you plan it that way.

A detailed discussion of corporate image is beyond the scope of this book. Our purpose is to help you see how your image affects your advertising, and vice versa. For cost estimates and calendars to help you manage your print collateral, refer to the templates and suggestions in Chapter 9. That discussion of direct mail is relevant to many aspects of the brochure, catalog, or newsletter production process. This chapter includes a pertinent template:

Chapter 11 Templates

Template 11-3, Newsletter Budget Cost Estimate Worksheet: This summarizes writing, layout, printing, and mailing costs, making use of Template 9-8A (Direct Mail Print Specifications Checklist) and Template 9-3 (Mailing List Cost Estimate Worksheet). If you consider your newsletter to be part of your marketing budget, carry these totals to the Master Budget, Template 1-10B. Integrate the newsletter schedule into the Master Calendar, Template 1-9B.

Tip: You need a corporate image that is in sync with your marketing plan. Your business review and your positioning work from Chapter 2, especially the "tone adjectives" you choose for your advertising, will have an impact on your corporate image. Review those sections, then ask yourself if your stationery looks appropriate for the company you're describing. If the answer is no, it's definitely time for a tune-up.

Chapter 12, Do You Need Help with Your Advertising? How to Hire and Work with Specialists

It's unlikely that you will do all of your advertising planning and execution yourself. Therefore, you're going to need to find and work with specialists who will help you reach your objectives. This chapter shows you how to make that search process productive. Read Chapter 12 to learn how you can become your agency's favorite client—and be rewarded with better work than those who pay far more may get.

Chapter 12 Templates

Template 12-1, Criteria for Reviewing Agencies: This gives questions you should ask yourself about the agencies you interview. Following the tips in this chapter will help you find a good match for your advertising partner.

Perhaps the most important tool this book offers to help you work with outside specialists is Template 1-9B, the Master Calendar. When you've filled out this template, you can be sure that you—and your agents—stay ahead of the deadlines on each component you've planned. If you are coordinating the efforts of different specialists, such as a writer, a graphic designer, and a printer, *you* will need to be the one who rides herd on the schedule.

Tip: When you shop for creative collaborators, look for a good match of expertise and personality. Print, direct mail, television— agencies will tend to grow in the areas of their inherent talents or capabilities. Make sure the work they show you reflects skill in the areas you need, then make sure you like the people you'll be working with. This relationship is like a partnership—you'll need trust and respect to do good work together. Look for a feeling of rapport.

Be Ready for Your Advertising to Work

Have you heard the saying, "Get your house in order before the party starts"? Don't be taken by surprise when advertising causes a growth spurt in your business.

What you do in your advertising will affect other areas of your business as well. One client of mine advertised a product with a tie-in to a radio program—a set of audiocassettes on the same subject as a call-in radio show. The call-in show was very popular, and the audiocassettes sold very well, too. Too well, in fact. The station switchboard was shut down by callers trying to order my client's product.

(Too many dialed the station's number, announced for the potential callers, rather than the product's 800 number, announced during the commercial break.) He lost a number of sales as a result—and lost some goodwill with the station. Some advance planning might have avoided this situation.

Early in the cycle of marketing your product or service, you must look ahead to the potential results. How will you track leads? How will you keep up with the orders? Imagine what you want the sales cycle to be, from first lead to repeat sales. Imagine *in detail* what will need to happen in every area of your business. Consider your operations: If the widget orders roll in, do you have the production capacity to make the new widgets? Will doing so require hiring new staff? A client of mine provides in-home care to the ill and disabled. Adding a client almost always means adding a new employee, too, as each client might require as much as round-the-clock attended care. This client must match advertising to clients with advertisements in the "help wanted" section.

Whether your successful marketing campaign means adding new personnel or not, consider the effect your advertising is going to have on your staff. Every employee is a sales representative in a way. What your employees have to say about their jobs, positive or negative, is a pervasive factor affecting you. Make sure they're informed of special promotions or new ad themes that are about to break. If you're following my advice, you're planning your promotional activities from three to twelve months in advance. Make your staff aware of the calendar. You will see the result in your esprit de corps.

Maximize your financial reward for marketing by harnessing the power of follow-through. Track your advertising results. Devise a system at the point of order entry that lets you track sales specific to any promotional strategy or ad campaign currently in place. I've talked about using codes on coupons as one method to track sales. I've pointed out other methods, too. You maximize your marketing effort when you plan a quantifiable objective, and measure and compare actual against projected results.

At this point there should be no mystery left in your mind about the sequence of advertising activity. You know how to set objectives, plan strategies, create executions. If you've browsed through this book, returned to the sections that interest you, and compiled your results in a plan, you're ready to go.

Put your knowledge to use... and let me know how it all works out.

Index